Commentaries on the Laws of England

William Blackstone

A Facsimile of the First Edition of 1765–1769

VOLUME IV

Of
Public Wrongs
(1769)

With an Introduction by Thomas A. Green

The University of Chicago Press

Chicago & London

Commentaries on the Laws of England, by
William Blackstone, is available in a clothbound
set and separate paperback volumes from the
University of Chicago Press.

Vol. 1 *Of the Rights of Persons*
Vol. 2 *Of the Rights of Things*
Vol. 3 *Of Private Wrongs*
Vol. 4 *Of Public Wrongs*

The University of Chicago Press, Chicago 60637
The University of Chicago Press, Ltd., London

95 94 93 92 91 90   5 4

ISBN: clothbound set
       0–226–05536–1

       paperback edition
       0–226–05538–8 (volume 1)
       0–226–05541–8 (volume 2)
       0–226–05543–4 (volume 3)
       0–226–05545–0 (volume 4)

LCN: 79–11753

INTRODUCTION TO BOOK IV

THE final volume of Blackstone's *Commentaries* sets forth a lucid survey of crime and criminal procedure informed by those propositions concerning English law and the relations between man and state that characterize the entire work. Perhaps no area of the law so tested Blackstone's settled and complacent views as did the criminal law, particularly the large and growing body of statutory capital crimes. In the end, Blackstone failed to demonstrate that English criminal law reflected a coherent set of principles, but his intricate and often internally contradictory attempt nevertheless constitutes a classic description of that law, and can still be read as such. Blackstone struggled to reconcile the severity of the criminal law with what he saw as the essentially humane inspiration of English law in general, and in this he was a man of his age. Moreover, he sought to show that, in practice, English criminal justice accorded with the principles of certainty and proportionality of punishment invoked by the leading Continental penal reformers. His recognition of the gulf between the ideal and the reality, however, led him to cast his introductory statement,[1] and much that followed, as a heartfelt, though muted and deferential, plea for reform of the laws of crimes and punishments.

In organization and coverage Blackstone's last volume is the least original of the four. It draws heavily upon earlier treatises on the pleas of the Crown, principally those by Hale[2] in the late seventeenth century and Hawkins[3] in the early eighteenth century, both of whom also dealt first with substantive crimes and then with criminal procedure. The sections on noncapital crimes, particularly those on offenses against the Crown, religion and public justice, and peace and trade, appear to borrow from Thomas Wood's *An Institute of the Laws of England*,[4] first published in 1720. Nevertheless, Blackstone's treatment far surpasses all earlier works on English criminal law. It is both comprehensive and unified, not only stating the law as it then stood, but also providing a philosophical setting and historical background for the criminal law.

What gives his work a special force and unity is Blackstone's insistence that criminal law ought to be "founded upon principles that are permanent, uniform and universal; and always conformable to the dictates of truth and justice, the feelings of humanity, and the indelible rights of mankind."[5] These principles of natural law and justice are invoked both to explain and to defend English law. Blackstone did not consider all legal rules and prohibitions to be propositions of natural law. He followed convention in characterizing those that expressed moral as well as legal commands as *mala in se*, but he recognized that there were as many or more *mala prohibita*, or mere positive commands. As to these, the moral claim to obedience arose only as an incident to society's right to create the duty, a right that flowed from the social compact.[6]

The procedures of criminal law belonged to this class of positive commands that derived their force from consent. But Blackstone sought to show that English criminal procedure, too, was consonant with principles of natural justice. In design and measure, it was suited to effect the purpose of all punishment: to serve as "a precaution against future offenses of the same kind,"[7] whether by correction or physical restraint of an offender or by deterrence of other, potential offenders.

Blackstone understood that, in its fortuitous provenance or unreasonable severity, much of the letter of English law was hard to justify by recourse to theories of natural justice, consent, or deterrence. Accordingly, he placed considerable weight upon those aspects of the actual application of the law that tended to reduce its inhumanity: natural justice was achieved through merciful application of the law. Blackstone largely suppressed his concern that a system which corrected for its cruelty by ad hoc recourse to mechanisms for excusing from punishment might sacrifice something both of the principle of certainty of punishment and of the related end of deterrence.[8] But even as he extolled the virtues of royal pardons and defended "pious perjury," he revealed his belief that English criminal law stood in considerable tension and in need of substantial reform.[9]

The Substantive Law of Crimes

Blackstone's introductory chapter on the substantive law of crimes, couched as a discussion of persons capable of committing

criminal acts, stresses the importance of free will. It is "the concurrence of the will, when it has its choice either to do or to avoid the
fact in question," that "renders human actions either praiseworthy
or culpable."[10] Men are free, their social obligations derived from
a freely given consent to social existence. But men have not consented to be punished for involuntary acts or acts of pure necessity.
Blackstone saw, however, that the will theory could be used to re-
sist much of the substantive law: might not poverty, he asks,
ground a defense of involuntarism or of necessity, especially in
cases of theft of food and clothing? Blackstone replies that property
would be rendered insecure by the alleged wants of others, "of
which wants no man can possibly be an adequate judge, but the
party himself who pleads them."[11] In any case, he continues, in
England there is no need for such self-help, as the poor were
provided for by civil magistrates. Finally, and characteristically,
in a more sympathetic reflection on the problem Blackstone in-
vokes the power of the Crown "to soften the law, and to extend
mercy in cases of peculiar hardship."[12]

Blackstone's treatment of specific crimes surveys three kinds of
offenses: offenses against God and religion; offenses directly against
the state, comprising those against the Crown and the prerogative
or against justice (broadly, obstructing justice), those against public peace (riots, affrays, and libels), and those against public trade
and public health and economy; and finally offenses against the
person, habitation, and private property generally. In his discussion of each kind of offense, Blackstone deals first with felony,
then with misdemeanor. There is no systematic segregation of the
historic pleas of the Crown from the more recent statutorily created offenses, and the unity of the entire work is thereby en-
hanced.[13] There are degrees of criminality, but all crimes, whether
statutory or common law, are first and foremost breaches of the
social bonds men have consented to protect.

For Blackstone, vertical lines of authority and obedience were
in the natural order of things. Those offenses against God and
religion over which secular authorities had jurisdiction were
attacks upon the ultimate source of authority in human society.
Although eager to assert that the laws concerning Roman Catholics
were "seldom exerted to their utmost rigor" (they were relics
of "the urgency of the times which produced them"),[14] Blackstone was passionately anti-Papist. He scorned what he called the
"slavish, blind devotion" of the Catholics to their Church, con-

trasting to it the "due obedience" that the Church of England inculcated: "The most stable foundation of legal and rational government is due subordination of rank, and a gradual scale of authority . . . ."[15] Catholicism, like the opposite excess of democracy, represented a perversion of the natural order.

In his discussion of treason, Blackstone strikes a similar note, characterizing the offense as an act of betrayal and treachery that strikes at the heart of social bonds and suspends all measure of affection otherwise due a person from those of higher station. High treason, an offense against majesty, is therefore the highest of crimes. Nevertheless, Blackstone warns that the very seriousness of the offense requires that it be "the most precisely ascertained."[16] History taught that too great a latitude in the power to define treasonous acts was an invitation to arbitrary and despotic government.

Blackstone's chapters on offenses against public justice, peace, trade, and health describe much of the vast misdemeanor jurisdiction of the justices of the peace that had been steadily increasing since the fourteenth century. The reader need only glance at the table of contents in order to sense the extent to which regulatory law pervaded politics, enterprise, and morals in the eighteenth century. The Elizabethan obsession with public order and the consequent management of private behavior had hardly abated by Blackstone's day. Blackstone shared the assumptions of the rulers of his tightly knit and closely regulated society. His paternalism and prudery were virtually unbounded. He thus insists upon the highest standards from public officials and from the practicing bar;[17] details with evident approbation the myriad prohibitions against even the most minor causes of public disorder;[18] and excoriates public nuisances of every sort, reserving his most moralistic tone for gaming, horse racing, and private lotteries, which tended "by necessary consequences to promote public idleness, theft, and debauchery" among the poor.[19] For Blackstone the virtues of industriousness, thrift, and common decency were more than ends in themselves: they were instrumental to the security of the property, liberty, and persons of all subjects of the realm.

In treating offenses against person and property, Blackstone pays careful attention both to the law in practice and to the theoretical distinctions between the capital and the noncapital forms of these crimes. He does not merely explain and defend; where appropriate, he is critical and counsels reform. The distinction between murder and manslaughter, or between capital and noncapital homicide, was a product of the sixteenth century. At the core of "murder" lay the concept of malice aforethought, but murder had even by Coke's day been further complicated by the concept of "implied malice."[20] Blackstone appears to approve of the law of implied malice. Moreover he offers only muted criticism of the presumption of murder in cases of a mother's concealment of the death of her child.[21] The discussion of noncapital homicide is comprehensive. He strongly endorses the law of justifiable homicide (e.g., slaying to prevent the commission of a serious crime), finding precedent for it in Jewish, Roman, and Greek law. Truly excusable homicide, whether committed in self-defense or through nonnegligent accident, also merits acquittal. Thus it appears from Blackstone's discussion that the courts were now acquitting outright those who earlier had to obtain a royal pardon. The line between true self-defense and manslaughter is defended despite its fuzziness. It most often depends on the question of retreat, he states, and the defendant's retreat is not a fiction, but results "from a real tenderness of shedding his brother's blood."[22]

Blackstone thus took the complex law of homicide much as he found it, endorsing both its strict rules of capital murder and its subtle gradations in noncapital forms. The distinctions were subtle but rational and to be taken seriously. It was for the prisoner to make out the "circumstances of justification, excuse or alleviation . . . to the satisfaction of the court and jury."[23]

The law of theft, by contrast, was altogether too severe. The unlawful taking of property worth twelve pence or more was capital. Thus the scope of capital theft had always been broad, and it had expanded steadily with inflation. Furthermore, a profusion of statutes, of which the Black Act of 1723 is only the most notorious,[24] created dozens of other capital felonies for threats to or destruction of property.[25] Blackstone questions the wisdom of capital punishment in such cases, citing More and Beccaria for the view that imprisonment with the obligation to labor and make restitution was the preferable sanction. He endorses the tendency of juries to undervalue goods, where only inflation had made a theft capital. For a jury to do so in other cases of theft, he states, is to indulge in "a kind of pious perjury"; he appears to regard such behavior as a lesser evil and as an indication of the need for reform of the law.[26]

Criminal Procedure

In Blackstone's discussion of substantive law we see the imprint of his political and social theory. We also see his pronounced bent toward comparative inquiry, albeit on a superficial level; he frequently defends English doctrines by reference to similar practices in ancient and in contemporary Continental legal systems. By contrast, his treatment of procedure is more historical than theoretical, and it is decidedly insular. Blackstone is quick to condemn long-vanished or vestigial English practices, drawing at once the two lessons of the barbarism and irrationality of much medieval procedure and the enlightened progress of his own day.

Blackstone stresses the importance of the principle that prevention is preferable to punishment, emphasizing thereby both humaneness and deterrence.[27] Like his contemporaries, he took for granted the role of justices of the peace in receiving complaints and requiring those complained of to produce sureties for their good behavior, practices that long predated but were substantially increased by Tudor vagrancy legislation.[28] Although Blackstone concedes that the magistrates' discretionary power was very great in this area, he indicates little concern about it.[29] Here, as elsewhere, his preoccupation with the maintenance of public order surfaces; the specter of riot and pilferage haunts the volume on public wrongs.

Blackstone is nevertheless scrupulously consistent in distinguishing punishment from what he considers prevention. He countenances cooperation with the modern forms of the ancient system of frankpledge as integral to one's natural social obligation; failure to make good on these obligations justifies restraints on liberty. Punishment for commission of a crime, on the other hand, requires sound proof. Blackstone insists upon rigorous adherence to the rules of arrest, committal, and bail: justices must state precisely the cause for apprehending a suspect and must grant him his freedom, on recognizance and pending trial, save in those few most serious cases where pretrial incarceration was necessary.[30] Similarly,

Blackstone states that indictment should not be treated casually, that the grand jury "ought to be thoroughly persuaded of the truth of an indictment . . . ."[31] He defends the legality of informations, so long as they are supported by "express direction from the court of kings bench,"[32] but inveighs against their former abuse by Star Chamber and at common law.

Blackstone's defense of jury trial as a safeguard against unjust restraints upon the liberty of the accused[33] is of a piece with his endorsement of strict rules regarding committal and indictment. He approves the disposition of the bench to discourage defendants from confessing their guilt; they should be urged to plead to the indictment and stand trial.[34] Blackstone approves of the liberal right to challenge jurors allowed to the defendant, but he fails to mention that actual practice was not nearly so liberal.[35]

Blackstone has surprisingly little to say about the nature of the criminal trial. He shows little awareness of contemporary changes that were making the trial a highly structured formal proceeding. Well into the eighteenth century, the typical felony trial was much like the one that Thomas Smith had described nearly two centuries before.[36] The trial was in large measure an altercation between accusing witnesses and the defendant himself. The bench interceded with questions of its own, commented freely upon the evidence, and frequently tried to influence the jury in its verdict. By Blackstone's time, however, a virtual transformation in trial procedure was under way. Blackstone was not alert to the slow rise of the law of criminal evidence. He overstates the role of counsel, perhaps generalizing from private law, which he knew from firsthand experience, and from the state trials. Blackstone believed that judges had "seldom scruple[d]" to allow counsel both to advise the accused on questions of law and "even to ask questions for him, with respect to matters of fact."[37] In truth, counsel had only very recently come to play this role and were thus only beginning to have a dramatic impact on the criminal trial.[38]

The Problem of Merciful Application of the Law

The grounds for appealing a conviction were in Blackstone's day still very narrow: writs of error lay only for errors on the face of the record, for instance, "notorious mistakes in the judgment" or

"other less palpable errors" in the formal record. In capital cases
the writ issued *ex gratia,* not as a matter of course.[39] This system
was tempered by a bench that not infrequently exercised a discretionary power to reprieve a sentence and to recommend to the
Crown either an absolute or a conditional pardon. The bench
might act not only for errors in form but also, states Blackstone,
"where the judge is not satisfied with the verdict, or the evidence
is suspicious, . . . or sometimes if it be a small felony, or any favor-
able circumstances appear in the criminal's character . . . ."[40] The
resulting disparity between the letter of the capital penal statutes
and actual sentencing policy has been noted by modern scholars.[41]
Blackstone, too, remarked it; indeed, it posed for him the central
problem of English criminal law.

Blackstone approved of the royal power to pardon, which was
as old as kingship itself and integral to the sacred royal duty to extend mercy where mercy is due.[42] At the same time, he sought to
demonstrate that English law embodied the principle of certainty
of punishment to which contemporary Continental publicists gave
so much weight. Noting that Beccaria opposed pardons because of
their intrinsically discretionary nature, Blackstone argues that the
English position was correct. Without royal pardons, judges and
juries would take upon themselves the "dangerous power . . . of
construing the criminal law by the spirit instead of the letter."[43]
Better to place the necessary power to mitigate in the Crown,
which occupies a station above that of the judiciary. The judge
is thus precluded from contradicting himself, from exercising a
power "to make and to unmake his decisions."[44] In criminal justice, as in much else, Blackstone concluded, monarchy was preferable to democracy: relative certainty of punishment, attention to
individual circumstances, divine mercy, all were possible within
the framework of the English constitution.

It is difficult, if not impossible, for the reader of the discourse on
public wrongs to conclude that Blackstone believed that his description of this aspect of English criminal process accorded with
the actual practice of the day. First, as we have seen, Blackstone
strongly doubted the wisdom and justice of the severity of the law
of theft. Though he much preferred penal reform, until reform
came about he saw no choice but to accept "pious perjury." It is
true that in the text Blackstone is silent about jury nullification
in cases not involving theft, but he was well aware that jury ac-

quittals were invulnerable to reversal and, following Hale, thought this a wise policy.[45] Moreover, though he makes no reference to those judicial jury instructions whose effect was to narrow capital statutes, he can hardly have been unaware of them;[46] and, as we have seen, he noted the extensive judicial powers of reprieve. Blackstone certainly believed that all power of mitigation ought to reside solely in the Crown, but surely he knew that in fact it did not.

Blackstone glossed over the serious problems that had been created by what was widely perceived as an overly severe system of criminal punishment, but he understood those problems and sought a remedy for them. Some modern scholars believe that this very severity of the law provided the ruling classes the critical leverage of nonenforcement from which they in turn reaped the gratitude and deference of those they ruled.[47] Yet Blackstone, recognizing the inevitable dangers of dispersed powers of mitigation, counseled reform. Though he thought some degree of royal mercy would always be necessary and desirable, he sought, through a more temperate law, to do away with the need for such mitigation by judges or at the common level of the jury. In this regard, the dramatic legal changes wrought in the nineteenth century by Benthamite reform legislation were more consonant than its proponents supposed with Blackstonian principles of criminal justice.[48]

Blackstone's instinctive conservatism regarding the locus of the power to mitigate proved, at least in one respect, to be in accord with the best interests of his class. Though he appears not to have foreseen the coming storm over the role of the jury in seditious libel prosecutions, Blackstone avoided for himself the dilemma posed for other admirers of the jury system who, having endorsed merciful jury verdicts in common-run felony cases, sanctioned judicial manipulation of the law in order to preclude such jury verdicts in political cases.[49]

Blackstone's Concluding Essay

Blackstone concluded his *Commentaries* with an essay—a Whig panegyric—entitled "Of the Rise, Progress and Gradual Improvements of the Laws of England."[50] Sweeping in scope, majestic in style, this final paean to the elegance, wisdom, and humanity of

English laws displays both Blackstone the optimistic and complacent eighteenth-century gentleman and Blackstone the proponent of measured reform. It was the duty of the nobility and gentlemen in Parliament "to sustain, to repair, to beautify this noble pile."[51]

The spirit and institutions of the English law, wrote Blackstone, were the product of three great periods: the Anglo-Saxon, the reign of Edward I, and the Restoration. The first produced the ancient constitution and English liberty; the second saw the elaboration of common law courts and doctrine, the forums and forms of the law that prevailed in Blackstone's day; the last washed away the vestiges of Norman enslavement and achieved, in the Habeas Corpus Act of 1679, the means to secure the liberty that Magna Charta had sought to guarantee centuries before.

Blackstone adhered to the myth of Anglo-Saxon liberties and heaped scorn on the Norman intruders. But unlike the radical mid-seventeenth-century law reformers, he did not deprecate the post-Conquest development of the common law. Rather he saw in this development the gradual freeing of Englishmen from Norman tyranny and the establishment of due process and responsible government in the hands of those fit to rule the realm. The Interregnum, by contrast, he reviled as an era of excess. He felt it best to "pass by the crude and abortive schemes for amending the laws in the times of confusion which followed [the Civil War]."[52]

Blackstone chose to dwell on the law, rather than on the arbitrary abuses of the law, in the Restoration period. He recognized that the long course of "the recovery of [Englishmen's] civil and political liberties" was not "fully and explicitly acknowledged and defined, till the aera of the happy revolution."[53] Like other "Old Whigs," Blackstone took his stand on the principles invoked and carried into effect at the time of the Glorious Revolution.[54] He listed many of the improvements made since that watershed, and still being made in his own day, but they were for him only inevitable elaborations upon the settlement of 1688–89. Blackstone put the best possible face even on those eighteenth-century innovations which he opposed. The great increase in capital offenses was counterbalanced by the merciful "extension of the benefit of clergy, by abolishing the pedantic criterion of reading,"[55] so that the unlettered, who were ignorant of the law, might have the same advantages as the learned, of whom more ought to be expected.[56]

Always the apologist, but also the rationalist, Blackstone believed that knowledge of the law would lead in the end to humaneness, freedom, and obedience.

THOMAS A. GREEN

NOTES

1. Blackstone, *Commentaries* IV:1ff, especially at 4–5.
2. M. Hale, *History of the Pleas of the Crown*, 2 vols. (not published until 1736).
3. W. Hawkins, *Pleas of the Crown*, 2 vols. (1716, 1721).
4. T. Wood, *An Institute of the Law of England*, 2 vols. (1720).
5. Blackstone IV:3.
6. Id. IV:8.
7. Id. IV:11.
8. Blackstone had Cesare Beccaria in mind when he wrote: "It is the sentiment of an ingenious writer, who seems to have well studied the springs of human action, that crimes are more effectually prevented by the *certainty*, than by the *severity*, of punishment." Id. IV:17.
9. This matter is considered further infra pp. x, xii.
10. Blackstone IV:20–21.
11. Id. IV:32.
12. Id.
13. Blackstone was not original in his melding of common law and statutory offenses; Hale and Hawkins, among others, had taken the same approach. It would have been difficult to do otherwise. Statutes had intervened so often over the centuries for narrow remedial purposes that there was no separate body of common law as opposed to statutory offenses. There was a continuum of lesser to greater statutory involvement with the common law of crimes, capped by a few strictly statutory offenses and their body of interpretative law. Blackstone's commentary on the nature and purpose of both statutory and common law, however, effected greater integration of the two forms than his predecessors had achieved.
14. Blackstone IV:57.
15. Id. IV:104ff.
16. Id. IV:75.

17. Id. IV:133–34.
18. Id. IV:142ff.
19. Id. IV:171.
20. Id. IV:200–201. For a discussion of the law relating to murder in the late sixteenth and early seventeenth centuries, see J. M. Kaye, "The Early History of Murder and Manslaughter," 83 *L.Q.R.* 569ff (1967). Blackstone drew heavily upon Sir Michael Foster's discussion of homicide. M. Foster, *Discourses upon a Few Branches of the Crown Law* (1762).
21. Id. IV:198. Here Blackstone discusses the provisions of 21 James 1, c. 27.
22. Id. IV:185.
23. Id. IV:201.
24. 9 George 1, c. 22. For a recent study of the act and of the politics and class interests involved in antipoaching legislation generally, see E. P. Thompson, *Whigs and Hunters* (1975).
25. L. Radzinowicz, *A History of English Criminal Law* I:3ff (1948).
26. Blackstone IV:239. This important and ambiguous passage reads: "It is true, the mercy of juries will often make them strain a point, and bring in larciny to be under the value of twelvepence, when it is really of much greater value: but this is a kind of pious perjury, and does not at all excuse our common law in this respect from the imputation of severity, but rather strongly confesses the charge."
27. Id. IV:248.
28. W. H. Holdsworth, *A History of English Law* IV:399ff (1922–66).
29. Blackstone IV:253.
30. Id. IV:293ff.
31. Id. IV:300.
32. Id. IV:307.
33. Id. IV:342–43.
34. Id. IV:324.
35. Id. IV:346ff. Blackstone noted that the Crown could not challenge except for cause but that the defendant might make up to twenty peremptory challenges in trials for felony and thirty-five in jury trials for misdemeanors. Challenges for "sufficient" cause were unlimited. Blackstone may have been more familiar with the great state trials, where challenges were not uncommon, than with common run felonies.
36. T. Smith, *De Republica Anglorum* 94ff (1583).
37. Blackstone IV:349–50.
38. On the criminal trial in the late seventeenth and early eighteenth centuries, see J. H. Langbein, "The Criminal Trial before the Lawyers," 45 *U. Chi. L. Rev.* 263–316 (1978); more generally, on crimi-

nal procedure, see J. H. Baker, "Criminal Courts and Procedure at Common Law, 1550–1800," in *Crime in England, 1550–1800* (J. S. Cockburn ed. 1977), at 15.

39. Blackstone IV:384–85.

40. Id. IV:387. On judicial recommendations for pardons, see Radzinowicz, op. cit. 112ff.

41. E.g., Radzinowicz, op. cit. Part II passim; D. Hay, "Property, Authority and the Criminal Law," 22ff in *Albion's Fatal Tree* (D. Hay et al. eds. 1975); J. M. Beattie, "Crime and the Courts in Surrey, 1736–1753" 183ff, in Cockburn, op. cit., at 155.

42. Blackstone IV:389–90.

43. Id. IV:390.

44. Id.

45. Id. IV:354–55.

46. Radzinowicz, op. cit. 83ff.

47. E.g., Hay, op. cit. The reasons for the multiplication of capital statutes in the eighteenth century are still poorly understood. G. R. Elton ("Introduction: Crime and the Historian," in Cockburn, op. cit. 4–5, 12) and J. Styles ("Criminal Records," 20 *Historical Journal* 977–81 [1977]) caution against the assumption that the statutes reflect class attitudes or new conceptions of property. Moreover, Elton suggests that the large number of acquittals may have resulted, at least in part, from an indictment process that was poorly equipped to filter out false allegations. Whatever the objective truth of this matter, Blackstone believed that the law was too severe and that mitigation was the inevitable result.

48. Blackstone's somewhat muted call for reform was followed by two other important reformist studies of the criminal law: W. Eden, *Principles of Penal Reform* (1770); H. Dagge, *Considerations on Criminal Law* (1772). Eden, who perhaps saw the problems posed by mitigation more clearly and gave them far greater emphasis than the others, was cited more frequently by the next generation of law reformers.

49. On the seditious libel prosecutions, see Holdsworth, op. cit. VIII:336ff.

50. Blackstone IV:400ff.

51. Id. IV:436.

52. Id. IV:431.

53. Id. IV:435.

54. For classic discussions of the "Old Whig" position, see E. Burke, *Appeal from the New to the Old Whigs* (1791); *Reflections on the Revolution in France* (1790; 1955 ed., at 18ff and 35ff). For the most recent discussion of Blackstone's place in the history of Anglo-American constitutional and legal thought, see D. Kennedy, "The

Structure of Blackstone's *Commentaries,*" 28 *Buffalo L. Rev.*
_____ (1979).
55. Blackstone IV:434.
56. Id. IV:363.

COMMENTARIES

ON THE

LAWS

OF

ENGLAND.

BOOK THE FOURTH.

BY

WILLIAM BLACKSTONE, Esq.
SOLICITOR GENERAL TO HER MAJESTY.

OXFORD,
PRINTED AT THE CLARENDON PRESS.
M. DCC. LXIX.

CONTENTS.

Book IV.
Of Public Wrongs.

CONTENTS.

CHAP.

CONTENTS.

CHAP.

CONTENTS.

CHAP.

CONTENTS.

A P P E N D I X.

I N D E X.

COMMENTARIES

ON THE

LAWS OF ENGLAND.

BOOK THE FOURTH.

OF PUBLIC WRONGS.

CHAPTER THE FIRST.

OF THE NATURE OF CRIMES; AND THEIR PUNISHMENT.

WE are now arrived at the fourth and laſt branch of theſe commentaries; which treats of *public wrongs*, or *crimes* and *miſdemeſnors*. For we may remember that, in the beginning of the preceding volume [a], wrongs were divided into two ſorts or ſpecies; the one *private*, and the other *public*. Private wrongs, which are frequently termed civil injuries, were the ſubject of that entire book: we are now therefore, laſtly, to proceed to the conſideration of public wrongs, or crimes and miſdemeſnors; with the means of their prevention and puniſhment. In the purſuit of which ſubject I ſhall conſider, in the firſt place, the general nature of crimes and puniſhments; ſecondly, the perſons capable of committing crimes; thirdly, their ſeveral degrees of guilt,

[a] Book III. ch. 1.

as principals or acceſſories; fourthly, the several ſpecies of crimes, with the puniſhment annexed to each by the laws of England; fifthly, the means of preventing their perpetration; and, ſixthly, the method of inflicting thoſe puniſhments, which the law has annexed to each ſeveral crime and miſdemeſnor.

First, as to the general nature of crimes and their puniſhment: the diſcuſſion and admeaſurement of which forms in every country the code of criminal law; or, as it is more uſually denominated with us in England, the doctrine of the *pleas of the crown:* ſo called, becauſe the king, in whom centers the majeſty of the whole community, is ſuppoſed by the law to be the perſon injured by every infraction of the public rights belonging to that community, and is therefore in all caſes the proper proſecutor for every public offence[b].

The knowlege of this branch of juriſprudence, which teaches the nature, extent, and degrees of every crime, and adjuſts to it it's adequate and neceſſary penalty, is of the utmoſt importance to every individual in the ſtate. For (as a very great maſter of the crown law[c] has obſerved upon a ſimilar occaſion) no rank or elevation in life, no uprightneſs of heart, no prudence or circumſpection of conduct, ſhould tempt a man to conclude, that he may not at ſome time or other be deeply intereſted in theſe reſearches. The infirmities of the beſt among us, the vices and ungovernable paſſions of others, the inſtability of all human affairs, and the numberleſs unforeſeen events, which the compaſs of a day may bring forth, will teach us (upon a moment's reflection) that to know with preciſion what the laws of our country have forbidden, and the deplorable conſequences to which a wilful diſobedience may expoſe us, is a matter of univerſal concern.

In proportion to the importance of the criminal law, ought alſo to be the care and attention of the legiſlature in properly

[b] See Vol. I. p. 268.   [c] Sir Michael Foſter. pref. to rep.

forming

forming and enforcing it. It fhould be founded upon principles
that are permanent, uniform, and univerfal ; and always conformable to the dictates of truth and juftice, the feelings of
humanity, and the indelible rights of mankind : though it
fometimes (provided there be no tranfgreffion of thefe eternal
boundaries) may be modified, narrowed, or enlarged, according to the local or occafional neceffities of the ftate which it is
meant to govern. And yet, either from a want of attention to
thefe principles in the firft concoction of the laws, and adopting
in their ftead the impetuous dictates of avarice, ambition, and
revenge ; from retaining the difcordant political regulations,
which fucceffive conquerors or factions have eftablifhed, in the
various revolutions of government ; from giving a lafting efficacy to fanctions that were intended to be temporary, and made
(as lord Bacon expreffes it) merely upon the fpur of the occafion ;
or from, laftly, too haftily employing fuch means as are greatly
difproportionate to their end, in order to check the progrefs of
fome very prevalent offence ; from fome, or from all, of thefe caufes
it hath happened, that the criminal law is in every country of
Europe more rude and imperfect than the civil. I fhall not here
enter into any minute enquiries concerning the local conftitutions
of other nations ; the inhumanity and miftaken policy of which
have been fufficiently pointed out by ingenious writers of their
own [d]. But even with us in England, where our crown-law is
with juftice fuppofed to be more nearly advanced to perfection ;
where crimes are more accurately defined, and penalties lefs
uncertain and arbitrary ; where all our accufations are public,
and our trials in the face of the world ; where torture is unknown, and every delinquent is judged by fuch of his equals,
againft whom he can form no exception nor even a perfonal
diflike ; --- even here we fhall occafionally find room to remark
fome particulars, that feem to want revifion and amendment.
Thefe have chiefly arifen from too fcrupulous an adherence to
fome rules of the antient common law, when the reafons have
ceafed upon which thofe rules were founded ; from not repeal-

Baron Montefquieu, marquis Beccaria, &c.

ing

ing such of the old penal laws as are either obsolete or absurd; and from too little care and attention in framing and passing new ones. The enacting of penalties, to which a whole nation shall be subject, ought not to be left as a matter of indifference to the passions or interests of a few, who upon temporary motives may prefer or support such a bill; but be calmly and maturely considered by persons, who know what provisions the law has already made to remedy the mischief complained of, who can from experience foresee the probable consequences of those which are now proposed, and who will judge without passion or prejudice how adequate they are to the evil. It is never usual in the house of peers even to read a private bill, which may affect the property of an individual, without first referring it to some of the learned judges, and hearing their report thereon [e]. And surely equal precaution is necessary, when laws are to be established, which may affect the property, the liberty, and perhaps even the lives, of thousands. Had such a reference taken place, it is impossible that in the eighteenth century it could ever have been made a capital crime, to break down (however maliciously) the mound of a fishpond, whereby any fish shall escape; or to cut down a cherry tree in an orchard [f]. Were even a committee appointed but once in an hundred years to revise the criminal law, it could not have continued to this hour a felony without benefit of clergy, to be seen for one month in the company of persons who call themselves, or are called, Egyptians [g].

I T is true, that these outrageous penalties, being seldom or never inflicted, are hardly known to be law by the public: but that rather aggravates the mischief, by laying a snare for the unwary. Yet they cannot but occur to the observation of any one, who hath undertaken the task of examining the great outlines of the English law, and tracing them up to their principles: and it is the duty of such a one to hint them with

---

[e] See Vol. II. p. 345.   [g] Stat. 5 Eliz. c. 20.
[f] Stat. 9 Geo. I. c. 22. 31 Geo. II. c. 42.

decency to thofe, whofe abilities and ftations enable them to apply the remedy. Having therefore premifed this apology for fome of the enfuing remarks, which might otherwife feem to favour of arrogance, I proceed now to confider (in the firft place) the general nature of *crimes*.

I. A CRIME, or mifdemefnor, is an act committed, or omitted, in violation of a public law, either forbidding or commanding it. This general definition comprehends both crimes and mifdemefnors; which, properly fpeaking, are mere fynonymous terms: though, in common ufage, the word, "crimes," is made to denote fuch offences as are of a deeper and more atrocious dye; while fmaller faults, and omiffions of lefs confequence, are comprized under the gentler name of "mifde-"mefnors" only.

THE diftinction of public wrongs from private, of crimes and mifdemefnors from civil injuries, feems principally to confift in this: that private wrongs, or civil injuries, are an infringement or privation of the civil rights which belong to individuals, confidered merely as individuals; public wrongs, or crimes and mifdemefnors, are a breach and violation of the public rights and duties, due to the whole community, confidered as a community, in it's focial aggregate capacity. As if I detain a field from another man, to which the law has given him a right, this is a civil injury, and not a crime; for here only the right of an individual is concerned, and it is immaterial to the public, which of us is in poffeffion of the land: but treafon, murder, and robbery are properly ranked among crimes; fince, befides the injury done to individuals, they ftrike at the very being of fociety; which cannot poffibly fubfift, where actions of this fort are fuffered to efcape with impunity.

IN all cafes the crime includes an injury: every public offence is alfo a private wrong, and fomewhat more; it affects the individual, and it likewife affects the community. Thus

treafon

treafon in imagining the king's death involves in it confpiracy
againft an individual, which is alfo a civil injury : but as this
fpecies of treafon in it's confequences principally tends to the
diffolution of government, and the deftruction thereby of the
order and peace of fociety, this denominates it a crime of the
higheft magnitude. Murder is an injury to the life of an individual ; but the law of fociety confiders principally the lofs
which the ftate fuftains by being deprived of a member, and
the pernicious example thereby fet, for others to do the like.
Robbery may be confidered in the fame view : it is an injury to
private property ; but, were that all, a civil fatisfaction in damages might atone for it : the *public* mifchief is the thing, for
the prevention of which our laws have made it a capital offence.
In thefe grofs and atrocious injuries the private wrong is fwallowed up in the public : we feldom hear any mention made of
fatisfaction to the individual ; the fatisfaction to the community
being fo very great. And indeed, as the public crime is not
otherwife avenged than by forfeiture of life and property, it is
impoffible afterwards to make any reparation for the private
wrong ; which can only be had from the body or goods of the
aggreffor. But there are crimes of an inferior nature, in which
the public punifhment is not fo fevere, but it affords room for
a private compenfation alfo : and herein the diftinction of crimes
from civil injuries is very apparent. For inftance ; in the cafe
of battery, or beating another, the aggreffor may be indicted
for this at the fuit of the king, for difturbing the public peace,
and be punifhed criminally by fine and imprifonment : and the
party beaten may alfo have his private remedy by action
of trefpafs for the injury, which he in particular fuftains, and
recover a civil fatisfaction in damages. So alfo, in cafe of a
public nufance, as digging a ditch acrofs a highway, this is
punifhable by indictment, as a common offence to the whole
kingdom and all his majefty's fubjects : but if any individual
fuftains any fpecial damage thereby, as laming his horfe, breaking his carriage, or the like, the offender may be compelled to
make

make ample fatisfaction, as well for the private injury, as for the public wrong.

UPON the whole we may obferve, that in taking cognizance of all wrongs, or unlawful acts, the law has a double view: *viz.* not only to redrefs the party injured, by either reftoring to him his right, if poffible; or by giving him an equivalent; the manner of doing which was the object of our enquiries in the preceding book of thefe commentaries: but alfo to fecure to the public the benefit of fociety, by preventing or punifhing every breach and violation of thofe laws, which the fovereign power has thought proper to eftablifh, for the government and tranquillity of the whole. What thofe breaches are, and how prevented or punifhed, are to be confidered in the prefent book.

II. THE nature of *crimes and mifdemefnors* in general being thus afcertained and diftinguifhed, I proceed in the next place to confider the general nature of *punifhmcnts:* which are evils or inconveniences confequent upon crimes and mifdemefnors; be-ing devifed, denounced, and inflicted by human laws, in con-fequence of difobedience or mifbehaviour in thofe, to regulate whofe conduct fuch laws were refpectively made. And herein we will briefly confider the *power,* the *end,* and the *meafure* of human punifhment.

1. As to the *power* of human punifhment, or the right of the temporal legiflator to inflict difcretionary penalties for crimes and mifdemefnors[h]. It is clear, that the right of punifhing crimes againft the law of nature, as murder and the like, is in a ftate of mere nature vefted in every individual. For it muft be vefted in fomebody; otherwife the laws of nature would be vain and fruitlefs, if none were empowered to put them in execution: and if that power is vefted in any *one,* it muft alfo be vefted in *all* mankind; fince all are by nature equal. Whereof

<hr>

[h] See Grotius, *de j. b. & p. l.* 2. *c.* 20. Puffendorf, L. of Nat. and N. b. 8. c. 3.

the firſt murderer Cain was ſo ſenſible, that we find him [i] ex-preſſing his apprehenſions, that *whoever* ſhould find him would ſlay him.   In a ſtate of ſociety this right is transferred from in-dividuals to the ſovereign power; whereby men are prevented from being judges in their own cauſes, which is one of the evils that civil government was intended to remedy.   Whatever power therefore individuals had of puniſhing offences againſt the law of nature, that is now veſted in the magiſtrate alone; who bears the ſword of juſtice by the conſent of the whole commu-nity.   And to this precedent natural power of individuals muſt be referred that right, which ſome have argued to belong to every ſtate, (though, in faſt, never exerciſed by any) of puniſh-ing not only their own ſubjects, but alſo foreign embaſſadors, even with death itſelf; in caſe they have offended, not indeed againſt the municipal laws of the country, but againſt the di-vine laws of nature, and become liable thereby to forfeit their lives for their guilt [k].

A s to offences merely againſt the laws of ſociety, which are only *mala prohibita,* and not *mala in ſe*; the temporal magiſ-trate is alſo empowered to infliſt coercive penalties for ſuch tranſgreſſions : and this by the conſent of individuals; who, in forming ſocieties, did either tacitly or expreſſly inveſt the ſove-reign power with a right of making laws, and of enforcing obedience to them when made, by exerciſing, upon their non-obſervance, ſeverities adequate to the evil.   The lawfulneſs therefore of puniſhing ſuch criminals is founded upon this prin-ciple, that the law by which they ſuffer was made by their own conſent; it is part of the original contraſt into which they en-tered, when firſt they engaged in ſociety; it was calculated for, and has long contributed to, their own ſecurity.

T h i s right therefore, being thus conferred by univerſal con-ſent, gives to the ſtate exaſtly the ſame power, and no more, over all it's members, as each individual member had naturally

[i] Gen. iv. 14.   [k] See Vol. I. pag. 254.

over

over himself or others. Which has occasioned some to doubt, how far a human legislature ought to inflict capital punishments for *positive* offences; offences against the municipal law only, and not against the law of nature; since no individual has, naturally, a power of inflicting death upon himself or others for actions in themselves indifferent. With regard to offences *mala in se*, capital punishments are in some instances inflicted by the immediate *command* of God himself to all mankind; as, in the case of murder, by the precept delivered to Noah, their common ancestor and representative[1], " whoso sheddeth man's blood, " by man shall his blood be shed." In other instances they are inflicted after the *example* of the creator, in his positive code of laws for the regulation of the Jewish republic; as in the case of the crime against nature. But they are sometimes inflicted without such express warrant or example, at the will and discretion of the human legislature; as for forgery, for robbery, and sometimes for offences of a lighter kind. Of these we are principally to speak: as these crimes are, none of them, offences against natural, but only against social, rights; not even robbery itself, unless it be a robbery from one's person : all others being an infringement of that right of property, which, as we have formerly seen[m], owes it's origin not to the law of nature, but merely to civil society.

THE practice of inflicting capital punishments, for offences of human institution, is thus justified by that great and good man, sir Matthew Hale[n]: " when offences grow enormous, frequent, " and dangerous to a kingdom or state, destructive or highly " pernicious to civil societies, and to the great insecurity and " danger of the kingdom or it's inhabitants, severe punishment " and even death itself is necessary to be annexed to laws in " many cases by the prudence of lawgivers." It is therefore the enormity, or dangerous tendency, of the crime, that alone can warrant any earthly legislature in putting him to death that

[1] Gen. ix. 6.
[m] Book II. ch. 1.
[n] 1 Hal. P. C. 13.

commits it. It is not it's frequency only, or the difficulty of
otherwife preventing it, that will excufe our attempting to prevent it by a wanton effufion of human blood. For, though the
end of punifhment is to deter men from offending, it never can
follow from thence, that it is lawful to deter them at any rate
and by any means; fince there may be unlawful methods of enforcing obedience even to the jufteft laws. Every humane legiflator will be therefore extremely cautious of eftablifhing laws
that inflict the penalty of death, efpecially for flight offences,
or fuch as are merely pofitive. He will expect a better reafon
for his fo doing, than that loofe one which generally is given;
that it is found by former experience that no lighter penalty will
be effectual. For is it found upon farther experience, that capital punifhments are more effectual? Was the vaft territory of
all the Ruffias worfe regulated under the late emprefs Elizabeth, than under her more fanguinary predeceffors? Is it now,
under Catherine II, lefs civilized, lefs focial, lefs fecure? And
yet we are affured, that neither of thefe illuftrious princeffes
have, throughout their whole adminiftration, inflicted the penalty of death: and the latter has, upon full experience of it's
being ufelefs, nay even pernicious, given orders for abolifhing it entirely throughout her extenfive dominions[o]. But indeed, were capital punifhments proved by experience to be a
fure and effectual remedy, that would not prove the neceffity
(upon which the juftice and propriety depend) of inflicting
them upon all occafions when other expedients fail. I fear
this reafoning would extend a great deal too far. For inftance,
the damage done to our public roads by loaded waggons is
univerfally allowed, and many laws have been made to prevent it; none of which have hitherto proved effectual. But
it does not therefore follow, that it would be juft for the legiflature to inflict death upon every obftinate carrier, who defeats or eludes the provifions of former ftatutes. Where the
evil to be prevented is not adequate to the violence of the
preventive, a fovereign that thinks ferioufly can never juftify

[o] Grand inftructions for framing a new code of laws for the Ruffian empire. §. 210.

such

fuch a law to the dictates of confcience and humanity. To fhed the blood of our fellow creature is a matter that requires the greateft deliberation, and the fulleft conviction of our own authority : for life is the immediate gift of God to man ; which neither he can refign, nor can it be taken from him, unlefs by the command or permiffion of him who gave it ; either exprefly revealed, or collected from the laws of nature or fociety by clear and indifputable demonftration.

I would not be underftood to *deny* the right of the legifla- ture in any country to inforce it's own laws by the death of the tranfgreffor, though perfons of fome abilities have *doubted* it ; but only to fuggeft a few hints for the confideration of fuch as are, or may hereafter become, legiflators. When a queftion arifes, whether death may be lawfully inflicted for this or that tranfgreffion, the wifdom of the laws muft decide it : and to this public judgment or decifion all private judgments muft fubmit ; elfe there is an end of the firft principle of all fociety and government. The guilt of blood, if any, muft lie at their doors, who mifinterpret the extent of their warrant ; and not at the doors of the fubject, who is bound to receive the inter- pretations, that are given by the fovereign power.

2. As to the *end*, or final caufe of human punifhments. This is not by way of atonement or expiation for the crime committed ; for that muft be left to the juft determination of the fupreme being : but as a precaution againft future offences of the fame kind. This is effected three ways : either by the amendment of the offender himfelf ; for which purpofe all cor- poral punifhments, fines, and temporary exile or imprifonment are inflicted : or, by deterring others by the dread of his ex- ample from offending in the like way, "*ut poena* (as Tully[p] " exprefles it) *ad paucos, metus ad omnes perveniat* ;" which gives rife to all ignominious punifhments, and to fuch execu- tions of juftice as are open and public : or, laftly, by depriving

[p] *pro Cluentio.* 46.

the

the party injuring of the power to do future mifchief; which
is effected by either putting him to death, or condemning
him to perpetual confinement, flavery, or exile. The fame one
end, of preventing future crimes, is endeavoured to be anfwered
by each of thefe three fpecies of punifhment. The public gains
equal fecurity, whether the offender himfelf be amended by
wholfome correction; or whether he be difabled from doing any
farther harm: and if the penalty fails of both thefe effects, as
it may do, ftill the terror of his example remains as a warning
to other citizens. The method however of inflicting punifhment ought always to be proportioned to the particular purpofe
it is meant to ferve, and by no means to exceed it: therefore
the pains of death, and perpetual difability by exile, flavery, or
imprifonment, ought never to be inflicted, but when the offender appears *incorrigible:* which may be collected either from
a repetition of minuter offences; or from the perpetration of
fome one crime of deep malignity, which of itfelf demonftrates
a difpofition without hope or probability of amendment ·, and
in fuch cafes it would be cruelty to the public, to defer the punifhment of fuch a criminal, till he had an opportunity of repeating perhaps the worft of villanies.

3. As to the *meafure* of human punifhments. From what
has been obferved in the former articles we may collect, that
the quantity of punifhment can never be abfolutely determined
by any ftanding invariable rule; but it muft be left to the arbi-
tration of the legiflature to inflict fuch penalties as are warranted
by the laws of nature and fociety, and fuch as appear to be the
beft calculated to anfwer the end of precaution againft future
offences.

HENCE it will be evident, that what fome have fo highly
extolled for it's equity, the *lex talionis* or law of retaliation, can
never be in all cafes an adequate or permanent rule of punifhment. In fome cafes indeed it feems to be dictated by natural
reafon; as in the cafe of confpiracies to do an injury, or falfe
accufations

accufations of the innocent: to which we may add that law of
the Jews and Egyptians, mentioned by Jofephus and Diodorus
Siculus, that whoever without fufficient caufe was found with
any mortal poifon in his cuftody, fhould himfelf be obliged to
take it. But, in general, the difference of perfons, place, time,
provocation, or other circumftances, may enhance or mitigate
the offence; and in fuch cafes retaliation can never be a proper
meafure of juftice. If a nobleman ftrikes a peafant, all mankind will fee, that if a court of juftice awards a return of the
blow, it is more than a juft compenfation. On the other hand,
retaliation may fometimes be too eafy a fentence; as, if a man
malicioufly fhould put out the remaining eye of him who had
loft one before, it is too flight a punifhment for the maimer to
lofe only one of his: and therefore the law of the Locrians,
which demanded an eye for an eye, was in this inftance judi-
cioufly altered; by decreeing, in imitation of Solon's laws[q], that
he who ftruck out the eye of a one-eyed man, fhould lofe both
his own in return. Befides, there are very many crimes, that
will in no fhape admit of thefe penalties, without manifeft abfurdity and wickednefs. Theft cannot be punifhed by theft,
defamation by defamation, forgery by forgery, adultery by adultery, and the like. And we may add, that thofe inftances,
wherein retaliation appears to be ufed, even by the divine authority, do not really proceed upon the rule of exact retribu-
tion, by doing to the criminal the fame hurt he has done to his
neighbour, and no more; but this correfpondence between the
crime and punifhment is barely a confequence from fome other
principle. Death is ordered to be punifhed with death; not
becaufe one is equivalent to the other, for that would be expiation, and not punifhment. Nor is death always an equivalent
for death: the execution of a needy decrepit affaffin is a poor
fatisfaction for the murder of a nobleman in the bloom of his
youth, and full enjoyment of his friends, his honours, and his
fortune. But the reafon upon which this fentence is grounded
feems to be, that this is the higheft penalty that man can inflict,

[q] Pott. Ant. b.1. c. 26.

and

and tends moft to the fecurity of the world; by removing one murderer from the earth, and fetting a dreadful example to deter others : fo that even this grand inftance proceeds upon other principles than thofe of retaliation. And truly, if any meafure of punifhment is to be taken from the damage fuftained by the fufferer, the punifhment ought rather to exceed than equal the injury : fince it feems contrary to reafon and equity, that the guilty (if convicted) fhould fuffer no more than the innocent has done before him; efpecially as the fuffering of the innocent is paft and irrevocable, that of the guilty is future, contingent, and liable to be efcaped or evaded. With regard indeed to crimes that are incomplete, which confift merely in the intention, and are not yet carried into act, as confpiracies and the like; the innocent has a chance to fruftrate or avoid the villany, as the confpirator has alfo a chance to efcape his punifhment : and this may be one reafon why the *lex talionis* is more proper to be inflicted, if at all, for crimes that confift in intention, than for fuch as are carried into act. It feems indeed confonant to natural reafon, and has therefore been adopted as a maxim by feveral theoretical writers [r], that the punifhment, due to the crime of which one falfely accufes another, fhould be inflicted on the perjured informer. Accordingly, when it was once attempted to introduce into England the law of retaliation, it was intended as a punifhment for fuch only as preferred malicious accufations againft others; it being enacted by ftatute 37 Edw. III. c. 18. that fuch as preferred any fuggeftions to the king's great council fhould put in fureties of taliation; that is, to incur the fame pain that the other fhould have had, in cafe the fuggeftion were found untrue. But, after one year's experience, this punifhment of taliation was rejected, and imprifonment adopted in it's ftead [s].

But though from what has been faid it appears, that there cannot be any regular or determinate method of rating the

---

[r] Beccar. c. 15.   [s] Stat. 38 Edw. III. c. 9.

quantity

quantity of punifhments for crimes, by any one uniform rule; but they muft be referred to the will and difcretion of the legiflative power: yet there are fome general principles, drawn from the nature and circumftances of the crime, that may be of fome affiftance in allotting it an adequate punifhment.

As, firft, with regard to the *object* of it: for the greater and more exalted the object of an injury is, the more care fhould be taken to prevent that injury, and of courfe under this aggravation the punifhment fhould be more fevere. Therefore treafon in confpiring the *king*'s death is by the Englifh law punifhed with greater rigour than even actually killing any private fubject. And yet, generally, a defign to tranfgrefs is not fo flagrant an enormity, as the actual completion of that defign. For evil, the nearer we approach it, is the more difagreeable and fhocking; fo that it requires more obftinacy in wickednefs to perpetrate an unlawful action, than barely to entertain the thought of it: and it is an encouragement to repentance and remorfe, even till the laft ftage of any crime, that it never is too late to retract; and that if a man ftops even here, it is better for him than if he proceeds: for which reafons an attempt to rob, to ravifh, or to kill, is far lefs penal than the actual robbery, rape, or murder. But in the cafe of a treafonable confpiracy, the object whereof is the king's majefty, the bare intention will deferve the higheft degree of feverity: not becaufe the intention is equivalent to the act itfelf; but becaufe the greateft rigour is no more than adequate to a treafonable purpofe of the heart, and there is no greater left to inflict upon the actual execution itfelf.

Again: the violence of paffion, or temptation, may fometimes alleviate a crime; as theft, in cafe of hunger, is far more worthy of compaffion, than when committed through avarice, or to fupply one in luxurious exceffes. To kill a man upon fudden and violent refentment is lefs penal, than upon cool deliberate malice. The age, education, and character of the offender; the repetition (or otherwife) of the offence; the time,

the

the place, the company wherein it was committed; all thefe, and a thoufand other incidents, may aggravate or extenuate the crime[t].

FARTHER: as punifhments are chiefly intended for the prevention of future crimes, it is but reafonable that among crimes of different natures thofe fhould be moft feverely punifh-ed, which are the moft deftructive of the public fafety and happinefs[v]: and, among crimes of an equal malignity, thofe which a man has the moft frequent and eafy opportunities of committing, which cannot be fo eafily guarded againft as others, and which therefore the offender has the ftrongeft inducement to commit: according to what Cicero obferves[u], " *ea funt* " *animadvertenda peccata maxime, quae difficillime praecaventur.*" Hence it is, that for a fervant to rob his mafter is in more cafes capital, than for a ftranger: if a fervant kills his mafter, it is a fpecies of treafon; in another it is only murder: to fteal a handkerchief, or other trifle, privately from one's perfon, is made capital; but to carry off a load of corn from an open field, though of fifty times greater value, is punifhed with tranfportation only. And in the ifland of Man, this rule was formerly carried fo far, that to take away an horfe or an ox was there no felony, but a trefpafs; becaufe of the difficulty in that little territory to conceal them or carry them off: but to fteal a pig or a fowl, which is eafily done, was a capital mifdemefnor, and the offender was punifhed with death[w].

LASTLY, as a conclufion to the whole, we may obferve that punifhments of unreafonable feverity, efpecially when indifcri-minately inflicted, have lefs effect in preventing crimes, and amending the manners of a people, than fuch as are more mer-ciful in general, yet properly intermixed with due diftinctions

---

[t] Thus Demofthenes (in his oration againft Midias) finely works up the aggravations of the infult he had received. " I was abufed, " fays he, by my enemy, in cold blood, out " of malice, not by heat of wine, in the " morning, publicly, before ftrangers as well " as citizens; and that in the temple, whi- " ther the duty of my office called me."

[v] Beccar. c. 6.

[u] *pro Sexto Rofcio*, 40.

[w] 4 Inft. 285.

of feverity. It is the fentiment of an ingenious writer, who feems to have well ftudied the fprings of human action[x], that crimes are more effectually prevented by the *certainty*, than by the *feverity*, of punifhment. For the exceffive feverity of laws (fays Montefquieu[y]) hinders their execution: when the punifhment furpaffes all meafure, the public will frequently out of humanity prefer impunity to it. Thus the ftatute 1 Mar. ft. 1. c. 1. recites in it's preamble, " that the ftate of every king confifts more af-
" furedly in the love of the fubject towards their prince, than
" in the dread of laws made with rigorous pains; and that laws
" made for the prefervation of the commonwealth without
" great penalties are more often obeyed and kept, than laws
" made with extreme punifhments." Happy had it been for the nation, if the fubfequent practice of that deluded princefs in matters of religion, had been correfpondent to thefe fentiments of herfelf and parliament, in matters of ftate and government! We may farther obferve that fanguinary laws are a bad fymptom of the diftemper of any ftate, or at leaft of it's weak conftitution. The laws of the Roman kings, and the twelve tables of the *decemviri*, were full of cruel punifhments: the Porcian law, which exempted all citizens from fentence of death, filently abrogated them all. In this period the republic flourifhed: under the emperors fevere punifhments were revived; and then the empire fell.

I T is moreover abfurd and impolitic to apply the fame punifhment to crimes of different malignity. A multitude of fanguinary laws (befides the doubt that may be entertained concerning the right of making them) do likewife prove a manifeft defect either in the wifdom of the legiflative, or the ftrength of the executive power. It is a kind of quackery in government, and argues a want of folid fkill, to apply the fame univerfal remedy, the *ultimum fupplicium*, to every cafe of difficulty. It is, it muft be owned, much *eafier* to extirpate than to amend mankind:

[x] Beccar. c. 7.   [y] Sp. L. b. 6. c. 13.

yet that magiſtrate muſt be eſteemed both a weak and a cruel ſurgeon, who cuts off every limb, which through ignorance or indolence he will not attempt to cure. It has been therefore ingeniouſly propoſed[z], that in every ſtate a ſcale of crimes ſhould be formed, with a correſponding ſcale of puniſhments, deſcending from the greateſt to the leaſt: but, if that be too romantic an idea, yet at leaſt a wiſe legiſlator will mark the principal diviſions, and not aſſign penalties of the firſt degree to offences of an inferior rank. Where men ſee no diſtinction made in the nature and gradations of puniſhment, the generality will be led to conclude there is no diſtinction in the guilt. Thus in France the puniſhment of robbery, either with or without murder, is the ſame[a]: hence it is, that though perhaps they are therefore ſubject to fewer robberies, yet they never rob but they alſo murder. In China murderers are cut to pieces, and robbers not: hence in that country they never murder on the highway, though they often rob. And in England, beſides the additional terrors of a ſpeedy execution, and a ſubſequent expoſure or diſſection, robbers have a hope of tranſportation, which ſeldom is extended to murderers. This has the ſame effect here as in China; in preventing frequent aſſaſſination and ſlaughter.

YET, though in this inſtance we may glory in the wiſdom of the Engliſh law, we ſhall find it more difficult to juſtify the frequency of capital puniſhment to be found therein; inflicted (perhaps inattentively) by a multitude of ſucceſſive independent ſtatutes, upon crimes very different in their natures. It is a melancholy truth, that among the variety of actions which men are daily liable to commit, no leſs than an hundred and ſixty have been declared by act of parliament[b] to be felonies without benefit of clergy; or, in other words, to be worthy of inſtant death. So dreadful a liſt, inſtead of diminiſhing, increaſes the number of

[z] Beccar. c. 6.
[a] Sp. L. b. 6. c. 16.

[b] See Ruffhead's index to the ſtatutes, (tit. felony) and the acts which have ſince been made.

offenders.

offenders. The injured, through compaffion, will often forbear to profecute : juries, through compaffion, will fometimes forget their oaths, and either acquit the guilty or mitigate the nature of the offence : and judges, through compaffion, will refbite one half of the convicts, and recommend them to the royal mercy. Among fo many chances of efcaping, the needy or hardened offender overlooks the multitude that fuffer ; he boldly engages in fome defperate attempt, to relieve his wants or fupply his vices ; and, if unexpectedly the hand of juftice overtakes him, he deems himfelf peculiarly unfortunate, in falling at laft a facrifice to thofe laws, which long impunity has taught him to contemn.

C H A P T E R   T H E   S E C O N D.

O F T H E PERSONS CAPABLE O F C O M M I T T I N G C R I M E S.

HAVING, in the preceding chapter, confidered in general the nature of crimes, and punifhments, we are next led, in the order of our diftribution, to enquire what perfons are, or are not, *capable* of committing crimes; or, which is all one, who are exempted from the cenfures of the law upon the commiffion of thofe acts, which in other perfons would be feverely punifhed. In the procefs of which enquiry, we muft have recourfe to particular and fpecial exceptions: for the general rule is, that no perfon fhall be excufed from punifhment for difobedience to the laws of his country, excepting fuch as are expreffly defined and exempted by the laws themfelves.

ALL the feveral pleas and excufes, which protect the committer of a forbidden act from the punifhment which is otherwife annexed thereto, may be reduced to this fingle confideration, the want or defect of *will*. An involuntary act, as it has no claim to merit, fo neither can it induce any guilt: the concurrence of the will, when it has it's choice either to do or to avoid the fact in queftion, being the only thing that renders
human

human actions either praiseworthy or culpable. Indeed, to make a complete crime, cognizable by human laws, there must be both a will and an act. For though, *in foro conscientiae*, a fixed design or will to do an unlawful act is almost as heinous as the commission of it, yet, as no temporal tribunal can search the heart, or fathom the intentions of the mind, otherwise than as they are demonstrated by outward actions, it therefore cannot punish for what it cannot know. For which reason in all temporal jurisdictions an *overt* act, or some open evidence of an intended crime, is necessary, in order to demonstrate the depravity of the will, before the man is liable to punishment. And, as a vitious will without a vitious act is no civil crime, so, on the other hand, an unwarrantable act without a vitious will is no crime at all. So that to constitute a crime against human laws, there must be, first, a vitious will; and, secondly, an unlawful act consequent upon such vitious will.

Now there are three cases, in which the will does not join with the act: 1. Where there is a defect of understanding. For where there is no discernment, there is no choice; and where there is no choice, there can be no act of the will, which is nothing else but a determination of one's choice, to do or to abstain from a particular action: he therefore, that has no understanding, can have no will to guide his conduct. 2. Where there is understanding and will sufficient, residing in the party; but not called forth and exerted at the time of the action done: which is the case of all offences committed by chance or ignorance. Here the will sits neuter; and neither concurs with the act, nor disagrees to it. 3. Where the action is constrained by some outward force and violence. Here the will counteracts the deed; and is so far from concurring with, that it loaths and disagrees to, what the man is obliged to perform. It will be the business of the present chapter briefly to consider all the several species of defect in will, as they fall under some one or other of these general heads: as infancy, idiocy, lunacy, and intoxication, which fall under the first class; misfortune, and
ignorance,

ignorance, which may be referred to the fecond; and compulfion or neceffity, which may properly rank in the third.

I. First, we will confider the cafe of *infancy*, or nonage; which is a defect of the underftanding. Infants, under the age of difcretion, ought not to be punifhed by any criminal profecution whatever[a]. What the age of difcretion is, in various nations is matter of fome variety. The civil law diftinguifhed the age of minors, or thofe under twenty five years old, into three ftages: *infantia*, from the birth till feven years of age; *pueritia*, from feven to fourteen; and *pubertas* from fourteen upwards. The period of *pueritia*, or childhood, was again fubdivided into two equal parts; from feven to ten and an half was *aetas infantiae proxima*; from ten and an half to fourteen was *aetas pubertati proxima*. During the firft ftage of infancy, and the next half ftage of childhood, *infantiae proxima*, they were not punifhable for any crime[b]. During the other half ftage of childhood, approaching to puberty, from ten and an half to fourteen, they were indeed punifhable, if found to be *doli capaces*, or capable of mifchief; but with many mitigations, and not with the utmoft rigor of the law. During the laft ftage (at the age of puberty, and afterwards) minors were liable to be punifhed, as well capitally, as otherwife.

The law of England does in fome cafes privilege an infant, under the age of twenty one, as to common mifdemefnors; fo as to efcape fine, imprifonment, and the like: and particularly in cafes of omiffion, as not repairing a bridge, or a highway, and other fimilar offences[c]: for, not having the command of his fortune till twenty one, he wants the capacity to do thofe things, which the law requires. But where there is any notorious breach of the peace, a riot, battery, or the like, (which infants, when full grown, are at leaft as liable as others to

[a] 1 Hawk. P. C. 2.
[b] *Inft.* 3. 20. 10.

[c] 1 Hal. P. C. 20, 21, 22.

commit

commit) for thefe an infant, above the age of fourteen, is
equally liable to fuffer, as a perfon of the full age of twenty one.

WITH regard to capital crimes, the law is ftill more minute
and circumfpect; diftinguifhing with greater nicety the feveral
degrees of age and difcretion. By the antient Saxon law, the
age of twelve years was eftablifhed for the age of poffible difcretion, when firft the underftanding might open[d]: and from
thence till the offender was fourteen, it was *aetas pubertati
proxima*, in which he might, or might not, be guilty of a crime,
according to his natural capacity or incapacity. This was the
dubious ftage of difcretion: but, under twelve, it was held
that he could not be guilty in will, neither after fourteen could
he be fuppofed innocent, of any capital crime which he in fact
committed. But by the law, as it now ftands, and has ftood at
leaft ever fince the time of Edward the third, the capacity of
doing ill, or contracting guilt, is not fo much meafured by
years and days, as by the ftrength of the delinquent's underftanding and judgment. For one lad of eleven years old may
have as much cunning as another of fourteen; and in thefe
cafes our maxim is, that "*malitia fupplet aetatem.*" Under feven
years of age indeed an infant cannot be guilty of felony[e]; for
then a felonious difcretion is almoft an impoffibility in nature:
but at eight years old he may be guilty of felony[f]. Alfo, under
fourteen, though an infant fhall be *prima facie* adjudged to be
doli incapax; yet if it appear to the court and jury, that he was
doli capax, and could difcern between good and evil, he may
be convicted and fuffer death. Thus a girl of thirteen has been
burnt for killing her miftrefs: and one boy of ten, and another
of nine years old, who had killed their companions, have been
fentenced to death, and he of ten years actually hanged; becaufe it appeared upon their trials, that the one hid himfelf,
and the other hid the body he had killed; which hiding manifefted a confcioufnefs of guilt, and a difcretion to difcern be-

---

[d] *LL. Athelftan.* Wilk. 65.   [f] Dalt. Juft. c. 147.
[e] Mirr. c. 4. §. 16. 1 Hal. P. C. 27.

tween good and evil[g]. And there was an inſtance in the laſt century, where a boy of eight years old was tried at Abingdon for firing two barns; and, it appearing that he had malice, revenge, and cunning, he was found guilty, condemned, and hanged accordingly[h]. Thus alſo, in very modern times, a boy of ten years old was convicted on his own confeſſion of murdering his bedfellow; there appearing in his whole behaviour plain tokens of a miſchievous diſcretion: and, as the ſparing this boy merely on account of his tender years might be of dangerous conſequence to the public, by propagating a notion that children might commit ſuch atrocious crimes with impunity, it was unanimouſly agreed by all the judges that he was a proper ſubject of capital puniſhment[i]. But, in all ſuch caſes, the evidence of that malice, which is to ſupply age, ought to be ſtrong and clear beyond all doubt or contradiction.

II. The ſecond caſe of a deficiency in will, which excuſes from the guilt of crimes, ariſes alſo from a defective or vitiated underſtanding, viz. in an *idiot* or a *lunatic*. For the rule of law as to the latter, which may eaſily be adapted alſo to the former, is, that "*furioſus furore ſolum punitur.*" In criminal caſes therefore idiots and lunatics are not chargeable for their own acts, if committed when under theſe incapacities: no, not even for treaſon itſelf[k]. Alſo, if a man in his ſound memory commits a capital offence, and before arraignment for it, he becomes mad, he ought not to be arraigned for it; becauſe he is not able to plead to it with that advice and caution that he ought. And if, after he has pleaded, the priſoner becomes mad, he ſhall not be tried; for how can he make his defence? If, after he be tried and found guilty, he loſes his ſenſes before judgment, judgment ſhall not be pronounced; and if, after judgment, he becomes of nonſane memory, execution ſhall be ſtayed: for peradventure, ſays the humanity of the Engliſh law, had the priſoner been of ſound memory, he might have alleged ſome-

[g] 1 Hal. P. C. 26, 27.　　　　[i] Foſter. 72.
[h] Emlyn on 1 Hal. P. C. 25.　　[k] 3 Inſt. 6.

thing

thing in ſtay of judgment or execution[1]. Indeed, in the bloody reign of Henry the eighth, a ſtatute was made[m], which enacted, that if a perſon, being *compos mentis,* ſhould commit high treaſon, and after fall into madneſs, he might be tried in his abſence, and ſhould ſuffer death, as if he were of perfect memory. But this ſavage and inhuman law was repealed by the ſtatute 1 & 2 Ph. & M. c. 10. "For, as is obſerved by ſir Edward "Coke[n], the execution of an offender is for example, *ut poena* "*ad paucos, metus ad omnes perveniat :* but ſo it is not when "a madman is executed ; but ſhould be a miſerable ſpectacle, "both againſt law, and of extreme inhumanity and cruelty, "and can be no example to others." But if there be any doubt, whether the party be *compos* or not, this ſhall be tried by a jury. And if he be ſo found, a total idiocy, or abſolute inſanity, excuſes from the guilt, and of courſe from the puniſhment, of any criminal action committed under ſuch deprivation of the ſenſes : but, if a lunatic hath lucid intervals of underſtanding, he ſhall anſwer for what he does in thoſe intervals, as if he had no deficiency[o]. Yet, in the caſe of abſolute madmen, as they are not anſwerable for their actions, they ſhould not be permitted the liberty of acting unleſs under proper control ; and, in particular, they ought not to be ſuffered to go looſe, to the terror of the king's ſubjects. It was the doctrine of our antient law, that perſons deprived of their reaſon might be confined till they recovered their ſenſes[p], without waiting for the forms of a commiſſion or other ſpecial authority from the crown : and now, by the vagrant acts[q], a method is chalked out for impriſoning, chaining, and ſending them to their proper homes.

III. THIRDLY ; as to artificial, voluntarily contracted madneſs, by *drunkenneſs* or intoxication, which, depriving men of their reaſon, puts them in a temporary phrenzy ; our law looks upon this as an aggravation of the offence, rather than as an

---

[l] 1 Hal. P. C. 34.
[m] 33 Hen. VIII. c. 20.
[n] 3 Inſt. 6.

[o] 1 Hal. P. C. 31.
[p] Bro. *Abr. tit. corone.* 101.
[q] 17 Geo. II. c. 5.

excufe for any criminal mifbehaviour. A drunkard, fays fir Edward Coke[r], who is *voluntarius daemon*, hath no privilege thereby; but what hurt or ill foever he doth, his drunkennefs doth aggravate it : *nam omne crimen ebrietas, et incendit, et detegit.* It hath been obferved, that the real ufe of ftrong liquors, and the abufe of them by drinking to excefs, depend much upon the temperature of the climate in which we live. The fame indulgence, which may be neceffary to make the blood move in Norway, would make an Italian mad. A German therefore, fays the prefident Montefquieu[s], drinks through cuftom, founded upon conftitutional neceffity ; a Spaniard drinks through choice, or out of the mere wantonnefs of luxury : and drunkennefs, he adds, ought to be more feverely punifhed, where it makes men mifchievous and mad, as in Spain and Italy, than where it only renders them ftupid and heavy, as in Germany and more northern countries. And accordingly, in the warmer climate of Greece, a law of Pittacus enacted, " that he who " committed a crime, when drunk, fhould receive a double pu- " nifhment;" one for the crime itfelf, and the other for the ebriety which prompted him to commit it[t]. The Roman law indeed made great allowances for this vice : " *per vinum delapfis* " *capitalis poena remittitur*[u]. But the law of England, confidering how eafy it is to counterfeit this excufe, and how weak an excufe it is, (though real) will not fuffer any man thus to privilege one crime by another[w].

IV. A FOURTH deficiency of will, is where a man commits an unlawful act by *misfortune* or *chance*, and not by defign. Here the will obferves a total neutrality, and does not co-operate with the deed; which therefore wants one main ingredient of a crime. Of this, when it affects the life of another, we fhall find more occafion to fpeak hereafter; at prefent only obferving, that if any accidental mifchief happens to follow from the per-

[r] 1 Inft. 247.
[s] Sp. L. b. 14. c. 10.
[t] Puff. L. of N. b. 8. c. 3.

[u] *Ff.* 49. 16. 6.
[w] Plowd. 19.

formance

formance of a *lawful* act, the party ftands excufed from all
guilt : but if a man be doing any thing *unlawful,* and a confequence enfues which he did not forefee or intend, as the death
of a man or the like, his want of forefight fhall be no excufe ;
for, being guilty of one offence, in doing antecedently what is
in itfelf unlawful, he is criminally guilty of whatever confequence may follow the firft mifbehaviour[x].

V. FIFTHLY, *ignorance* or *miftake* is another defect of will ;
when a man, intending to do a lawful act, does that which is
unlawful. For here the deed and the will acting feparately,
there is not that conjunction between them, which is neceffary
to form a criminal act. But this muft be an ignorance or miftake of fact, and not an error in point of law. As if a man,
intending to kill a thief or houfebreaker in his own houfe, by
miftake kills one of his own family, this is no criminal action[y]:
but if a man thinks he has a right to kill a perfon excommunicated or outlawed, wherever he meets him, and does fo; this
is wilful murder. For a miftake in point of law, which every
perfon of difcretion not only may, but is bound and prefumed
to know, is in criminal cafes no fort of defence. *Ignorantia
juris, quod quifque tenetur fcire, neminem excufat,* is as well the
maxim of our own law[z], as it was of the Roman[a].

VI. A SIXTH fpecies of defect of will is that arifing from
compulfion and inevitable *neceffity.* Thefe are a conftraint upon
the will, whereby a man is urged to do that which his judgment difapproves ; and which, it is to be prefumed, his will (if
left to itfelf) would reject. As punifhments are therefore only
inflicted for the abufe of that free-will, which God has given
to man, it is highly juft and equitable that a man fhould be
excufed for thofe acts, which are done through unavoidable
force and compulfion.

[x] 1 Hal. P. C. 39.　　　　　　　[z] Plowd. 343.
[y] Cro. Car. 538.　　　　　　　　[a] Ff. 22. 6. 9.

1. O F this nature, in the firſt place, is the obligation of *civil ſubjection*, whereby the inferior is conſtrained by the ſuperior to act contrary to what his own reaſon and inclination would ſuggeſt: as when a legiſlator eſtabliſhes iniquity by a law, and commands the ſubject to do an act contrary to religion or ſound morality. How far this excuſe will be admitted *in foro conſcientiae*, or whether the inferior in this caſe is not bound to obey the divine, rather than the human law, it is not my buſineſs to decide ; though the queſtion I believe, among the caſuiſts, will hardly bear a doubt. But, however that may be, obedience to the laws in being is undoubtedly a ſufficient extenuation of civil guilt before the municipal tribunal. The ſheriff, who burnt Latimer and Ridley, in the bigotted days of queen Mary, was not liable to puniſhment from Elizabeth, for executing ſo horrid an office ; being juſtified by the commands of that magiſtracy, which endeavoured to reſtore ſuperſtition under the holy auſpices of it's mercileſs ſiſter, perſecution.

A s to perſons in private relations ; the principal caſe, where conſtraint of a ſuperior is allowed as an excuſe for criminal miſconduct, is with regard to the matrimonial ſubjection of the wife to her huſband : for neither a ſon or a ſervant are excuſed for the commiſſion of any crime, whether capital or otherwiſe, by the command or coercion of the parent or maſter [b]; though in ſome caſes the command or authority of the huſband, either expreſs or implied, will privilege the wife from puniſhment, even for capital offences. And therefore if a woman commit theft, burglary, or other civil offences againſt the laws of ſociety, by the coercion of her huſband ; or merely by his command, which the law conſtrues a coercion ; or even in his company, his example being equivalent to a command ; ſhe is not guilty of any crime : being conſidered as acting by compulſion and not of her own will [c]. Which doctrine is at leaſt a thouſand years old in this kingdom, being to be found among the laws of

[b] 1 Hawk. P. C. 3.   [c] 1 Hal. P. C. 45.

king

king Ina the Weſt Saxon [d]. And it appears that, among the northern nations on the continent, this privilege extended to any
woman tranſgreſſing in concert with a man, and to any ſervant
that committed a joint offence with a freeman : the male or
freeman only was puniſhed, the female or ſlave diſmiſſed ;
" *proculdubio quod alterum libertas, alterum neceſſitas impelleret* [e]."
But (beſides that in our law, which is a ſtranger to ſlavery, no
impunity is given to ſervants, who are as much free agents as
their maſters) even with regard to wives, this rule admits of an
exception in crimes that are *mala in ſe*, and prohibited by the
law of nature, as murder and the like : not only becauſe theſe
are of a deeper dye ; but alſo, ſince in a ſtate of nature no one
is in ſubjection to another, it would be unreaſonable to ſcreen
an offender from the puniſhment due to natural crimes, by the
refinements and ſubordinations of civil ſociety. In treaſon alſo,
(the higheſt crime which a member of ſociety can, as ſuch, be
guilty of) no plea of coverture ſhall excuſe the wife ; no pre-
ſumption of the huſband's coercion ſhall extenuate her guilt [f]:
as well becauſe of the odiouſneſs and dangerous conſequence of
the crime itſelf, as becauſe the huſband, having broken through
the moſt ſacred tie of ſocial community by rebellion againſt the
ſtate, has no right to that obedience from a wife, which he
himſelf as a ſubject has forgotten to pay. In inferior miſdemeſnors alſo, we may remark another exception ; that a wife
may be indicted and ſet in the pillory *with* her huſband, for
keeping a brothel : for this is an offence touching the domeſtic
oeconomy or government of the houſe, in which the wife has
a principal ſhare ; and is alſo ſuch an offence as the law pre-
ſumes to be generally conducted by the intrigues of the female
ſex [g]. And in all caſes, where the wife offends alone, without
the company or command of her huſband, ſhe is reſponſible for
her offence, as much as any feme-ſole.

---

[d] *cap.* 57.
[e] Stiernhook *de jure Suecn. l.* 2. *c.* 4.

[f] 1 Hal. P. C. 47.
[g] 1 Hawk. P. C. 2, 3.

2. AN-

2. ANOTHER species of compulsion or necessity is what our law calls *duress per minas* [h]; or threats and menaces, which induce a fear of death or other bodily harm, and which take away for that reason the guilt of many crimes and misdemesnors; at least before the human tribunal. But then that fear, which compels a man to do an unwarrantable action, ought to be just and well grounded; such, " *qui cadere possit in virum constantem,* " *non timidum et meticulosum,*" as Bracton expresses it [i], in the words of the civil law [k]. Therefore, in time of war or rebellion, a man may be justified in doing many treasonable acts by compulsion of the enemy or rebels, which would admit of no excuse in the time of peace [l]. This however seems only, or at least principally, to hold as to positive crimes, so created by the laws of society; and which therefore society may excuse; but not as to natural offences, so declared by the law of God, wherein human magistrates are only the executioners of divine punishment. And therefore though a man be violently assaulted, and hath no other possible means of escaping death, but by killing an innocent person; this fear and force shall not acquit him of murder; for he ought rather to die himself, than escape by the murder of an innocent [m]. But in such a case he is permitted to kill the assailant; for there the law of nature, and self-defence it's primary canon, have made him his own protector.

3. THERE is a third species of necessity, which may be distinguished from the actual compulsion of external force or fear; being the result of reason and reflection, which act upon and constrain a man's will, and oblige him to do an action, which without such obligation would be criminal. And that is, when a man has his choice of two evils set before him, and, being under a necessity of choosing one, he chuses the least

[h] See Vol. I. pag. 131.
[i] *l. 2. f.* 16.
[k] *Ff.* 4. 2. 5, & 6.

[l] 1 Hal. P. C. 50.
[m] *Ibid.* 51.

pernicious

pernicious of the two. Here the will cannot be faid freely to
exert itfelf, being rather paffive, than active ; or, if active, it is
rather in rejecting the greater evil than in choofing the lefs. Of
this fort is that neceffity, where a man by the commandment
of the law is bound to arreft another for any capital offence, or
to difperfe a riot, and refiftance is made to his authority : it is
here juftifiable and even neceffary to beat, to wound, or perhaps to kill the offenders, rather than permit the murderer to
efcape, or the riot to continue. For the prefervation of the
peace of the kingdom, and the apprehending of notorious malefactors, are of the utmoft confequence to the public ; and
therefore excufe the felony, which the killing would otherwife amount to [n].

4. T H E R E is yet another cafe of neceffity, which has occafioned great fpeculation among the writers upon general law ;
viz. whether a man in extreme want of food or clothing may
juftify ftealing either, to relieve his prefent neceffities. And
this both Grotius [o] and Puffendorf [p], together with many other
of the foreign jurifts, hold in the affirmative ; maintaining by
many ingenious, humane, and plaufible reafons, that in fuch
cafes the community of goods by a kind of tacit conceffion of
fociety is revived. And fome even of our own lawyers have
held the fame [q] ; though it feems to be an unwarranted doctrine,
borrowed from the notions of fome civilians : at leaft it is now
antiquated, the law of England admitting no fuch excufe at
prefent [r]. And this it's doctrine is agreeable not only to the
fentiments of many of the wifeft antients, particularly Cicero [s],
who holds that " *fuum cuique incommodum ferendum eft, potius*
" *quam de alterius commodis detrahendum ;*" but alfo to the Jewifh
law, as certified by king Solomon himfelf [t] : " if a thief fteal to
" fatisfy his foul when he is hungry, he fhall reftore fevenfold,

---

[n] 1 Hal. P. C. 53.
[o] *de jure b. & p. l.* 2. *c.* 2.
[p] L. of Nat. and N. l. 2. c. 6.
[q] Briton, c. 10. Mirr. c. 4. §. 16.

[r] 1 Hal. P. C. 54.
[s] *de off. l.* 3. *c.* 5.
[t] Prov. vi. 30.

" and

" and shall give all the substance of his house:" which was the ordinary punishment for theft in that kingdom. And this is founded upon the highest reason: for men's properties would be under a strange insecurity, if liable to be invaded according to the wants of others; of which wants no man can possibly be an adequate judge, but the party himself who pleads them. In this country especially, there would be a peculiar impropriety in admitting so dubious an excuse: for by our laws such sufficient provision is made for the poor by the power of the civil magistrate, that it is impossible that the most needy stranger should ever be reduced to the necessity of thieving to support nature. This case of a stranger is, by the way, the strongest instance put by baron Puffendorf, and whereon he builds his principal arguments: which, however they may hold upon the continent, where the parsimonious industry of the natives orders every one to work or starve, yet must lose all their weight and efficacy in England, where charity is reduced to a system, and interwoven in our very constitution. Therefore our laws ought by no means to be taxed with being unmerciful, for denying this privilege to the necessitous; especially when we consider, that the king, on the representation of his ministers of justice, hath a power to soften the law, and to extend mercy in cases of peculiar hardship. An advantage which is wanting in many states, particularly those which are democratical: and these have in it's stead introduced and adopted, in the body of the law itself, a multitude of circumstances tending to alleviate it's rigour. But the founders of our constitution thought it better to vest in the crown the power of pardoning particular objects of compassion, than to countenance and establish theft by one general undistinguishing law.

VII. In the several cases before-mentioned, the incapacity of committing crimes arises from a deficiency of the will. To these we may add one more, in which the law supposes an incapacity of doing wrong from the excellence and perfection of the person;

fon ; which extend as well to the will as to the other qualities of his mind. I mean the cafe of the king : who, by virtue of his royal prerogative, is not under the coercive power of the law ; which will not fuppofe him capable of committing a folly, much lefs a crime. We are therefore, out of reverence and decency, to forbear any idle enquiries, of what would be the confequence if the king were to act thus and thus : fince the law deems fo highly of his wifdom and virtue, as not even to prefume it poffible for him to do any thing inconfiftent with his ftation and dignity ; and therefore has made no provifion to remedy fuch a grievance. But of this fufficient was faid in a former volume ᵂ, to which I muft refer the reader.

ᵘ 1 Hal. P. C. 44.　　　　　　ᵂ Book I. ch. 7. pag. 244.

CHAPTER THE THIRD.

OF PRINCIPALS AND ACCESSORIES.

IT having been shewn in the preceding chapter what persons
are, or are not, upon account of their situation and circumstances, capable of committing crimes, we are next to make a
few remarks on the different degrees of guilt among persons
that are capable of offending; *viz.* as *principal*, and as *accessory*.

I. A MAN may be *principal* in an offence in two degrees.
A principal, in the first degree, is he that is the actor, or absolute perpetrator of the crime; and, in the second degree, he
who is present, aiding, and abetting the fact to be done[a].
Which *presence* need not always be an actual immediate standing by, within sight or hearing of the fact; but there may be
also a constructive presence, as when one commits a robbery or
murder, and another keeps watch or guard at some convenient
distance[b]. And this rule hath also other exceptions: for, in
case of murder by poisoning, a man may be a principal felon,
by preparing and laying the poison, or giving it to another (who
is ignorant of it's poisonous quality[c]) for that purpose; and yet
not administer it himself, nor be present when the very deed of
poisoning is committed[d]. And the same reasoning will hold,

a 1 Hal. P. C. 615.   c *Ibid.* 349.
b Foster. 350.   d 3 Inst. 138.

with

with regard to other murders committed in the abſence of the murderer, by means which he had prepared before-hand, and which probably could not fail of their miſchievous effect. As by laying a trap or pitfall for another, whereby he is killed; letting out a wild beaſt, with an intent to do miſchief, or exciting a madman to commit murder, ſo that death thereupon enſues; in every of theſe caſes the party offending is guilty of murder as a principal, in the firſt degree. For he cannot be called an acceſſory, that neceſſarily pre-ſuppoſing a principal; and the poiſon, the pitfall, the beaſt, or the madman cannot be held principals, being only the inſtruments of death. As therefore he muſt be certainly guilty, either as principal or acceſſory, and cannot be ſo as acceſſory, it follows that he muſt be guilty as principal: and if principal, then in the firſt degree; for there is no other criminal, much leſs a ſuperior in the guilt, whom he could aid, abet, or aſſiſt[e].

II. AN *acceſſory* is he who is not the chief actor in the offence, nor preſent at it's performance, but is ſomeway concerned therein, either *before* or *after* the fact committed. In conſidering the nature of which degree of guilt, we will, firſt, examine, what offences admit of acceſſories, and what not: ſecondly, who may be an acceſſory *before* the fact: thirdly, who may be an acceſſory *after* it: and, laſtly, how acceſſories, conſidered merely as ſuch, and diſtinct from principals, are to be treated.

1. AND, firſt, as to what offences admit of acceſſories, and what not. In high treaſon there are no acceſſories, but all are principals: the ſame acts, that make a man acceſſory in felony, making him a principal in high treaſon, upon account of the heinouſneſs of the crime[f]. Beſides it is to be conſidered, that the bare intent to commit treaſon is many times actual treaſon; as imagining the death of the king, or conſpiring to take away his crown. And, as no one can adviſe and abet ſuch a crime without an intention to have it done, there can be no acceſſories

[e] 1 Hal. P. C. 617.　2 Hawk. P. C. 315.　[f] 3 Inſt. 138.　1 Hal. P. C. 613.

E 2　　　　　　　　　　　　before

before the fact; fince the very advice and abetment amount to principal treafon. But this will not hold in the inferior fpecies of high treafon, which do not amount to the legal idea of compaffing the death of the king, queen, or prince. For in thofe no advice to commit them, unlefs the thing be actually performed, will make a man a principal traitor[s]. In petit treafon, murder, and felonies of all kinds, there may be acceffories: except only in thofe offences, which by judgment of law are fudden and unpremeditated, as manflaughter and the like; which therefore cannot have any acceffories *before* the fact[h]. But in petit larciny, or minute thefts, and all other crimes under the degree of felony, there are no acceffories; but all perfons concerned therein, if guilty at all, are principals[i]: the fame rule holding with regard to the higheft and loweft offences; though upon different reafons. In treafon all are principals, *propter odium delicti*; in trefpafs all are principals, becaufe the law, *quae de minimis non curat*, does not defcend to diftinguifh the different fhades of guilt in petty mifdemefnors. It is a maxim, that *accefforius fequitur naturam fui principalis*[k]: and therefore an acceffory cannot be guilty of a higher crime than his principal; being only punifhed, as a partaker of his guilt. So that if a fervant inftigates a ftranger to kill his mafter, this being murder in the ftranger as principal, of courfe the fervant is acceffory only to the crime of murder; though, had he been prefent and affifting, he would have been guilty as principal of petty treafon, and the ftranger of murder[l].

2. A s to the fecond point, who may be an acceffory *before* the fact; fir Matthew Hale[m] defines him to be one, who being abfent at the time of the crime committed, doth yet procure, counfel, or command another to commit a crime. Herein abfence is neceffary to make him an acceffory; for if fuch procurer, or the like, be prefent, he is guilty of the crime as prin-

---

  [s] Fofter. 342.   [k] 3 Inft. 139.
  [h] 1 Hal. P. C. 615.   [l] 2 Hawk. P. C. 315.
  [i] *Ibid.* 613.   [m] 1 Hal. P. C. 615, 616.

cipal.

cipal. If A then advifes B to kill another, and B does it in the abfence of A, now B is principal, and A is acceffory in the murder. And this holds, even though the party killed be not *in rerum natura* at the time of the advice given. As if A, the reputed father, advifes B the mother of a baftard child, unborn, to ftrangle it when born, and fhe does fo; A is acceffory to this murder[n]. And it is alfo fettled[o], that whoever procureth a felony to be committed, though it be by the intervention of a third perfon, is an acceffory before the fact. It is likewife a rule, that he who in any wife commands or counfels another to commit an unlawful act, is acceffory to all that enfues upon that unlawful act; but is not acceffory to any act diftinct from the other. As if A commands B to beat C, and B beats him fo that he dies; B is guilty of murder as principal, and A as acceffory. But if A commands B to burn C's houfe; and he, in fo doing, commits a robbery; now A, though acceffory to the burning, is not acceffory to the robbery, for that is a thing of a diftinct and unconfequential nature[p]. But if the felony committed be the fame in fubftance with that which is commanded, and only varying in fome circumftantial matters; as if, upon a command to poifon Titius, he is ftabbed or fhot, that he dies; the commander is ftill acceffory to the murder, for the fubftance of the thing commanded was the death of Titius, and the manner of it's execution is a mere collateral circumftance[q].

3. AN acceffory *after* the fact may be, where a perfon, knowing a felony to have been committed, receives, relieves, comforts, or affifts the felon[r]. Therefore, to make an acceffory *ex poft facto*, it is in the firft place requifite that he knows of the felony committed[s]. In the next place, he muft receive, relieve, comfort, or affift him. And, generally, any affiftance whatever given to a felon, to hinder his being apprehended,

[n] Dyer. 186.
[o] Fofter. 125.
[p] 1 Hal. P. C. 617.

[q] 2 Hawk. P. C. 316.
[r] 1 Hal. P. C. 618.
[s] 2 Hawk. P. C. 319.

tried,

tried, or fuffering punifhment, makes the affiftor an acceffory. As furnifhing him with a horfe to efcape his purfuers, money or victuals to fupport him, a houfe or other fhelter to conceal him, or open force and violence to refcue or protect him [t]. So likewife to convey inftruments to a felon to enable him to break gaol, or to bribe the gaoler to let him efcape, makes a man an acceffory to the felony. But to relieve a felon in gaol with clothes or other neceffaries, is no offence: for the crime imputable to this fpecies of acceffory is the hindrance of public juftice, by affifting the felon to efcape the vengeance of the law [u]. To buy or receive ftolen goods, knowing them to be ftolen, falls under none of thefe defcriptions: it was therefore at common law, a mere mifdemefnor, and made not the receiver acceffory to the theft, becaufe he received the *goods* only, and not the *felon* [w]: but now by the ftatutes 5 Ann. c. 31. and 4 Geo. I. c. 11. all fuch receivers are made acceffories, and may be tranfported for fourteen years. In France this is punifhed with death: and the Gothic conftitutions diftinguifhed alfo three forts of thieves, " *unum qui confilium daret, alterum qui* " *contrectaret, tertium qui receptaret et occuleret; pari poenae fin-* " *gulos obnoxios* [x].

THE felony muft be complete at the time of the affiftance given; elfe it makes not the affiftant an acceffory. As if one wounds another mortally, and after the wound given, but before death enfues, a perfon affifts or receives the delinquent: this does not make him acceffory to the homicide, for till death enfues there is no felony committed [y]. But fo ftrict is the law where a felony is actually complete, in order to do effectual juftice, that the neareft relations are not fuffered to aid or receive one another. If the parent affifts his child, or the child his parent, if the brother receives his brother, the mafter his fervant, or the fervant his mafter, or even if the hufband relieves

[t] 2 Hawk. P. C. 317, 318.
[u] 1 Hal. P. C. 620, 621.
[w] 1 Hal. P. C. 620.
[x] Stiernhook *de jure Goth. l.* 3. *c.* 5.
[y] 2 Hawk. P. C. 320.

his

his wife, who have any of them committed a felony, the receivers become acceſſories *ex poſt facto*[z]. But a feme covert cannot become an acceſſory by the receipt and concealment of her huſband; for ſhe is preſumed to act under his coercion, and therefore ſhe is not bound, neither ought ſhe, to diſcover her lord[a].

4. THE laſt point of enquiry is, how acceſſories are to be treated, conſidered diſtinct from principals. And the general rule of the antient law (borrowed from the Gothic conſtitutions[b]) is this, that acceſſories ſhall ſuffer the ſame puniſhment as their principals: if one be liable to death, the other is alſo liable[c]: as, by the laws of Athens, delinquents and their abettors were to receive the ſame puniſhment[d]. Why then, it may be aſked, are ſuch elaborate diſtinctions made between acceſſories and principals, if both are to ſuffer the ſame puniſhment? For theſe reaſons. 1. To diſtinguiſh the nature and denomination of crimes, that the accuſed may know how to defend himſelf when indicted: the commiſſion of an actual robbery being quite a different accuſation, from that of harbouring the robber. 2. Becauſe, though by the antient common law the rule is as before laid down, that both ſhall be puniſhed alike, yet now by the ſtatutes relating to the benefit of clergy a diſtinction is made between them: acceſſories *after* the fact being ſtill allowed the benefit of clergy in all caſes; which is denied to the principals, and acceſſories *before* the fact, in many caſes; as in petit treaſon, murder, robbery, and wilful burning[e]. And perhaps if a diſtinction were conſtantly to be made between the puniſhment of principals and acceſſories, even *before* the fact, the latter to be treated with a little leſs ſeverity than the former, it might prevent the perpetration of many crimes, by increaſing the difficulty of finding a perſon to execute the deed itſelf; as his danger would be greater than that of his accomplices, by

[z] 3 Inſt. 108. 2 Hawk. P. C. 320.   [c] 3 Inſt. 188.
[a] 1 Hal. P. C. 621.   Pott. Antiq. b. 1. c. 26.
[b] See Stiernho. k. 167.   1 Hal. P. C. 615.

reafon of the difference of his punifhment[1].   3. Becaufe formerly no man could be tried as acceffory, till after the principal
was convicted, or at leaft at the fame time with him : though
that law is now much altered, as will be fhewn more fully in it's
proper place.   4. Becaufe, though a man be indicted as acceffory
and acquitted, he may afterwards be indicted as principal ; for
an acquittal of receiving or counfelling a felon is no acquittal
of the felony itfelf : but it is matter of fome doubt, whether, if
a man be acquitted as principal, he can be afterwards indicted
as acceffory *before* the fact ; fince thofe offences are frequently
very near allied, and therefore an acquittal of the guilt of one
may be an acquittal of the other alfo[g]. But it is clearly held,
that one acquitted as principal may be indicted as an acceffory
after the fact ; fince that is always an offence of a different
fpecies of guilt, principally tending to evade the public juftice,
and is fubfequent in it's commencement to the other.   Upon
thefe reafons the diftinction of principal and acceffory will appear
to be highly neceffary ; though the punifhment is ftill much the
fame with regard to principals, and fuch acceffories as offend
a priori.

Beccar. c. 37.

g 1 Hal. P. C. 625, 626. 2 Hawk. P. C. 373.
Fofter. 361.

CHAPTER THE FOURTH.

OF OFFENCES AGAINST GOD AND RELIGION.

IN the prefent chapter we are to enter upon the detail of the
feveral fpecies of crimes and mifdemefnors, with the punifhment annexed to each by the laws of England. It was obferved, in the beginning of this book [a], that crimes and mifdemefnors are a breach and violation of the public rights and
duties, owing to the whole community, confidered as a community, in it's focial aggregate capacity. And in the very entrance of thefe commentaries [b] it was fhewn, that human laws
can have no concern with any but focial and relative duties;
being intended only to regulate the conduct of man, confidered
under various relations, as a member of civil fociety. All crimes
ought therefore to be eftimated merely according to the mif-
chiefs which they produce in civil fociety [c]: and, of confequence, private vices, or the breach of mere abfolute duties,
which man is bound to perform confidered only as an individual, are not, cannot be, the object of any municipal law; any
farther than as by their evil example, or other pernicious effects,
they may prejudice the community, and thereby become a fpecies of public crimes. Thus the vice of drunkennefs, if committed privately and alone, is beyond the knowlege and of courfe
beyond the reach of human tribunals: but if committed publicly, in the face of the world, it's evil example makes it liable

[a] See pag. 5.   [c] Beccar. ch. 8.
[b] See Vol. I. pag. 123, 124.

to temporal cenfures. The vice of lying, which confifts (ab-
ftractedly taken) in a criminal violation of truth, and therefore
in any fhape is derogatory from found morality, is not however
taken notice of by our law, unlefs it carries with it fome public
inconvenience, as fpreading falfe news; or fome focial injury,
as flander and malicious profecution, for which a private recom-
pence is given. And yet drunkennefs and lying are *in foro con-*
fcientiae as thoroughly criminal when they are not, as when they
are, attended with public inconvenience. The only difference
is, that both public and private vices are fubject to the vengeance of eternal juftice; and public vices are befides liable to
the temporal punifhments of human tribunals.

On the other hand, there are fome mifdemefnors, which are
punifhed by the municipal law, that are in themfelves nothing
criminal, but are made fo by the pofitive conftitutions of the
ftate for public convenience. Such as poaching, exportation of
wool, and the like. Thefe are naturally no offences at all;
but their whole criminality confifts in their difobedience to
the fupreme power, which has an undoubted right for the well-
being and peace of the community to make fome things unlawful, which were in themfelves indifferent. Upon the whole
therefore, though part of the offences to be enumerated in the
following fheets are offences againft the revealed law of God,
others againft the law of nature, and fome are offences againft
neither; yet in a treatife of municipal law we muft confider
them all as deriving their particular guilt, here punifhable, from
the law of man.

Having premifed this caution, I fhall next proceed to
diftribute the feveral offences, which are either directly or by
confequence injurious to civil fociety, and therefore punifhable
by the laws of England, under the following general heads:
firft, thofe which are more immediately injurious to God and
his holy religion; fecondly, fuch as violate and tranfgrefs the
law of nations; thirdly, fuch as more efpecially affect the fovereign

reign executive power of the ſtate, or the king and his government ; fourthly, ſuch as more directly infringe the rights of the
public or common wealth ; and, laſtly, ſuch as derogate from
thoſe rights and duties, which are owing to particular individuals, and in the preſervation and vindication of which the community is deeply intereſted.

FIRST then, of ſuch crimes and miſdemeſnors, as more immediately offend Almighty God, by openly tranſgreſſing the precepts of religion either natural or revealed ; and mediately, by
their bad example and conſequence, the law of ſociety alſo ;
which conſtitutes that guilt in the action, which human tribunals are to cenſure.

I. Of this ſpecies the firſt is that of *apoſtacy*, or a total renunciation of chriſtianity, by embracing either a falſe religion,
or no religion at all. This offence can only take place in ſuch
as have once profeſſed the true religion. The perverſion of a
chriſtian to judaiſm, paganiſm, or other falſe religion, was
puniſhed by the emperors Conſtantius and Julian with confiſcation of goods[d] ; to which the emperors Theodoſius and Valen-
nian added capital puniſhment, in caſe the apoſtate endeavoured
to pervert others to the ſame iniquity[e]. A puniſhment too ſevere for any temporal laws to inflict : and yet the zeal of our
anceſtors imported it into this country ; for we find by Bracton[f],
that in his time apoſtates were to be burnt to death. Doubtleſs
the preſervation of chriſtianity, as a national religion, is, ab-
ſtracted from it's own intrinſic truth, of the utmoſt conſequence
to the civil ſtate : which a ſingle inſtance will ſufficiently demonſtrate. The belief of a future ſtate of rewards and puniſhments, the entertaining juſt ideas of the moral attributes of the
ſupreme being, and a firm perſuaſion that he ſuperintends and
will finally compenſate every action in human life (all which
are clearly revealed in the doctrines, and forcibly inculcated by
the precepts, of our ſaviour Chriſt) theſe are the grand founda-

[d] *Cod.* 1. 7. 1.
[e] *Ibid.* 6.

[f] *l.* 3. *c.* 9.

tion

tion of all judicial oaths; which call God to witnefs the truth of thofe facts, which perhaps may be only known to him and the party attefting: all moral evidence therefore, all confidence in human veracity, muft be weakened by irreligion, and overthrown by infidelity. Wherefore all affronts to chriftianity, or endeavours to depreciate it's efficacy, are highly deferving of human punifhment. But yet the lofs of life is a heavier penalty than the offence, taken in a civil light, deferves: and, taken in a fpiritual light, our laws have no jurifdiction over it. This punifhment therefore has long ago become obfolete; and the offence of apoftacy was for a long time the object only of the ecclefiaftical courts, which corrected the offender *pro falute animae*. But about the clofe of the laft century, the civil liberties to which we were then reftored being ufed as a cloke of malicioufnefs, and the moft horrid doctrines fubverfive of all religion being publicly avowed both in difcourfe and writings, it was found neceffary again for the civil power to interpofe, by not admitting thofe mifcreants [g] to the privileges of fociety, who maintained fuch principles as deftroyed all moral obligation. To this end it was enacted by ftatute 9 & 10 W. III. c.32. that if any perfon educated in, or having made profeffion of, the chriftian religion, fhall by writing, printing, teaching, or advifed fpeaking, deny the chriftian religion to be true, or the holy fcriptures to be of divine authority, he fhall upon the firft offence be rendered incapable to hold any office or place of truft; and, for the fecond, be rendered incapable of bringing any action, being guardian, executor, legatee, or purchafer of lands, and fhall fuffer three years imprifonment without bail. To give room however for repentance; if, within four months after the firft conviction, the delinquent will in open court publicly renounce his error, he is difcharged for that once from all difabilities.

II. A s e c o n d offence is that of *herefy*; which confifts not in a total denial of chriftianity, but of fome of it's effential

[g] *Mefcreyantz* in our antient law-books is the name of unbelievers.

doctrines,

doctrines, publicly and obstinately avowed; being defined, "*sententia rerum divinarum humano sensu excogitata, palam docta,* "*et pertinaciter defensa*[h]." And here it must also be acknowleged that particular modes of belief or unbelief, not tending to over-turn christianity itself, or to sap the foundations of morality, are by no means the object of coercion by the civil magistrate. What doctrines shall therefore be adjudged heresy, was left by our old constitution to the determination of the ecclesiastical judge; who had herein a most arbitrary latitude allowed him. For the general definition of an heretic given by Lyndewode[i], ex-tends to the smallest deviations from the doctrines of holy church: "*haereticus est qui dubitat de fide catholica, et qui negligit servare ea,* "*quae Romana ecclesia statuit, seu servare decreverat.*" Or, as the statute 2 Hen. IV. c. 15. expresses it in English, "teachers of "erroneous opinions, contrary to the faith and blessed determi-"nations of the holy church." Very contrary this to the usage of the first general councils, which defined all heretical doctrines with the utmost precision and exactness. And what ought to have alleviated the punishment, the uncertainty of the crime, seems to have enhanced it in those days of blind zeal and pious cruelty. It is true, that the sanctimonious hypocrisy of the canonists went at first no farther than enjoining penance, ex-communication, and ecclesiastical deprivation, for heresy; though afterwards they proceeded boldly to imprisonment by the ordi-nary, and confiscation of goods *in pios usus.* But in the mean time they had prevailed upon the weakness of bigotted princes to make the civil power subservient to their purposes, by making heresy not only a temporal, but even a capital offence: the Romish ecclesiastics determining, without appeal, whatever they pleased to be heresy, and shifting off to the secular arm the odium and drudgery of executions; with which they themselves were too tender and delicate to intermeddle. Nay they pre-tended to intercede and pray, on behalf of the convicted heretic, *ut citra mortis periculum sententia circa eum moderetur*[k]:	well knowing at the fame time that they were delivering the unhappy victim to certain death. Hence the capital punifhments inflicted on the antient Donatifts and Manichaeans by the emperors Theodofius and Juftinian [l]: hence alfo the conftitution of the emperor Frederic mentioned by Lyndewode [m], adjudging all perfons without diftinction to be burnt with fire, who were convicted of herefy by the ecclefiaftical judge. The fame emperor, in another conftitution [n], ordained that if any temporal lord, when admonifhed by the church, fhould neglect to clear his territories of heretics within a year, it fhould be lawful for good catholics to feife and occupy the lands, and utterly to exterminate the heretical poffeffors. And upon this foundation was built that arbitrary power, fo long claimed and fo fatally exerted by the pope, of difpofing even of the kingdoms of refractory princes to more dutiful fons of the church. The immediate event of this conftitution was fomething fingular, and may ferve to illuftrate at once the gratitude of the holy fee, and the juft punifhment of the royal bigot: for upon the authority of this very conftitution, the pope afterwards expelled this very emperor Frederic from his kingdom of Sicily, and gave it to Charles of Anjou [o].

CHRISTIANITY being thus deformed by the daemon of perfecution upon the continent, we cannot expect that our own ifland fhould be entirely free from the fame fcourge. And therefore we find among our antient precedents [p] a writ *de haeretico comburendo*, which is thought by fome to be as antient as the common law itfelf. However it appears from thence, that the conviction of herefy by the common law was not in any petty ecclefiaftical court, but before the archbifhop himfelf in a provincial fynod; and that the delinquent was delivered over to the king to do as he fhould pleafe with him: fo that the crown had a control over the fpiritual power, and might pardon the convict by iffuing

[l] *Cod. l.* 1. *tit.* 5.
[m] *c. de haereticis.*
[n] *Cod.* 1. 5. 4.

[o] Baldus *in Cod.* 1. 5. 4.
[p] F. N. B. 269.

no procefs againſt him ; the writ *de haeretico comburendo* being not a writ of courſe, but iſſuing only by the ſpecial direction of the king in council [q].

But in the reign of Henry the fourth, when the eyes of the chriſtian world began to open, and the ſeeds of the proteſtant religion (though under the opprobrious name of lollardy [r]) took root in this kingdom ; the clergy, taking advantage from the king's dubious title to demand an increaſe of their own power, obtained an act of parliament [s], which ſharpened the edge of perſecution to it's utmoſt keenneſs. For, by that ſtatute, the dioceſan alone, without the intervention of a ſynod, might convict of heretical tenets ; and unleſs the convict abjured his opinions, or if after abjuration he relapſed, the ſheriff was bound *ex officio*, if required by the biſhop, to commit the unhappy victim to the flames, without waiting for the conſent of the crown. By the ſtatute 2 Hen. V. c. 7. lollardy was alſo made a temporal offence, and indictable in the king's courts ; which did not thereby gain an excluſive, but only a concurrent juriſdiction with the biſhop's conſiſtory.

Afterwards, when the final reformation of religion began to advance, the power of the ecclefiaſtics was ſomewhat moderated : for though what hereſy *is*, was not then preciſely defined, yet we are told in ſome points what it *is not:* the ſtatute 25 Hen. VIII. c. 14. declaring, that offences againſt the ſee of Rome are not hereſy ; and the ordinary being thereby reſtrained from proceeding in any caſe upon mere ſuſpicion ; that is, unleſs the party be accuſed by two credible witneſſes, or an indictment of hereſy be firſt previouſly found in the king's courts of common law. And yet the ſpirit of perſecution was not then abated, but only diverted into a lay chanel. For in ſix years afterwards, by ſtatute 31 Hen. VIII. c. 14. the bloody law of the ſix articles was made, which eſtabliſhed the ſix moſt conteſted points of popery, tran-

---

[q] 1 Hal. P. C. 395.

[r] So called not from *lolium*, or tares, (which was afterwards deviſed, in order to juſtify the burning of them from Matth.

xiii. 30.) but from one Walter Lolhard, a German reformer. Mod. Un. Hiſt. xxvi. 13. Spelm. *Gloſſ.* 371.

[s] 2 Hen. IV. c. 15.

ſub-

substantiation, communion in one kind, the celibacy of the clergy, monastic vows, the sacrifice of the mass, and auricular confession ; which points were " determined and resolved by the " most godly study, pain, and travail of his majesty : for which " his most humble and obedient subjects, the lords *spiritual* and " temporal and the commons, in parliament assembled, did not " only render and give unto his highness their most high and " hearty thanks," but did also enact and declare all oppugners of the first to be heretics, and to be burnt with fire ; and of the five last to be felons, and to suffer death. The same statute established a new and mixed jurisdiction of clergy and laity for the trial and conviction of heretics ; the reigning prince being then equally intent on destroying the supremacy of the bishops of Rome, and establishing all other their corruptions of the christian religion.

I shall not perplex this detail with the various repeals and revivals of these sanguinary laws in the two succeeding reigns ; but shall proceed directly to the reign of queen Elizabeth ; when the reformation was finally established with temper and decency, unsullied with party rancour, or personal caprice and resentment. By statute 1 Eliz. c. 1. all former statutes relating to heresy are repealed, which leaves the jurisdiction of heresy as it stood at common law ; *viz.* as to the infliction of common censures, in the ecclesiastical courts ; and, in case of burning the heretic, in the provincial synod only [l]. Sir Matthew Hale is indeed of a different opinion, and holds that such power resided in the diocesan also ; though he agrees, that in either case the writ *de haeretico comburendo* was not demandable of common right, but grantable or otherwise merely at the king's discretion [u]. But the principal point now gained, was, that by this statute a boundary is for the first time set to what shall be accounted heresy ; nothing for the future being to be so determined, but only such tenets, which have been heretofore so declared, 1. By the words of the canonical scriptures ; 2. By the first four general councils, or such others

[l] 5 Rep. 23. 12 Rep. 56 92.   [u] 1 Hal. P. C. 405.

as

as have only ufed the words of the holy fcriptures; or, 3. Which fhall hereafter be fo declared by the parliament, with the affent of the clergy in convocation. Thus was herefy reduced to a greater certainty than before; though it might not have been the worfe to have defined it in terms ftill more precife and particular: as a man continued ftill liable to be burnt, for what perhaps he did not underftand to be herefy, till the ecclefiaftical judge fo interpreted the words of the canonical fcriptures.

FOR the writ *de haeretico comburendo* remained ftill in force; and we have inftances of it's being put in execution upon two anabaptifts in the feventeenth of Elizabeth, and two Arians in the ninth of James the firft. But it was totally abolifhed, and herefy again fubjected only to ecclefiaftical correction, *pro falute animae*, by virtue of the ftatute 29 Car. II. c. 9. For in one and the fame reign, our lands were delivered from the flavery of military tenures; our bodies from arbitrary imprifonment by the *habeas corpus* act; and our minds from the tyranny of fuperftitious bigotry, by demolifhing this laft badge of perfecution in the Englifh law.

IN what I have now faid I would not be underftood to derogate from the juft rights of the national church, or to favour a loofe latitude of propagating any crude undigefted fentiments in religious matters. Of propagating, I fay; for the bare entertaining them, without an endeavour to diffufe them, feems hardly cognizable by any human authority. I only mean to illuftrate the excellence of our prefent eftablifhment, by looking back to former times. Every thing is now as it fhould be: unlefs perhaps that herefy ought to be more ftrictly defined, and no profecution permitted, even in the ecclefiaftical courts, till the tenets in queftion are by proper authority previoufly declared to be heretical. Under thefe reftrictions, it feems neceffary for the fupport of the national religion, that the officers of the church fhould have power to cenfure heretics, but not to exterminate or deftroy them. It has alfo been thought proper for the civil magiſtrate again to interpoſe, with regard to one ſpecies of hereſy, very prevalent in modern times : for by ſtatute 9 & 10 W. III. c. 32. if any perſon educated in the chriſtian religion, or profeſſing the ſame, ſhall by writing, printing, teaching, or adviſed ſpeaking, deny any one of the perſons in the holy trinity to be God, or maintain that there are more Gods than one, he ſhall undergo the ſame penalties and incapacities, which were juſt now mentioned to be inflicted on apoſtacy by the ſame ſtatute. And thus much for the crime of hereſy.

III. ANOTHER ſpecies of offences againſt religion are thoſe which affect the *eſtabliſhed church*. And theſe are either poſitive, or negative. Poſitive, as by reviling it's ordinances : or negative, by non-conformity to it's worſhip. Of both of theſe in their order.

1. AND, firſt, of the offence of *reviling the ordinances* of the church. This is a crime of a much groſſer nature than the other of mere non-conformity : ſince it carries with it the utmoſt indecency, arrogance, and ingratitude : indecency, by ſetting up private judgment in oppoſition to public ; arrogance, by treating with contempt and rudeneſs what has at leaſt a better chance to be right, than the ſingular notions of any particular man ; and ingratitude, by denying that indulgence and liberty of conſcience to the members of the national church, which the retainers to every petty conventicle enjoy. However it is provided by ſtatutes 1 Edw. VI. c. 1. and 1 Eliz. c. 1. that whoever reviles the ſacrament of the lord's ſupper ſhall be puniſhed by fine and impriſonment : and by the ſtatute 1 Eliz. c. 2. if any *miniſter* ſhall ſpeak any thing in derogation of the book of common prayer, he ſhall be impriſoned ſix months, and forfeit a year's value of his benefice ; and for the ſecond offence he ſhall be deprived. And if *any perſon* whatſoever ſhall in plays, ſongs, or other open words, ſpeak any thing in derogation, depraving, or deſpiſing of the ſaid book, he ſhall forfeit for the firſt offence an hundred marks ; for the ſecond four hundred ; and for the

third

third shall forfeit all his goods and chattels, and suffer imprisonment for life. These penalties were framed in the infancy of our
present establishment ; when the disciples of Rome and of Ge-
neva united in inveighing with the utmost bitterness against the
English liturgy : and the terror of these laws (for they seldom,
if ever, were fully executed) proved a principal means, under
providence, of preserving the purity as well as decency of our
national worship.   Nor can their continuance to this time be
thought too severe and intolerant ; when we consider, that they
are levelled at an offence, to which men cannot now be prompted
by any laudable motive ; not even by a mistaken zeal for reformation : since from political reasons, sufficiently hinted at in a
former volume ᵛ, it would now be extremely unadvisable to
make any alterations in the service of the church ; unless it
could be shewn that some manifest impiety or shocking absurdity
would follow from continuing it in it's present form.   And
therefore the virulent declamations of peevish or opinionated men
on topics so often refuted, and of which the preface to the liturgy
is itself a perpetual refutation, can be calculated for no other
purpose, than merely to disturb the consciences, and poison the
minds of the people.

2. NON-CONFORMITY to the worship of the church is the
other, or negative branch of this offence.   And for this there is
much more to be pleaded than for the former ; being a matter of
private conscience, to the scruples of which our present laws have
shewn a very just and christian indulgence.   For undoubtedly all
persecution and oppression of weak consciences, on the score of
religious persuasions, are highly unjustifiable upon every principle
of natural reason, civil liberty, or sound religion.   But care must
be taken not to carry this indulgence into such extremes, as may
endanger the national church : there is always a difference to be
made between toleration and establishment.

NON-CONFORMISTS are of two sorts : first, such as absent
themselves from the divine worship in the established church,

ᵛ Vol. I. pag. 98.

through

through total irreligion, and attend the fervice of no other perfuafion. Thefe by the ftatutes of 1 Eliz. c. 2. 23 Eliz. c. 1. and
3 Jac. I. c. 4. forfeit one fhilling to the poor every lord's day
they fo abfent themfelves, and 20 *l.* to the king if they continue
fuch default for a month together. And if they keep any inmate, thus irreligioufly difpofed, in their houfes, they forfeit
10 *l. per* month.

T H E fecond fpecies of non-conformifts are thofe who offend
through a miftaken or perverfe zeal. Such were efteemed by our
laws, enacted fince the time of the reformation, to be papifts
and proteftant diffenters : both of which were fuppofed to be
equally fchifmatics in departing from the national church ; with
this difference, that the papifts divide from us upon material,
though erroneous, reafons ; but many of the diffenters upon
matters of indifference, or, in other words, upon no reafon at
all. However the laws againft the former are much more fevere
than againft the latter ; the principles of the papifts being de-
fervedly looked upon to be fubverfive of the civil government,
but not thofe of the proteftant diffenters. As to the papifts,
their tenets are undoubtedly calculated for the introduction of all
flavery, both civil and religious : but it may with juftice be
queftioned, whether the fpirit, the doctrines, and the practice
of the fectaries are better calculated to make men good fubjects.
One thing is obvious to obferve, that thefe have once within the
compafs of the laft century, effected the ruin of our church and
monarchy ; which the papifts have attempted indeed, but have
never yet been able to execute. Yet certainly our anceftors were
miftaken in their plans of compulfion and intolerance. The fin
of fchifm, as fuch, is by no means the object of temporal coercion and punifhment. If through weaknefs of intellect, through
mifdirected piety, through perverfenefs and acerbity of temper,
or (which is often the cafe) through a profpect of fecular advantage in herding with a party, men quarrel with the ecclefiaftical
eftablifhment, the civil magiftrate has nothing to do with it ;
unlefs their tenets and practice are fuch as threaten ruin or difturbance

turbance to the ſtate.　He is bound indeed to protect the eſtabliſhed church, by admitting none but it's genuine members to offices of truſt and emolument : for, if every ſect was to be indulged in a free communion of civil employments, the idea of a national eſtabliſhment would at once be deſtroyed, and the epiſcopal church would be no longer the church of England. But, this point being once ſecured, all perſecution for diverſity of opinions, however ridiculous or abſurd they may be, is contrary to every principle of ſound policy and civil freedom.　The names and ſubordination of the clergy, the poſture of devotion, the materials and colour of the miniſter's garment, the joining in a known or an unknown form of prayer, and other matters of the ſame kind, muſt be left to the option of every man's private judgment.

WITH regard therefore to *proteſtant diſſenters*, although the experience of their turbulent diſpoſition in former times occaſioned ſeveral diſabilities and reſtrictions (which I ſhall not undertake to juſtify) to be laid upon them by abundance of ſtatutes [w], yet at length the legiſlature, with a ſpirit of true magnanimity, extended that indulgence to theſe ſectaries, which they themſelves, when in power, had held to be countenancing ſchiſm, and denied to the church of England.　The penalties are all of them ſuſpended by the ſtatute 1 W. & M. ſt. 2. c. 18. commonly called the toleration act ; which exempts all diſſenters (except papiſts, and ſuch as deny the trinity) from all penal laws relating to religion, provided they take the oaths of allegiance and ſupremacy, and ſubſcribe the declaration againſt popery, and repair to ſome congregation regiſtered in the biſhop's court or at the ſeſſions, the doors whereof muſt be always open :　and diſſenting teachers are alſo to ſubſcribe the thirty nine articles, except thoſe relating to church government and infant baptiſm.　Thus are all perſons, who will approve themſelves no papiſts or oppugners of the trinity, left at full liberty to act as their conſcience ſhall direct them, in the matter of religious worſhip.　But by ſtatute

[w] 31 Eliz. c. 1.　17 Car. II. c. 2.　22 Car. II. c. 1.

5 Geo. I.

5 Geo. I. c. 4. no mayor, or principal magiſtrate, muſt appear at any diſſenting meeting with the enſigns of his office[x], on pain of diſability to hold that or any other office : the legiſlature judging it a matter of propriety, that a mode of worſhip, ſet up in oppoſition to the national, when allowed to be exerciſed in peace, ſhould be exerciſed alſo with decency, gratitude, and humility.

A s to *papiſts*, what has been ſaid of the proteſtant diſſenters would hold equally ſtrong for a general toleration of them ; provided their ſeparation was founded only upon difference of opinion in religion, and their principles did not alſo extend to a ſubverſion of the civil government. If once they could be brought to renounce the ſupremacy of the pope, they might quietly enjoy their ſeven ſacraments, their purgatory, and auricular confeſſion ; their worſhip of reliques and images ; nay even their tranſub-ſtantiation. But while they acknowlege a foreign power, ſupe-rior to the ſovereignty of the kingdom, they cannot complain if the laws of that kingdom will not treat them upon the foot-ing of good ſubjects.

L e t us therefore now take a view of the laws in force againſt the papiſts ; who may be divided into three claſſes, perſons pro-feſſing popery, popiſh recuſants convict, and popiſh prieſts. 1. Perſons profeſſing the popiſh religion, beſides the former pe-nalties for not frequenting their pariſh church, are by ſeveral ſtatutes, too numerous to be here recited[y], diſabled from taking any lands either by deſcent or purchaſe, after eighteen years of age, until they renounce their errors ; they muſt at the age of twenty one regiſter their eſtates before acquired, and all future conveyances and wills relating to them ; they are incapable of preſenting to any advowſon, or granting to any other perſon any

---

[x] Sir Humphrey Edwin, a lord mayor of London, had the imprudence ſoon after the toleration-act to go to a preſbyterian meet-ing-houſe in his formalities : which is allu-ded to by dean Swift, in his *tale of a tub,* under the allegory of *Jack* getting on a great horſe, and eating cuſtard.

[y] See Hawkins's pleas of the crown, and Burn's juſtice.

avoid-

avoidance of the fame, in prejudice of the two univerfities; they may not keep or teach any fchool under pain of perpetual imprifonment; they are liable alfo in fome inftances to pay double taxes; and, if they willingly fay or hear mafs, they forfeit the one two hundred, the other one hundred marks, and each fhall fuffer a year's imprifonment. Thus much for perfons, who, from the misfortune of family prejudices or otherwife, have conceived an unhappy attachment to the Romifh church from their infancy, and publicly profefs it's errors. But if any evil induftry is ufed to rivet thefe errors upon them, if any perfon fends another abroad to be educated in the popifh religion, or to refide in any religious houfe abroad for that purpofe, or contributes any thing to their maintenance when there; both the fender, the fent, and the contributor, are difabled to fue in law or equity, to be executor or adminiftrator to any perfon, to take any legacy or deed of gift, and to bear any office in the realm, and fhall forfeit all their goods and chattels, and likewife all their real eftate for life. And where thefe errors are alfo aggravated by apoftacy, or perverfion, where a perfon is reconciled to the fee of Rome or procures others to be reconciled, the offence amounts to high treafon. 2. Popifh recufants, convicted in a court of law of not attending the fervice of the church of England, are fubject to the following difabilities, penalties, and forfeitures, over and above thofe before-mentioned. They can hold no office or employment; they muft not keep arms in their houfes, but the fame may be feifed by the juftices of the peace; they may not come within ten miles of London, on pain of 100 *l*; they can bring no action at law, or fuit in equity; they are not permitted to travel above five miles from home, unlefs by licence, upon pain of forfeiting all their goods; and they may not come to court, under pain of 100 *l*. No marriage or burial of fuch recufant, or baptifm of his child, fhall be had otherwife than by the minifters of the church of England, under other fevere penalties. A married woman, when recufant, fhall forfeit two thirds of her dower or jointure, may not be executrix or adminiftratrix to her hufband, nor have any part of his goods; and during the

coverture

coverture may be kept in prifon, unlefs her hufband redeems her
at the rate of 10 *l.* a month, or the third part of all his lands.
And, laftly, as a feme-covert recufant may be imprifoned, fo all
others muft, within three months after conviction, either fubmit
and renounce their errors, or, if required fo to do by four juftices,
muft abjure and renounce the realm : and if they do not depart, or if they return without the king's licence, they fhall be
guilty of felony, and fuffer death as felons. There is alfo an
inferior fpecies of recufancy, (refufing to make the declaration
againft popery enjoined by ftatute 30 Car. II. ft. 2. when tendered
by the proper magiftrate) which, if the party refides within ten
miles of London, makes him an abfolute recufant convict ; or,
if at a greater diftance, fufpends him from having any feat in
parliament, keeping arms in his houfe, or any horfe above the
value of five pounds. This is the ftate, by the laws now in being, of a lay papift. But, 3. The remaining fpecies or degree,
viz. popifh priefts, are in a ftill more dangerous condition. By
ftatute 11 & 12 W. III. c. 4. popifh priefts or bifhops, celebra-
ting mafs or exercifing any parts of their functions in England,
except in the houfes of embaffadors, are liable to perpetual imprifonment. And by the ftatute 27 Eliz. c. 2. any popifh prieft,
born in the dominions of the crown of England, who fhall come
over hither from beyond fea, or fhall be in England three days
without conforming and taking the oaths, is guilty of high treafon : and all perfons harbouring him are guilty of felony without the benefit of clergy.

THIS is a fhort fummary of the laws againft the papifts, under their three feveral claffes, of perfons profeffing the popifh
religion, popifh recufants convict, and popifh priefts. Of which
the prefident Montefquieu obferves [z], that they are fo rigorous,
though not profeffedly of the fanguinary kind, that they do all
the hurt that can poffibly be done in cold blood. But in anfwer
to this it may be obferved, (what foreigners who only judge
from our ftatute book are not fully apprized of) that thefe laws

[z] Sp. L. b. 19. c. 27.

are

are seldom exerted to their utmost rigor: and indeed, if they were, it would be very difficult to excuse them. For they are rather to be accounted for from their history, and the urgency of the times which produced them, than to be approved (upon a cool review) as a standing system of law. The restless machinations of the jesuits during the reign of Elizabeth, the turbulence and uneasiness of the papists under the new religious establishment, and the boldness of their hopes and wishes for the succession of the queen of Scots, obliged the parliament to counteract so dangerous a spirit by laws of a great, and perhaps necessary, severity. The powder-treason, in the succeeding reign, struck a panic into James I, which operated in different ways: it occasioned the enacting of new laws against the papists; but deterred him from putting them in execution. The intrigues of queen Henrietta in the reign of Charles I, the prospect of a popish successor in that of Charles II, the assassination-plot in the reign of king William, and the avowed claim of a popish pretender to the crown, will account for the extension of these penalties at those several periods of our history. But if a time should ever arrive, and perhaps it is not very distant, when all fears of a pretender shall have vanished, and the power and influence of the pope shall become feeble, ridiculous, and despicable, not only in England but in every kingdom of Europe; it probably would not then be amiss to review and soften these rigorous edicts; at least till the *civil* principles of the roman-catholics called again upon the legislature to renew them: for it ought not to be left in the breast of every merciless bigot, to drag down the vengeance of these occasional laws upon inoffensive, though mistaken, subjects; in opposition to the lenient inclinations of the civil magistrate, and to the destruction of every principle of toleration and religious liberty.

IN order the better to secure the established church against perils from non-conformists of all denominations, infidels, turks, jews, heretics, papists, and sectaries, there are however two bulwarks erected; called the *corporation* and *test* acts: by the

former of which [a] no perfon can be legally elected to any office
relating to the government of any city or corporation, unlefs,
within a twelvemonth before, he has received the facrament of
the lord's fupper according to the rites of the church of England : and he is alfo enjoined to take the oaths of allegiance
and fupremacy at the fame time that he takes the oath of office :
or, in default of either of thefe requifites, fuch election fhall be
void. The other, called the teft act [b], directs all officers civil
and military to take the oaths and make the declaration againft
tranfubftantiation, in the court of king's bench or chancery,
the next term, or at the next quarter feffions, or (by fubfequent
ftatutes) within fix months, after their admiffion ; and alfo
within the fame time to receive the facrament of the lord's fupper, according to the ufage of the church of England, in fome
public church immediately after divine fervice and fermon, and
to deliver into court a certificate thereof figned by the minifter
and church-warden, and alfo to prove the fame by two credible
witneffes ; upon forfeiture of 500 l, and difability to hold the
faid office. And of much the fame nature with thefe is the ftatute 7 Jac. I. c. 2. which permits no perfons to be naturalized
or reftored in blood, but fuch as undergo a like teft : which teft
having been removed in 1753, in favour of the Jews, was the
next feffion of parliament reftored again with fome precipitation.

THUS much for offences, which ftrike at our national religion, or the doctrine and difcipline of the church of England
in particular. I proceed now to confider fome grofs impieties
and general immoralities, which are taken notice of and punifhed
by our municipal law ; frequently in concurrence with the ecclefiaftical, to which the cenfure of many of them does alfo of right
appertain ; though with a view fomewhat different : the fpiritual court punifhing all finful enormities for the fake of reforming the private finner, *pro falute animae* ; while the temporal
courts refent the public affront to religion and morality, on

[a] Stat. 13 Car. II. ft. 2. c. 1.   [b] Stat. 25 Car. II. c. 2.

which

which all government muſt depend for ſupport, and correct more for the ſake of example than private amendment.

IV. THE fourth ſpecies of offences therefore, more immediately againſt God and religion, is that of *blaſphemy* againſt the Almighty, by denying his being or providence; or by contumelious reproaches of our Saviour Chriſt. Whither alſo may be referred all profane ſcoffing at the holy ſcripture, or expoſing it to contempt and ridicule. Theſe are offences puniſhable at common law by fine and impriſonment, or other infamous corporal puniſhment[c]: for chriſtianity is part of the laws of England[d].

V. SOMEWHAT allied to this, though in an inferior degree, is the offence of profane and common *ſwearing* and *curſing*. By the laſt ſtatute againſt which, 19 Geo. II. c. 21. which repeals all former ones, every labourer, ſailor, or ſoldier ſhall forfeit 1 *s.* for every profane oath or curſe, every other perſon under the degree of a gentleman 2 *s.* and every gentleman or perſon of ſuperior rank 5 *s.* to the poor of the pariſh; and, on a ſecond conviction, double; and, for every ſubſequent conviction, treble the ſum firſt forfeited; with all charges of conviction: and in default of payment ſhall be ſent to the houſe of correction for ten days. Any juſtice of the peace may convict upon his own hearing, or the teſtimony of one witneſs; and any conſtable or peace officer, upon his own hearing, may ſecure any offender and carry him before a juſtice, and there convict him. If the juſtice omits his duty, he forfeits 5 *l.* and the conſtable 40 *s.* And the act is to be read in all pariſh churches, and public chapels, the ſunday after every quarter day, on pain of 5 *l.* to be levied by warrant from any juſtice. Beſides this puniſhment for taking God's name in vain in common diſcourſe, it is enacted by ſtatute 3 Jac. I. c. 21. that if in any ſtage play, interlude, or ſhew, the name of the holy trinity, or any of the perſons therein,

ᵗ Hawk. P. C. 7.   ᵈ 1 Ventr. 293. 2 Strange, 834.

be jeftingly or profanely ufed, the offender fhall forfeit 10 *l*, one moiety to the king, and the other to the informer.

VI. A SIXTH fpecies of offences againſt God and religion, of which our antient books are full, is a crime of which one knows not well what account to give. I mean the offence of *witchcraft, conjuration, inchantment,* or *forcery.* To deny the poffibility, nay, actual exiftence, of witchcraft and forcery, is at once flatly to contradict the revealed word of God, in various paffages both of the old and new teftament: and the thing itſelf is a truth to which every nation in the world hath in it's turn borne teftimony, by either examples feemingly well attefted, or prohibitory laws, which at leaft fuppofe the poffibility of a commerce with evil fpirits. The civil law punifhes with death not only the forcerers themfelves, but alfo thofe who confult them [e]; imitating in the former the exprefs law of God [f], "thou fhalt not fuffer a "witch to live." And our own laws, both before and fince the conqueft, have been equally penal; ranking this crime in the fame clafs with herefy, and condemning both to the flames [g]. The prefident Montefquieu [h] ranks them alfo both together, but with a very different view: laying it down as an important maxim, that we ought to be very circumfpect in the profecution of magic and herefy; becaufe the moft unexceptionable conduct, the pureft morals, and the conftant practice of every duty in life, are not a fufficient fecurity againft the fufpicion of crimes like thefe. And indeed the ridiculous ftories that are generally told, and the many impoftures and delufions that have been difcovered in all ages, are enough to demolifh all faith in fuch a dubious crime; if the contrary evidence were not alfo extremely ftrong. Wherefore it feems to be the moft eligible way to conclude, with an ingenious writer of our own [i], that in general there has been fuch a thing as witchcraft; though one cannot give credit to any particular modern inftance of it.

---

[e] *Cod. l. 9. t.* 18.
[f] Exod. xxii. 18.
[g] 3 Inft. 44.

[h] Sp. L. b. 12. c 5.
[i] Mr Addifon, Spect. N° 117.

OUR forefathers were ſtronger believers, when they enacted by
ſtatute 33 Hen.VIII. c. 8. all witchcraft and ſorcery to be felony
without benefit of clergy; and again by ſtatute 1 Jac.I. c. 12. that
all perſons invoking any evil ſpirit, or conſulting, covenanting
with, entertaining, employing, feeding, or rewarding any evil
ſpirit; or taking up dead bodies from their graves to be uſed in
any witchcraft, ſorcery, charm, or inchantment; or killing or
otherwiſe hurting any perſon by ſuch infernal arts; ſhould be
guilty of felony without benefit of clergy, and ſuffer death. And,
if any perſon ſhould attempt by ſorcery to diſcover hidden trea-
ſure, or to reſtore ſtolen goods, or to provoke unlawful love, or
to hurt any man or beaſt, though the ſame were not effected,
he or ſhe ſhould ſuffer impriſonment and pillory for the firſt offence, and death for the ſecond. Theſe acts continued in force
till lately, to the terror of all antient females in the kingdom :
and many poor wretches were ſacrificed thereby to the prejudice
of their neighbours, and their own illuſions; not a few having,
by ſome means or other, confeſſed the fact at the gallows. But
all executions for this dubious crime are now at an end; our legiſlature having at length followed the wiſe example of Louis
XIV in France, who thought proper by an edict to reſtrain the
tribunals of juſtice from receiving informations of witchcraft[k].
And accordingly it is with us enacted by ſtatute 9 Geo. II. c. 5.
that no proſecution ſhall for the future be carried on againſt any
perſon for conjuration, witchcraft, ſorcery, or inchantment. But
the miſdemeſnor of perſons pretending to uſe witchcraft, tell
fortunes, or diſcover ſtolen goods by ſkill in the occult ſciences,
is ſtill deſervedly puniſhed with a year's impriſonment, and
ſtanding four times in the pillory.

VII. A SEVENTH ſpecies of offenders in this claſs are all *religious impoſtors:* ſuch as falſely pretend an extraordinary com-

[k] Voltaire *Siecl. Louis xiv*. Mod. Univ.
Hiſt. xxv. 215. Yet Vouglans, *(de droit
criminel,* 353. 459.) ſtill reckons up ſorcery
and witchcraft among the crimes puniſhable in France.

miſſion

miſſion from heaven ; or terrify and abuſe the people with falſe denunciations of judgments. Theſe, as tending to ſubvert all religion, by bringing it into ridicule and contempt, are puniſhable by the temporal courts with fine, impriſonment, and infamous corporal puniſhment [1].

VIII. Simony, or the corrupt preſentation of any one to an eccleſiaſtical benefice for gift or reward, is alſo to be conſidered as an offence againſt religion ; as well by reaſon of the ſacredneſs of the charge which is thus profanely bought and ſold, as becauſe it is always attended with perjury in the perſon preſented [m]. The ſtatute 31 Eliz. c. 6. (which, ſo far as it relates to the forfeiture of the right of preſentation, was conſidered in a former book [n]) enacts, that if any patron, for money or any other corrupt conſideration or promiſe, directly or indirectly given, ſhall preſent, admit, inſtitute, induct, inſtall, or collate any perſon to an eccleſiaſtical benefice or dignity, both the giver and taker ſhall forfeit two years value of the benefice or dignity ; one moiety to the king, and the other to any one who will ſue for the ſame. If perſons alſo corruptly reſign or exchange their benefices, both the giver and taker ſhall in like manner forfeit double the value of the money or other corrupt conſideration. And perſons who ſhall corruptly ordain or licence any miniſter, or procure him to be ordained or licenced, (which is the true idea of ſimony) ſhall incur a like forfeiture of forty pounds ; and the miniſter himſelf of ten pounds, beſides an incapacity to hold any eccleſiaſtical preferment for ſeven years afterwards. Corrupt elections and reſignations in colleges, hoſpitals, and other eleemoſynary corporations, are alſo puniſhed by the ſame ſtatute with forfeiture of the double value, vacating the place or office, and a devolution of the right of election for that turn to the crown.

[1] 1 Hawk. P. C. 7.　　　　　　　[n] See Vol. II. pag. 279.
[m] 3 Inſt. 156.

IX. Profa-

IX. Profanation of the lord's day, or *sabbath-breaking*, is a ninth offence against God and religion, punished by the municipal laws of England. For, besides the notorious indecency and scandal, of permitting any secular business to be publicly transacted on that day, in a country professing christianity, and the corruption of morals which usually follows it's profanation, the keeping one day in seven holy, as a time of relaxation and refreshment as well as for public worship, is of admirable service to a state, considered merely as a civil institution. It humanizes by the help of conversation and society the manners of the lower classes; which would otherwise degenerate into a sordid ferocity and savage selfishness of spirit: it enables the industrious workman to pursue his occupation in the ensuing week with health and chearfulness: it imprints on the minds of the people that sense of their duty to God, so necessary to make them good citizens; but which yet would be worn out and defaced by an unremitted continuance of labour, without any stated times of recalling them to the worship of their maker. And therefore the laws of king Athelstan ° forbad all merchandizing on the lord's day, under very severe penalties. And by the statute 27 Hen. VI. c. 5. no fair or market shall be held on the principal festivals, good friday, or any sunday (except the four sundays in harvest) on pain of forfeiting the goods exposed to sale. And, since, by the statute 1 Car. I. c. 1. no persons shall assemble, out of their own parishes, for any sport whatsoever upon this day; nor, in their parishes, shall use any bull or bear baiting, interludes, plays, or other *unlawful* exercises, or pastimes; on pain that every offender shall pay 3 *s.* 4 *d.* to the poor. This statute does not prohibit, but rather impliedly allows, any innocent recreation or amusement, within their respective parishes, even on the lord's day, after divine service is over. But by statute 29 Car. II. c. 7. no person is allowed to *work* on the lord's day, or use any boat or barge, or expose any goods to sale; except meat in public houses, milk at certain hours, and works of ne-

° *c.* 24.

cessity

ceffity or charity, on forfeiture of 5 _s_. Nor fhall any drover, carrier, or the like, travel upon that day, under pain of twenty fhillings.

X. Drunkenness is alfo punifhed by ftatute 4 Jac. I. c. 5. with the forfeiture of 5 _s_; or the fitting fix hours in the ftocks: by which time the ftatute prefumes the offender will have regained his fenfes, and not be liable to do mifchief to his neighbours. And there are many wholfome ftatutes, by way of prevention, chiefly paffed in the fame reign of king James I, which regulate the licencing of ale-houfes, and punifh perfons found tippling therein; or the mafters of fuch houfes permitting them.

XI. The laft offence which I fhall mention, more immediately againft religion and morality, and cognizable by the temporal courts, is that of open and notorious _lewdnefs:_ either by frequenting houfes of ill fame, which is an indictable offence[p]; or by fome groffly fcandalous and public indecency, for which the punifhment is by fine and imprifonment[q]. In the year 1650, when the ruling powers found it for their intereft to put on the femblance of a very extraordinary ftrictnefs and purity of morals, not only inceft and wilful adultery were made capital crimes; but alfo the repeated act of keeping a brothel, or committing fornication, were (upon a fecond conviction) made felony without benefit of clergy[r]. But at the reftoration, when men from an abhorrence of the hypocrify of the late times fell into a contrary extreme, of licentioufnefs, it was not thought proper to renew a law of fuch unfafhionable rigour. And thefe offences have been ever fince left to the feeble coercion of the fpiritual court, according to the rules of the canon law; a law which has treated the offence of incontinence, nay even adultery itfelf, with a great degree of tendernefs and lenity; owing perhaps to the celibacy of it's firft compilers. The temporal

[p] Poph. 208.   [r] Scobell. 121.
[q] 1 Siderf. 168.

                                        courts

courts therefore take no cognizance of the crime of adultery, otherwife than as a private injury[s].

But, before we quit this fubject, we muft take notice of the temporal punifhment for having *baftard children*, confidered in a criminal light; for with regard to the maintenance of fuch illegitimate offspring, which is a civil concern, we have formerly fpoken at large[t]. By the ftatute 18 Eliz. c. 3. two juftices may take order for the punifhment of the mother and reputed father; but what that punifhment fhall be, is not therein afcertained : though the contemporary expofition was, that a corporal punifhment was intended[u]. By ftatute 7 Jac. I. c. 4. a fpecific punifhment (*viz.* commitment to the houfe of correction) is inflicted on the woman only. But in both cafes, it feems that the penalty can only be inflicted, if the baftard becomes chargeable to the parifh : for otherwife the very maintenance of the child is confidered as a degree of punifhment. By the laft mentioned ftatute the juftices may commit the mother to the houfe of correction, there to be punifhed and fet on work for one year ; and, in cafe of a fecond offence, till fhe find fureties never to offend again.

[s] See Vol. III. pag. 139.　　　　　[u] Dalt. juft. ch. 11.
[t] See Vol. I. pag. 458.

C H A P T E R   T H E   F I F T H.

O f   O F F E N C E S   A G A I N S T   T H E   L A W   O F   N A T I O N S.

ACCORDING to the method marked out in the preceding chapter, we are next to confider the offences more
immediately repugnant to that univerfal law of fociety, which
regulates the mutual intercourfe between one ftate and another;
thofe, I mean, which are particularly animadverted on, as fuch,
by the Englifh law.

THE law of nations is a fyftem of rules, deducible by natural reafon, and eftablifhed by univerfal confent among the civilized inhabitants of the world [a]; in order to decide all difputes,
to regulate all ceremonies and civilities, and to infure the ob-
fervance of juftice and good faith, in that intercourfe which
muft frequently occur between two or more independent ftates,
and the individuals belonging to each [b]. This general law is
founded upon this principle, that different nations ought in time
of peace to do one another all the good they can; and, in time
of war, as little harm as poffible, without prejudice to their
own real interefts [c]. And, as none of thefe ftates will allow a
fuperiority in the other, therefore neither can dictate or prefcribe
the rules of this law to the reft; but fuch rules muft neceffarily

[a] *Ff.* 1. 1. 9.
[b] See Vol. I. pag. 43.
[c] Sp. L. b. 1. c. 3.

refult

refult from thofe principles of natural juftice, in which all the learned of every nation agree: or they depend upon mutual compacts or treaties between the refpective communities; in the conftruction of which there is alfo no judge to refort to, but the law of nature and reafon, being the only one in which all the contracting parties are equally converfant, and to which they are equally fubject..

In arbitrary ftates this law, wherever it contradicts or is not provided for by the municipal law of the country, is enforced by the royal power.: but fince in England no royal power can introduce a new law, or fufpend the execution of the old, therefore the law of nations (wherever any queftion arifes which is properly the object of it's jurifdiction) is here adopted in it's full extent by the common law, and is held to be a part of the law of the land.. And thofe acts of parliament, which have from time to time been made to enforce this univerfal law, or to facilitate the execution of it's decifions, are not to be confidered as introductive of any new rule, but merely as declaratory of the old fundamental conftitutions of the kingdom; without which it muft ceafe to be a part of the civilized world. Thus in mercantile queftions, fuch as bills of exchange and the like; in all marine caufes, relating to freight, average, demurrage, infurances, bottomry, and others of a fimilar nature; the law-merchant[d], which is a branch of the law of nations, is regularly and conftantly adhered to. So too in all difputes relating to prizes, to fhipwrecks, to hoftages, and ranfom bills, there is no other rule of decifion but this great univerfal law, collected from hiftory and ufage, and fuch writers of all nations and languages as are generally approved and allowed of..

But, though in civil tranfactions and queftions of property between the fubjects of different ftates, the law of nations has much fcope and extent, as adopted by the law of England; yet the prefent branch of our enquiries will fall within a narrow

d See Vol. I. pag. 273.

compafs,

compass, as offences againſt the law of nations can rarely be the objeᴄt of the criminal law of any particular ſtate. For offences againſt this law are principally incident to whole ſtates or nations: in which caſe recourſe can only be had to war; which is an appeal to the God of hoſts, to puniſh ſuch infraᴄtions of public faith, as are committed by one independent people againſt another: neither ſtate having any ſuperior juriſdiᴄtion to reſort to upon earth for juſtice. But where the individuals of any ſtate violate this general law, it is then the intereſt as well as duty of the government under which they live, to animadvert upon them with a becoming ſeverity, that the peace of the world may be maintained. For in vain would nations in their colleᴄtive capacity obſerve theſe univerſal rules, if private ſubjeᴄts were at liberty to break them at their own diſcretion, and involve the two ſtates in a war. It is therefore incumbent upon the nation injured, firſt to demand ſatisfaᴄtion and juſtice to be done on the offender, by the ſtate to which he belongs; and, if that be refuſed or negleᴄted, the ſovereign then avows himſelf an accomplice or abettor of his ſubjeᴄt's crime, and draws upon his community the calamities of foreign war.

T H E principal offences againſt the law of nations, animadverted on as ſuch by the municipal laws of England, are of three kinds; 1. Violation of ſafe-conduᴄts; 2. Infringement of the rights of embaſſadors; and, 3. Piracy.

I. A s to the firſt, *violation* of *ſafe-conduᴄts* or *paſſports*, expreſſly granted by the king or his embaſſadors ᵉ to the ſubjeᴄts of a foreign power in time of mutual war; or, committing aᴄts of hoſtility againſt ſuch as are in amity, league, or truce with us, who are here under a general implied ſafe-conduᴄt; theſe are breaches of the public faith, without the preſervation of which there can be no intercourſe or commerce between one nation and another: and ſuch offences may, according to the writers upon the law of nations, be a juſt ground

ᵉ See Vol. I. pag. 260.

of a national war; since it is not in the power of the foreign prince to cause justice to be done to his subjects by the very individual delinquent, but he must require it of the whole community. And as during the continuance of any safe-conduct, either exprefs or implied, the foreigner is under the protection of the king and the law; and, more especially, as it is one of the articles of *magna carta* [f], that foreign merchants shall be intitled to safe-conduct and security throughout the kingdom; there is no question but that any violation of either the person or property of such foreigner may be punished by indictment in the name of the king, whose honour is more particularly engaged in supporting his own safe-conduct. And, when this malicious rapacity was not confined to private individuals, but broke out into general hostilities, by the statute 2 Hen. V. st. 1. c. 6. breaking of truce and safe-conducts, or abetting and receiving the truce-breakers, was (in affirmance and support of the law of nations) declared to be high treason against the crown and dignity of the king; and conservators of truce and safe-conducts were appointed in every port, and impowered to hear and determine such treasons (when committed at sea) according to the antient marine law then practised in the admiral's court: and, together with two men learned in the law of the land, to hear and determine according to that law the same treasons, when committed within the body of any county. Which statute, so far as it made these offences amount to treason, was suspended by 14 Hen. VI. c. 8. and repealed by 20 Hen. VI. c. 11. but revived by 29 Hen. VI. c. 2. which gave the same powers to the lord chancellor, associated with either of the chief justices, as belonged to the conservators of truce and their assessors; and enacted that, notwithstanding the party be convicted of treason, the injured stranger should have restitution out of his effects, prior to any claim of the crown. And it is farther enacted by the statute 31 Hen. VI. c. 4. that if any of the king's subjects attempt or offend, upon the sea, or in any port within the king's obeysance, against any stranger in amity, league, or truce, or under safe-conduct; and

[f] 9 *Hen. III. c.* 30. See Vol. I. pag. 259, &c.

especially

especially by attaching his person, or spoiling him, or robbing him of his goods; the lord chancellor, with any of the justices of either the king's bench or common pleas, may cause full restitution and amends to be made to the party injured.

I T is to be observed, that the suspending and repealing acts of 14 & 20 Hen. VI, and also the reviving act of 29 Hen. VI, were only temporary; so that it should seem that, after the expiration of them all, the statute 2 Hen. V continued in full force: but yet it is considered as extinct by the statute 14 Edw. IV. c. 4. which revives and confirms all statutes and ordinances made before the accession of the house of York against breakers of amities, truces, leagues, and safe-conducts, with an express exception to the statutes of 2 Hen. V. But (however that may be) I apprehend it was finally repealed by the general statutes of Edward VI and queen Mary, for abolishing new-created treasons; though sir Matthew Hale seems to question it as to treasons committed on the sea [s]. But certainly the statute of 31 Hen. VI remains in full force to this day.

II. As to the rights of *embassadors*, which are also established by the law of nations, and are therefore matter of universal concern, they have formerly been treated of at large [h]. It may here be sufficient to remark, that the common law of England recognizes them in their full extent, by immediately stopping all legal process, sued out through the ignorance or rashness of individuals, which may intrench upon the immunities of a foreign minister or any of his train. And, the more effectually to enforce the law of nations in this respect, when violated through wantonness or insolence, it is declared by the statute 7 Ann. c. 12. that all process whereby the person of any embassador, or of his domestic or domestic servant, may be arrested, or his goods distreined or seised, shall be utterly null and void; and that all persons prosecuting, soliciting, or executing such process, being convicted by confession or the oath of one

s 1 Hal. P. C. 262.   h See Vol. I. pag. 253.

witness,

witnefs, before the lord chancellor and the chief juftices, or any two of them, fhall be deemed violaters of the laws of nations, and difturbers of the public repofe; and fhall fuffer fuch penalties and corporal punifhment as the faid judges, or any two of them, fhall think fit[i]. Thus, in cafes of extraordinary outrage, for which the law hath provided no fpecial penalty, the legiflature hath intrufted to the three principal judges of the kingdom an unlimited power of proportioning the punifhment to the crime.

III. LASTLY, the crime of *piracy,* or robbery and depredation upon the high feas, is an offence againft the univerfal law of fociety; a pirate being, according to fir Edward Coke[k], *hoftis humani generis.* As therefore he has renounced all the benefits of fociety and government, and has reduced himfelf afrefh to the favage ftate of nature, by declaring war againft all mankind, all mankind muft declare war againft him: fo that every community hath a right, by the rule of felf-defence, to inflict that punifhment upon him, which every individual would in a ftate of nature have been otherwife entitled to do, for any invafion of his perfon or perfonal property.

BY the antient common law, piracy, if committed by a fubject, was held to be a fpecies of treafon, being contrary to his natural allegiance; and by an alien to be felony only: but now, fince the ftatute of treafons, 25 Edw. III. c. 2. it is held to be only felony in a fubject[l]. Formerly it was only cognizable by the admiralty courts, which proceed by the rules of the civil law[m]. But, it being inconfiftent with the liberties of the nation, that any man's life fhould be taken away, unlefs by the judgment of his peers, or the common law of the land, the ftatute 28 Hen.VIII. c.15. eftablifhed a new jurifdiction for this purpofe; which proceeds according to the courfe of the common law, and of which we fhall fay more hereafter.

[i] See the occafion of making this ftatute; Vol. I. pag. 255.
[k] 3 Inft. 113.
[l] *Ibid.*
[m] 1 Hawk. P. C. 98.

THE

The offence of piracy, by common law, confifts in committing thofe acts of robbery and depredation upon the high feas, which, if committed upon land, would have amounted to felony there [n]. But, by ftatute, fome other offences are made piracy alfo: as, by ftatute 11 & 12 W. III. c. 7. if any natural born fubject commits any act of hoftility upon the high feas, againft others of his majefty's fubjects, under colour of a commiffion from any foreign power; this, though it would only be an act of war in an alien, fhall be conftrued piracy in a fubject. And farther, any commander, or other feafaring perfon, betraying his truft, and running away with any fhip, boat, ordnance, ammunition, or goods; or yielding them up voluntarily to a pirate; or confpiring to do thefe acts; or any perfon confining the commander of a veffel, to hinder him from fighting in defence of his fhip, or to caufe a revolt on board; fhall, for each of thefe offences, be adjudged a pirate, felon, and robber, and fhall fuffer death, whether he be principal or acceffory. By the ftatute 8 Geo. I. c. 24. the trading with known pirates, or furnifhing them with ftores or ammunition, or fitting out any veffel for that purpofe, or in any wife confulting, combining, confederating, or correfponding with them; or the forcibly boarding any merchant veffel, though without feifing or carrying her off, and deftroying or throwing any of the goods overboard; fhall be deemed piracy: and all acceffories to piracy, are declared to be principal pirates, and felons without benefit of clergy. By the fame ftatutes alfo, (to encourage the defence of merchant veffels againft pirates) the commanders or feamen wounded, and the widows of fuch feamen as are flain, in any piratical engagement, fhall be entitled to a bounty, to be divided among them, not exceeding one fiftieth part of the value of the cargo on board: and fuch wounded feamen fhall be entitled to the penfion of Greenwich hofpital; which no other feamen are, except only fuch as have ferved in a fhip of war. And if the commander fhall behave cowardly, by not defending the fhip,

[n] 1 Hawk. P. C. 100.

if

if she carries guns or arms, or shall discharge the mariners from fighting, so that the ship falls into the hands of pirates, such commander shall forfeit all his wages, and suffer six months imprisonment.

THESE are the principal cases, in which the statute law of England interposes, to aid and enforce the law of nations, as a part of the common law; by inflicting an adequate punishment upon offences against that universal law, committed by private persons. We shall proceed in the next chapter to consider offences, which more immediately affect the sovereign executive power of our own particular state, or the king and government; which species of crimes branches itself into a much larger extent, than either of those of which we have already treated.

Chapter the sixth.

Of HIGH TREASON.

THE third general divifion of crimes confifts of fuch, as more efpecially affect the fupreme executive power, or the king and his government; which amount either to a total renunciation of that allegiance, or at the leaft to a criminal neglect of that duty, which is due from every fubject to his fovereign. In a former part of thefe commentaries [a] we had occafion to mention the nature of allegiance, as the tie or *ligamen* which binds every fubject to be true and faithful to his fovereign *liege* lord the king, in return for that protection which is afforded him; and truth and faith to bear of life and limb, and earthly honour; and not to know or hear of any ill intended him, without defending him therefrom. And this allegiance, we may remember, was diftinguifhed into two forts or fpecies: the one natural and perpetual, which is inherent only in natives of the king's dominions; the other local and temporary, which is incident to aliens alfo. Every offence therefore more immediately affecting the royal perfon, his crown, or dignity, is in fome degree a breach of this duty of allegiance, whether natural and innate, or local and acquired by refidence: and thefe may be diftinguifhed into four kinds; 1. Treafon. 2. Felonies injurious to the king's prerogative. 3. *Praemunire.* 4. Other mifprifions and contempts. Of which crimes the firft and principal is that of treafon.

[a] Book I. ch. 10.

TREASON, *proditio*, in it's very name (which is borrowed from the French) imports a betraying, treachery, or breach of faith. It therefore happens only between allies, faith the mirror[b]: for treason is indeed a general appellation, made use of by the law, to denote not only offences against the king and government, but also that accumulation of guilt which arises whenever a superior reposes a confidence in a subject or inferior, between whom and himself there subsists a natural, a civil, or even a spiritual relation; and the inferior so abuses that confidence, so forgets the obligations of duty, subjection, and allegiance, as to destroy the life of any such his superior or lord. This is looked upon as proceeding from the same principle of treachery in private life, as would have urged him who harbours it to have conspired in public against his liege lord and sovereign: and therefore for a wife to kill her lord or husband, a servant his lord or master, and an ecclesiastic his lord or ordinary; these, being breaches of the lower allegiance, of private and domestic faith, are denominated *petit* treasons. But when disloyalty so rears it's crest, as to attack even majesty itself, it is called by way of eminent distinction *high* treason, *alta proditio*; being equivalent to the *crimen laesae majestatis* of the Romans, as Glanvil[c] denominates it also in our English law.

As this is the highest civil crime, which (considered as a member of the community) any man can possibly commit, it ought therefore to be the most precisely ascertained. For if the crime of high treason be indeterminate, this alone (says the president Montesquieu) is sufficient to make any government degenerate into arbitrary power[d]. And yet, by the antient common law, there was a great latitude left in the breast of the judges, to determine what was treason, or not so: whereby the creatures of tyrannical princes had opportunity to create abundance of constructive treasons; that is, to raise, by forced and arbitrary

[b] *c*. 1. §. 7.　　　[d] Sp. L. b. 12. c. 7.
[c] *l*. 1. *c*. 2.

conſtructions, offences into the crime and puniſhment of treaſon, which never were ſuſpected to be ſuch. Thus the *accroaching,* or attempting to exerciſe, royal power (a very uncertain charge) was in the 21 Edw. III. held to be treaſon in a knight of Hertfordſhire, who forcibly aſſaulted and detained one of the king's ſubjects till he paid him 90*l*[e]: a crime, it muſt be owned, well deſerving of puniſhment; but which ſeems to be of a complexion very different from that of treaſon. Killing the king's father, or brother, or even his meſſenger, has alſo fallen under the ſame denomination[f]. The latter of which is almoſt as tyrannical a doctrine as that of the imperial conſtitution of Arcadius and Honorius, which determines that any attempts or deſigns againſt the miniſters of the prince ſhall be treaſon[g]. But however, to prevent the inconveniences which began to ariſe in England from this multitude of conſtructive treaſons, the ſtatute 25 Edw. III. c. 2. was made; which defines what offences only for the future ſhould be held to be treaſon : in like manner as the *lex Julia majeſtatis* among the Romans, promulged by Auguſtus Caeſar, comprehended all the antient laws, that had before been enacted to puniſh tranſgreſſors againſt the ſtate[h]. This ſtatute muſt therefore be our text and guide, in order to examine into the ſeveral ſpecies of high treaſon. And we ſhall find that it comprehends all kinds of high treaſon under ſeven diſtinct branches.

1. "WHEN a man doth compaſs or imagine the death of our " lord the king, of our lady his queen, or of their eldeſt ſon " and heir." Under this deſcription it is held that a queen regnant (ſuch as queen Elizabeth and queen Anne) is within the words of the act, being inveſted with royal power and entitled to the allegiance of her ſubjects[i]: but the huſband of ſuch a

[e] 1 Hal. P. C. 80.
[f] Britt. c. 22. 1 Hawk. P. C. 34.
[g] *Qui de nece virorum illuſtrium, qui conſiliis et conſiſtorio noſtro interſunt, ſenatorum etiam (nam et ipſi pars corporis noſtri ſunt) vel cujuſlibet poſtremo, qui militat nobiſcum, cogitaverit: (eadem enim ſeveritate voluntatem*

ſceleris, qua effectum, puniri jura voluerunt) ipſe quidem, utpote majeſtatis reus, gladio feriatur, bonis ejus omnibus fiſco noſtro addictis. (Cod. 9. 8. 5.)
[h] Gravin. Orig. 1. §. 34.
[i] 1 Hal. P. C. 101.

queen

queen is not comprized within thefe words, and therefore no treafon can be committed againft him[k]. The king here intended is the king in poffeffion, without any refpect to his title: for it is held, that a king *de facto* and not *de jure*, or in other words an ufurper that hath got poffeffion of the throne, is a king within the meaning of the ftatute; as there is a temporary allegiance due to him, for his adminiftration of the government, and temporary protection of the public: and therefore treafons committed againft Henry VI were punifhed under Edward IV, though all the line of Lancafter had been previoufly declared ufurpers by act of parliament. But the moft rightful heir of the crown, or king *de jure* and not *de facto*, who hath never had plenary poffeffion of the throne, as was the cafe of the houfe of York during the three reigns of the line of Lancafter, is not a king within this ftatute, againft whom treafons may be committed[l]. And a very fenfible writer on the crown-law carries the point of poffeffion fo far, that he holds[m], that a king out of poffeffion is fo far from having any right to our allegiance, by any other title which he may fet up againft the king in being, that we are bound by the duty of our allegiance to refift him. A doctrine which he grounds upon the ftatute 11 Hen. VII. c. 1. which is declaratory of the common law, and pronounces all fubjects excufed from any penalty or forfeiture, which do affift and obey a king *de facto*. But, in truth, this feems to be confounding all notions of right and wrong; and the confequence would be, that when Cromwell had murdered the elder Charles, and ufurped the power (though not the name) of king, the people were bound in duty to hinder the fon's reftoration: and were the king of Poland or Morocco to invade this kingdom, and by any means to get poffeffion of the crown (a term, by the way, of very loofe and indiftinct fignification) the fubject would be bound by his allegiance to fight for his natural prince to-day, and by the fame duty of allegiance to fight againft him to-morrow. The true diftinction feems to be,

[k] 3 Inft. 7. 1 Hal. P. C. 106.   [m] 1 Hawk. P. C. 36
[l] 3 Inft. 7. 1 Hal. P. C. 104.

that

that the ſtatute of Henry the ſeventh does by no means *command* any oppoſition to a king *de jure*; but *excuſes* the obedience paid to a king *de facto*. When therefore a uſurper is in poſſeſſion, the ſubject is *excuſed* and *juſtified* in obeying and giving him aſſiſtance : otherwiſe, under a uſurpation, no man could be ſafe; if the lawful prince had a right to hang him for obedience to the powers in being, as the uſurper would certainly do for diſobedience. Nay farther, as the maſs of people are imperfect judges of title, of which in all caſes poſſeſſion is *prima facie* evidence, the law compels no man to yield obedience to that prince, whoſe right is by want of poſſeſſion rendered uncertain and diſputable, till providence ſhall think fit to interpoſe in his favour, and decide the ambiguous claim : and therefore, till he is entitled to ſuch allegiance by poſſeſſion, no treaſon can be committed againſt him. Laſtly, a king who has reſigned his crown, ſuch reſignation being admitted and ratified in parliament, is according to ſir Matthew Hale no longer the object of treaſon[n]. And the ſame reaſon holds, in caſe a king abdicates the government; or, by actions ſubverſive of the conſtitution, virtually renounces the authority which he claims by that very conſtitution : ſince, as was formerly obſerved[o], when the fact of abdication is once eſtabliſhed, and determined by the proper judges, the conſequence neceſſarily follows, that the throne is thereby vacant, and he is no longer king.

LET us next ſee, what is a *compaſſing* or *imagining* the death of the king, *&c.* Theſe are ſynonymous terms ; the word *compaſs* ſignifying the purpoſe or deſign of the mind or will[p], and not, as in common ſpeech, the carrying ſuch deſign to effect[q]. And therefore an accidental ſtroke, which may mortally wound the ſovereign, *per infortunium*, without any traiterous intent, is no treaſon : as was the caſe of ſir Walter Tyrrel, who, by the

[n] 1 Hal. P. C. 104.

[o] Vol. I. pag. 212.

[p] By the antient law *compaſſing* or intending the death of any man, demonſtra-

ted by ſome evident fact, was equally penal as homicide itſelf. (3 Inſt. 5.)

[q] 1 Hal. P. C. 107.

command

command of king William Rufus, fhooting at a hart, the arrow glanced againft a tree, and killed the king upon the fpot[r]. But, as this compaffing or imagination is an act of the mind, it cannot poffibly fall under any judicial cognizance, unlefs it be demonftrated by fome open, or *overt*, act. And yet the tyrant Dionyfius is recorded[s] to have executed a fubject, barely for dreaming that he had killed him; which was held for a fufficient proof, that he had thought thereof in his waking hours. But fuch is not the temper of the Englifh law; and therefore in this, and the three next fpecies of treafon, it is neceffary that there appear an open or *overt* act of a more full and explicit nature, to convict the traitor upon. The ftatute expreffly requires, that the accufed " be thereof upon fufficient proof attainted of fome " open act by men of his own condition." Thus, to provide weapons or ammunition for the purpofe of killing the king, is held to be a palpable overt act of treafon in imagining his death[t]. To confpire to imprifon the king by force, and move towards it by affembling company, is an overt act of compaffing the king's death[u]; for all force, ufed to the perfon of the king, in it's confequence may tend to his death, and is a ftrong prefumption of fomething worfe intended than the prefent force, by fuch as have fo far thrown off their bounden duty to their fovereign : it being an old obfervation, that there is generally but a fhort interval between the prifons and the graves of princes. There is no queftion alfo, but that taking any meafures to render fuch treafonable purpofes effectual, as affembling and confulting on the means to kill the king, is a fufficient overt act of high treafon[w].

How far mere *words*, fpoken by an individual, and not relative to any treafonable act or defign then in agitation, fhall amount to treafon, has been formerly matter of doubt. We have two inftances, in the reign of Edward the fourth, of per-

[r] 3 Inft. 6　　　　　　　　　[u] 1 Hal. P. C. 109.
[s] Plutarch. *in vit.*　　　　　[w] 1 Hawk. P. C. 38. 1 Hal. P. C. 119.
[t] 3 Inft. 12.

fons

fons executed for treafonable words : the one a citizen of London, who faid he would make his fon heir of the *crown*, being
the fign of the houfe in which he lived; the other a gentleman,
whofe favourite buck the king killed in hunting, whereupon he
wifhed it, horns and all, in the king's belly. Thefe were ef-
teemed.hard cafes : and the chief juftice Markham rather chofe
to leave his place than affent to the latter judgment[x]. But now
it feems clearly to be agreed, that, by the common law and the
ftatute of Edward III, words fpoken amount only to a high mifdemefnor, and no treafon. For they may be fpoken in heat,
without any intention, or be miftaken, perverted, or mif-remem-
bered by the hearers; their meaning depends always on their
connexion with other words, and things; they may fignify dif-
ferently even according to the tone of voice, with which they
are delivered; and fometimes filence itfelf is more expreffive
than any difcourfe. As therefore there can be nothing more
equivocal and ambiguous than words, it would indeed be unreafonable to make them amount to high treafon. And accordingly in 4 Car. I. on a reference to all the judges, concerning
fome very atrocious words fpoken by one Pyne, they certified
to the king, " that though the words were as wicked as might
" be, yet they were no treafon : for, unlefs it be by fome par-
" ticular ftatute, no words will be treafon[y]." If the words be
fet down in writing, it argues more deliberate intention; and
it has been held that writing is an overt act of treafon; for
fcribere eft agere. But even in this cafe the bare words are not
the treafon, but the deliberate act of writing them. And fuch
writing, though unpublifhed, has in fome arbitrary reigns convicted it's author of treafon : particularly in the cafes of one
Peacham a clergyman, for treafonable paffages in a fermon never preached[z]; and of Algernon Sidney, for fome papers found
in his clofet : which, had they been plainly relative to any
previous formed defign of dethroning or murdering the king,
might doubtlefs have been properly read in evidence as overt

[x] 1 Hal. P. C. 115.   [z] *Ibid.*
[y] Cro. Car. 125.

acts

acts of that treason, which was specially laid in the indictment[a]. But, being merely speculative, without any intention (so far as appeared) of making any public use of them, the convicting the authors of treason upon such an insufficient foundation has been universally disapproved. Peacham was therefore pardoned: and, though Sidney indeed was executed, yet it was to the general discontent of the nation; and his attainder was afterwards reversed by parliament. There was then no manner of doubt, but that the publication of such a treasonable writing was a sufficient overt act of treason at the common law[b]; though of late even that has been questioned.

2. THE second species of treason is, "if a man do violate "the king's companion, or the king's eldest daughter unmarried, "or the wife of the king's eldest son and heir." By the king's companion is meant his wife; and by violation is understood carnal knowlege, as well without force, as with it: and this is high treason in both parties, if both be consenting; as some of the wives of Henry the eighth by fatal experience evinced. The plain intention of this law is to guard the blood royal from any suspicion of bastardy, whereby the succession to the crown might be rendered dubious: and therefore, when this reason ceases, the law ceases with it; for to violate a queen or princess dowager is held to be no treason[c]: in like manner as, by the feodal law, it was a felony and attended with a forfeiture of the fief, if the vasal vitiated the wife or daughter of his lord[d]; but not so if he only vitiated his widow[e].

3. THE third species of treason is, "if a man do levy war "against our lord the king in his realm." And this may be done by taking arms, not only to dethrone the king, but under pretence to reform religion, or the laws, or to remove evil counsellors, or other grievances whether real or pretended[f]. For the

[a] Foster. 198.
[b] 1 Hal. P. C. 118. 1 Hawk. P. C. 38.
[c] 3 Inst. 9.
[d] *Feud. l. 1. t. 5.*
[e] *Ibid. t. 21.*
[f] 1 Hawk. P. C. 37.

law does not, neither can it, permit any private man, or fet of men, to interfere forcibly in matters of fuch high importance; efpecially as it has eftablifhed a fufficient power, for thefe pur- pofes, in the high court of parliament: neither does the con- ftitution juftify any private or particular refiftance for **private or** particular grievances; though in cafes of national oppreffion the nation has very juftifiably rifen as one man, to vindicate the original contract fubfifting between the king and his people. To refift the king's forces by defending a caftle againft them, is a levying of war: and fo is an infurrection with an avowed de- fign to pull down *all* inclofures, *all* brothels, and the like; the univerfality of the defign making it a rebellion againft the ftate, an ufurpation of the powers of government, and an infolent in- vafion of the king's authority[g]. But a tumult with a view to pull down a particular houfe, or lay open a particular enclofure, amounts at moft to a riot; this being no general defiance of public government. So, if two fubjects quarrel and levy war againft each other, it is only a great riot and contempt, and no treafon. Thus it happened between the earls of Hereford and Glocefter in 20 Edw. I. who raifed each a little army, and com- mitted outrages upon each others lands, burning houfes, attended with the lofs of many lives: yet this was held to be no high treafon, but only a great mifdemefnor[h]. A bare confpiracy to levy war does not amount to this fpecies of treafon; but (if particularly pointed at the perfon of the king or his govern- ment) it falls within the firft, of compaffing or imagining the king's death[i].

4. "IF a man be adherent to the king's enemies in his "realm, giving to them aid and comfort in the realm, or elfe- "where," he is alfo declared guilty of high treafon. This muft likewife be proved by fome overt act, as by giving them intel- ligence, by fending them provifions, by felling them arms, by treacheroufly furrendering a fortrefs, or the like[k]. By enemies

[g] 1 Hal. P. C. 132.
[h] *Ibid.* 136.

[i] 3 Inft. 9. Fofter. 211. 213.
[k] 3 Inft. 10.

are

are here underſtood the ſubjects of foreign powers with whom
we are at open war. As to foreign pirates or robbers, who may
happen to invade our coaſts, without any open hoſtilities between their nation and our own, and without any commiſſion
from any prince or ſtate at enmity with the crown of Great
Britain, the giving them any aſſiſtance is alſo clearly treaſon ;
either in the light of adhering to the public enemies of the king
and kingdom [l], or elſe in that of levying war againſt his majeſty. And, moſt indiſputably, the ſame acts of adherence or aid,
which (when applied to foreign enemies) will conſtitute treaſon
under this branch of the ſtatute, will (when afforded to our
own fellow-ſubjects in actual rebellion at home) amount to high
treaſon under the deſcription of levying war againſt the king [m].
But to relieve a rebel, fled out of the kingdom, is no treaſon :
for the ſtatute is taken ſtrictly, and a rebel is not an *enemy* ; an
enemy being always the ſubject of ſome foreign prince, and
one who owes no allegiance to the crown of England [n]. And
if a perſon be under circumſtances of actual force and conſtraint, through a well-grounded apprehenſion of injury to his
life or perſon, this fear or compulſion will excuſe his even joining with either rebels or enemſes *in* the kingdom, provided he
leaves them whenever he hath a ſafe opportunity [o].

5. "I f a man counterfeit the king's great or privy ſeal,"
this is alſo high treaſon. But if a man takes wax bearing the
impreſſion of the great ſeal off from one patent, and fixes it to
another, this is held to be only an abuſe of the ſeal, and not a
counterfeiting of it ; as was the caſe of a certain chaplain, who
in ſuch manner framed a diſpenſation for non-reſidence. But
the knaviſh artifice of a lawyer much exceeded this of the divine. One of the clerks in chancery glewed together two pieces
of parchment ; on the uppermoſt of which he wrote a patent,
to which he regularly obtained the great ſeal, the label going
through both the ſkins. He then diſſolved the cement ; and

[l] Foſter. 219.
[m] *Ibid.* 216.

[n] 1 Hawk. P. C. 38.
[o] Foſter. 216.

taking off the written patent, on the blank ſkin wrote a freſh patent, of a different import from the former, and publiſhed it as true. This was held no counterfeiting of the great ſeal, but only a great miſpriſion; and ſir Edward Coke[p] mentions it with ſome indignation, that the party was living at that day.

6. THE ſixth ſpecies of treaſon under this ſtatute, is "if a "man counterfeit the king's money; and if a man bring falſe "money into the realm counterfeit to the money of England, "knowing the money to be falſe." As to the firſt branch, counterfeiting the king's money; this is treaſon, whether the falſe money be uttered in payment or not. Alſo if the king's own minters alter the ſtandard or alloy eſtabliſhed by law, it is treaſon. But gold and ſilver money only are held to be within this ſtatute[q]. With regard likewiſe to the ſecond branch, importing foreign counterfeit money, in order to utter it here; it is held that uttering it, without importing it, is not within the ſtatute[r]. But of this we ſhall preſently ſay more.

7. THE laſt ſpecies of treaſon, aſcertained by this ſtatute, is "if a man ſlay the chancellor, treaſurer, or the king's juſtices "of the one bench or the other, juſtices in eyre, or juſtices of "aſſize, and all other juſtices aſſigned to hear and determine, "being in their places doing their offices." Theſe high magiſtrates, as they repreſent the king's majeſty during the execution of their offices, are therefore for the time equally regarded by the law. But this ſtatute extends only to the actual killing of them, and not to wounding, or a bare attempt to kill them. It extends alſo only to the officers therein ſpecified; and therefore the barons of the exchequer, as ſuch, are not within the protection of this act[s].

THUS careful was the legiſlature, in the reign of Edward the third, to ſpecify and reduce to a certainty the vague notions of

p 3 Inſt. 16.
q 1 Hawk. P. C. 42.
r *Ibid.* 43.
s 1 Hal. P. C. 231.

treaſon,

treafon, that had formerly prevailed in our courts. But the act
does not ftop here, but goes on. " Becaufe other like cafes of
" treafon may happen in time to come, which cannot be thought
" of nor declared at prefent, it is accorded, that if any other
" cafe fuppofed to be treafon, which is not above fpecified, doth
" happen before any judge ; the judge fhall tarry without going
" to judgment of the treafon, till the caufe be fhewed and de-
" clared before the king and his parliament, whether it ought
" to be judged treafon, or other felony." Sir Matthew Hale[t] is
very high in his encomiums on the great wifdom and care of the
parliament, in thus keeping judges within the proper bounds and
limits of this act, by not fuffering them to run out (upon their
own opinions) into conftructive treafons, though in cafes that
feem to them to have a like parity of reafon ; but referving
them to the decifion of parliament. This is a great fecurity to
the public, the judges, and even this facred act itfelf ; and leaves
a weighty *memento* to judges to be careful, and not overhafty
in letting in treafons by conftruction or interpretation, efpecially
in new cafes that have not been refolved and fettled.   2. He
obferves, that as the authoritative decifion of thefe *cafus omiffi*
is referved to the king and parliament, the moft regular way to
do it is by a new declarative act : and therefore the opinion of
any one or of both houfes, though of very refpectable weight,
is not that folemn declaration referred to by this act, as the only
criterion for judging of future treafons.

In confequence of this power, not indeed originally granted
by the ftatute of Edward III, but conftitutionally inherent
in every fubfequent parliament, (which cannot be abridged of
any rights by the act of a precedent one) the legiflature was extremely liberal in declaring new treafons in the unfortunate reign
of king Richard the fecond : as, particularly, the killing of an
embaffador was made fo ; which feems to be founded upon better
reafon than the multitude of other points, that were then ftrained
up to this high offence : the moft arbitrary and abfurd of all

[t] 1 Hal. P. C. 259.

which

which was by the ftatute 21 Ric. II. c. 3. which made the bare
purpofe and intent of killing or depofing the king, without any
overt act to demonftrate it, high treafon. And yet fo little effect
have over-violent laws to prevent any crime, that within two
years afterwards this very prince was both depofed and murdered.
And, in the firft year of his fucceffor's reign, an act was paffed[u],
reciting "that no man knew how he ought to behave himfelf,
" to do, fpeak, or fay, for doubt of fuch pains of treafon : and
" therefore it was accorded that in no time to come any treafon be
" judged, otherwife than was ordained by the ftatute of king
" Edward the third." This at once fwept away the whole load
of extravagant treafons introduced in the time of Richard the
fecond.

BUT afterwards, between the reign of Henry the fourth and
queen Mary, and particularly in the bloody reign of Henry the
eighth, the fpirit of inventing new and ftrange treafons was revived ; among which we may reckon the offences of clipping
money ; breaking prifon or refcue, when the prifoner is committed for treafon ; burning houfes to extort money ; ftealing
cattle by Welchmen ; counterfeiting foreign coin ; wilful poifoning ; execrations againft the king ; calling him opprobrious
names by public writing ; counterfeiting the fign manual or
fignet ; refufing to abjure the pope ; deflowering, or marrying
without the royal licence, any of the king's children, fifters,
aunts, nephews, or nieces ; bare folicitation of the chaftity of
the queen or princefs, or advances made by themfelves ; marrying with the king, by a woman not a virgin, without previoufly difcovering to him fuch her unchafte life ; judging or
believing (manifefted by any overt act) the king to have been
lawfully married to Anne of Cleve ; derogating from the king's
royal ftile and title ; impugning his fupremacy ; and affembling
riotoufly to the number of twelve, and not difperfing upon proclamation : all which new-fangled treafons were totally abrogated by the ftatute 1 Mar. c. 1. which once more reduced all

---

[u] Stat. 1 Hen. IV. c. 10.

treafons

treafons to the ftandard of the ftatute 25 Edw. III. Since which time, though the legiflature has been more cautious in creating new offences of this kind, yet the number is very confiderably encreafed, as we fhall find upon a fhort review.

THESE new treafons, created fince the ftatute 1 Mar. c. 1. and not comprehended under the defcription of ftatute 25 Edw. III, I fhall comprize under three heads. 1. Such as relate to papifts. 2. Such as relate to falfifying the coin or other royal fignatures. 3. Such as are created for the fecurity of the proteftant fucceffion in the houfe of Hanover.

1. THE firft fpecies, relating to *papifts,* was confidered in the preceding chapter, among the penalties incurred by that branch of non-conformifts to the national church; wherein we have only to remember that by ftatute 5 Eliz. c. 1. to defend the pope's jurifdiction in this realm is, for the firft time, a heavy mifdemefnor; and, if the offence be repeated, it is high treafon. Alfo by ftatute 27 Eliz. c. 2. if any popifh prieft, born in the dominions of the crown of England, fhall come over hither from beyond the feas; or fhall tarry here three days without conforming to the church; he is guilty of high treafon. And by ftatute 3 Jac. I. c. 4. if any natural born fubject be withdrawn from his allegiance, and reconciled to the pope or fee of Rome, or any other prince or ftate, both he and all fuch as procure fuch reconciliation fhall incur the guilt of high treafon. Thefe were mentioned under the divifion before referred to, as fpiritual offences, and I now repeat them as temporal ones alfo: the reafon of diftinguifhing thefe overt acts of popery from all others, by fetting the mark of high treafon upon them, being certainly on a civil, and not on a religious, account. For every popifh prieft of courfe renounces his allegiance to his temporal fovereign upon taking orders; that being inconfiftent with his new engagements of canonical obedience to the pope: and the fame may be faid of an obftinate defence of his authority here, or a formal reconciliation to the fee of Rome, which the ftatute

tute conftrues to be a withdrawing from one's natural allegiance ; and therefore, befides being reconciled " to the pope," it alfo adds " or any other prince or ftate."

2. W I T H regard to treafons relative to the *coin* or other *royal fignatures,* we may recollect that the only two offences refpecting the coinage, which are made treafon by the ftatute 25 Edw. III. are the actual counterfeiting the gold and filver coin of this king-dom ; or the importing fuch counterfeit money with intent to utter it, knowing it to be falfe. But thefe not being found fuf-ficient to reftrain the evil practices of coiners and falfe moneyers, other ftatutes have been fince made for that purpofe. The crime itfelf is made a fpecies of high treafon ; as being a breach of al-legiance, by infringing the king's prerogative, and affuming one of the attributes of the fovereign, to whom alone it belongs to fet the value and determination of coin made at home, or to fix the currency of foreign money : and befides, as all money which bears the ftamp of the kingdom is fent into the world upon the public faith, as containing metal of a particular weight and ftan-dard, whoever falfifies this is an offender againft the ftate, by contributing to render that public faith fufpected. And upon the fame reafons, by a law of the emperor Conftantine [w], falfe coiners were declared guilty of high treafon, and were con-demned to be burned alive : as, by the laws of Athens [x], all counterfeiters, debafers, and diminifhers of the current coin were fubjected to capital punifhment. However, it muft be owned, that this method of reafoning is a little overftrained : counterfeiting or debafing the coin being ufually practiced, rather for the fake of private and unlawful lucre, than out of any dif-affection to the fovereign. And therefore both this and it's kind-red fpecies of treafon, that of counterfeiting the feals of the crown or other royal fignatures, feem better denominated by the later civilians a branch of the *crimen falfi* or forgery (in which they are followed by Glanvil [y], Bracton [z], and Fleta [a]) than by

[w] *C.* 9. 24. 2. *Cod. Theod. de falfa moneta, l.* 9.

[x] Pott. Ant. l. 1. c. 26.

[y] *l.* 14. *c.* 7.

[z] *l.* 3. *c.* 3. §. 1 & 2.

[a] *l.* 1. *c.* 22.

Con-

Conftantine and our Edward the third, a fpecies of the *crimen laefae majeftatis* or high treafon. For this confounds the diftinction and proportion of offences; and, by affixing the fame ideas of guilt upon the man who coins a leaden groat and him who affaffinates his fovereign, takes off from that horror which ought to attend the very mention of the crime of high treafon, and makes it more familiar to the fubject. Before the ftatute 25 Edw. III. the offence of counterfeiting the coin was held to be only a fpecies of petit treafon [b]: but fubfequent acts in their new extenfions of the offence have followed the example of that, and have made it equally high treafon as an endeavour to fubvert the government, though not quite equal in it's punifhment.

In confequence of the principle thus adopted, the ftatute 1 Mar. c. 1. having at one blow repealed all intermediate treafons created fince the 25 Edw. III. it was thought expedient by ftatute 1 Mar. ft. 2. c. 6. to revive two fpecies thereof; *viz.* 1. That if any perfon falfely forge or counterfeit any fuch kind of coin of gold or filver, as is not the proper coin of this realm, but fhall be current within this realm by confent of the crown; or, 2. fhall falfely forge or counterfeit the fign manual, privy fignet, or privy feal; fuch offences fhall be deemed high treafon. And by ftatute 1 & 2 P. & M. c. 11. if any perfons do bring into this realm fuch falfe or counterfeit foreign money, being current here, knowing the fame to be falfe, and fhall utter the fame in payment, they fhall be deemed offenders in high treafon. The money referred to in thefe ftatutes muft be fuch as is abfolutely current here, in all payments, by the king's proclamation; of which there is none at prefent, Portugal money being only taken by confent, as approaching the neareft to our ftandard, and falling in well enough with our divifions of money into pounds and fhillings: therefore to counterfeit it is no high treafon, but another inferior offence. Clipping or defacing the genuine coin was not hitherto included in thefe ftatutes; though an offence equally pernicious to trade, and an equal infult upon

[b] 1 Hal. P. C. 224.

the prerogative, as well as perfonal affront to the fovereign ;
whofe very image ought to be had in reverence by all loyal fubjects.   And therefore, among the Romans [c], defacing or even
melting down the emperor's ftatues was made treafon by the
Julian law ; together with other offences of the like fort, according to that vague appendix, " *aliudve quid fimile fi admiferint*."
And now, in England, by ftatute 5 Eliz. c. 11. clipping, wafhing,
rounding, or filing, for wicked gain's fake, any of the money
of this realm, or other money fuffered to be current here, fhall
be adjudged high treafon ; and by ftatute 18 Eliz. c. 1. the fame
offence is defcribed in other more general words ; *viz.* impair-
ing, diminifhing, falfifying, fcaling, and lightening ; and made
liable to the fame penalties.   By ftatute 8 & 9 W. III. c. 26.
made perpetual by 7 Ann. c. 25. whoever fhall knowingly make
or mend, or affift in fo doing, or fhall buy or fell, or have in
his poffeffion, any inftruments proper only for the coinage of
money ; or fhall convey fuch inftruments out of the king's mint ;
fhall be guilty of high treafon : which is by much the fevereft
branch of the coinage law.   The ftatute goes on farther, and
enacts, that to mark any coin on the edges with letters, or
otherwife, in imitation of thofe ufed in the mint ; or to colour,
gild, or cafe over any coin refembling the current coin, or even
round blanks of bafe metal ; fhall be conftrued high treafon.
And, laftly, by ftatute 15 & 16 Geo. II. c. 28. if any perfon
colours or alters any filver current coin of this kingdom, to
make it refemble a gold one ; or any copper coin, to make it
refemble a filver one ; this is alfo high treafon : but the offender fhall be pardoned, in cafe he difcovers and convicts two
other offenders of the fame kind.

3. THE other new fpecies of high treafon is fuch as is created for the fecurity of the *proteftant fucceffion*, over and above
fuch treafons againft the king and government as were comprized under the ftatute 25 Edw. III. For this purpofe, after
the act of fettlement was made, for transferring the crown to

[c] *Ff.* 48. 4. 6.

the

the illuftrious houfe of Hanover, it was enacted by ftatute
13 & 14 W. III. c. 3. that the pretended prince of Wales, who
was then thirteen years of age, and had affumed the title of
king James III, fhould be attainted of high treafon; and it was
made high treafon for any of the king's fubjects by letters, mef-
fages, or otherwife, to hold correfpondence with him, or any
perfon employed by him, or to remit any money for his ufe,
knowing the fame to be for his fervice. And by ftatute 17Geo.II.
c. 39. it is enacted, that if any of the fons of the pretender
fhall land or attempt to land in this kingdom, or be found in
Great Britain, or Ireland, or any of the dominions belonging
to the fame, he fhall be judged attainted of high treafon, and
fuffer the pains thereof. And to correfpond with them, or remit money for their ufe, is made high treafon in the fame manner as it was to correfpond with the father. By the ftatute
1 Ann. ft. 2. c. 17. if any perfon fhall endeavour to deprive or
hinder any perfon, being the next in fucceffion to the crown
according to the limitations of the act of fettlement, from fucceeding to the crown, and fhall malicioufly and directly attempt
the fame by any overt act, fuch offence fhall be high treafon.
And by ftatute 6 Ann. c. 7. if any perfon fhall malicioufly, advifedly, and directly, by writing or printing, maintain and affirm, that any other perfon hath any right or title to the crown
of this realm, otherwife than according to the act of fettlement;
or that the kings of this realm with the authority of parliament
are not able to make laws and ftatutes, to bind the crown and
the defcent thereof; fuch perfon fhall be guilty of high treafon.
This offence (or indeed maintaining this doctrine in any wife,
that the king and parliament cannot limit the crown) was once
before made high treafon, by ftatute 13 Eliz. c. 1. during the
life of that princefs. And after her deceafe it continued a high
mifdemefnor, punifhable with forfeiture of goods and chattels,
even in the moft flourifhing aera of indefeafible hereditary right
and *jure divino* fucceffion. But it was again raifed into high
treafon, by the ftatute of Anne before-mentioned, at the time
of a projected invafion in favour of the then pretender; and

upon

upon this ftatute one Matthews, a printer, was convicted and executed in 1719, for printing a treafonable pamphlet intitled *vox populi vox Dei*[d].

Thus much for the crime of treafon, or *laefae majeftatis*, in all it's branches; which confifts, we may obferve, originally, in groffly counteracting that allegiance, which is due from the fubject by either birth or refidence: though, in fome inftances, the zeal of our legiflators to ftop the progrefs of fome highly pernicious practices has occafioned them a little to depart from this it's primitive idea. But of this enough has been hinted already: it is now time to pafs on from defining the crime to defcribing it's punifhment.

The punifhment of high treafon in general is very folemn and terrible. 1. That the offender be drawn to the gallows, and not be carried or walk; though ufually a fledge or hurdle is allowed, to preferve the offender from the extreme torment of being dragged on the ground or pavement[e]. 2. That he be hanged by the neck, and then cut down alive. 3. That his entrails be taken out, and burned, while he is yet alive. 4. That his head be cut off. 5. That his body be divided into four parts. 6. That his head and quarters be at the king's difpofal[f].

The king may, and often doth, difcharge all the punifhment, except beheading, efpecially where any of noble blood are attainted. For, beheading being part of the judgment, that may be executed, though all the reft be omitted by the king's command[g]. But where beheading is no part of the judgment, as in murder or other felonies, it hath been faid that the king cannot change the judgment, although at the requeft of the party,

[d] State Tr. IX. 680.

[e] 1 Hal. P. C. 382.

[f] This punifhment for treafon fir Edward Coke tells us, is warranted by divers examples in fcripture; for Joab was drawn, Bithan was hanged, Judas was embowelled, and fo of the reft. (3 Inft. 211.)

[g] 1 Hal. P. C. 351.

from

from one fpecies of death to another[h]. But of this we fhall fay more hereafter.

In the cafe of coining, which is a treafon of a different complexion from the reft, the punifhment is milder for male offenders ; being only to be drawn, and hanged by the neck till dead[i]. But in treafons of every kind the punifhment of women is the fame, and different from that of men. For, as the natural modefty of the fex forbids the expofing and publicly mangling their bodies, their fentence (which is to the full as terrible to fenfe as the other) is to be drawn to the gallows, and there to be burned alive[k].

The confequences of this judgment, (attainder, forfeiture, and corruption of blood) muft be referred to the latter end of this book, when we fhall treat of them all together, as well in treafon as in other offences.

[h] 3 Inft. 52.
[i] 1 Hal. P. C. 351.

[k] 2 Hal. P. C. 399.

CHAPTER THE SEVENTH.

OF FELONIES, INJURIOUS TO THE KING'S PREROGATIVE.

AS, according to the method I have adopted, we are next to confider fuch felonies as are more immediately injurious to the king's prerogative, it will not be amifs here, at our firft entrance upon this crime, to enquire briefly into the nature and meaning of *felony*; before we proceed upon any of the particular branches, into which it is divided.

FELONY, in the general acceptation of our Englifh law, comprizes every fpecies of crime, which occafioned at common law the forfeiture of lands or goods. This moft frequently happens in thofe crimes, for which a capital punifhment either is or was liable to be inflicted: for thofe felonies, which are called clergyable, or to which the benefit of clergy extends, were antiently punifhed with death in all lay, or unlearned, offenders; though now by the ftatute-law that punifhment is for the firft offence univerfally remitted. Treafon itfelf, fays fir Edward Coke [a], was antiently comprized under the name of felony: and in confirmation of this we may obferve, that the ftatute of treafons, 25 Edw. III. c. 2. fpeaking of fome dubious crimes, directs a

[a] 3 Inft. 15.

reference

reference to parliament; that it may be there adjudged, "whe-
" ther they be treaſon, or *other* felony." All treaſons therefore,
ſtrictly ſpeaking, are felonies; though all felonies are not treaſon.
And to this alſo we may add, that all offences, now capital, are
in ſome degree or other felony: and this is likewiſe the caſe
with ſome other offences, which are not puniſhed with death;
as ſuicide, where the party is already dead; homicide by chance-
medly, or in ſelf-defence; and petit larceny, or pilfering; all
which are (ſtrictly ſpeaking) felonies, as they ſubject the com-
mitters of them to forfeitures. So that upon the whole the only
adequate definition of felony ſeems to be that which is before
laid down; *viz.* an offence which occaſions a total forfeiture of
either lands, or goods, or both, at the common law; and to
which capital or other puniſhment may be ſuperadded, according
to the degree of guilt.

To explain this matter a little farther: the word *felony*, or
felonia, is of undoubted feodal original, being frequently to be
met with in the books of feuds, *&c*; but the derivation of it
has much puzzled the juridical lexicographers, Prateus, Calvi-
nus, and the reſt: ſome deriving it from the Greek, φηλος, an
impoſtor or deceiver; others from the Latin, *fallo, fefelli*, to
countenance which they would have it called *fallonia*. Sir Edward Coke, as his manner is, has given us a ſtill ſtranger etymology[b]; that it is *crimen animo felleo perpetratum*, with a bitter
or galliſh inclination. But all of them agree in the deſcription,
that it is ſuch a crime as works a forfeiture of all the offender's
lands, or goods. And this gives great probability to ſir Henry
Spelman's Teutonic or German derivation of it[c]: in which language indeed, as the word is clearly of feodal original, we ought
rather to look for it's ſignification, than among the Greeks and
Romans. *Fe-lon* then, according to him, is derived from two
northern words; **fee**, which ſignifies (we well know) the fief,
feud, or beneficiary eſtate; and **lon**, which ſignifies price or
value. Felony is therefore the ſame as *pretium feudi*, the conſi-

---

[b] 1 Inſt. 391.　　　　　　　　　[c] Gloſſar. *tit. Felon.*

deration

deration for which a man gives up his fief; as we fay in common fpeech, fuch an act is as much as your life, or eftate, is worth. In this fenfe it will clearly fignify the feodal forfeiture, or act by which an eftate is forfeited, or efcheats, to the lord.

To confirm this we may obferve, that it is in this fenfe, of forfeiture to the lord, that the feodal writers conftantly ufe it. For all thofe acts, whether of a criminal nature or not, which at this day are generally forfeitures of copyhold eftates[d], are ftiled *feloniae* in the feodal law : " *fcilicet, per quas feudum amittitur*[e]." As, " *fi domino defervire noluerit*[f] ; *fi per annum et diem ceffaverit* " *in petenda inveftitura*[g] ; *fi dominum ejuravit, i. e. negavit fe a* " *domino feudum habere*[h] ; *fi a domino, in jus eum vocante, ter ci-* " *tatus non comparuerit*[i] ;" all thefe, with many others, are ftill caufes of forfeiture in our copyhold eftates, and were denominated felonies by the feodal conftitutions. So likewife injuries of a more fubftantial or criminal nature were denominated felonies, that is, forfeitures: as affaulting or beating the lord[k]; vitiating his wife or daughter, " *fi dominum cucurbitaverit, i. e. cum uxore ejus concubue-* " *rit*[l] ;" all thefe are efteemed felonies, and the latter is exprefsly fo denominated, " *fi fecerit feloniam, dominum forte cucurbitando*[m]." And as thefe contempts, or fmaller offences, were felonies or acts of forfeiture, of courfe greater crimes, as murder and robbery, fell under the fame denomination. On the other hand the lord might be guilty of felony, or forfeit his feignory to the vaffal, by the fame acts as the vaffal would have forfeited his feud to the lord. " *Si dominus commifit feloniam, per quam vafallus amitteret* " *feudum fi eam commiferit in dominum, feudi proprietatem etiam* " *dominus perdere debet*[n]." One inftance given of this fort of fe-lony in the lord is beating the fervant of his vafal, fo as that he lofes his fervice; which feems merely in the nature of a civil

---

[d] See Vol. II. pag. 284.
[e] *Feud. l. 2. t. 26. in calc.*
[f] *Feud. l. 1. t. 21.*
[g] *Feud. l. 2. t. 24.*
[h] *Feud. l. 2. t. 34. l. 2. t. 26. §. 3.*

[i] *Feud. l. 2. t. 22.*
[k] *Feud. l. 2. t. 24. §. 2.*
[l] *Feud. l. 1. t. 5.*
[m] *Feud. l. 2. t. 38.* Britton. *l. 1. c. 22.*
[n] *Feud. l. 2. t. 26 & 47.*

injury,

injury, so far as it respects the vasal. And all these felonies were to be determined " *per laudamentum sive judicium parium suorum*" in the lord's court; as with us forfeitures of copyhold lands are presentable by the homage in the court-baron.

FELONY, and the act of forfeiture to the lord, being thus synonymous terms in the feodal law, we may easily trace the reason why, upon the introduction of that law into England, those crimes which induced such forfeiture or escheat of lands (and, by a small deflexion from the original sense, such as induced the forfeiture of goods also) were denominated felonies. Thus it was said, that suicide, robbery, and rape, were felonies; that is, the consequence of such crimes was forfeiture; till by long use we began to signify by the term of felony the actual crime committed, and not the penal consequence. And upon this system only can we account for the cause, why treason in antient times was held to be a species of felony: *viz.* because it induced a forfeiture.

HENCE it follows, that capital punishment does by no means enter into the true idea and definition of felony. Felony may be without inflicting capital punishment, as in the cases instanced of self-murder, excusable homicide, and petit larciny: and it is possible that capital punishments may be inflicted, and yet the offence be no felony; as in the case of heresy by the common law, which, though capital, never worked any forfeiture of lands or goods °, an inseparable incident to felony. And of the same nature is the punishment of standing mute, without pleading to an indictment; which is capital, but without any forfeiture, and therefore such standing mute is no felony. In short the true criterion of felony is forfeiture; for, as sir Edward Coke justly observes P, in all felonies which are punishable with death, the offender loses all his lands in fee-simple, and also his goods and chattels; in such as are not so punishable, his goods and chattels only.

° 3 Inst. 43.   P 1 Inst. 391.

THE idea of felony is indeed so generally connected with that of capital punishment, that we find it hard to separate them; and to this usage the interpretations of the law do now conform. And therefore if a statute makes any new offence felony, the law [q] implies that it shall be punished with death, *viz.* by hanging, as well as with forfeiture: unless the offender prays the benefit of clergy; which all felons are entitled once to have unless the same is expressly taken away by statute. And, in compliance herewith, I shall for the future consider it also in the same light, as a generical term, including all capital crimes below treason; having premised thus much concerning the true nature and original meaning of felony, in order to account for the reason of those instances I have mentioned, of felonies that are not capital, and capital offences that are not felonies: which seem at first view repugnant to the general idea which we now entertain of felony, as a crime to be punished by death; whereas properly it is a crime to be punished by forfeiture, and to which death may, or may not be, though it generally is, superadded.

I PROCEED now to consider such felonies, as are more immediately injurious to the king's prerogative. These are, 1. Offences relating to the coin, not amounting to treason. 2. Offences against the king's council. 3. The offence of serving a foreign prince. 4. The offence of imbezzling the king's armour or stores of war. To which may be added a fifth, 5. Desertion from the king's armies in time of war.

1. OFFENCES relating to the *coin*, under which may be ranked some inferior misdemesnors not amounting to felony, are thus declared by a series of statutes, which I shall recite in the order of time. And, first, by statute 27 Edw. I. c. 3. none shall bring pollards and crockards, which were foreign coins of base metal, into the realm, on pain of forfeiture of life and goods. By statute 9 Edw. III. st. 2. no sterling money shall be melted

[q] 1 Hawk. P. C. 107.　2 Hawk. P. C. 444.

down,

down, upon pain of forfeiture thereof. By ſtatute 14 Eliz. c. 3.
ſuch as forge any foreign coin, although it be not made current
here by proclamation, ſhall (with their aiders and abettors) be
guilty of miſpriſion of treaſon: a crime which we ſhall hereafter conſider. By ſtatute 13 & 14 Car. II. c. 31. the offence of
melting down any current ſilver money ſhall be puniſhed with
forfeiture of the ſame, and alſo the double value: and the offender, if a freeman of any town, ſhall be disfranchiſed; if not,
ſhall ſuffer ſix months impriſonment. By ſtatute 6 & 7 W. III.
c. 17. if any perſon buys or ſells, or knowingly has in his cuſtody, any clippings or filings of the coin, he ſhall forfeit the
ſame and 500 l; one moiety to the king, and the other to the
informer; and be branded in the cheek with the letter R. By
ſtatute 8 & 9 W. III. c. 26. if any perſon ſhall blanch, or whiten,
copper for ſale; (which makes it reſemble ſilver) or buy or ſell
or offer to ſale any malleable compoſition, which ſhall be heavier
than ſilver, and look, touch, and wear like gold, but be beneath
the ſtandard: or if any perſon ſhall receive or pay any counterfeit or diminiſhed money of this kingdom, not being cut in
pieces, (an operation which every man is thereby empowered to
perform) at a leſs rate than it ſhall import to be of: (which de-
monſtrates a conſciouſneſs of it's baſeneſs, and a fraudulent deſign) all ſuch perſons ſhall be guilty of felony. But theſe pre-
cautions not being found ſufficient to prevent the uttering of falſe
or diminiſhed money, which was only a miſdemeſnor at common
law, it is enacted by ſtatute 15 & 16 Geo. II. c. 28. that if any
perſon ſhall tender in payment any counterfeit coin, knowing it
ſo to be, he ſhall for the firſt offence be impriſoned ſix months;
and find ſureties for his good behaviour for ſix months more:
for the ſecond offence, ſhall be impriſoned and find ſureties for
two years: and, for the third offence, ſhall be guilty of felony
without benefit of clergy. Alſo if a perſon knowingly tenders
in payment any counterfeit money, and at the ſame time has
more in his cuſtody; or ſhall, within ten days after, knowingly
tender other falſe money; he ſhall for the firſt offence be impriſoned one year, and find ſureties for his good behaviour for two

years

years longer; and for the second, be guilty of felony without benefit of clergy. By the same statute it is also enacted, that, if any person counterfeits the copper coin, he shall suffer two years imprisonment, and find sureties for two years more. Thus much for offences relating to the coin, as well misdemesnors as felonies, which I thought it most convenient to consider in one and the same view.

2. FELONIES, against the king's *council*[r], are; first, by statute 3 Hen. VII. c. 14. if any sworn servant of the king's houshold conspires or confederates to kill any lord of this realm, or other person, sworn of the king's council, he shall be guilty of felony. Secondly, by statute 9 Ann. c. 16. to assault, strike, wound, or attempt to kill, any privy counsellor in the execution of his office, is made felony without benefit of clergy.

3. FELONIES in *serving foreign states*, which service is generally inconsistent with allegiance to one's natural prince, are restrained and punished by statute 3 Jac. I. c. 4. which makes it felony for any person whatever to go out of the realm, to serve any foreign prince, without having first taken the oath of allegiance before his departure. And it is felony also for any gentleman, or person of higher degree, or who hath borne any office in the army, to go out of the realm to serve such foreign prince or state, without previously entering into a bond with two sureties, not to be reconciled to the see of Rome, or enter into any conspiracy against his natural sovereign. And farther, by statute 9 Geo. II. c. 30. enforced by statute 29 Geo. II. c. 17. if any subject of Great Britain shall enlist himself, or if any person shall procure him to be enlisted, in any foreign service, or detain or embark him for that purpose, without licence under the king's sign manual, he shall be guilty of felony without benefit of clergy: but if the person, so enlisted or enticed, shall discover his seducer within fifteen days, so as he may be apprehended and convicted of the same, he shall himself be indem-

[r] See Vol. I. pag. 332.

nified.

nified. By ftatute 29 Geo. II. c.17. it is moreover enacted, that to ferve under the French king, as à military officer, fhall be felony without benefit of clergy; and to enter into the Scotch brigade, in the Dutch fervice, without previoufly taking the oaths of allegiance and abjuration, fhall be a forfeiture of 500 *l.*

4. FELONY, by *imbezzling* the king's *armour* or warlike *ftores*, is fo declared to be by ftatute 31 Eliz. c. 4. which enacts, that if any perfon having the charge or cuftody of the king's armour, ordnance, ammunition, or habiliments of war; or of any victual provided for victualling the king's foldiers or mariners; fhall, either for gain, or to impede his majefty's fervice, imbezzle the fame to the value of twenty fhillings, fuch offence fhall be felony. And the ftatute 22 Car. II. c. 5. takes away the benefit of clergy from this offence, fo far as it relates to naval ftores. Other inferior imbezzlements and mifdemefnors, that fall under this denomination, are punifhed by ftatute 1 Geo. I. c. 25. with fine and imprifonment.

5. DESERTION from the king's armies in time of war, whether by land or fea, in England or in parts beyond the feas, is by the ftanding laws of the land (exclufive of the annual acts of parliament to punifh mutiny and defertion) and particularly by ftatute 18 Hen. VI. c.19. and 5 Eliz. c. 5. made felony, but not without benefit of clergy. But by the ftatute 2 & 3 Edw. VI. c. 2. clergy is taken away from fuch deferters, and the offence is made triable by the juftices of every fhire. The fame ftatutes punifh other inferior military offences with fines, imprifonment, and other penalties.

CHAPTER   THE   EIGHTH.

Of   PRAEMUNIRE.

A THIRD ſpecies of offence more immediately affecting
the king and his government, though not ſubject to capital puniſhment, is that of *praemunire:* ſo called from the words
of the writ preparatory to the proſecution thereof; "*praemunire*[a]
"*facias A. B.*" forewarn A. B. that he appear before us to anſwer the contempt wherewith he ſtands charged; which contempt is particularly recited in the preamble to the writ[b]. It
took it's original from the exorbitant power claimed and exerciſed in England by the pope, which even in the days of blind
zeal was too heavy for our anceſtors to bear.

It may juſtly be obſerved, that religious principles, which
(when genuine and pure) have an evident tendency to make their
profeſſors better citizens as well as better men, have (when perverted and erroneous) been uſually ſubverſive of civil government, and been made both the cloak and the inſtrument of every
pernicious deſign that can be harboured in the heart of man.
The unbounded authority that was exerciſed by the Druids in
the weſt, under the influence of pagan ſuperſtition, and the
terrible ravages committed by the Saracens in the eaſt, to pro-
pagate the religion of Mahomet, both witneſs to the truth of

[a] A barbarous word for *praemonere.*   [b] Old *Nat. Brev.* 101. *edit.* 1534.

that

that antient univerfal obfervation; that, in all ages and in all countries, civil and ecclefiaftical tyranny are mutually productive of each other. And it is the glory of the church of England, as well as a ftrong prefumptive argument in favour of the purity of her faith, that fhe hath been (as her prelates on a trying occafion once expreffed it [c]) in her principles and practice ever moft unqueftionably loyal. The clergy of her perfuafion, holy in their doctrines and unblemifhed in their lives and converfation, are alfo moderate in their ambition, and entertain juft notions of the ties of fociety and the rights of civil government. As in matters of faith and morality they acknowlege no guide but the fcriptures, fo, in matters of external polity and of private right, they derive all their title from the civil magiftrate; they look up to the king as their head, to the parliament as their lawgiver, and pride themfelves in nothing fo juftly, as in being true members of the church, emphatically *by law* eftablifhed. Whereas the principles of thofe who differ from them, as well in one extreme as the other, are equally and totally deftructive of thofe ties and obligations by which all fociety is kept together; equally encroaching on thofe rights, which reafon and the original contract of every free ftate in the univerfe have vefted in the fovereign power; and equally aiming at a diftinct independent fupremacy of their own, where fpiritual men and fpiritual caufes are concerned. The dreadful effects of fuch a religious bigotry, when actuated by erroneous principles, even of the proteftant kind, are fufficiently evident from the hiftory of the anabaptifts in Germany, the covenanters in Scotland, and that deluge of fectaries in England, who murdered their fovereign, overturned the church and monarchy, fhook every pillar of law, juftice, and private property, and moft devoutly eftablifhed a kingdom of the faints in their ftead. But thefe horrid devaftations, the effects of mere madnefs or of zeal that was nearly allied to it, though violent and tumultuous, were but of a fhort duration. Whereas the progrefs of the papal policy, long actuated by the fteady counfels of fucceffive pontiffs,

[c] Addrefs to James II. 1687.

took

took deeper root, and was at length in some places with difficulty, in others never yet, extirpated. For this we might call to witness the black intrigues of the Jesuits, so lately triumphant over Christendom, but now universally abandoned by even the Roman catholic powers: but the subject of our present chapter rather leads us to consider the vast strides, which were formerly made in this kingdom by the popish clergy; how nearly they arrived to effecting their grand design; some few of the means they made use of for establishing their plan; and how almost all of them have been defeated or converted to better purposes, by the vigour of our free constitution, and the wisdom of successive parliaments.

THE antient British church, by whomsoever planted, was a stranger to the bishop of Rome, and all his pretended authority. But, the pagan Saxon invaders having driven the professors of christianity to the remotest corners of our island, their own conversion was afterwards effected by Augustin the monk, and other missionaries from the court of Rome. This naturally introduced some few of the papal corruptions in point of faith and doctrine; but we read of no civil authority claimed by the pope in these kingdoms, till the aera of the Norman conquest: when the then reigning pontiff having favoured duke William in his projected invasion, by blessing his host and consecrating his banners, he took that opportunity also of establishing his spiritual encroachments; and was even permitted so to do by the policy of the conqueror, in order more effectually to humble the Saxon clergy and aggrandize his Norman prelates: prelates, who, being bred abroad in the doctrine and practice of slavery, had contracted a reverence and regard for it, and took a pleasure in rivetting the chains of a free-born people.

THE most stable foundation of legal and rational government is a due subordination of rank, and a gradual scale of authority; and tyranny also itself is most surely supported by a regular increase of despotism, rising from the slave to the sultan: with this

this difference however, that the meafure of obedience in the one is grounded on the principles of fociety, and is extended no farther than reafon and neceffity will warrant; in the other it is limited only by abfolute will and pleafure, without permitting the inferior to examine the title upon which it is founded. More effectually therefore to enflave the confciences and minds of the people, the Romifh clergy themfelves paid the moft implicit obedience to their own fuperiors or prelates; and they, in their turns, were as blindly devoted to the will of the fovereign pon-tiff, whofe decifions they held to be infallible, and his authority co-extenfive with the chriftian world. Hence his legates *a latere* were introduced into every kingdom of Europe, his bulles and decretal epiftles became the rule both of faith and difcipline, his judgment was the final refort in all cafes of doubt or difficulty, his decrees were enforced by anathemas and fpiritual cenfures, he dethroned even kings that were refractory, and denied to whole kingdoms (when undutiful) the exercife of chriftian or-dinances, and the benefits of the gofpel of God.

BUT, though the being fpiritual head of the church was a thing of great found, and of greater authority, among men of confcience and piety, yet the court of Rome was fully apprized that (among the bulk of mankind) power cannot be maintained without property; and therefore it's attention began very early to be rivetted upon every method that promifed pecuniary advan-tage. The doctrine of purgatory was introduced, and with it the purchafe of maffes to redeem the fouls of the deceafed. New-fangled offences were created, and indulgences were fold to the wealthy, for liberty to fin without danger. The canon law took cognizance of crimes, injoined penance *pro falute animae*, and commuted that penance for money. Non-refidence and pluralities among the clergy, and marriages among the laity related within the feventh degree, were ftrictly prohibited by canon; but difpenfations were feldom denied to thofe who could afford to buy them. In fhort, all the wealth of chriftendom was gradually drained, by a thoufand chanels, into the coffers of the holy fee.

THE eftablifhment alfo of the feodal fyftem in moft of the governments of Europe, whereby the lands of all private proprietors were declared to be holden of the prince, gave a hint to the court of Rome for ufurping a fimilar authority over all the preferments of the church; which began firft in Italy, and gradually fpread itfelf to England. The pope became a feodal lord; and all ordinary patrons were to hold their right of patronage under this univerfal fuperior. Eftates held by feodal tenure, being originally gratuitous donations, were at that time denominated *beneficia*: their very name as well as conftitution was borrowed, and the care of the fouls of a parifh thence came to be denominated a *benefice*. Lay fees were conferred by inveftiture or delivery of corporal poffeffion; and fpiritual benefices, which at firft were univerfally donatives, now received in like manner a fpiritual inveftiture, by inftitution from the bifhop, and induction under his authority. As lands efcheated to the lord, in defect of a legal tenant, fo benefices lapfed to the bifhop upon non-prefentation by the patron, in the nature of a fpiritual efcheat. The annual tenths collected from the clergy were equivalent to the feodal render, or rent referved upon a grant; the oath of canonical obedience was copied from the oath of fealty required from the vafal by his fuperior; and the *primer feifins* of our military tenures, whereby the firft profits of an heir's eftate were cruelly extorted by his lord, gave birth to as cruel an exaction of firft-fruits from the beneficed clergy. And the occafional aids and talliages, levied by the prince on his vafals, gave a handle to the pope to levy, by the means of his legates *a latere*, peter-pence and other taxations.

AT length the holy father went a ftep beyond any example of either emperor or feodal lord. He referved to himfelf, by his own apoftolical authority[d], the prefentation to all benefices which

[d] *Extrav. l. 3. t. 2. c. 13.*

became

beeame vacant while the incumbent was attending the court of Rome upon any occaſion, or on his journey thither, or back again ; and moreover ſuch alſo as became vacant by his promotion to a biſhoprick or abbey : " *etiamſi ad illa perſonae conſue-* " *verint et debuerint per electionem aut quemvis alium modum aſſumi."* And this laſt, the canoniſts declared, was no detriment at all to the patron, being only like the change of a life in a feodal eſtate by the lord. Diſpenſations to avoid theſe vacancies begat the doctrine of *commendams :* and papal *proviſions* were the previous nomination to ſuch benefices, by a kind of anticipation, before they became actually void ; though afterwards indiſcriminately applied to any right of patronage exerted or uſurped by the pope. In conſequence of which the beſt livings were filled by Italian and other foreign clergy, equally unſkilled in and averſe to the laws and conſtitution of England. The very nomination to biſhopricks, that antient prerogative of the crown, was wreſted from king Henry the firſt, and afterwards from his ſucceſſor king John ; and ſeemingly indeed conferred on the chapters belonging to each ſee : but by means of the frequent appeals to Rome, through the intricacy of the laws which regulated canonical elections, was eventually veſted in the pope. And, to ſum up this head with a tranſaction moſt unparalleled and aſtoniſhing in it's kind, pope Innocent III had at length the effrontery to demand, and king John had the meanneſs to conſent to, a reſignation of his crown to the pope, whereby England was to become for ever St Peter's patrimony ; and the daſtardly monarch re-accepted his ſceptre from the hands of the papal legate, to hold as the vaſal of the holy ſee, at the annual rent of a thouſand marks.

ANOTHER engine ſet on foot, or at leaſt greatly improved, by the court of Rome, was a maſterpiece of papal policy. Not content with the ample proviſion of tithes, which the law of the land had given to the parochial clergy, they endeavoured to graſp at the lands and inheritances of the kingdom, and (had not the legiſlature withſtood them) would by this time have probably

been

been masters of every foot of ground in the kingdom. To this end they introduced the monks of the Benedictine and other rules, men of four and austere religion, separated from the world and it's concerns by a vow of perpetual celibacy, yet fascinating the minds of the people by pretences to extraordinary sanctity, while all their aim was to aggrandize the power and extend the influence of their grand superior the pope. And as, in those times of civil tumult, great rapines and violence were daily committed by overgrown lords and their adherents, they were taught to believe, that founding a monastery a little before their deaths would atone for a life of incontinence, disorder, and bloodshed. Hence innumerable abbeys and religious houses were built within a century after the conquest, and endowed, not only with the tithes of parishes which were ravished from the secular clergy, but also with lands, manors, lordships, and extensive baronies. And the doctrine inculcated was, that whatever was so given to, or purchased by, the monks and friers, was consecrated to God himself; and that to alienate or take it away was no less than the sin of sacrilege.

I MIGHT here have enlarged upon other contrivances, which will occur to the recollection of the reader, set on foot by the court of Rome, for effecting an entire exemption of it's clergy from any intercourse with the civil magistrate: such as the separation of the ecclesiastical court from the temporal; the appointment of it's judges by merely spiritual authority, without any interpolition from the crown; the exclusive jurisdiction it claimed over all ecclesiastical persons and causes; and the *privilegium clericale*, or benefit of clergy, which delivered all clerks from any trial or punishment except before their own tribunal. But the history and progress of ecclesiastical courts [e], as well as of purchases in mortmain [f], have already been fully discussed in the preceding volumes: and we shall have an opportunity of examining at large the nature of the *privilegium clericale* in the progress of the present book. And therefore I shall only observe

e See Vol. III. pag. 61. f See Vol. II. pag. 268.

at

at prefent, that notwithftanding this plan of pontifical power was fo deeply laid, and fo indefatigably purfued by the unwearied politics of the court of Rome through a long fucceffion of ages; notwithftanding it was polifhed and improved by the united endeavours of a body of men, who engroffed all the learning of Europe for centuries together; notwithftanding it was firmly and refolutely executed by perfons the beft calculated for eftablifhing tyranny and defpotifm, being fired with a bigoted enthufiafm, (which prevailed not only among the weak and fimple, but even among thofe of the beft natural and acquired endowments) unconnected with their fellow-fubjects, and totally indifferent what might befal that pofterity to which they bore no endearing relation; --- yet it vanifhed into nothing, when the eyes of the people were a little enlightened, and they fet themfelves with vigour to oppofe it. So vain and ridiculous is the attempt to live in fociety, without acknowleging the obligations which it lays us under; and to affect an intire independence of that civil ftate, which protects us in all our rights, and gives us every other liberty, that only excepted of defpifing the laws of the community.

HAVING thus in fome degree endeavoured to trace out the original and fubfequent progrefs of the papal ufurpations in England, let us now return to the ftatutes of *praemunire*, which were framed to encounter this overgrown yet encreafing evil. King Edward I, a wife and magnanimous prince, fet himfelf in earneft to fhake off this fervile yoke[g]. He would not fuffer his bifhops to attend a general council, till they had fworn not to receive the papal benediction. He made light of all papal bulles and proceffes: attacking Scotland in defiance of one; and feifing the temporalties of his clergy, who under pretence of another refufed to pay a tax impofed by parliament. He ftrengthened the ftatutes of mortmain; thereby clofing the great gulph, in which all the lands of the kingdom were in danger of being fwallowed.

[g] Dav. 83, &c.

And,

And, one of his fubjects having obtained a bulle of excommunication againſt another, he ordered him to be executed as a traitor, according to the antient law [h]. And in the thirty fifth year
of his reign was made the firſt ſtatute againſt papal proviſions,
which, according to ſir Edward Coke [i], is the foundation of all
the fubfequent ſtatutes of *praemunire*; which we rank as an offence immediately againſt the king, becauſe every encouragement of the papal power is a diminution of the authority of
the crown.

I N the weak reign of Edward the ſecond the pope again
endeavoured to encroach, but the parliament manfully withſtood
him; and it was one of the principal articles charged againſt
that unhappy prince, that he had given allowance to the bulles
of the ſee of Rome. But Edward the third was of a temper
extremely different; and, to remedy theſe inconveniences firſt
by gentle means, he and his nobility wrote an expoſtulation to
the pope: but receiving a menacing and contemptuous anſwer,
withal acquainting him, that the emperor, (who a few years
before at the diet of Nuremberg, *A. D.* 1323, had eſtabliſhed
a law againſt proviſions [k]) and alſo the king of France, had lately
fubmitted to the holy ſee; the king replied, that if both the
emperor and the French king ſhould take the pope's part, he
was ready to give battel to them both, in defence of the liberties of his crown. Hereupon more ſharp and penal laws were
enacted againſt proviſors [l], which enact ſeverally, that the court
of Rome ſhall preſent or collate to no biſhoprick or living in
England; and that whoever diſturbs any patron in the preſentation to a living by virtue of a papal proviſion, ſuch proviſor
ſhall pay fine and ranſom to the king at his will; and be impriſoned till he renounces ſuch proviſion: and the ſame puniſhment is inflicted on ſuch as cite the king, or any of his fubjects,

---

[h] Bro. *Abr. tit. Coron.* 115. *Treaſon.* 14.
5 Rep. part 1. fol. 12. 3 Aſſ. 19.
[i] 2 Inſt. 583.
[k] Mod. Univ. Hiſt. xxix. 293.

[l] Stat. 25 Edw. III. ſt. 6. 27 Edw. III.
ſt. 1. c. 1. 38 Edw. III. ſt. 1. c. 4. & ſt. 2.
c. 1, 2, 3, 4.

to anfwer in the court of Rome. And when the holy fee refented thefe proceedings, and pope Urban V attempted to revive the vafalage and annual rent to which king John had fubjected his kingdom, it was unanimoufly agreed by all the eftates of the realm in parliament affembled, 40 Edw. III. that king John's donation was null and void, being without the concurrence of parliament, and contrary to his coronation oath : and all the temporal noblity and commons engaged, that if the pope fhould endeavour by procefs or otherwife to maintain thefe ufurpations, they would refift and withftand him with all their power[m].

In the reign of Richard the fecond, it was found neceffary to fharpen and ftrengthen thefe laws, and therefore it was enacted by ftatutes 3 Ric. II. c. 3. and 7 Ric. II. c. 12. firft, that no alien fhould be capable of letting his benefice to farm ; in order to compel fuch, as had crept in, at leaft to refide on their preferments : and, afterwards, that no alien fhould be capable to be prefented to any ecclefiaftical preferment, under the penalty of the ftatutes of provifors. By the ftatute 12 Ric. II. c. 15. all liegemen of the king, accepting of a living by any foreign provifion, are put out of the king's protection, and the benefice made voʻd. To which the ftatute 13 Ric. II. ft. 2. c. 2. adds banifhment and forfeiture of lands and goods : and by c. 3. of the fame ftatute, any perfon bringing over any citation or excommunication from beyond fea, on account of the execution of the foregoing ftatutes of provifors, fhall be imprifoned, forfeit his goods and lands, and moreover fuffer pain of life and member.

In the writ for the execution of all thefe ftatutes the words *praemunire facias,* being (as was faid) ufed to command a citation of the party, have denominated in common fpeech, not only the writ, but the offence itfelf of maintaining the papal power, by the name of *praemunire.* And accordingly the next ftatute I fhall mention, which is generally referred to by all fubfequent

[m] Seld. *in Flet.* 10. 4.

ftatutes, is ufually called the ftatute of *praemunire*. It is the ftatute 16 Ric. II. c. 5. which enacts, that whoever procures at Rome, or elfewhere, any tranflations, proceffes, excommunications, bulles, inftruments, or other things which touch the king, againft him, his crown, and realm, and all perfons aiding and affifting therein, fhall be put out of the king's protection, their lands and goods forfeited to the king's ufe, and they fhall be attached by their bodies to anfwer to the king and his council; or procefs of *praemunire facias* fhall be made out againft them, as in other cafes of provifors.

By the ftatute 2 Hen. IV. c. 3. all perfons who accept any provifion from the pope, to be exempt from canonical obedience to their proper ordinary, are alfo fubjected to the penalties of *praemunire*. And this is the laft of our antient ftatutes touching this offence; the ufurped civil power of the bifhop of Rome being pretty well broken down by thefe ftatutes, as his ufurped religious power was in about a century afterwards: the fpirit of the nation being fo much raifed againft foreigners, that about this time, in the reign of Henry the fifth, the alien priories, or abbies for foreign monks, were fuppreffed, and their lands given to the crown. And no farther attempts were afterwards made in fupport of thefe foreign jurifdictions.

A LEARNED writer, before referred to, is therefore greatly miftaken, when he fays [n], that in Henry the fixth's time the archbifhop of Canterbury and other bifhops offered to the king a large fupply, if he would confent that all laws againft provifors, and efpecially the ftatute 16 Ric. II. might be repealed; but that this motion was rejected. This account is incorrect in all it's branches. For, firft, the application, which he probably means, was made not by the bifhops only, but by the unanimous confent of a provincial fynod, affembled in 1439, 18 Hen. VI. that very fynod which at the fame time refufed to confirm and allow a papal bulle, which then was laid before them. Next, the

[n] Dav. 96.

purport

purport of it was not to procure a repeal of the statutes against provisors, or that of Richard II in particular; but to request that the penalties thereof, which by a forced construction were applied to all that sued in the spiritual, and even in many temporal, courts of this realm, might be turned against the proper objects only; those who appealed to Rome or to any foreign jurisdictions: the tenor of the petition being, " that those " penalties should be taken to extend only to those that com- " menced any suits or procured any writs or public instruments " at Rome, or elsewhere out of England; and that no one " should be prosecuted upon that statute for any suit in the spi- " ritual courts or lay jurisdictions of this kingdom." Lastly, the motion was so far from being rejected, that the king promised to recommend it to the next parliament, and in the mean time that no one should be molested upon this account. And the clergy were so satisfied with their success, that they granted to the king a whole tenth upon this occasion[o].

AND indeed so far was the archbishop, who presided in this synod, from countenancing the usurped power of the pope in this realm, that he was ever a firm opposer of it. And, particularly, in the reign of Henry the fifth, he prevented the king's brother from being then made a cardinal, and legate *a latere* from the pope; upon the mere principle of it's being within the mischief of papal provisions, and derogatory from the liberties of the English church and nation. For, as he expressed himself to the king in his letter upon that subject, " he was " bound to oppose it by his ligeance, and also to quit himself " to God, and the church of this land, of which God and the " king had made him governor." This was not the language of a prelate addicted to the slavery of the see of Rome; but of one, who was indeed of principles so very opposite to the papal usurpations, that in the year preceding this synod, 17 Hen. VI. he refused to consecrate a bishop of Ely, that was nominated by pope Eugenius IV. A conduct quite consonant to his former

[o] Wilk. *Concil. Mag. Brit.* III. 533.

behaviour, in 6 Hen. VI, when he refused to obey the commands of pope Martin V, who had required him to exert his endeavours to repeal the statute of *praemunire* ; (" *execrabile illud statutum*," as the holy father phrases it) which refusal so far exasperated the court of Rome against him, that at length the pope issued a bulle to suspend him from his office and authority, which the archbishop disregarded, and appealed to a general council. And so sensible were the nation of their primate's merit, that the lords spiritual, and temporal, and also the university of Oxford, wrote letters to the pope in his defence ; and the house of commons addressed the king, to send an embassador forthwith to his holiness, on behalf of the archbishop, who had incurred the displeasure of the pope for opposing the excessive power of the court of Rome [r].

THIS then is the original meaning of the offence, which we call *praemunire* ; viz. introducing a foreign power into this land, and creating *imperium in imperio*, by paying that obedience to papal process, which constitutionally belonged to the king alone, long before the reformation in the reign of Henry the eighth : at which time the penalties of *praemunire* were indeed extended to more papal abuses than before; as the kingdom then entirely renounced the authority of the see of Rome, though not all the corrupted doctrines of the Roman church. And therefore by the several statutes of 24 Hen. VIII. c. 12. and 25 Hen. VIII. c. 19 & 21. to appeal to Rome from any of the king's courts, which (though illegal before) had at times been connived at ; to sue to Rome for any licence or dispensation ; or to obey any process from thence ; are made liable to the pains of *praemunire*. And, in order to restore to the king in effect the nomination of vacant bishopricks, and yet keep up the established forms, it is

---

[r] See Wilk. *Concil. Mag. Br.* Vol. III. *passim.* and Dr Duck's life of archbishop Chichele, who was the prelate here spoken of, and the munificent founder of All Souls college in Oxford : in vindication of whose memory the author hopes to be excused this digression; if indeed it be a digression, to shew how contrary to the sentiments of so learned and pious a prelate, even in the days of popery, those usurpations were, which the statutes of *praemunire* and provisors were made to restrain.

enacted

enacted by ftatute 25 Hen. VIII. c. 20. that if the dean and chapter refufe to elect the perfon named by the king, or any archbifhop or bifhop to confirm or confecrate him, they fhall fall within the penalties of the ftatutes of *praemunire*. Alfo by ftatute 5 Eliz. c. 1. to refufe the oath of fupremacy will incur the pains of *praemunire*; and to defend the pope's jurifdiction in this realm, is a *praemunire* for the firft offence, and high treafon for the fecond. So too, by ftatute 13 Eliz. c. 2. to import any *agnus Dei*, croffes, beads, or other fuperftitious things pretended to be hallowed by the bifhop of Rome, and tender the fame to be ufed; or to receive the fame with fuch intent, and not dif-cover the offender; or if a juftice of the peace, knowing thereof, fhall not within fourteen days declare it to a privy counfellor; they all incur a *praemunire*. But importing, or felling mafs books or other popifh books, is by ftatute 3 Jac. I. c. 5. §. 25. only a penalty of forty fhillings. Laftly, to contribute to the mainte-nance of a jefuit's college, or any popifh feminary whatever, beyond fea; or any perfon in the fame; or to contribute to the maintenance of any jefuit or popifh prieft in England, is by fta-tute 27 Eliz. c. 2. made liable to the penalties of *praemunire*.

THUS far the penalties of *praemunire* feem to have kept within the proper bounds of their original inftitution, the depreffing the power of the pope: but, they being pains of no inconfiderable confequence, it has been thought fit to apply the fame to other heinous offences; fome of which bear more, and fome lefs re-lation to this original offence, and fome no relation at all.

THUS, 1. By the ftatute 1 & 2 Ph. & Mar. c. 8. to moleft the poffeffors of abbey lands granted by parliament to Henry the eighth, and Edward the fixth, is a *praemunire*. 2. So likewife is the offence of acting as a broker or agent in any ufurious con-tract, where above ten *per cent*. intereft is taken, by ftatute 13 Eliz. c. 10. 3. To obtain any ftay of proceedings, other than by arreft of judgment or writ of error, in any fuit for a monopoly, is likewife a *praemunire*, by ftatute 21 Jac. I. c. 3.

4. To

4. To obtain an exclufive patent for the fole making or importation of gunpowder or arms, or to hinder others from importing them, is alfo a *praemunire* by two ftatutes ; the one 16 Car. I.
c. 21. the other 1 Jac. II. c. 8.　　5. On the abolition, by ftatute
12 Car. II. c. 24. of purveyance [q], and the prerogative of pre-
emption, or taking any victual, beafts, or goods for the king's ufe,
at a ftated price, without confent of the proprietor, the exertion of
any fuch power for the future was declared to incur the penalties
of *praemunire*.　6. To affert, malicioufly and advifedly, by fpeaking or writing, that both or either houfe of parliament have a
legiflative authority without the king, is declared a *praemunire*
by ftatute 13 Car. II. c. 1.　　7. By the *habeas corpus* act alfo,
31 Car. II. c. 2. it is a *praemunire*, and incapable of the king's
pardon, befides other heavy penalties [r], to fend any fubject of
this realm a prifoner into parts beyond the feas.　8. By the ftatute 1 W. & M. ft. 1. c. 8. perfons of eighteen years of age,
refufing to take the new oaths of allegiance, as well as fupremacy, upon tender by the proper magiftrate, are fubject to the
penalties of a *praemunire* ; and by ftatute 7 & 8 W. III. c. 24.
ferjeants, counfellors, proctors, attorneys, and all officers of
courts, practifing without having taken the oaths of allegiance
and fupremacy, and fubfcribing the declaration againft popery,
are guilty of a *praemunire*, whether the oaths be tendered or no.
9. By the ftatute 6 Ann. c. 7. to affert malicioufly and directly,
by preaching, teaching, or advifed fpeaking, that the then pretended prince of Wales, or any perfon other than according to
the acts of fettlement and union, hath any right to the throne
of thefe kingdoms ; or that the king and parliament cannot
make laws to limit the defcent of the crown ; fuch preaching,
teaching, or advifed fpeaking is a *praemunire :* as writing, printing, or publifhing the fame doctrines amounted, we may remember, to high treafon.　10. By ftatute 6 Ann. c. 23. if the
affembly of peers of Scotland, convened to elect their fixteen
reprefentatives in the Britifh parliament, fhall prefume to treat

------

[q] See Vol. I. pag. 287.　　　　　　[r] See Vol. I. pag. 138. Vol. III. pag. 137.

of

of any other matter fave only the election, they incur the penalties of a *praemunire*. 11. The laft offence that has been made a *praemunire*, was by ftatute 6 Geo. I. c. 18. the year after the infamous fouth fea project had beggared half the nation. This therefore makes all unwarrantable undertakings by unlawful fubfcriptions, then commonly known by the name of bubbles, fubject to the penalties of a *praemunire*.

HAVING thus enquired into the nature and feveral fpecies of *praemunire*, it's punifhment may be gathered from the foregoing ftatutes, which are thus fhortly fummed up by fir Edward Coke[s] : " that, from the conviction, the defendant fhall " be out of the king's protection, and his lands and tenements, " goods and chattels forfeited to the king : and that his body " fhall remain in prifon *at the king's pleafure* ; or (as other autho- " rities have it) *during life*[t] :" both which amount to the fame thing ; as the king by his prerogative may any time remit the whole, or any part of the punifhment, except in the cafe of tranfgreffing the ftatute of *habeas corpus*. Thefe forfeitures, here inflicted, do not (by the way) bring this offence within our former definition of felony ; being inflicted by particular ftatutes, and not by the common law. But fo odious, fir Edward Coke adds, was this offence of *praemunire*, that a man that was attainted of the fame might have been flain by any other man without danger of law : becaufe it was provided by law[u], that any man might do to him as to the king's enemy ; and any man may lawfully kill an enemy. However, the pofition itfelf, that it is at any time lawful to kill an enemy, is by no means tenable : it is only lawful, by the law of nature and nations, to kill him in the heat of battel, or for neceffary felf-defence. And, to obviate fuch favage and miftaken notions, the ftatute 5 Eliz. c. 1. provides, that it fhall not be lawful to kill any perfon attainted in a *praemunire*, any law, ftatute, opinion, or expofi-

---

[s] 1 Inft. 129.
[t] 1 Bulftr. 199.

[u] Stat. 25 Edw. III. ft. 5. c. 22.

tion

tion of law to the contrary notwithſtanding. But ſtill ſuch delinquent, though protected as a part of the public from public wrongs, can bring no action for any private injury, how atrocious ſoever ; being ſo far out of the protection of the law, that it will not guard his civil rights, nor remedy any grievance which he as an individual may ſuffer. And no man, knowing him to be guilty, can with ſafety give him comfort, aid, or relief [w].

[w] 1 Hawk. P. C. 55.

CHAPTER THE NINTH.

Of MISPRISIONS AND CONTEMPTS, AFFECTING THE KING AND GOVERNMENT.

THE fourth fpecies of offences, more immediately againſt the king and government, are intitled miſpriſions and contempts.

MISPRISIONS (a term derived from the old French, *meſpris*, a neglect or contempt) are, in the acceptation of our law, generally underſtood to be all ſuch high offences as are under the degree of capital, but nearly bordering thereon: and it is ſaid, that a miſpriſion is contained in every treaſon and felony whatſoever; and that, if the king ſo pleaſe, the offender may be proceeded againſt for the miſpriſion only[a]. And upon the ſame principle, while the juriſdiction of the ſtar-chamber ſubſiſted, it was held that the king might remit a proſecution for treaſon, and cauſe the delinquent to be cenſured in that court, merely for a high miſdemeſnor: as happened in the caſe of Roger earl of Rutland, in 43 Eliz. who was concerned in the earl of Eſſex's rebellion[b]. Miſpriſions are generally divided into two ſorts; negative, which conſiſt in the concealment of ſomething which ought to be revealed; and poſitive, which conſiſt in the commiſſion of ſomething which ought not to be done.

[a] Yearb. 2 *Ric. III.* 10. Staundf. P. C. 37. 1 Hawk. P. C. 55, 56.

[b] Hudſon of the court of ſtar-chamber. *MS. in Muſ. Brit.*

I. Of

I. O f the firſt, or negative kind, is what is called *miſpriſion of treaſon*; conſiſting in the bare knowlege and concealment of treaſon, without any degree of aſſent thereto: for any aſſent makes the party a principal traitor; as indeed the concealment, which was conſtrued aiding and abetting, did at the common law: in like manner as the knowlege of a plot againſt the ſtate, and not revealing it, was a capital crime at Florence, and other ſtates of Italy[c]. But it is now enacted by the ſtatute 1 & 2 Ph. & Mar. c. 10. that a bare concealment of treaſon ſhall be only held a miſpriſion. This concealment becomes criminal, if the party apprized of the treaſon does not, as ſoon as conveniently may be, reveal it to ſome judge of aſſiſe or juſtice of the peace[d]. But if there be any probable circumſtances of aſſent, as if one goes to a treaſonable meeting, knowing beforehand that a con-ſpiracy is intended againſt the king; or, being in ſuch company once by accident, and having heard ſuch treaſonable conſpiracy, meets the ſame company again, and hears more of it, but con-ceals it; this is an implied aſſent in law, and makes the con-cealer guilty of principal high treaſon[e].

T h e r e is alſo one poſitive miſpriſion of treaſon, created ſo by act of parliament. The ſtatute 13 Eliz. c. 2. enacts, that thoſe who forge foreign coin, not current in this kingdom, their aiders, abettors, and procurers, ſhall all be guilty of miſpriſion of treaſon. For, though the law would not put foreign coin upon quite the ſame footing as our own; yet, if the circum-ſtances of trade concur, the falſifying it may be attended with conſequences almoſt equally pernicious to the public; as the counterfeiting of Portugal money would be at preſent: and therefore the law has made it an offence juſt below capital, and that is all. For the puniſhment of miſpriſion of treaſon is loſs of the profits of lands during life, forfeiture of goods, and im-priſonment during life[f]. Which total forfeiture of the goods

c Guicciard. Hiſt. b. 3 & 13.   e 1 Hawk. P. C. 56.
d 1 Hal. P. C. 372.   f 1 Hal. P. C. 374.

was

was originally inflicted while the offence amounted to principal treason, and of course included in it a felony, by the common law; and therefore is no exception to the general rule laid down in a former chapter [g], that wherever an offence is punished by such total forfeiture it is felony at the common law.

MISPRISION *of felony* is also the concealment of a felony which a man knows, but never assented to; for, if he assented, this makes him either principal, or accessory. And the punishment of this, in a public officer, by the statute Westm. 1. 3 Edw. I. c. 9. is imprisonment for a year and a day; in a common person, imprisonment for a less discretionary time; and, in both, fine and ransom at the king's pleasure: which pleasure of the king must be observed, once for all, not to signify any extrajudicial will of the sovereign, but such as is declared by his representatives, the judges in his courts of justice; " *volun-* " *tas regis in curia, non in camera* [h]."

THERE is also another species of negative misprisions; namely, the *concealing of treasure-trove*, which belongs to the king or his grantees, by prerogative royal: the concealment of which was formerly punishable by death [j]; but now only by fine and imprisonment [i].

II. MISPRISIONS, which are merely positive, are generally denominated *contempts* or *high misdemesnors*; of which

1. THE first and principal is the *mal-administration* of such high officers, as are in public trust and employment. This is usually punished by the method of parliamentary impeachment: wherein such penalties, short of death, are inflicted, as to the wisdom of the house of peers shall seem proper; consisting usually of banishment, imprisonment, fines, or perpetual disability. Hitherto also may be referred the offence of *imbezzling the*

g See pag. 94.　　　　　　　　　j Glanv. *l.* 1. *c.* 2.
h 1 Hal. P. C. 375.　　　　　　i 3 Inst. 133.

public money, called among the Romans *peculatus,* which the Julian law punifhed with death in a magiftrate, and with deportation, or banifhment, in a private perfon [k]. With us it is not a capital crime, but fubjects the committer of it to a difcretionary fine and imprifonment. Other mifprifions are, in general, fuch contempts of the executive magiftrate, as demonftrate themfelves by fome arrogant and undutiful behaviour towards the king and government. Thefe are

2. CONTEMPTS againft the king's *prerogative.* As, by refufing to affift him for the good of the public; either in his councils, by advice, if called upon; or in his wars, by perfonal fervice for defence of the realm, againft a rebellion or invafion [l]. Under which clafs may be ranked the neglecting to join the *poffe comitatus,* or power of the county, being thereunto required by the fheriff or juftices, according to the ftatute 2 Hen. V. c. 8. which is a duty incumbent upon all that are fifteen years of age, under the degree of nobility, and able to travel [m]. Contempts againft the prerogative may alfo be, by preferring the interefts of a foreign potentate to thofe of our own, or doing or receiving any thing that may create an undue influence in favour of fuch extrinfic power; as, by taking a penfion from any foreign prince without the confent of the king [n]. Or, by difobeying the king's lawful commands; whether by writs iffuing out of his courts of juftice, or by a fummons to attend his privy council, or by letters from the king to a fubject commanding him to return from beyond the feas, (for difobedience to which his lands fhall be feifed till he does return, and himfelf afterwards punifhed) or by his writ of *ne exeat regnum,* or proclamation, commanding the fubject to ftay at home [o]. Difobedience to any of thefe commands is a high mifprifion and contempt: and fo, laftly, is difobedience to any act of parliament, where no particular penalty is affigned; for then it is punifhable, like the reft of

[k] *Inft.* 4. 18. 9.
[l] 1 Hawk. P. C. 59.
[m] Lamb. Eir. 315.

[n] 3 Inft. 144.
[o] See Vol. I. pag. 266.

thefe

these contempts, by fine and imprisonment, at the discretion of the king's courts of justice [p].

3. CONTEMPTS and misprisions against the king's *person* and *government*, may be by speaking or writing against them, cursing or wishing him ill, giving out scandalous stories concerning him, or doing any thing that may tend to lessen him in the esteem of his subjects, may weaken his government, or may raise jealousies between him and his people. It has been also held an offence of this species to drink to the pious memory of a traitor; or for a clergyman to absolve persons at the gallows, who there persist in the treasons for which they die: these being acts which impliedly encourage rebellion. And for this species of contempt a man may not only be fined and imprisoned, but suffer the pillory or other infamous corporal punishment [q]: in like manner as, in the antient German empire, such persons as endeavoured to sow sedition, and disturb the public tranquillity, were condemned to become the objects of public notoriety and derision, by carrying a dog upon their shoulders from one great town to another. The emperors Otho I. and Frederic Barbarossa inflicted this punishment on noblemen of the highest rank [r].

4. CONTEMPTS against the king's *title*, not amounting to treason or *praemunire*, are the denial of his right to the crown in common and unadvised discourse; for, if it be by advisedly speaking, we have seen [s] that it amounts to a *praemunire*. This heedless species of contempt is however punished by our law with fine and imprisonment. Likewise if any person shall in any wise hold, affirm, or maintain, that the common laws of this realm, not altered by parliament, ought not to direct the right of the crown of England; this is a misdemesnor, by statute 13 Eliz. c. 1. and punishable with forfeiture of goods and chattels. A contempt may also arise from refusing or neglecting to take the oaths, appointed by statute for the better securing the

[p] 1 Hawk. P. C. 60.
[q] *Ibid.*
[r] Mod. Un. Hist. xxix. 28. 119.
[s] See pag. 91.

govern-

government; and yet acting in a public office, place of truft, or other capacity, for which the faid oaths are required to be taken; *viz.* thofe of allegiance, fupremacy, and abjuration: which muft be taken within fix calendar months after admiffion. The penalties for this contempt, inflicted by ftatute 1 Geo. I. ft. 2. c. 13. are very little, if any thing, fhort of thofe of a *praemunire:* being an incapacity to hold the faid offices, or any other; to profecute any fuit; to be guardian or executor; to take any legacy or deed of gift; and to vote at any election for members of parliament: and after conviction the offender fhall alfo forfeit 500 *l.* to him or them that will fue for the fame. Members on the foundation of any college in the two univerfities, who by this ftatute are bound to take the oaths, muft alfo regifter a certificate thereof in the college regifter, within one month after; otherwife, if the electors do not remove him, and elect another within twelve months, or after, the king may nominate a perfon to fucceed him by his great feal or fign manual. Befides thus taking the oaths for offices, any two juftices of the peace may by the fame ftatute fummon, and tender the oaths to, any perfon whom they fhall fufpect to be difaffected; and every perfon refufing the fame, who is properly called a non-juror, fhall be adjudged a popifh recufant convict, and fubjected to the fame penalties that were mentioned in a former chapter [t]; which in the end may amount to the alternative of abjuring the realm, or fuffering death as a felon.

5. C o n t e m p t s againft the king's *palaces* or *courts of juftice* have always been looked upon as high mifprifions: and by the antient law, before the conqueft, fighting in the king's palace, or before the king's judges, was punifhed with death [v]. So too, in the old Gothic conftitution, there were many places privileged by law, *quibus major reverentia et fecuritas debetur, ut templa et judicia, quae fancta habebantur,* --- *arces et aula regis,* --- *denique locus quilibet praefente aut adventante rege* [u]. And at

---

[t] See pag. 55.
[v] 3 Inft. 140. *LL. Alured. cap.* 7. & 34.

[u] Stiernh. *de jure Goth. l.* 3. *c.* 3.

prefent, with us, by the ftatute 33 Hen. VIII. c. 12. malicious
ftriking in the king's palace, wherein his royal perfon refides,
whereby blood is drawn, is punifhable by perpetual imprifonment, and fine at the king's pleafure; and alfo with lofs of the
offender's right hand, the folemn execution of which fentence
is prefcribed in the ftatute at length.

But *ftriking* in the king's fuperior courts of juftice, in
Weftminfter-hall, or at the affifes, is made ftill more penal than
even in the king's palace. The reafon feems to be, that thofe
courts being antiently held in the king's palace, and before the
king himfelf, ftriking there included the former contempt againft
the king's palace, and fomething more; *viz.* the difturbance of
public juftice. For this reafon, by the antient common law before the conqueft [w], ftriking in the king's courts of juftice, or
drawing a fword therein, was a capital felony: and our modern
law retains fo much of the antient feverity, as only to exchange
the lofs of life for the lofs of the offending limb. Therefore a
ftroke or a blow in fuch court of juftice, whether blood be drawn
or not, or even affaulting a judge, fitting in the court, by drawing a weapon, without any blow ftruck, is punifhable with the
lofs of the right hand, imprifonment for life, and forfeiture of
goods and chattels, and of the profits of his lands during life [x].
A *refcue* alfo of a prifoner from any of the faid courts, without
ftriking a blow, is punifhed with perpetual imprifonment, and
forfeiture of goods, and of the profits of lands during life [y]:
being looked upon as an offence of the fame nature with the laft;
but only, as no blow is actually given, the amputation of the
hand is excufed. For the like reafon an affray, or riot, near the
faid courts, but out of their actual view, is punifhed only with
fine and imprifonment [z].

[w] LL. Inae. c. 6. LL. Canut. c. 56. LL.
Alured. c. 7.
[x] Staundf. P. C. 38. 3 Inft. 140, 141.

[y] 1 Hawk. P. C. 57.
[z] Cro. Car. 373.

N o t

N O T only such as are guilty of an actual violence, but of threatening or reproachful words to any judge sitting in the courts, are guilty of a high misprision, and have been punished with large fines, imprisonment, and corporal punishment [a]. And, even in the inferior courts of the king, an affray, or contemptuous behaviour, is punishable with a fine by the judges there sitting; as by the steward in a court-leet, or the like [b].

LIKEWISE all such, as are guilty of any injurious treatment to those who are immediately under the protection of a court of justice, are punishable by fine and imprisonment: as if a man assaults or threatens his adversary for suing him, a counsellor or attorney for being employed against him, a juror for his verdict, or a gaoler or other ministerial officer for keeping him in custody, and properly executing his duty [c]: which offences, when they proceeded farther than bare threats, were punished in the Gothic constitutions with exile and forfeiture of goods [d].

LASTLY, to endeavour to dissuade a witness from giving evidence; to disclose an examination before the privy council; or, to advise a prisoner to stand mute; (all of which are impediments of justice) are high misprisions, and contempts of the king's courts, and punishable by fine and imprisonment. And antiently it was held, that if one of the grand jury disclosed to any person indicted the evidence that appeared against him, he was thereby made accessory to the offence, if felony; and in treason a principal. And at this day it is agreed, that he is guilty of a high misprision [e], and liable to be fined and imprisoned [f].

[a] Cro. Car. 503.
[b] 1 Hawk. P. C. 58.
[c] 3 Inst. 141, 142.
[d] Stiernh. *de jure Goth. l. 3. c. 3.*

[e] See Barr. 212. 27 Ass. pl. 44. §. 4. fol. 138.
[f] 1 Hawk. P. C. 59.

CHAPTER THE TENTH.

OF OFFENCES AGAINST PUBLIC JUSTICE.

THE order of our diftribution will next lead us to take into confideration fuch crimes and mifdemefnors as more efpecially affect the *common-wealth*, or public polity of the kingdom : which however, as well as thofe which are peculiarly pointed againft the lives and fecurity of private fubjects, are alfo offences againft the king, as the *pater-familias* of the nation ; to whom it appertains by his regal office to protect the community, and each individual therein, from every degree of injurious violence, by executing thofe laws, which the people themfelves in conjunction with him have enacted ; or at leaft have confented to, by an agreement either exprefsly made in the perfons of their reprefentatives, or by a tacit and implied confent prefumed and proved by immemorial ufage.

THE fpecies of crimes, which we have now before us, is fubdivided into fuch a number of inferior and fubordinate claffes, that it would much exceed the bounds of an elementary treatife, and be infupportably tedious to the reader, were I to examine them all minutely, or with any degree of critical accuracy. I fhall therefore confine myfelf principally to general definitions or defcriptions of this great variety of offences, and to the punifhments inflicted by law for each particular offence ; with now and then a few incidental obfervations : referring the ftudent for

more

more particulars to other voluminous authors; who have treated of thefe fubjeets with greater precifion and more in detail, than is confiftent with the plan of thefe commentaries.

The crimes and mifdemefnors, that more efpecially affeet the common-wealth, may be divided into five fpecies; *viz.* offences againft public *juftice*, againft the public *peace*, againft public *trade*, againft the public *health*, and againft the public *police* or *oeconomy*: of each of which we will take a curfory view in their order.

First then, of offences againft public *juftice*: fome of which are felonious, whofe punifhment may extend to death; others only mifdemefnors. I fhall begin with thofe that are moft penal, and defcend gradually to fuch as are of lefs malignity.

1. Imbezzling or vacating *records*, or falfifying certain other proceedings in a court of judicature, is a felonious offence againft public juftice. It is enaeted by ftatute 8 Hen. VI. c. 12. that if any clerk, or other perfon, fhall wilfully take away, withdraw, or avoid any record, or procefs in the fuperior courts of juftice in Weftminfter-hall, by reafon whereof the judgment fhall be reverfed or not take effeet; it is felony not only in the principal aetors, but alfo in their procurers, and abettors. Likewife by ftatute 21 Jac. I. c. 26. to acknowlege any fine, recovery, deed enrolled, ftatute, recognizance, bail, or judgment, in the name of another perfon not privy to the fame, is felony without benefit of clergy. Which law extends only to proceedings in the courts themfelves: but by ftatute 4 W. & M. c. 4. to perfonate any other perfon before any commiffioner authorized to take bail in the country is alfo felony. For no man's property would be fafe, if records might be fuppreffed or falfified, or perfons' names be falfely ufurped in courts, or before their public officers.

2. To

2. To prevent abuses by the extensive power, which the law is obliged to repose in gaolers, it is enacted by statute 14 Edw. III. c. 10. that if any *gaoler* by too great duress of imprisonment makes any prisoner that he hath in ward, become an *approver* or an appellor against his will; that is, as we shall see hereafter, to accuse and turn evidence against some other person; it is felony in the gaoler. For, as sir Edward Coke [a] observes, it is not lawful to induce or excite any man even to a just accusation of another; much less to do it by duress of imprisonment; and least of all by a gaoler, to whom the prisoner is committed for safe custody.

3. A THIRD offence against public justice is *obstructing* the execution of lawful *process*. This is at all times an offence of a very high and presumptuous nature; but more particularly so, when it is an obstruction of an arrest upon criminal process. And it hath been holden, that the party opposing such arrest becomes thereby *particeps criminis*; that is, an accessory in felony, and a principal in high treason [b]. Formerly one of the greatest obstructions to public justice, both of the civil and criminal kind, was the multitude of pretended privileged places, where indigent persons assembled together to shelter themselves from justice, (especially in London and Southwark) under the pretext of their having been antient palaces of the crown, or the like [c]: all of which sanctuaries for iniquity are now demolished, and the opposing of any process therein is made highly penal, by the statutes 8 & 9 W. III. c. 27. 9 Geo. I. c. 28. and 11 Geo. I. c. 22. which enact, that persons opposing the execution of any process in such pretended privileged places within the bills of mortality, or abusing any officer in his endeavours to execute his duty therein, so that he receives bodily hurt, shall be guilty of felony, and transported for seven years.

---

[a] 3 Inst. 91.
[b] 1 Hawk. P. C. 121.

[c] Such as *White-Friers*, and it's environs; the *Savoy*; and the *Mint* in Southwark.

4. AN *efcape* of a perfon arrefted upon criminal procefs, by
eluding the vigilance of his keepers before he is put in hold, is
alfo an offence againft public juftice, and the party himfelf is
punifhable by fine or imprifonment[d]. But the officer permitting
fuch efcape, either by negligence or connivance, is much more
culpable than the prifoner; the natural defire of liberty pleading
ftrongly in his behalf, though he ought in ftrictnefs of law to
fubmit himfelf quietly to cuftody, till cleared by the due courfe
of juftice. Officers therefore who, after arreft, *negligently* permit a felon to efcape, are alfo punifhable by fine[e]; but *voluntary* efcapes, by confent and connivance of the officer, are a
much more ferious offence: for it is generally agreed that fuch
efcapes amount to the fame kind of offence, and are punifhable
in the fame degree, as the offence of which the prifoner is
guilty, and for which he is in cuftody, whether treafon, felony,
or trefpafs. And this, whether he were actually committed to
gaol, or only under a bare arreft[f]. But the officer cannot be
thus punifhed, till the original delinquent is actually found
guilty or convicted, by verdict, confeffion, or outlawry, of the
crime for which he was fo committed or arrefted: otherwife it
might happen, that the officer might be punifhed for treafon or
felony, and the perfon arrefted and efcaping might turn out to
be an innocent man. But, before the conviction of the principal party, the officer thus neglecting his duty may be fined and
imprifoned for a mifdemefnor[g].

5. BREACH of prifon by the offender himfelf, when committed for *any* caufe, was felony at the common law[h]: or even
confpiring to break it[i]. But this feverity is mitigated by the ftatute *de frangentibus prifonam*, 1 Edw. II. which enacts, that no
perfon fhall have judgment of life or member, for breaking pri-

[d] 2 Hawk. P. C. 122.
[e] 1 Hal. P. C. 600.
[f] 1 Hal. P. C. 590. 2 Hawk. P. C. 134.
[g] 1 Hal. P. C. 588,9. 2 Hawk. P.C. 134,5.
[h] 1 Hal. P. C. 607.
[i] Bract. *l.* 3. *c.* 9.

fon,

son, unless committed for some capital offence. So that to break prison, when lawfully committed for any treason or felony, remains still felony as at the common law; and to break prison, when lawfully confined upon any other inferior charge, is still punishable as a high misdemesnor by fine and imprisonment. For the statute, which ordains that such offence shall be no longer capital, never meant to exempt it entirely from every degree of punishment [k].

6. RESCUE is the forcibly freeing another from an arrest or imprisonment; and is always the same offence in the stranger so rescuing, as it would have been in the party himself to have broken prison [l]. A rescue therefore of one apprehended for felony, is felony; for treason, treason; and for a misdemesnor, a misdemesnor also. But here, as upon voluntary escapes, the principal must first be attainted before the rescuer can be punished: and for the same reason; because perhaps in fact it may turn out that there has been no offence committed [m]. By the statute, 16 Geo. II. c. 31. to assist a prisoner in custody for treason or felony with any arms, instruments of escape, or disguise, without the knowlege of the gaoler; or any way to assist such prisoner to attempt an escape, though no escape be actually made, is felony, and subjects the offender to transportation for seven years. And by the statutes 25 Geo. II. c. 37. and 27 Geo. II. c. 15. to rescue, or attempt to rescue, any person committed for murder, or for any of the offences enumerated in that act, or in the black act 9 Geo. I. c. 22. is felony without benefit of clergy.

7. ANOTHER capital offence against public justice is the *returning from transportation*, or being seen at large in Great Britain before the expiration of the term for which the offender was sentenced to be transported. This is made felony without

[k] 2 Hawk. P. C. 128.
[l] *Ibid.* 139.

[m] 1 Hal. P. C. 607.

benefit

benefit of clergy by ftatutes 4 Geo. I. c. 11. 6 Geo. I. c. 23. and 8 Geo. III. c. 15.

8. AN eighth is that of *taking a reward*, under pretence of *helping* the owner to his *ftolen goods*. This was a contrivance carried to a great length of villainy in the beginning of the reign of George the firft: the confederates of the felons thus difpo-fing of ftolen goods, at a cheap rate, to the owners themfelves, and thereby ftifling all farther enquiry. The famous Jonathan Wild had under him a well difciplined corps of thieves, who brought in all their fpoils to him; and he kept a fort of public office for reftoring them to the owners at half price. To prevent which audacious practice, to the ruin and in defiance of public juftice, it was enacted by ftatute 4 Geo. I. c. 11. that whoever fhall take a reward under the pretence of helping any one to ftolen goods, fhall fuffer as the felon who ftole them; unlefs he caufe fuch principal felon to be apprehended and brought to trial, and fhall alfo give evidence againft him. Wild, upon this ftatute, (ftill continuing in his old practice) was at laft convicted and executed.

9. RECEIVING of ftolen goods, *knowing them to be ftolen,* is alfo a high mifdemefnor and affront to public juftice. We have feen in a former chapter[n], that this offence, which is only a mifdemefnor at common law, by the ftatutes 3 & 4 W. & M. c. 9. and 5 Ann. c. 31. makes the offender acceffory to the theft and felony. But becaufe the acceffory cannot in general be tried, unlefs with the principal, or after the principal is convicted, the receivers by that means frequently eluded juftice. To re-medy which, it is enacted by ftatute 1 Ann. c. 9. and 5 Ann. c. 31. that fuch receivers may ftill be profecuted for a mifde-mefnor, and punifhed by fine and imprifonment, though the principal felon be not before taken, fo as to be profecuted and convicted. And, in cafe of receiving ftolen lead, iron, and certain other metals, fuch offence is by ftatute 29 Geo. II. c. 30.

[n] See pag. 38.

punifh-punishable by transportation for fourteen years[o]. So that now the prosecutor has two methods in his choice: either to punish the receivers for the misdemesnor immediately, before the thief is taken[p]; or to wait till the felon is convicted, and then punish them as accessories to the felony. But it is provided by the same statutes, that he shall only make use of one, and not both of these methods of punishment. By the same statute also 29 Geo. II. c. 30. persons having lead, iron, and other metals in their custody, and not giving a satisfactory account how they came by the same, are guilty of a misdemesnor and punishable by fine or imprisonment.

10. OF a nature somewhat similar to the two last is the offence of *theft-bote*, which is where the party robbed not only knows the felon, but also takes his goods again, or other amends, upon agreement not to prosecute. This is frequently called compounding of felony, and formerly was held to make a man an accessory; but is now punished only with fine and imprisonment[q]. This perversion of justice, in the old Gothic constitutions, was liable to the most severe and infamous punishment. And the Salic law "*latroni eum similem habuit, qui furtum celare* "*vellet, et occulte sine judice compositionem ejus admittere*[r]." By statute 25 Geo. II. c. 36. even to advertise a reward for the return of things stolen, with no questions asked, or words to the same purport, subjects the advertiser and the printer to a forfeiture of 50 *l.* each.

11. COMMON *barretry* is the offence of frequently exciting and stirring up suits and quarrels between his majesty's subjects, either at law or otherwise[s]. The punishment for this offence, in a common person, is by fine and imprisonment: but if the offender (as is too frequently the case) belongs to the profession

[o] See also statute 2 Geo. III. c. 28. §. 12. for the punishment of receivers of goods stolen by bum-boats, &c. in the Thames.

[p] Foster. 373.

[q] 1 Hawk. P. C. 125.

[r] Stiernh. *de jure Goth. l.* 3. *c.* 5.

[s] 1 Hawk. P. C. 243.

of

of the law, a barretor, who is thus able as well as willing to do
mifchief, ought alfo to be difabled from practifing for the future[t]. Hereunto may be referred an offence of equal malignity
and audacioufnefs; that of fuing another in the name of a fictitious plaintiff; either one not in being at all, or one who is ignorant of the fuit. This offence, if committed in any of the
king's fuperior courts, is left, as a high contempt, to be punifhed
at their difcretion. But in courts of a lower degree, where the
crime is equally pernicious, but the authority of the judges not
equally extenfive, it is directed by ftatute 8 Eliz. c. 2. to be
punifhed by fix months imprifonment, and treble damages to
the party injured.

12. MAINTENANCE is an offence, that bears a near relation
to the former; being an officious intermeddling in a fuit that no
way belongs to one, by maintaining or affifting either party with
money or otherwife, to profecute or defend it[u]: a practice, that
was greatly encouraged by the firft introduction of ufes[w]. This
is an offence againft public juftice, as it keeps alive ftrife and
contention, and perverts the remedial procefs of the law into an
engine of oppreffion. And therefore, by the Roman law, it was
a fpecies of the *crimen falfi* to enter into any confederacy, or do
any act to fupport another's lawfuit, by money, witneffes, or
patronage[x]. A man may however maintain the fuit of his near
kinfman, fervant, or poor neighbour, out of charity and compaffion, with impunity. Otherwife the punifhment by common
law is fine and imprifonment[y]; and, by the ftatute 32 Hen. VIII.
c. 9. a forfeiture of ten pounds.

13. CHAMPERTY, *campi-partitio*, is a fpecies of maintenance, and punifhed in the fame manner[z]: being a bargain with
a plaintiff or defendant *campum partire*, to divide the land or
other matter fued for between them, if they prevail at law;

[t] 1 Hawk. P. C. 244.
[u] *Ibid.* 249.
[w] Dr & St. 203.

[x] *Ff.* 48. 10. 20.
[y] 1 Hawk. P. C. 255.
[z] *Ibid.* 257.

where-

whereupon the champertor is to carry on the party's suit at his own expenſe[a]. Thus *champart*, in the French law, ſignifies a ſimilar diviſion of profits, being a part of the crop annually due to the landlord by bargain or cuſtom. In our ſenſe of the word, it ſignifies the purchaſing of a ſuit, or right of ſuing: a practice ſo much abhorred by our law, that it is one main reaſon why a *choſe* in action, or thing of which one hath the right but not the poſſeſſion, is not aſſignable at common law; becauſe no man ſhould purchaſe any pretence to ſue in another's right. Theſe peſts of civil ſociety, that are perpetually endeavouring to diſturb the repoſe of their neighbours, and officiouſly interfering in other men's quarrels, even at the hazard of their own fortunes, were ſeverely animadverted on by the Roman law: " *qui improbe coeunt* " *in alienam litem, ut quicquid ex communicatione in rem ipſius re-* " *dactum fuerit, inter eos communicaretur, lege Julia de vi privata* " *tenentur*[b];" and they were puniſhed by the forfeiture of a third part of their goods, and perpetual infamy. Hitherto alſo muſt be referred the proviſion of the ſtatute 32 Hen. VIII. c. 9. that no one ſhall ſell or purchaſe any pretended right or title to land, unleſs the vendor hath received the profits thereof for one whole year before ſuch grant, or hath been in actual poſſeſſion of the land, or of the reverſion or remainder; on pain that both purchaſor and vendor ſhall each forfeit the value of ſuch land to the king and the proſecutor. Theſe offences relate chiefly to the commencement of *civil* ſuits: but

14. THE *compounding of informations* upon penal ſtatutes are an offence of an equivalent nature in *criminal* cauſes; and are, beſides, an additional miſdemeſnor againſt public juſtice, by contributing to make the laws odious to the people. At once therefore to diſcourage malicious informers, and to provide that offences, when once diſcovered, ſhall be duly proſecuted, it is enacted by ſtatute 18 Eliz. c. 5. that if any perſon, informing under pretence of any penal law, makes any compoſition without leave of the court, or takes any money or promiſe from the

---

[a] Stat. of conſpirat. 33 Edw. I.　　　　[b] *Ff*. 48. 7. 6.

defendant

defendant to excufe him (which demonftrates his intent in com-
mencing the profecution to be merely to ferve his own ends,
and not for the public good) he fhall forfeit 10 *l*, fhall ftand
two hours on the pillory, and fhall be for ever difabled to fue
on any popular or penal ftatute.

15. A CONSPIRACY alfo to indict an innocent man of felony
falfely and malicioufly, who is accordingly indicted and acquitted, is a farther abufe and perverfion of public juftice; for
which the party injured may either have a civil action by writ
of confpiracy, (of which we fpoke in the preceding book[c]) or
the confpirators, for there muft be at leaft two to form a confpiracy, may be indicted at the fuit of the king, and were by
the antient common law[d] to receive what is called the *villenous*
judgment; *viz.* to lofe their *liberam legem*, whereby they are
difcredited and difabled to be jurors or witneffes; to forfeit
their goods and chattels, and lands for life; to have thofe lands
wafted, their houfes rafed, their trees rooted up, and their own
bodies committed to prifon[e]. But it now is the better opinion,
that the villenous judgment is by long difufe become obfolete;
it not having been pronounced for fome ages: but inftead thereof
the delinquents are ufually fentenced to imprifonment, fine, and
pillory. To this head may be referred the offence of fending
letters, threatening to accufe any perfon of a crime punifhable
with death, tranfportation, pillory, or other infamous punifhment, with a view to extort from him any money or other valuable chattels. This is punifhable by ftatute 30 Geo. II. c.24.
at the difcretion of the court, with fine, imprifonment, pillory,
whipping, or tranfportation for feven years.

16. THE next offence againft public juftice is when the fuit
is paft it's commencement, and come to trial. And that is the
crime of wilful and corrupt *perjury*; which is defined by fir Edward Coke[f], to be a crime committed when a *lawful* oath is ad-

---

See Vol. III. pag. 126.
[d] Bro. *Abr. t. conspiracy.* 28.

[e] 1 Hawk. P. C. 193.
[f] 3 Inft. 164.

miniftred, in fome *judicial* proceeding, to a perfon who fwears *wilfully, abfolutely* and *falfely,* in a matter *material* to the iffue or point in queftion. The law takes no notice of any perjury but fuch as is committed in fome court of juftice, having power to adminifter an oath ; or before fome magiftrate or proper officer, invefted with a fimilar authority, in fome proceedings relative to a civil fuit or a criminal profecution : for it efteems all other oaths unneceffary at leaft, and therefore will not punifh the breach of them. For which reafon it is much to be queftioned how far any magiftrate is juftifiable in taking a voluntary *affidavit* in any extrajudicial matter, as is now too frequent upon every petty occafion : fince it is more than poffible, that by fuch idle oaths a man may frequently *in foro confcientiae* incur the guilt, and at the fame time evade the temporal penalties, of perjury. The perjury muft alfo be wilful, pofitive, and abfolute ; not upon furprize, or the like : it alfo muft be in fome point material to the queftion in difpute ; for if it only be in fome trifling collateral circumftance, to which no regard is paid, it is no more penal than in the voluntary extrajudicial oaths before-mentioned. *Subornation* of perjury is the offence of procuring another to take fuch a falfe oath, as conftitutes perjury in the principal. The punifhment of perjury and fubornation, at common law, has been various. It was antiently death ; afterwards banifhment, or cutting out the tongue ; then forfeiture of goods ; and now it is fine and imprifonment, and never more to be capable of bearing teftimony [g]. But the ftatute 5 Eliz. c. 9. (if the offender be profecuted thereon) inflicts the penalty of perpetual infamy, and a fine of 40 *l.* on the fuborner ; and, in default of payment, imprifonment for fix months, and to ftand with both ears nailed to the pillory. Perjury itfelf is thereby punifhed with fix months imprifonment, perpetual infamy, and a fine of 20 *l.* or to have both ears nailed to the pillory. But the profecution is ufually carried on for the offence at common law ; efpecially as, to the penalties before inflicted, the ftatute 2 Geo. II. c. 25. fuper-adds a power, for the court to order the offender to be fent to the

[g] 3 Inft. 163.

houfe of correction for feven years, or to be tranfported for the fame period; and makes it felony without benefit of clergy to return or efcape within the time. It has fometimes been wifhed, that perjury, at leaft upon capital accufations, whereby another's life has been or might have been deftroyed, was alfo rendered capital, upon a principle of retaliation; as it is univerfally by the laws of France[h]. And certainly the odioufnefs of the crime pleads ftrongly in behalf of the French law. But it is to be confidered, that there they admit witneffes to be heard only on the fide of the profecution, and ufe the rack to extort a confeffion from the accufed. In fuch a conftitution therefore it is neceffary to throw the dread of capital punifhment into the other fcale, in order to keep in awe the witneffes for the crown; on whom alone the prifoner's fate depends: fo naturally does one cruel law beget another. But corporal and pecuniary punifhments, exile and perpetual infamy, are more fuited to the genius of the Englifh law, where the fact is openly difcuffed between witneffes on *both* fides, and the evidence for the crown may be contradicted and difproved by thofe of the prifoner. Where indeed the death of an innocent perfon has actually been the confequence of fuch wilful perjury, it falls within the guilt of deliberate murder, and deferves an equal punifhment: which our antient law in fact inflicted[i]. But the mere attempt to deftroy life by other means not being capital, there is no reafon that an attempt by perjury fhould: much lefs that this crime fhould in *all* judicial cafes be punifhed with death. For to multiply capital punifhments leffens their effect, when applied to crimes of the deepeft dye; and, deteftable as perjury is, it is not by any means to be compared with fome other offences, for which only death can be inflicted: and therefore it feems already (except perhaps in the inftance of deliberate murder by perjury) very properly punifhed by our prefent law; which has adopted the opinion of Cicero[k], derived from the law of the twelve tables, "*perjurii poena divina, ex-* "*itium; humana, dedecus.*"

[h] Montefq. Sp. L. b. 29. ch. 11.   [k] *de Leg.* 2. 9.
[i] Britton. c. 5.

17. Bri-

17. BRIBERY is the next species of offence against public juſtice; which is when a judge, or other perſon concerned in the adminiſtration of juſtice, takes any undue reward to influence his behaviour in his office[1]. In the eaſt it is the cuſtom never to petition any ſuperior for juſtice, not excepting their kings, without a preſent. This is calculated for the genius of deſpotic countries; where the true principles of government are never underſtood, and it is imagined that there is no obligation from the ſuperior to the inferior, no relative duty owing from the governor to the governed. The Roman law, though it contained many ſevere injunctions againſt bribery, as well for ſelling a man's vote in the ſenate or other public aſſembly, as for the bartering of common juſtice, yet, by a ſtrange indulgence in one inſtance, it tacitly encouraged this practice; allowing the magiſtrate to receive ſmall preſents, provided they did not in the whole exceed a hundred crowns in the year[m]: not conſidering the inſinuating nature and gigantic progreſs of this vice, when once admitted. Plato therefore more wiſely, in his ideal republic[n], orders thoſe who take preſents for doing their duty to be puniſhed in the ſevereſt manner: and by the laws of Athens he that offered was alſo proſecuted, as well as he that received a bribe[o]. In England this offence of taking bribes is puniſhed, in inferior officers, with fine and impriſonment; and in thoſe who offer a bribe, though not taken, the ſame[p]. But in judges, eſpecially the ſuperior ones, it hath been always looked upon as ſo heinous an offence, that the chief juſtice Thorpe was hanged for it in the reign of Edward III. By a ſtatute[q] 11 Hen. IV, all judges and officers of the king, convicted of bribery, ſhall forfeit treble the bribe, be puniſhed at the king's will, and be diſcharged from the king's ſervice for ever. And ſome notable examples have been made in parliament, of perſons in the

[1] 1 Hawk. P. C. 168.
[m] Ff. 48. 11. 6.
[n] de Leg. l. 12.

[o] Pott. Antiqu. b. 1. c. 23.
[p] 3 Inſt. 147.
[q] Ibid. 146.

higheſt

higheſt ſtations, and otherwiſe very eminent and able, but contaminated with this ſordid vice.

18. Emr racery is an attempt to influence a jury corruptly to one ſide by promiſes, perſuaſions, entreaties, money, entertainments, and the like[r]. The puniſhment for the perſon embracing is by fine and impriſonment; and, for the juror ſo embraced, if it be by taking money, the puniſhment is (by divers ſtatutes of the reign of Edward III) perpetual infamy, impriſonment for a year, and forfeiture of the tenfold value.

19. The *falſe verdict* of jurors, whether occaſioned by embracery or not, was antiently conſidered as criminal, and therefore exemplarily puniſhed by attaint in the manner formerly mentioned[ˢ].

20. Another offence of the ſame ſpecies is the *negligence of public officers,* entruſted with the adminiſtration of juſtice, as ſheriffs, coroners, conſtables, and the like: which makes the offender liable to be fined; and in very notorious caſes will amount to a forfeiture of his office, if it be a beneficial one[t]. Alſo the omitting to apprehend perſons, offering ſtolen iron, lead, and other metals to ſale, is a miſdemeſnor and puniſhable by a ſtated fine, or impriſonment, in purſuance of the ſtatute 29 Geo. II. c. 30.

21. There is yet another offence againſt public juſtice, which is a crime of deep malignity; and ſo much the deeper, as there are many opportunities of putting it in practice, and the power and wealth of the offenders may often deter the injured from a legal proſecution. This is the *oppreſſion* and tyrannical partiality of judges, juſtices, and other *magiſtrates,* in the adminiſtration and under the colour of their office. However, when proſecuted, either by impeachment in parliament,

[r] 1 Hawk. P. C. 259.   [t] 1 Hawk. P. C. 168.
[ˢ] See Vol. III. pag. 402.

or

or by information in the court of king's bench, (according to the rank of the offenders) it is sure to be severely punished with forfeiture of their offices, fines, imprisonment, or other discretionary censures, regulated by the nature and aggravations of the offence committed.

22. LASTLY, *extortion* is an abuse of public justice, which consists in any officer's unlawfully taking, by colour of his office, from any man, any money or thing of value, that is not due to him, or more than is due, or before it is due ". The punishment is fine and imprisonment, and sometimes a forfeiture of the office.

" 1 Hawk. P. C. 170.

CHAPTER THE ELEVENTH.

OF OFFENCES AGAINST THE PUBLIC PEACE.

WE are next to confider offences againft the public *peace*;
the confervation of which is intrufted to the king and
his officers, in the manner and for the reafons which were formerly mentioned at large[a]. Thefe offences are either fuch as are
an actual breach of the peace; or conftructively fo, by tending
to make others break it. Both of thefe fpecies are alfo either
felonious, or not felonious. The felonious breaches of the peace
are ftrained up to that degree of malignity by virtue of feveral
modern ftatutes: and, particularly,

1. THE *riotous affembling* of *twelve* perfons, or more, and
not difperfing upon proclamation. This was firft made high
treafon by ftatute 3 & 4 Edw. VI. c. 5. when the king was a minor, and a change in religion to be effected: but that ftatute
was repealed by ftatute 1 Mar. c. 1. among the other treafons
created fince the 25 Edw. III; though the prohibition was in
fubftance re-enacted, with an inferior degree of punifhment, by
ftatute 1 Mar. ft. 2. c. 12. which made the fame offence a fingle
felony. Thefe ftatutes fpecified and particularized the nature of
the riots they were meant to fupprefs; as, for example, fuch as
were fet on foot with intention to offer violence to the privy
council, or to change the laws of the kingdom, or for certain
other fpecific purpofes: in which cafes, if the perfons were

[a] Vol. I. pag. 117. 268. 350.

com-

commanded by proclamation to difperfe, and they did not, it was
by the ftatute of Mary made felony, but within the benefit of
clergy ; and alfo the act indemnified the peace officers and their
affiftants, if they killed any of the mob in endeavouring to fupprefs fuch riot. This was thought a neceffary fecurity in that
fanguinary reign, when popery was intended to be re-eftablifhed,
which was like to produce great difcontents : but at firft it was
made only for a year, and was afterwards continued for that
queen's life. And, by ftatute 1 Eliz. c. 16. when a reformation
in religion was to be once more attempted, it was revived and
continued duting her life alfo ; and then expired. From the
acceffion of James the firft to the death of queen Anne, it was
never once thought expedient to revive it : but, in the firft year
of George the firft, it was judged neceffary, in order to fupport
the execution of the act of fettlement, to renew it, and at one
ftroke to make it perpetual, with large additions. For, whereas
the former acts exprefsly defined and fpecified what fhould be
accounted a riot, the ftatute 1 Geo. I. c. 5. enacts, generally,
that if any twelve perfons are unlawfully affembled to the difturbance of the peace, and any one juftice of the peace, fheriff,
under-fheriff, or mayor of a town, fhall think proper to command them by proclamation to difperfe, if they contemn his
orders and continue together for one hour afterwards, fuch contempt fhall be felony without benefit of clergy. And farther,
if the reading of the proclamation be by force oppofed, or the
reader be in any manner wilfully hindered from the reading of
it, fuch oppofers and hinderers are felons, without benefit of
clergy : and all perfons to whom fuch proclamation *ought to have
been made*, and knowing of fuch hindrance, and not difperfing, are
felons, without benefit of clergy. There is the like indemnifying
claufe, in cafe any of the mob be unfortunately killed in the endeavour to difperfe them ; being copied from the act of queen
Mary. And, by a fubfequent claufe of the new act, if any perfons, fo riotoufly affembled, begin even before proclamation to
pull down any church, chapel, meeting-houfe, dwelling-houfe,
or out-houfes, they fhall be felons without benefit of clergy.

2. By

2. BY ftatute 1 Hen.VII. c. 7. *unlawful hunting* in any legal foreft, park, or warren, not being the king's property, *by night,* or with *painted faces,* was declared to be fingle felony. But now by the ftatute 9 Geo. I. c. 22. to appear armed in any open place by day, or night, with faces blacked or otherwife *difguifed,* or (being fo difguifed) to hunt, wound, kill, or fteal any deer, to rob a warren, or to fteal fifh, is felony without benefit of clergy. I mention this offence in this place, not on account of the damage thereby done to private property, but of the manner in which that damage is committed; namely, with the face blacked or with other difguife, to the breach of the public peace and the terror of his majefty's fubjects.

3. ALSO by the fame ftatute 9 Geo. I. c. 22. amended by ftatute 27 Geo. II. c. 15. knowingly to fend any *letter* without a name, or with a fictitious name, *demanding* money, venifon, or any other valuable thing, or *threatening* (without any demand) to kill, or fire the houfe of, any perfon, is made felony, without benefit of clergy. This offence was formerly high treafon, by the ftatute 8 Hen.V. c. 6.

4. To pull down or deftroy any *turnpike-gate,* or fence thereunto belonging, by the ftatute 1 Geo. II. c. 19. is punifhed with public whipping, and three months imprifonment; and to deftroy the toll-houfes, or any *fluice or lock* on a navigable river, is made felony to be punifhed with tranfportation for feven years. By the ftatute 5 Geo. II. c. 33. the offence of deftroying turnpike-gates or fences, is made felony alfo, with tranfportation for feven years. And, laftly, by ftatute 8 Geo. II. c. 20. the offences of deftroying both turnpikes upon roads, and fluices upon rivers, are made felony, without benefit of clergy; and may be tried as well in an adjacent county, as that wherein the fact is committed. The remaining offences againft the public peace are merely mifdemefnors, and no felonies : as,

5. AF-

5. AFFRAYS (from *affraier*, to terrify) are the fighting of two or more perfons in fome public place, to the terror of his majefty's fubjects: for, if the fighting be in private, it is no *affray* but an *affault* [b]. Affrays may be fuppreffed by any private perfon prefent, who is juftifiable in endeavouring to part the combatants, whatever confequence may enfue [c]. But more efpecially the conftable, or other fimilar officer, however denominated, is bound to keep the peace; and to that purpofe may break open doors to fupprefs an affray, or apprehend the affrayers; and may either carry them before a juftice, or imprifon them by his own authority for a convenient fpace till the heat is over; and may then perhaps alfo make them find fureties for the peace [d]. The punifhment of common affrays is by fine and imprifonment; the meafure of which muft be regulated by the circumftances of the cafe: for, where there is any material aggravation, the punifhment proportionably increafes. As where two perfons coolly and deliberately engage in a duel: this being attended with an apparent intention and danger of murder, and being a high contempt of the juftice of the nation, is a ftrong aggravation of the affray, though no mifchief has actually enfued [e]. Another aggravation is, when thereby the officers of juftice are difturbed in the due execution of their office: or where a refpect to the particular place ought to reftrain and regulate men's behaviour, more than in common ones; as in the king's court, and the like. And upon the fame account alfo all affrays in a church or church-yard are efteemed very heinous offences, as being indignities to him to whofe fervice thofe places are confecrated. Therefore mere quarrelfome words, which are neither an affray nor an offence in any other place, are penal here. For it is enacted by ftatute 5 & 6 Edw. VI. c. 4. that if any perfon fhall, by words only, quarrel, chide, or brawl, in a church or church-yard, the ordinary fhall fufpend him, if a layman, *ab ingreffu ecclefiae*; and, if a clerk in orders,

[b] 1 Hawk. P. C 134.
Ibid. 136.
[d] Ibid. 137.
[e] Ibid. 138.

from the miniſtration of his office during pleaſure. And, if any perſon in ſuch church or church-yard proceeds to ſmite or lay violent hands upon another, he ſhall be excommunicated *ipſo facto*; or if he ſtrikes him with a weapon, or draws any weapon with intent to ſtrike, he ſhall beſides excommunication (being convicted by a jury) have one of his ears cut off; or, having no ears, be branded with the letter F in his cheek. *Two* perſons may be guilty of an affray : but,

6. R I O T S, *routs*, and *unlawful aſſemblies* muſt have *three* perſons at leaſt to conſtitute them. An *unlawful aſſembly* is when three, or more, do aſſemble themſelves together to do an unlawful act, as to pull down incloſures, to deſtroy a warren or the game therein; and part without doing it, or making any motion towards it[f]. A *rout* is where three or more meet to do an unlawful act upon a common quarrel, as forcibly breaking down fences upon a right claimed of common, or of way; and make ſome advances towards it[g]. A *riot* is where three or more actually do an unlawful act of violence, either with or without a common cauſe or quarrel[h]: as if they beat a man; or hunt and kill game in another's park, chaſe, warren, or liberty; or do any other unlawful act with force and violence; or even do a lawful act, as removing a nuſance, in a violent and tumultuous manner. The puniſhment of unlawful aſſemblies, if to the number of twelve, we have juſt now ſeen may be capital, according to the circumſtances that attend it; but, from the number of three to eleven, is by fine and impriſonment only. The ſame is the caſe in riots and routs by the common law; to which the pillory in very enormous caſes has been ſometimes ſuperadded[i]. And by the ſtatute 13 Hen. IV. c. 7. any two juſtices, together with the ſheriff or under-ſheriff of the county, may come with the *poſſe comitatus*, if need be, and ſuppreſs any ſuch riot, aſſembly, or rout, arreſt the rioters, and record upon the ſpot the nature and circumſtances of the whole tranſaction;

[f] 3 Inſt. 176.
[g] Bro. *Abr. t. Riot.* 4. 5.

[h] 3 Inſt. 176.
[i] 1 Hawk. P. C. 159.

which

which record alone fhall be a fufficient conviction of the offenders. In the interpretation of which ftatute it hath been holden,
that all perfons, noblemen and others, except women, clergymen, perfons decrepit, and infants under fifteen, are bound to
attend the juftices in fuppreffing a riot, upon pain of fine and
imprifonment; and that any battery, wounding, or killing the
rioters, that may happen in fuppreffing the riot, is juftifiable [j].
So that our antient law, previous to the modern riot act, feems
pretty well to have guarded againft any violent breach of the
public peace; efpecially as any riotous affembly on a public or
general account, as to redrefs grievances or pull down all inclofures, and alfo refifting the king's forces if fent to keep the
peace, may amount to overt acts of high treafon, by levying
war againft the king.

7. NEARLY related to this head of riots is the offence of
tumultuous petitioning; which was carried to an enormous height
in the times preceding the grand rebellion. Wherefore by ftatute 13 Car. II. ft. 1. c. 5. it is enacted, that not more than
twenty names fhall be figned to any petition to the king or either
houfe of parliament, for any alteration of matters eftablifhed by
law in church or ftate; unlefs the contents thereof be previoufly
approved, in the country, by three juftices, or the majority of
the grand jury at the affifes or quarter feffions; and, in London,
by the lord mayor, aldermen, and common council [k]: and that
no petition fhall be delivered by a company of more than ten
perfons: on pain in either cafe of incurring a penalty not exceeding 100 l, and three months imprifonment.

8. AN eighth offence againft the public peace is that of a
forcible entry or *detainer*; which is committed by violently taking
or keeping poffeffion, with menaces, force, and arms, of lands
and tenements, without the authority of law. This was for-

<hr />

j 1 Hal. P. C. 495. 1 Hawk. P. C. 161.
k This may be one reafon (among others)
why the corporation of London has, fince
the reftoration, ufually taken the lead in
petitions to parliament for the alteration of
any eftablifhed law.

merly

merly allowable to every perfon diffeifed, or turned out of poffeffion, unlefs his entry was taken away or barred by his own
neglect, or other circumftances ; which were explained more at
large in a former volume[1]. But this being found very prejudicial to the public peace, it was thought neceffary by feveral ftatutes to reftrain all perfons from the ufe of fuch violent methods,
even of doing themfelves juftice ; and much more if they have
no juftice in their claim[m]. So that the entry now allowed by
law is a peaceable one ; that forbidden is fuch as is carried on
and maintained with force, with violence, and unufual weapons.
By the ftatute 5 Ric. II. ft. 1. c. 8. all forcible entries are punifhed
with imprifonment and ranfom at the king's will. And by the
feveral ftatutes of 15 Ric. II. c. 2. 8 Hen. VI. c. 9. 31 Eliz.
c. 11. and 21 Jac. I. c. 15. upon any forcible entry, or forcible
detainer after peaceable entry, into any lands, or benefices of the
church, one or more juftices of the peace, taking fufficient
power of the county, may go to the place, and there record the
force upon his own view, as in cafe of riots ; and upon fuch
conviction may commit the offender to gaol, till he makes fine
and ranfom to the king. And moreover the juftice or juftices
have power to fummon a jury, to try the forcible entry or detainer complained of : and, if the fame be found by that jury,
then befides the fine on the offender, the juftices fhall make reftitution by the fheriff of the poffeffion, without inquiring into
the merits of the title ; for the force is the only thing to be
tried, punifhed, and remedied by them : and the fame may be
done by indictment at the general feffions. But this provifion
does not extend to fuch as endeavour to maintain poffeffion by
force, where they themfelves, or their anceftors, have been in
the peaceable enjoyment of the lands and tenements, for three
years immediately preceding.

9. THE offence of *riding* or *going armed*, with dangerous or
unufual weapons, is a crime againft the public peace, by terri-
fying the good people of the land ; and is particularly prohibited

[1] See Vol. III. pag. 174, &c.   [m] 1 Hawk. P. C. 141.

by

by the ftatute of Northampton, 2 Edw. III. c. 3. upon pain of forfeiture of the arms, and imprifonment during the king's pleafure: in like manner as, by the laws of Solon, every Athenian was finable who walked about the city in armour[n].

10. SPREADING *falfe news*, to make difcord between the king and nobility, or concerning any great man of the realm, is punifhed by common law[o] with fine and imprifonment; which is confirmed by ftatutes Weftm. 1. 3 Edw. I. c. 34. 2 Ric. II. ft. 1. c. 5. and 12 Ric. II. c. 11.

11. FALSE and *pretended prophecies*, with intent to difturb the peace, are equally unlawful, and more penal; as they raife enthufiaftic jealoufies in the people, and terrify them with imaginary fears. They are therefore punifhed by our law, upon the fame principle that fpreading of public news of any kind, without communicating it firft to the magiftrate, was prohibited by the antient Gauls[p]. Such falfe and pretended prophecies were punifhed capitally by ftatute 1 Edw. VI. c. 12. which was repealed in the reign of queen Mary. And now by the ftatute 5 Eliz. c. 15. the penalty for the firft offence is a fine of 100 *l*, and one year's imprifonment; for the fecond, forfeiture of all goods and chattels, and imprifonment during life.

12. BESIDES actual breaches of the peace, any thing that tends to provoke or excite others to break it, is an offence of the fame denomination. Therefore *challenges to fight*, either by word or letter, or to be the bearer of fuch challenge, are punifhable by fine and imprifonment, according to the circumftances of the offence[q]. If this challenge arifes on account of any mo-

---

[n] Pott. Antiqu. b. 1. c. 26.
[o] 2 Inft. 226. 3 Inft. 198.
[p] " *Habent legibus fanctum, fi quis quid de republica a finitimis rumore aut fama acceperit, uti ad magiftratum deferat, neve cum alio communicet: quod faepe homines temerarios*

" *atque imperitos falfis rumoribus terreri, et ad facinus impelli, et de fummis rebus confilium capere, cognitum eft.*" Caef. de bell. Gall. lib. 6. cap. 19.
[q] 1 Hawk. P. C. 135. 138.

ney

ney won at gaming, or if any aſſault or affray happen upon
ſuch account, the offender, by ſtatute 9 Ann. c. 14. ſhall forfeit all his goods to the crown, and ſuffer two years impriſonment.

13. O f a nature very ſimilar to challenges are *libels, libelli
famoſi,* which, taken in their largeſt and moſt extenſive ſenſe,
ſignify any writings, pictures, or the like, of an immoral or
illegal tendency ; but, in the ſenſe under which we are now to
conſider them, are malicious defamations of any perſon, and eſpecially a magiſtrate, made public by either printing, writing,
ſigns, or pictures, in order to provoke him to wrath, or expoſe
him to public hatred, contempt, and ridicule ʳ. The direct
tendency of theſe libels is the breach of the public peace, by
ſtirring up the objects of them to revenge, and perhaps to blood-
ſhed. The communication of a libel to any one perſon is a
publication in the eye of the law ˢ : and therefore the ſending
an abuſive private letter to a man is as much a libel as if it
were openly printed, for it equally tends to a breach of the
peace ᵗ. For the ſame reaſon it is immaterial with reſpect to the
eſſence of a libel, whether the matter of it be true or falſe ᵘ ;
ſince the provocation, and not the falſity, is the thing to be
puniſhed criminally : though, doubtleſs, the falſhood of it may
aggravate it's guilt, and enhance it's puniſhment. In a civil action, we may remember, a libel muſt appear to be falſe, as well
as ſcandalous ʷ ; for, if the charge be true, the plaintiff has
received no private injury, and has no ground to demand a com-
penſation for himſelf, whatever offence it may be againſt the
public peace : and therefore, upon a civil action, the truth of
the accuſation may be pleaded in bar of the ſuit. But, in a
criminal proſecution, the tendency which all libels have to
create animoſities, and to diſturb the public peace, is the ſole
conſideration of the law. And therefore, in ſuch proſecutions,

ʳ 1 Hawk. P. C. 193.
ˢ Moor. 813.
ᵗ 2 Brownl. 151. 12 Rep. 35. Hob. 215.

Poph. 139. 1 Hawk. P. C. 195.
ᵘ Moor. 627. 5 Rep. 125. 11 Mod. 99.
ʷ See Vol. III. pag. 125.

the

the only facts to be confidered are, firft, the making or publifhing of the book or writing; and fecondly, whether the
matter be criminal: and, if both thefe points are againft the
defendant, the offence againft the public is complete. The
punifhment of fuch libellers, for either making, repeating,
printing, or publifhing the libel, is fine, and fuch corporal
punifhment as the court in their difcretion fhall inflict; regarding the quantity of the offence, and the quality of the offender [x]. By the law of the twelve tables at Rome, libels, which
affected the reputation of another, were made a capital offence:
but, before the reign of Auguftus, the punifhment became
corporal only [y]. Under the emperor Valentinian [z] it was again
made capital, not only to write, but to publifh, or even to
omit deftroying them. Our law, in this and many other refpects, correfponds rather with the middle age of Roman jurifprudence, when liberty, learning, and humanity, were in their
full vigour, than with the cruel edicts that were eftablifhed in
the dark and tyrannical ages of the antient *decemviri*, or the
later emperors.

IN this, and the other inftances which we have lately confidered, where blafphemous, immoral, treafonable, fchifmati-
cal, feditious, or fcandalous libels are punifhed by the Englifh
law, fome with a greater, others with a lefs degree of feverity;
the *liberty of the prefs*, properly underftood, is by no means in-
fringed or violated. The liberty of the prefs is indeed effential
to the nature of a free ftate: but this confifts in laying no *pre-*
vious reftraints upon publications, and not in freedom from
cenfure for criminal matter when publifhed. Every freeman
has an undoubted right to lay what fentiments he pleafes before
the public: to forbid this, is to deftroy the freedom of the

---

[x] 1 Hawk. P. C. 196.
[y] ———————————— *Quinetiam lex*
Poenaque lata, malo quae nollet carmine quenquam
Defcribi: —— *vertere modum formidine* fuftis. Hor. ad Aug. 152.
[z] *Cod.* 9. 36.

prefs : but if he publishes what is improper, mischievous, or illegal, he must take the consequence of his own temerity. To subject the prefs to the reftrictive power of a licenfer, as was formerly done, both before and fince the revolution ᵃ, is to subject all freedom of fentiment to the prejudices of one man, and make him the arbitrary and infallible judge of all controverted points in learning, religion, and government. But to punifh (as the law does at prefent) any dangerous or offenfive writings, which, when publifhed, fhall on a fair and impartial trial be adjudged of a pernicious tendency, is neceffary for the prefervation of peace and good order, of government and religion, the only folid foundations of civil liberty. Thus the will of individuals is ftill left free ; the abufe only of that free will is the object of legal punifhment. Neither is any reftraint hereby laid upon freedom of thought or enquiry : liberty of private fentiment is ftill left ; the diffeminating, or making public, of bad fentiments, deftructive of the ends of fociety, is the crime which fociety corrects. A man (fays a fine writer on this fubject) may be allowed to keep poifons in his clofet, but not publicly to vend them as cordials. And to this we may

---

ᵃ The art of printing, foon after it's introduction, was looked upon (as well in England as in other countries) as merely a matter of ftate, and fubject to the coercion of the crown. It was therefore regulated with us by the king's proclamations, prohibitions, charters of privilege and of licence, and finally by the decrees of the court of ftarchamber; which limited the number of printers, and of preffes which each fhould employ, and prohibited new publications unlefs previoufly approved by proper licenfers. On the demolition of this odious jurifdiction in 1641, the long parliament of Charles I, after their rupture with that prince, affumed the fame powers as the ftarchamber exercifed with refpect to the licenfing of books ; and in 1643, 1647, 1649, and 1652, (Scobell. i. 44, 134. ii. 88,

230.) iffued their ordinances for that purpofe, founded principally on the ftarchamber decree of 1637. In 1662 was paffed the ftatute 13 & 14 Car. II. c. 33. which (with fome few alterations) was copied from the parliamentary ordinances. This act expired in 1679, but was revived by ftatute 1 Jac. II. c. 17. and continued till 1692. It was then continued for two years longer by ftatute 4 W. & M. c. 24. but, though frequent attempts were made by the government to revive it, in the fubfequent part of that reign, (Com. Journ. 11 Feb. 1694. 26 Nov. 1695. 22 Oct. 1696. 9 Feb. 1697. 31 Jan. 1698.) yet the parliament refifted it fo ftrongly, that it finally expired, and the prefs became properly free, in 1694; and has ever fince fo continued.

add,

add, that the only plaufible argument heretofore ufed for reftraining the juft freedom of the prefs, "that it was neceffary
"to prevent the daily abufe of it," will entirely lofe it's force,
when it is fhewn (by a feafonable exertion of the laws) that the
prefs cannot be abufed to any bad purpofe, without incurring a
fuitable punifhment : whereas it never can be ufēd to any good
one, when under the control of an infpector. So true will it be
found, that to cenfure the licentioufnefs, is to maintain the liberty, of the prefs.

CHAPTER   THE   TWELFTH.

OF **OFFENCES** AGAINST **PUBLIC TRADE.**

OFFENCES againſt public *trade*, like thoſe of the preceding claſſes, are either felonious, or not felonious. Of
the firſt ſort are,

1. OWLING, ſo called from it's being uſually carried on in
the night, which is the offence of tranſporting wool or ſheep
out of this kingdom, to the detriment of it's ſtaple manufacture.
This was forbidden at common law [a], and more particularly by
ſtatute 11 Edw. III. c. 1. when the importance of our woollen
manufacture was firſt attended to; and there are now many later
ſtatutes relating to this offence, the moſt uſeful and principal of
which are thoſe enacted in the reign of queen Elizabeth, and
ſince. The ſtatute 8 Eliz. c. 3. makes the tranſportation of live
ſheep, or embarking them on board any ſhip, for the firſt offence forfeiture of goods, and impriſonment for a year, and that
at the end of the year the left hand ſhall be cut off in ſome public market, and ſhall be there nailed up in the openeſt place;
and the ſecond offence is felony. The ſtatutes 12 Car. II. c. 32.
and 7 & 8 W. III. c. 28. make the exportation of wool, ſheep,
or fuller's earth, liable to pecuniary penalties, and the forfeiture
of the intereſt of the ſhip and cargo by the owners, if privy;

[a] Mirr. c. 1. §. 3.

and

and confifcation of goods, and three years imprifonment to the mafter and all the mariners. And the ftatute 4 Geo. I. c. 11. (amended and farther enforced by 12 Geo. II. c. 21. and 19 Geo. II. c. 34.) makes it tranfportation for feven years, if the penalties be not paid.

2. SMUGGLING, or the offence of importing goods without paying the duties impofed thereon by the laws of the cuftoms and excife, is an offence generally connected and carried on hand in hand with the former. This is reftrained by a great variety of ftatutes, which inflict pecuniary penalties and feifure of the goods for clandeftine fmuggling; and affix the guilt of felony, with tranfportation for feven years, upon more open, daring, and avowed practices: but the laft of them, 19 Geo. II. c. 34. is for this purpofe *inftar omnium*; for it makes all forcible acts of fmuggling, carried on in defiance of the laws, or even in difguife to evade them, felony without benefit of clergy: enacting, that if three or more perfons fhall affemble, with fire arms or other offenfive weapons, to affift in the illegal exportation or importation of goods, or in refcuing the fame after feifure, or in refcuing offenders in cuftody for fuch offences; or fhall pafs with fuch goods in difguife; or fhall wound, fhoot at, or affault any officers of the revenue when in the execution of their duty; fuch perfons fhall be felons, without the benefit of clergy. As to that branch of the ftatute, which required any perfon, charged upon oath as a fmuggler, under pain of death, to furrender himfelf upon proclamation, it feems to be expired; as the fubfequent ftatutes[b], which continue the original act to the prefent time, do in terms continue only fo much of the faid act, as relates to the *punifhment* of the offenders, and not to the extraordinary method of apprehending or caufing them to furrender: and for offences of this pofitive fpecies, where punifhment (though neceffary) is rendered fo by the laws themfelves, which by impofing high duties on commodities increafe the temptation

---

[b] Stat. 26 Geo. II. c. 32. 32 Geo. II. c. 18. 4 Geo. III. c. 12.

to evade them, we cannot furely be too cautious in inflicting the penalty of death [c].

3. ANOTHER offence againft public trade is fraudulent *bankruptcy*, which was fufficiently fpoken of in a former volume [d]; when we thoroughly examined the nature of thefe unfortunate traders. I fhall therefore here barely mention over again fome abufes incident to bankruptcy, *viz.* the bankrupt's neglect of furrendering himfelf to his creditors; his non-conformity to the directions of the feveral ftatutes; his concealing or imbezzling his effects to the value of 20 *l*; and his withholding any books or writings with intent to defraud his creditors: all which the policy of our commercial country has made capital in the offender; or, felony without benefit of clergy. And indeed it is allowed in general, by fuch as are the moft averfe to the infliction of capital punifhment, that the offence of fraudulent bankruptcy, being an atrocious fpecies of the *crimen falfi*, ought to be put upon a level with thofe of forgery and falfifying the coin [e]. To this head we may alfo fubjoin, that by ftatute 32 Geo. II. c. 28. it is felony punifhable by tranfportation for feven years, if a prifoner, charged in execution for any debt under 100 *l*, neglects or refufes on demand to difcover and deliver up his effects for the benefit of his creditors. And thefe are the only felonious offences againft public trade; the refidue being mere mifdemefnors: as,

4. USURY, which is an unlawful contract upon the loan of money, to receive the fame again with exorbitant increafe. Of this alfo we had occafion to difcourfe at large in a former volume [f]. We there obferved that by ftatute 37 Hen. VIII. c. 9. the rate of intereft was fixed at 10 *l. per cent. per annum:* which the ftatute 13 Eliz. c.8. confirms; and ordains, that all brokers fhall be guilty of a *praemunire* that tranfact any contracts for more, and the fecurities themfelves fhall be void. The ftatute

---

[c] See Vol. I. pag. 317. Beccar. ch. 33.   [e] Beccar. ch. 34.
[d] See Vol. II. pag. 481, 482.   [f] See Vol. II. pag. 455, &c.

21 Jac. I.

21 Jac. I. c. 17. reduced intereſt to eight *per cent* ; and, it having been lowered in 1650, during the uſurpation, to ſix *per cent*, the ſame reduction was re-enacted after the reſtoration by ſtatute 12 Car. II. c. 13. and, laſtly, the ſtatute 12 Ann. ſt. 2. c. 16. has reduced it to five *per cent*. Wherefore not only all contracts for taking more are in themſelves totally void, but alſo the lender ſhall forfeit treble the money borrowed. Alſo if any ſcrivener or broker takes more than five ſhillings *per cent*. procuration-money, or more than twelve-pence for making a bond, he ſhall forfeit 20 *l.*, with coſts, and ſhall ſuffer impriſonment for half a year.

5. CHEATING is another offence, more immediately againſt public trade; as that cannot be carried on without a punctilious regard to common honeſty, and faith between man and man. Hither therefore may be referred that prodigious multitude of ſtatutes, which are made to prevent deceits in particular trades, and which are chiefly of uſe among the traders themſelves. For ſo cautious has the legiſlature been, and ſo thoroughly abhors all indirect practices, that there is hardly a conſiderable fraud incident to any branch of trade, but what is reſtrained and puniſhed by ſome particular ſtatute. The offence alſo of *breaking the aſſiſe* of bread, or the rules laid down by law, and particularly by ſtatute 31 Geo. II. c. 29. and 3 Geo. III. c. 11. for aſcertaining it's price in every given quantity, is reducible to this head of cheating : as is likewiſe in a peculiar manner the offence of ſelling by *falſe weights and meaſures*; the ſtandard of which fell under our conſideration in a former volume [g]. The puniſhment of bakers breaking the aſſiſe, was antiently to ſtand in the pillory, by ſtatute 51 Hen. III. ſt. 6. and for brewers (by the ſame act) to ſtand in the tumbrel or dungcart [h]: which, as we learn from domeſday book, was the puniſhment for knaviſh brewers in the city of Cheſter ſo early as the reign of Edward the confeſſor. " *Malam cerviſiam faciens, in cathedra ponebatur ſtercoris* [i]." But

[g] See Vol. I. pag. 274.
[h] 3 Inſt. 219.
[i] Seld. tit. of hon. b. 2. c. 5. §. 3.

now the general punishment for all frauds of this kind, if indicted (as they may be) at common law, is by fine and imprisonment: though the easier and more usual way is by levying on a summary conviction, by distress and sale, the forfeitures imposed by the several acts of parliament. Lastly, any deceitful practice, in cozening another by artful means, whether in matters of trade or otherwise, as by playing with false dice, or the like, is punishable with fine, imprisonment, and pillory[k]. And by the statutes 33 Hen. VIII. c. 1. and 30 Geo. II. c. 24. if any man defrauds another of any valuable chattels by colour of any false token, counterfeit letter, or false pretence, or pawns or disposes of another's goods without the consent of the owner, he shall suffer such punishment by imprisonment, fine, pillory, transportation, whipping, or other corporal pain, as the court shall direct.

6. THE offence of *forestalling* the market is also an offence against public trade. This, which (as well as the two following) is also an offence at common law[l], is described by statute 5 & 6 Edw. VI. c. 14. to be the buying or contracting for any merchandize or victual coming in the way to market; or dissuading persons from bringing their goods or provisions there; or persuading them to enhance the price, when there: any of which practices make the market dearer to the fair trader.

7. REGRATING is described by the same statute to be the buying of corn, or other dead victual, in any market, and selling them again in the same market, or within four miles of the place. For this also enhances the price of the provisions, as every successive seller must have a successive profit.

8. ENGROSSING, by the same statute, is the getting into one's possession, or buying up, of corn or other dead victuals, with intent to sell them again. This must of course be injurious to the public, by putting it in the power of one or two rich men to raise the price of provisions at their own discretion.

[k] 1 Hawk. P. C. 188.   [l] 2 Hawk. P. C. 235.

And

And the penalty for thefe three offences by this ftatute (which is the laft that hath been made concerning them) is the forfeiture of the goods or their value, and two months imprifonment for the firft offence ; double value and fix months imprifonment for the fecond ; and, for the third, the offender fhall forfeit all his goods, be fet in the pillory, and imprifoned at the king's pleafure. Among the Romans thefe offences, and other malepractices to raife the price of provifions, were punifhed by a pecuniary mulct. " *Poena viginti aureorum ftatuitur adverfus eum,* " *qui contra annonam fecerit, focietatemve coierit quo annona carior* " *fiat* [m]."

9. MONOPOLIES are much the fame offence in other branches of trade, that engroffing is in provifions : being a licence or privilege allowed by the king for the fole buying and felling, making, working, or ufing, of any thing whatfoever ; whereby the fubject in general is reftrained from that liberty of manufacturing or trading which he had before [n]. Thefe had been carried to an enormous height during the reign of queen Elizabeth ; and were heavily complained of by fir Edward Coke [o], in the beginning of the reign of king James the firft : but were in great meafure remedied by ftatute 21 Jac. I. c. 3. which declares fuch monopolies to be contrary to law and void ; (except as to patents, not exceeding the grant of fourteen years, to the authors of new inventions ;) and monopolifts are punifhed with the forfeiture of treble damages and double cofts, to thofe whom they attempt to difturb ; and if they procure any action, brought againft them for thefe damages, to be ftayed by any extrajudicial order, other than of the court wherein it is brought, they incur the penalties of *praemunire*. Combinations alfo among victuallers or artificers, to raife the price of provifions, or any commodities, or the rate of labour, are in many cafes feverely punifhed by particular ftatutes ; and, in general, by ftatute 2 & 3 Edw. VI. c. 15. with the forfeiture of 10 *l*, or twenty days imprifonment,

[m] *Ff.* 48. 12. 2.
[z] 1 Hawk. P. C. 231.
[o] 3 Inft. 181.

with

with an allowance of only bread and water, for the firſt offence; 20 *l.* or the pillory, for the ſecond; and 40 *l.* for the third, or elſe the pillory, loſs of one ear, and perpetual infamy. In the ſame manner, by a conſtitution of the emperor Zeno[p], all monopolies and combinations to keep up the price of merchandize, proviſions, or workmanſhip, were prohibited upon pain of forfeiture of goods and perpetual baniſhment.

10. To exerciſe a *trade* in any town, without having previouſly ſerved as an *apprentice* for ſeven years[q], is looked upon to be detrimental to public trade, upon the ſuppoſed want of ſufficient ſkill in the trader; and therefore is puniſhed by ſtatute 5 Eliz. c. 4. with the forfeiture of forty ſhillings by the month.

11. LASTLY, to prevent the deſtruction of our home manufactures, by *tranſporting and ſeducing our artiſts* to ſettle abroad, it is provided by ſtatute 5 Geo. I. c. 27. that ſuch as ſo entice or ſeduce them ſhall be fined 100 *l,* and be impriſoned three months; and for the ſecond offence ſhall be fined at diſcretion, and be impriſoned a year: and the artificers, ſo going into foreign countries, and not returning within ſix months after warning given them by the Britiſh embaſſador where they reſide, ſhall be deemed aliens, and forfeit all their lands and goods, and ſhall be incapable of any legacy or gift. By ſtatute 23 Geo. II. c. 13. the ſeducers incur, for the firſt offence, a forfeiture of 500 *l.* for each artificer contracted with to be ſent abroad, and impriſonment for twelve months; and for the ſecond, 1000 *l,* and are liable to two years impriſonment: and if any perſon exports any tools or utenſils uſed in the ſilk or woollen manufactures, he forfeits the ſame and 200 *l,* and the captain of the ſhip (having knowlege thereof) 100 *l:* and if any captain of a king's ſhip, or officer of the cuſtoms, knowingly ſuffers ſuch exportation, he forfeits 100 *l.* and his employment; and is for ever made incapable of bearing any public office.

[p] *Cod.* 4. 59. 1.   [q] See Vol. I. pag. 427.

CHAPTER THE THIRTEENTH.

OF OFFENCES AGAINST THE PUBLIC HEALTH, AND THE PUBLIC POLICE OR OECONOMY.

THE fourth fpecies of offences, more efpecially affecting the commonwealth, are fuch as are againft the public *health* of the nation; a concern of the higheft importance, and for the prefervation of which there are in many countries fpecial magiftrates or curators appointed.

1. THE firft of thefe offences is a felony; but, by the bleffing of providence for more than a century paft, incapable of being committed in this nation. For by ftatute 1 Jac. I. c. 31. it is enacted, that if any perfon infected with the plague, or dwelling in any infected houfe, be commanded by the mayor or conftable, or other head officer of his town or vill, to keep his houfe, and fhall venture to difobey it; he may be inforced, by the watchmen appointed on fuch melancholy occafions, to obey fuch neceffary command: and, if any hurt enfue by fuch inforcement, the watchmen are thereby indemnified. And farther, if fuch perfon fo commanded to confine himfelf goes abroad, and converfes in company, if he has no plague fore upon him, he fhall be punifhed as a vagabond by whipping, and be bound to his good behaviour: but, if he has any infectious fore upon him uncured, he then fhall be guilty of felony. By the ftatute

26 Geo. II. c. 6. (explained and amended by 29 Geo. II. c. 8.) the method of performing *quarentine*, or forty days probation, by ſhips coming from infected countries, is put in a much more regular and effectual order than formerly; and maſters of ſhips, coming from infected places and diſobeying the directions there given, or having the plague on board and concealing it, are guilty of felony without benefit of clergy. The ſame penalty alſo attends perſons eſcaping from the *lazarets*, or places wherein quarentine is to be performed; and officers and watchmen neglecting their duty; and perſons conveying goods or letters from ſhips performing quarentine.

2. A SECOND, but much inferior, ſpecies of offence againſt public health is the ſelling of *unwholſome proviſions*. To prevent which the ſtatute 51 Hen. III. ſt. 6. and the ordinance for bakers, c. 7. prohibit the ſale of corrupted wine, contagious or unwholſome fleſh, or fleſh that is bought of a Jew; under pain of amercement for the firſt offence, pillory for the ſecond, fine and impriſonment for the third, and abjuration of the town for the fourth. And by the ſtatute 12 Car. II. c. 25. §. 11. any brewing or adulteration of wine is puniſhed with the forfeiture of 100 *l*, if done by the wholeſale merchant; and 40 *l*, if done by the vintner or retale trader. Theſe are all the offences which may properly be ſaid to reſpect the public health.

V. THE laſt ſpecies of offences which eſpecially affect the commonwealth are thoſe againſt the public *police* and *oeconomy*. By the public police and oeconomy I mean the due regulation and domeſtic order of the kingdom: whereby the individuals of the ſtate, like members of a well-governed family, are bound to conform their general behaviour to the rules of propriety, good neighbourhood, and good manners; and to be decent, induſtrious, and inoffenſive in their reſpective ſtations. This head of offences muſt therefore be very miſcellaneous, as it comprizes all ſuch crimes as eſpecially affect public ſociety, and are not comprehended under any of the four preceding ſpecies. Theſe

amount,

amount, fome of them to felony, and others to mifdemefnors
only. Among the former are,

1. THE offence of *clandefline marriages:* for by the ftatute
26 Geo. II. c. 33. 1. To folemnize marriage in any other place
befides a church, or public chapel wherein banns have been ufually publifhed, except by licence from the archbifhop; --- and,
2. To folemnize marriage in fuch church or chapel without due
publication of banns, or licence obtained from a proper authority; --- do both of them not only render the marriage void,
but fubject the perfon folemnizing it to felony, punifhed by
tranfportation for fourteen years: as, by three former ftatutes[a],
he and his affiftants were fubject to a pecuniary forfeiture of
100 *l.* 3. To make a falfe entry in a marriage regifter; to alter
it when made; to forge, or counterfeit, fuch entry, or a marriage licence, or aid and abet fuch forgery; to utter the fame
as true, knowing it to be counterfeit; or to deftroy or procure
the deftruction of any regifter, in order to vacate any marriage,
or fubject any perfon to the penalties of this act; all thefe offences, knowingly and wilfully committed, fubject the party to
to the guilt of felony, without benefit of clergy.

2. ANOTHER felonious offence, with regard to this holy eftate of matrimony, is what our law corruptly calls *bigamy;* which
properly fignifies being twice married, but with us is ufed as fynonymous to *polygamy,* or having a plurality of wives at once[b].
Such fecond marriage, living the former hufband or wife, is fim-
ply void, and a mere nullity, by the ecclefiaftical law of England:
and yet the legiflature has thought it juft to make it felony, by
reafon of it's being fo great a violation of the public oeconomy and
decency of a well ordered ftate. For polygamy can never be endured under any rational civil eftablifhment, whatever fpecious
reafons may be urged for it by the eaftern nations, the fallaciouf-
nefs of which has been fully proved by many fenfible writers:

[a] 6 & 7 W. III. c. 6.　7 & 8 W. III. c. 35.　　[b] 3 Inft. 88.
10 Ann. c. 19. §. 1-6.

　　　　　　　　　　　　　　but

but in northern countries the very nature of the climate seems to reclaim again∫t it ; it never having obtained in this part of the world, even from the time of our German ance∫tors ; who, as Tacitus informs us[c], " *prope ∫oli barbarorum ∫ingulis uxoribus* " *contenti ∫unt."* It is therefore puni∫hed by the laws both of antient and modern Sweden with death[d]. And with us in England it is enacted by ∫tatute 1 Jac. I. c. 11. that if any per∫on, being married, do afterwards marry again, the former hu∫band or wife being alive, it is felony; but within the benefit of clergy. The fir∫t wife in this ca∫e ∫hall not be admitted as an evidence again∫t her hu∫band, becau∫e ∫he is the true wife ; but the ∫econd may, for ∫he is indeed no wife at all[e]; and ∫o, *vice ver∫a,* of a ∫econd hu∫band. This act makes an exception to five ca∫es, in which ∫uch ∫econd marriage, though in the three fir∫t it is void, is yet no felony. 1. Where either party hath been continually *abroad* for ∫even years, whether the party in England hath notice of the other's being living or no. 2. Where either of the parties hath been ab∫ent from the other ∫even years, *within* this kingdom, and the remaining party hath had no notice of the other's being alive within that time. 3. Where there is a divorce or ∫eparation *a men∫a et thoro* by ∫entence in the eccle∫ia∫tical court. 4. Where the fir∫t marriage is declared ab∫olutely void by any ∫uch ∫entence, and the parties loo∫ed *a vinculo.* Or, 5. Where either of the parties was under the age of con∫ent at the time of the fir∫t marriage : for in ∫uch ca∫e the fir∫t marriage was voidable by the di∫agreement of either party, which this ∫econd marriage very clearly amounts to. But, if at the age of con∫ent the parties had agreed to the marriage, which completes the contract, and is indeed the real marriage ; and afterwards one of them ∫hould marry again ; I ∫hould apprehend that ∫uch ∫econd marriage would be within the rea∫on and penalties of the act.

[c] *de mor. Germ.* 18.
[d] Stiernh. *de jure Sueon. l.* 3. *c.* 2.
[e] 1 Hal. P. C. 693.

3. A THIRD

3. A THIRD ſpecies of felony againſt the good order and oeconomy of the kingdom, is by idle *ſoldiers* and *mariners wandering* about the realm, or perſons pretending ſo to be, and abuſing the name of that honourable profeſſion [f]. Such a one, not having a teſtimonial or paſs from a juſtice of the peace, limiting the time of his paſſage; or exceeding the time limited for fourteen days, unleſs he falls ſick; or forging ſuch teſtimonial; is by ſtatute 39 Eliz. c. 17. made guilty of felony, without benefit of clergy. This ſanguinary law, though in practice deſervedly antiquated, ſtill remains a diſgrace to our ſtatute-book: yet attended with this mitigation, that the offender may be delivered, if any honeſt freeholder or other perſon of ſubſtance will take him into his ſervice, and he abides in the ſame for one year; unleſs licenced to depart by his employer, who in ſuch caſe ſhall forfeit ten pounds.

4. OUTLANDISH perſons calling themſelves *Egyptians*, or *gypſies*, are another object of the ſeverity of ſome of our unrepealed ſtatutes. Theſe are a ſtrange kind of commonwealth among themſelves of wandering impoſtors and jugglers, who made their firſt appearance in Germany about the beginning of the ſixteenth century, and have ſince ſpread themſelves all over Europe. Munſter, it is true [g], who is followed and relied upon by Spelman [h], fixes the time of their firſt appearance to the year 1417; but, as he owns, that the firſt whom he ever ſaw were in 1524, it is probably an error of the preſs for 1517: eſpecially as other hiſtorians [j] inform us, that when ſultan Selim conquered Egypt, in the year 1517, ſeveral of the natives refuſed to ſubmit to the Turkiſh yoke; but, being at length ſubdued and baniſhed, they agreed to diſperſe in ſmall parties all over the world, where their ſuppoſed ſkill in the black art gave them an univerſal reception, in that age of ſuperſtition and credulity. In the compaſs of a very few years they gained ſuch a number of idle proſelytes,

[f] 3 Inſt. 85.
[g] *Coſmogr. l.* 3.
[h] *Gloſſ.* 193.
[j] Mod. Univ. Hiſt. xliii. 271.

(who

(who imitated their language and complexion, and betook themfelves to the fame arts of chiromancy, begging, and pilfering)
that they became troublefome and even formidable to moft of
the ftates of Europe. Hence they were expelled from France
in the year 1560, and from Spain in 1591 [i]. And the government in England took the alarm much earlier: for in 1530, they
are defcribed by ftatute 22 Hen. VIII. c. 10. as "outlandifh
" people, calling themfelves Egyptians, ufing no craft nor feat
" of merchandize, who have come into this realm and gone from
" fhire to fhire and place to place in great company, and ufed
" great, fubtil, and crafty means to deceive the people; bearing
" them in hand, that they by palmeftry could tell men's and
" women's fortunes; and fo many times by craft and fubtilty
" have deceived the people of their money, and alfo have com-
" mitted many heinous felonies and robberies." Wherefore they
are directed to avoid the realm, and not to return under pain of
imprifonment, and forfeiture of their goods and chattels; and,
upon their trials for any felony which they may have committed,
they fhall not be intitled to a jury *de medietate linguae*. And afterwards, it is enacted by ftatutes 1 & 2 Ph. & M. c. 4. and
5 Eliz. c. 20. that if any fuch perfons fhall be imported into
this kingdom, the importer fhall forfeit 40 *l*. And if the Egyptians themfelves remain one month in this kingdom; or if any
perfon, being fourteen years old, (whether natural born fubject
or ftranger) which hath been feen or found in the fellowfhip
of fuch Egyptians, or which hath difguifed him or herfelf like
them, fhall remain in the fame one month, at one or feveral
times; it is felony without benefit of clergy: and fir Matthew
Hale informs us [k], that at one Suffolk affifes no lefs than thirteen gy fies were executed upon thefe ftatutes, a few years before the reftoration. But, to the honour of our national humanity, there are no inftances more modern than this, of carrying thefe laws into practice.

---

[i] Dufrefne. *Glofſ. I.* 200.　　　　　　[k] 1 Hal. P. C. 671.

5. To

5. T o defcend next to offences, whofe punifhment is fhort of death. *Common nufances* are a fpecies of offences againft the public order and oeconomical regimen of the ftate; being either the doing of a thing to the annoyance of all the king's fubjects, or the neglecting to do a thing which the common good requires[1]. The nature of *common* nufances, and their diftinction from *private* nufances, were explained in the preceding volume[m]; when we confidered more particularly the nature of the private fort, as a civil injury to individuals. I fhall here only remind the ftudent, that common nufances are fuch inconvenient or troublefome offences, as annoy the whole community in general, and not merely fome particular perfon; and therefore are indictable only, and not actionable; as it would be unreafonable to multiply fuits, by giving every man a feparate right of action, for what damnifies him in common only with the reft of his fellow fubjects. Of this nature are, 1. Annoyances in *highways*, *bridges*, and public *rivers*, by rendering the fame inconvenient or dangerous to pafs: either pofitively, by actual obftructions; or negatively, by want of reparations. For both of thefe, the perfons fo obftructing, or fuch individuals as are bound to repair and cleanfe them, or (in default of thefe laft) the parifh at large, may be indicted, diftreined to repair and amend them, and in fome cafes fined. Where there is an houfe erected, or an inclofure made, upon any part of the king's demefnes, or of an highway, or common ftreet, or public water, or fuch like public things, it is properly called a *purpreflure*[n]. 2. All thofe kinds of nufances, (fuch as offenfive trades and manufactures) which when injurious to a private man are actionable, are, when detrimental to the public, punifhable by public profecution, and fubject to fine according to the quantity of the mifdemefnor: and particularly the keeping of hogs in any city or market town is indictable as a public nufance[o].

[1] 1 Hawk. P. C. 197.
[m] Vol. III. pag. 216.

[n] Co. Litt. 277. from the French *pourpris*, an inclofure.
[o] Salk. 460.

3. All

3. All diforderly *inns* or *ale-houfes, bawdy-houfes, gaming-houfes, ftage-plays* unlicenced, booths and ftages for *rope-dancers, moun-tebanks,* and the like, are public nufances, and may upon indict-ment be fuppreffed and fined[p]. Inns, in particular, being in-tended for the lodging and receipt of travellers, may be indict-ed, fuppreffed, and the inn-keepers fined, if they refufe to en-tertain a traveller without a very fufficient caufe : for thus to fruftrate the end of their inftitution is held to be diforderly be-haviour[q]. Thus too the hofpitable laws of Norway punifh, in the fevereft degree, fuch inn-keepers as refufe to furnifh accom-modations at a juft and reafonable price[r]. 4. By ftatute 10 & 11 W. III. c. 17. all *lotteries* are declared to be public nufances, and all grants, patents, or licences for the fame to be contrary to law. 5. *Cottages* are held to be common nufances, if erected fingly on the wafte, being harbours for thieves and other idle and diffolute perfons. Therefore it is enacted by ftatute 31 Eliz. c. 7. that no perfon fhall erect a cottage, unlefs he lays to it four acres of freehold land of inheritance to be occupied there-with, on pain to forfeit to the king 10 *l.* for it's erection, and 40 *s. per* month for it's continuance : and no owner or occu-pier of a cottage fhall fuffer any inmates therein, or more fami-lies than one to inhabit there, on pain to forfeit 1 o *s. per* month to the lord of the leet. This feems, upon our prefent more enlarged notions, a hard and impolitic law ; depriving the peo-ple of houfes to dwell in, and confequently preventing the po-puloufnefs of towns and parifhes : which, though it is gene-rally endeavoured to be guarded againft, through a fatal rural policy, (being fometimes, when the poor are ill-managed, an intolerable hardfhip) yet, taken in a national view, and on a fuppofition of proper induftry and good parochial government, is a very great advantage to any kingdom. But indeed this, like moft other rigid or inconvenient laws, is rarely put in execution. 6. The making and felling of *fireworks* and *fquibs,* or throwing them about in any ftreet, is, on account of the danger that may

---

[p] 1 Hawk. P. C. 198. 225.   [r] Stiernh. *de jure Sueon. l. 2. c. 9.*
[q] 1 Hawk. P. C. 225.

enfue to any thatched or timber buildings, declared to be a common nufance, by ftatute 9 & 10 W. III. c. 7. and therefore is punifhable by fine. 7. *Eaves-droppers*, or fuch as liften under walls or windows, or the eaves of a houfe, to hearken after dif-courfe, and thereupon to frame flanderous and mifchievous tales, are a common nufance and prefentable at the court-leet[s]: or are indictable at the feffions, and punifhable by fine and finding fu-reties for the good behaviour[t]. 8. Laftly, a *common fcold, communis rixatrix*, (for our law-latin confines it to the feminine gender) is a public nufance to her neighbourhood. For which offence fhe may be indicted[u]; and, if convicted, fhall [w] be fen-tenced to be placed in a certain engine of correction called the trebucket, caftigatory, or *cucking* ftool, which in the Saxon lan-guage fignifies the fcolding ftool; though now it is frequently corrupted into *ducking* ftool, becaufe the refidue of the judgment is, that, when fhe is fo placed therein, fhe fhall be plunged in the water for her punifhment[x].

6. IDLENESS in any perfon whatfoever is alfo a high offence againft the public oeconomy. In China it is a maxim, that if there be a man who does not work, or a woman that is idle, in the empire, fomebody muft fuffer cold or hunger: the produce of the lands not being more than fufficient, with culture, to maintain the inhabitants; and therefore, though the idle perfon may fhift off the want from himfelf, yet it muft in the end fall fome-where. The court alfo of Areopagus at Athens punifhed idle-nefs, and exerted a right of examining every citizen in what manner he fpent his time; the intention of which was[y], that the Athenians, knowing they were to give an account of their oc-cupations, fhould follow only fuch as were laudable, and that there might be no room left for fuch as lived by unlawful arts. The civil law expelled all fturdy vagrants from the city[z]: and,

[s] Kitch. of courts. 20.
[t] *Ibid.* 1 Hawk. P. C. 132.
[u] 6 Mod. 213.
[w] 1 Hawk. P. C. 198. 200.

[x] 3 Inft. 219.
[y] Valer. Maxim. *l.* 2. *c.* 6.
[z] *Nov.* 80. *c.* 5.

in our own law, all idle perſons or vagabonds, whom our antient ſtatutes deſcribe to be " ſuch as wake on the night, and ſleep on " the day, and haunt cuſtomable taverns, and ale-houſes, and " routs about; and no man wot from whence they come, ne " whither they go;" or ſuch as are moſt particularly deſcribed by ſtatute 17 Geo. II. c. 5. and divided into three claſſes, *idle* and *diſorderly* perſons, *rogues* and *vagabonds*, and *incorrigible rogues*; --- all theſe are offenders againſt the good order, and blemiſhes in the government, of any kingdom. They are there-fore all puniſhed, by the ſtatute laſt-mentioned; that is to ſay, idle and diſorderly perſons with one month's impriſonment in the houſe of correction; rogues and vagabonds with whipping and impriſonment not exceeding ſix months; and incorrigible rogues with the like diſcipline and confinement, not exceeding two years: the breach and eſcape from which confinement in one of an inferior claſs, ranks him among incorrigible rogues; and in a rogue (before incorrigible) makes him a felon, and liable to be tranſported for ſeven years. Perſons harbouring vagrants are liable to a fine of forty ſhillings, and to pay all expenſes brought upon the pariſh thereby; in the ſame manner as, by our antient laws, whoever harboured any ſtranger for more than two nights, was anſwerable to the public for any offence that ſuch his inmate might commit[a].

7. Under the head of public oeconomy may alſo be pro-perly ranked all ſumptuary laws againſt *luxury*, and extravagant expenſes in dreſs, diet, and the like; concerning the general utility of which to a ſtate, there is much controverſy among the political writers. Baron Monteſquieu lays it down[b], that luxury is neceſſary in monarchies, as in France; but ruinous to demo-cracies, as in Holland. With regard therefore to England, whoſe government is compounded of both ſpecies, it may ſtill be a dubious queſtion, how far private luxury is a public evil; and, as ſuch, cognizable by public laws. And indeed our legiſ-

---

[a] *LL. Edw. c.* 27. Bracton. *l.* 3. *tr.* 2.   [b] Sp. L. b. 7. c. 2 & 4.
c. 10. ſ. 2.

lators

lators have feveral times changed their fentiments as to this point : for formerly there were a multitude of penal laws exift-ing, to reftrain excefs in apparel[c]; chiefly made in the reigns of Edward the third, Edward the fourth, and Henry the eighth, againft piked fhoes, fhort doublets, and long coats; all of which were repealed by ftatute 1 Jac. I. c. 25. But, as to excefs in diet, there ftill remains one antient ftatute unrepealed, 10 Edw. III. ft. 3. which ordains that no man fhall be ferved, at dinner or fupper, with more than two courfes ; except upon fome great holydays there fpecified, in which he may be ferved with three.

8. NEXT to that of luxury, naturally follows the offence of *gaming*, which is generally introduced to fupply or retrieve the expenfes occafioned by the former : it being a kind of tacit con-feffion, that the company engaged therein do, in general, exceed the bounds of their refpective fortunes ; and therefore they caft lots to determine upon whom the ruin fhall at prefent fall, that the reft may be faved a little longer. But, taken in any light, it is an offence of the moft alarming nature ; tending by necef-fary confequence to promote public idlenefs, theft, and debau-chery among thofe of a lower clafs : and, among perfons of a fuperior rank, it hath frequently been attended with the fudden ruin and defolation of antient and opulent families, an abandoned proftitution of every principle of honour and virtue, and too often hath ended in felf-murder. To reftrain this pernicious vice, among the inferior fort of people, the ftatute 33 Hen. VIII. c. 9. was made ; which prohibits to all but gentlemen the games of tennis, tables, cards, dice, bowls, and other unlawful diverfions there fpecified[d], unlefs in the time of chriftmas, under pecuniary pains and imprifonment. And the fame law, and alfo the ftatute 30 Geo. II. c. 24. inflict pecuniary penalties, as well upon the mafter of any public houfe wherein fervants are permitted to game, as upon the fervants themfelves who are found to be ga-ming there. But this is not the principal ground of modern

[c] 3 Inft. 199.
[d] Logetting in the fields, flide-thrift or coyting.
fhove-groat, cloyfh-cayls, half-bowl, and

com-

complaint: it is the gaming in high life, that demands the attention of the magiftrate; a paffion to which every valuable confideration is made a facrifice, and which we feem to have inherited from our anceftors the antient Germans; whom Tacitus[c] defcribes to have been bewitched with the fpirit of play to a moft exorbitant degree. " They addict themfelves, fays he, to dice, " (which is wonderful) when fober, and as a ferious employ-" ment; with fuch a mad defire of winning or lofing, that, when " ftript of every thing elfe, they will ftake at laft their libetty, " and their very felves. The lofer goes into a voluntary flavery, " and, though younger and ftronger than his antagonift, fuffers " himfelf to be bound and fold. And this perfeverance in fo bad " a caufe they call the point of honour: *ea eft in re prava per-* " *vicacia, ipfi fidem vocant.*" One would almoft be tempted to think Tacitus was defcribing a modern Englifhman. When men are thus intoxicated with fo frantic a fpirit, laws will be of little avail: becaufe the fame falfe fenfe of honour, that prompts a man to facrifice himfelf, will deter him from appealing to the magiftrate. Yet it is proper that laws fhould be, and be known publicly, that gentlemen may learn what penalties they wilfully incur, and what a confidence they repofe in fharpers; who, if fuccefsful in play, are certain to be paid with honour, or, if unfuccefsful, have it in their power to be ftill greater gainers by informing. For by ftatute 16 Car. II. c. 7. if any perfon by playing or betting fhall lofe more than 100 *l.* at one time, he fhall not be compellable to pay the fame; and the winner fhall forfeit treble the value, one moiety to the king, the other to the informer. The ftatute 9 Ann. c. 14. enacts, that all bonds and other fecurities, given for money won at play, or money lent at the time to play withal, fhall be utterly void: that all mortgages and incumbrances of lands, made upon the fame confideration, fhall be and enure to the ufe of the heir of the mortgagor: that, if any perfon at one time lofes 10 *l.* at play, he may fue the winner, and recover it back by action of debt at law; and, in cafe the lofer does not, any other perfon may fue the win-

<hr />

[c] *de mor. Germ. c.* 24.

ner

ner for treble the fum fo loft; and the plaintiff in either cafe may examine the defendant himfelf upon oath : and that in any of thefe fuits no privilege of parliament fhall be allowed. The ftatute farther enacts, that if any perfon cheats at play, and at one time wins more than 10 *l.* or any valuable thing, he may be indicted thereupon, and fhall forfeit five times the value, fhall be deemed infamous, and fuffer fuch corporal punifhment as in cafe of wilful perjury. By feveral ftatutes of the reign of king George II [f], all private lotteries by tickets, cards, or dice, (and particularly the games of faro, baffet, ace of hearts, hazard, paffage, rolly polly, and all other games with dice, except bag-gammon) are prohibited under a penalty of 200 *l.* for him that fhall erect fuch lotteries, and 50 *l.* a time for the players. Public lotteries, unlefs by authority of parliament, and all manner of ingenious devices, under the denomination of fales or otherwife, which in the end are equivalent to lotteries, were before prohibited by a great variety of ftatutes [g] under heavy pecuniary penalties. But particular defcriptions will ever be lame and deficient, unlefs all games of mere chance are at once prohibited ; the inventions of fharpers being fwifter than the punifhment of the law, which only hunts them from one device to another. The ftatute 13 Geo. II. c. 19. to prevent the multiplicity of horfe races, another fund of gaming, directs that no plates or matches under 50 *l.* value fhall be run, upon penalty of 200 *l.* to be paid by the owner of each horfe running, and 100 *l.* by fuch as advertife the plate. By ftatute 18 Geo. II. c. 34. the ftatute 9 Ann. is farther enforced, and fome deficiences fupplied : the forfeitures of that act may now be recovered in a court of equity ; and, moreover, if any man be convicted upon information or indictment of winning or lofing at any fitting 10 *l,* or 20 *l.* within twenty four hours, he fhall forfeit five times the fum. Thus careful has the legiflature been to prevent this deftructive vice : which may fhew that our laws againft gaming

[f] 12 Geo. II. c. 28. 13 Geo. II. c. 19.   §.56. 10 Ann. c.26. §.109. 8 Geo. I. c. 2.
18 Geo. II. c. 34.   §.36,37. 9 Geo. I. c.19. §. 4, 5.   6 Geo. II.
[g] 10 & 11 W. III. c. 17.   9 Ann. c. 6.   c.35. §. 29, 30.

are

are not fo deficient, as ourfelves and our magiftrates in putting thofe laws in execution.

9. Lastly, there is another offence, fo conftituted by a variety of acts of parliament, which are fo numerous and fo confufed, and the crime itfelf of fo queftionable a nature, that I fhall not detain the reader with many obfervations thereupon. And yet it is an offence which the fportfmen of England feem to think of the higheft importance; and a matter, perhaps the only one, of general and national concern: affociations having been formed all over the kingdom to prevent it's deftructive progrefs. I mean the offence of deftroying fuch beafts and fowls, as are ranked under the denomination of *game:* which, we may remember, was formerly obferved [h], (upon the old principles of the foreft law) to be a trefpafs and offence in all perfons alike, who have not authority from the crown to kill game (which is royal property) by the grant of either a free warren, or at leaft a manor of their own. But the laws, called the game laws, have alfo inflicted additional punifhments (chiefly pecuniary) on perfons guilty of this general offence, unlefs they be people of fuch rank or fortune as is therein particularly fpecified. All perfons therefore, of what property or diftinction foever, that kill game out of their own territories, or even upon their own eftates, without the king's licence expreffed by the grant of a franchife, are guilty of the firft original offence, of encroaching on the royal prerogative. And thofe indigent perfons who do fo, without having fuch rank or fortune as is generally called a qualification, are guilty not only of the original offence, but of the aggravations alfo, created by the ftatutes for preferving the game: which aggravations are fo feverely punifhed, and thofe punifhments fo implacably inflicted, that the offence againft the king is feldom thought of, provided the miferable delinquent can make his peace with the lord of the manor. This offence, thus aggravated, I have ranked under the prefent head, becaufe the only rational footing, upon which we can confider it as a

---

[h] See Vol. II. pag. 417, &c.   [i] Burn's Juftice, tit. Game. §. 3.

crime,

crime, is that in low and indigent perfons it promotes idlenefs, and takes them away from their proper employments and callings; which is an offence againft the public police and oeconomy of the commonwealth.

THE ftatutes for preferving the game are many and various, and not a little obfcure and intricate; it being remarked[i], that in one ftatute only, 5 Ann. c. 14. there is falfe grammar in no fewer than fix places, befides other miftakes: the occafion of which, or what denomination of perfons were probably the penners of thefe ftatutes, I fhall not at prefent enquire. It is in general fufficient to obferve, that the *qualifications* for killing game, as they are ufually called, or more properly the *exemptions* from the penalties inflicted by the ftatute law, are, 1. The having a freehold eftate of 100 *l. per annum*; there being fifty times the property required to enable a man to kill a partridge, as to vote for a knight of the fhire: 2. A leafehold for ninety nine years of 150 *l. per annum*: 3. Being the fon and heir apparent of an efquire (a very loofe and vague defcription) or perfon of fuperior degree: 4. Being the owner, or keeper, of a foreft, park, chafe, or warren. For unqualified perfons tranfgreffing thefe laws, by killing game, keeping engines for that purpofe, or even having game in their cuftody, or for perfons (however qualified) that kill game, or have it in poffeffion, at unfeafonable times of the year, there are various penalties affigned, corporal and pecuniary, by different ftatutes[k]; on any of which, but only on one at a time, the juftices may convict in a fummary way, or profecutions may be carried on at the affifes. And, laftly, by ftatute 28 Geo. II. c. 12. no perfon, however qualified to *kill*, may make merchandize of this valuable privilege, by *felling* or expofing to fale any game, on pain of like forfeiture as if he had no qualification.

[k] Burn's Juftice, tit. Game.

CHAPTER THE FOURTEENTH.

OF HOMICIDE.

IN the ten preceding chapters we have confidered, firft, fuch crimes and mifdemefnors as are more immediately injurious to God and his holy religion; fecondly, fuch as violate or tranfgrefs the law of nations; thirdly, fuch as more efpecially affect the king, the father and reprefentative of his people; fourthly, fuch as more directly infringe the rights of the public or commonwealth, taken in it's collective capacity; and are now, laftly, to take into confideration thofe which in a more peculiar manner affect and injure *individuals* or private fubjects.

WERE thefe injuries indeed confined to individuals only, and did they affect none but their immediate objects, they would fall abfolutely under the notion of private wrongs; for which a fatisfaction would be due only to the party injured: the manner of obtaining which was the fubject of our enquiries in the preceding volume. But the wrongs, which we are now to treat of, are of a much more extenfive confequence; 1. Becaufe it is impoffible they can be committed without a violation of the laws of nature; of the moral as well as political rules of right: 2. Becaufe they include in them almoft always a breach of the public peace: 3. Becaufe by their example and evil tendency they threaten and endanger the fubverfion of all civil fociety.

ciety. Upon thefe accounts it is, that, befides the private fatisfaction due and given in many cafes to the individual, by action
for the private wrong, the government alfo calls upon the offender
to fubmit to public punifhment for the public crime. And the
profecution of thefe offences is always at the fuit and in the name
of the king, in whom by the texture of our conftitution the
jus gladii, or executory power of the law, entirely refides. Thus
too, in the old Gothic conftitution, there was a threefold punifhment inflicted on all delinquents : firft, for the private wrong to
the party injured; fecondly, for the offence againft the king by
difobedience to the laws; and thirdly, for the crime againft the
public by their evil example[a]. Of which we may trace the
groundwork, in what Tacitus tells us of his Germans[b]; that,
whenever offenders were fined, " *pars mulctae regi, vel civitati,*
" *pars ipfi qui vindicatur vel propinquis ejus, exfolvitur.*"

THESE crimes and mifdemefnors againft private fubjects are
principally of three kinds; againft their *perfons*, their *habitations*, and their *property*.

OF crimes injurious to the *perfons* of private fubjects, the
moft principal and important is the offence of taking away that
life, which is the immediate gift of the great creator; and
which therefore no man can be entitled to deprive himfelf or
another of, but in fome manner either exprefsly commanded in,
or evidently deducible from, thofe laws which the creator has
given us; the divine laws, I mean, of either nature or revelation. The fubject therefore of the prefent chapter will be, the
offence of *homicide* or deftroying the life of man, in it's feveral
ftages of guilt, arifing from the particular circumftances of mitigation or aggravation which attend it.

NOW homicide, or the killing of any human creature, is of
three kinds; *juftifiable, excufable*, and *felonious*. The firft has
no fhare of guilt at all; the fecond very little; but the third is

---

[a] Stiernhook. *l. 1. c. 5.*   [b] *de mor. Germ. c. 12.*

the higheſt crime againſt the law of nature, that man is capable of committing.

I. Justifiable homicide is of divers kinds.

1. Such as is owing to ſome unavoidable *neceſſity*, without any will, intention, or deſire, and without any inadvertence or negligence, in the party killing, and therefore without any ſhadow of blame. As, for inſtance, by virtue of ſuch an office as obliges one, in the execution of public juſtice, to put a malefactor to death, who hath forfeited his life by the laws and verdict of his country. This is an act of neceſſity, and even of civil duty; and therefore not only juſtifiable, but commendable, where the law requires it. But the law muſt *require* it, otherwiſe it is not juſtifiable: therefore wantonly to kill the greateſt of malefactors, a felon or a traitor, attainted or outlawed, deliberately, uncompelled, and extrajudicially, is murder[c]. For as Bracton[d] very juſtly obſerves, " *iſtud homicidium ſi fit ex livore,* " *vel delectatione effundendi humanum ſanguinem, licet juſte occidatur* " *iſte, tamen occiſor peccat mortaliter, propter intentionem corrup-* " *tam.*" And farther, if judgment of death be given by a judge not authorized by lawful commiſſion, and execution is done accordingly, the judge is guilty of murder[e]. And upon this account ſir Matthew Hale himſelf, though he accepted the place of a judge of the common pleas under Cromwell's government (ſince it is neceſſary to decide the diſputes of civil property in the worſt of times) yet declined to ſit on the crown ſide at the aſſiſes, and try priſoners; having very ſtrong objections to the legality of the uſurper's commiſſion[f]: a diſtinction perhaps rather too refined; ſince the puniſhment of crimes is at leaſt as neceſſary to ſociety, as maintaining the boundaries of property. Alſo ſuch judgment, when legal, muſt be executed by the proper officer, or his appointed deputy; for no one elſe is *required* by law to do it, which requiſition it is, that juſtifies

c 1 Hal. P. C. 497.   e 1 Hawk. P. C. 70. 1 Hal. P. C. 497.
d *fol.* 120.   f Burnet in his life.

the

the homicide. If another perſon doth it of his own head, it is held to be murder[g]: even though it be the judge himſelf[h]. It muſt farther be executed, *ſervato juris ordine*; it muſt purſue the ſentence of the court. If an officer beheads one who is adjudged to be hanged, or *vice verſa*, it is murder[i]: for he is merely miniſterial, and therefore only juſtified when he acts under the authority and compulſion of the law; but, if a ſheriff changes one kind of death for another, he then acts by his own authority, which extends not to the commiſſion of homicide: and, beſides, this licence might occaſion a very groſs abuſe of his power. The king indeed may remit part of a ſentence; as, in the caſe of treaſon, all but the beheading: but this is no change, no introduction of a new puniſhment; and in the caſe of felony, where the judgment is *to be hanged*, the king (it hath been ſaid) cannot legally order even a peer to be beheaded[k]. But this doctrine will be more fully conſidered in a ſubſequent chapter.

AGAIN: in ſome caſes homicide is juſtifiable, rather by the *permiſſion*, than by the abſolute *command* of the law: either for the *advancement* of public *juſtice*, which without ſuch indemnification would never be carried on with proper vigour; or, in ſuch inſtances where it is committed for the *prevention* of ſome atrocious *crime*, which cannot otherwiſe be avoided.

2. HOMICIDES, committed for the *advancement* of public *juſtice*, are; 1. Where an officer, in the execution of his office, either in a civil or criminal caſe, kills a perſon that aſſaults and reſiſts him[l]. 2. If an officer, or any private perſon, attempts to take a man charged with felony, and is reſiſted; and, in the endeavour to take him, kills him[m]. This is of a piece with the old Gothic conſtitutions, which (Stiernhook informs us[n]) "*furem, ſi aliter capi non poſſet, occidere permittunt.*" 3. In caſe

g 1 Hal. P. C. 501. 1 Hawk. P. C. 70.
h Dalt. Juſt. c. 150.
i Finch. L. 31. 3 Inſt. 52. 1 Hal. P. C. 501.
k 3 Inſt. 52. 212.
l 1 Hal. P. C. 494. 1 Hawk. P. C. 71.
m 1 Hal. P. C. 494.
n *de jure Goth. l.* 3. *c.* 5.

of a riot, or rebellious affembly, the officers endeavouring to difperfe the mob are juftifiable in killing them, both at common law°, and by the riot act, 1 Geo. I. c. 5. 4. Where the prifoners in a gaol, or going to gaol, affault the gaoler or officer, and he in his defence kills any of them, it is juftifiable, for the fake of preventing an efcape P. 5. If trefpaffers in forefts, parks, chafes, or warrens, will not furrender themfelves to the keepers, they may be flain; by virtue of the ftatute 21 Edw. I. ft. 2. *de malefactoribus in parcis*, and 3 & 4 W. & M. c. 10. But, in all thefe cafes, there muft be an apparent neceffity on the officer's fide; *viz.* that the party could not be arrefted or apprehended, the riot could not be fuppreffed, the prifoners could not be kept in hold, the deer-ftealers could not but efcape, unlefs fuch homicide were committed: otherwife, without fuch abfolute neceffity, it is not juftifiable. 6. If the champions in a trial by battel killed either of them the other, fuch homicide was juftifiable, and was imputed to the juft judgment of God, who was thereby prefumed to have decided in favour of the truth q.

3. In the next place, fuch homicide, as is committed for the *prevention* of any forcible and atrocious *crime*, is juftifiable by the law of nature r; and alfo by the law of England, as it ftood fo early as the time of Bracton s, and as it is fince declared by ftatute 24 Hen. VIII. c. 5. If any perfon attempts a robbery or murder of another, or attempts to break open a houfe *in the night time*, (which extends alfo to an attempt to burn it t,) and fhall be killed in fuch attempt, the flayer fhall be acquitted and difcharged. This reaches not to any crime unaccompanied with force, as picking of pockets, or to the breaking open of any houfe *in the day time*, unlefs it carries with it an attempt of robbery alfo. So the Jewifh law, which punifhed no theft with death, makes homicide only juftifiable, in cafe of *nocturnal* houfebreaking: "if a thief be found breaking up, and he be fmitten

° 1 Hal. P. C. 495. 1 Hawk. P. C. 161.   r Puff. L. of N. l. 2. c. 5.
P 1 Hal. P. C. 496.   s *fol.* 155.
q 1 Hawk. P. C. 71.   t 1 Hal. P. C. 488.

"that

"that he die, no blood shall be shed for him : but if the sun
" be risen upon him, there shall blood be shed for him; for he
" should have made full restitution ᵘ." At Athens, if any theft
was committed by night, it was lawful to kill the criminal, if
taken in the fact ᵂ: and, by the Roman law of the twelve tables,
a thief might be slain by night with impunity; or even by day,
if he armed himself with any dangerous weapon ˣ : which
amounts very nearly to the same as is permitted by our own
constitutions.

THE Roman law also justifies homicide, when committed in
defence of the chastity either of oneself or relations ʸ : and so
also, according to Selden ᶻ, stood the law in the Jewish republic.
The English law likewise justifies a woman, killing one who
attempts to ravish her ª : and so too the husband or father may
justify killing a man, who attempts a rape upon his wife or
daughter; but not if he takes them in adultery by consent, for
the one is forcible and felonious, but not the other ᵇ.   And I
make no doubt but the forcibly attempting a crime, of a still
more detestable nature, may be equally resisted by the death of
the unnatural aggressor. For the one uniform principle that runs
through our own, and all other laws, seems to be this : that
where a crime, in itself capital, is endeavoured to be committed
by force, it is lawful to repel that force by the death of the party
attempting. But we must not carry this doctrine to the same vi-
sionary length that Mr Locke does; who holds ᶜ, " that all man-
" ner of force without right upon a man's person, puts him in a
" state of war with the aggressor; and, of consequence, that,
" being in such a state of war, he may lawfully kill him that
" puts him under this unnatural restraint." However just this
conclusion may be in a state of uncivilized nature, yet the law

ᵘ Exod. xxii. 2.
ᵂ Potter. Antiqu. b. 1. c. 24.
ˣ Cic. *pro Milone.* 3. *Ff.* 9. 2. 4.
ʸ " *Divus Hadrianus rescripsit, eum qui*
" *stuprum sibi vel suis inferentem occidit, di-*
" *mittendum.*" (*Ff.* 48. 8. 1.)
ᶻ *de legib. Hebræor. l.* 4. *c.* 3.
ª Bac. Elem. 34. 1 Hawk. P. C. 71.
ᵇ 1 Hal. P. C. 485, 486.
ᶜ Ess. on gov. p. 2. c. 3.

of

of England, like that of every other well-regulated community, is too tender of the public peace, too careful of the lives of the fubjects, to adopt fo contentious a fyftem ; nor will fuffer with impunity any crime to be *prevented* by death, unlefs the fame, if committed, would alfo be *punifhed* by death.

I n thefe inftances of *juftifiable* homicide, you will obferve that the flayer is in no kind of fault whatfoever, not even in the minuteft degree ; and is therefore to be totally acquitted and difcharged, with commendation rather than blame. But that is not quite the cafe in *excufable* homicide, the very name whereof imports fome fault, fome error, or omiffion ; fo trivial however, that the law excufes it from the guilt of felony, though in ftrictnefs it judges it deferving of fome little degree of punifhment.

II. Excusable homicide is of two forts; either *per infortunium,* by mifadventure ; or *fe defendendo,* upon a principle of felf-prefervation. We will firft fee wherein thefe two fpecies of homicide are diftinct, and then wherein they agree.

1. Homicide *per infortunium,* or *mifadventure,* is where a man, doing a lawful act, without any intention of hurt, unfortunately kills another : as where a man is at work with a hatchet, and the head thereof flies off and kills a ftander by ; or, where a perfon, qualified to keep a gun, is fhooting at a mark, and undefignedly kills a man [d] : for the act is lawful, and the effect is merely accidental. So where a parent is moderately correcting his child, a mafter his fervant or fcholar, or an officer punifhing a criminal, and happens to occafion his death, it is only mifadventure ; for the act of correction was lawful : but if he exceeds the bounds of moderation, either in the manner, the inftrument, or the quantity of punifhment, and death enfues, it is manflaughter at leaft, and in fome cafes (according to the circumftances) murder [e] ; for the act of immoderate correction is un-

[d] 1 Hawk. P. C. 73, 74.   [e] 1 Hal. P. C. 473, 474.

lawful.

lawful. Thus by an edict of the emperor Conftantine [f], when the rigor of the Roman law with regard to flaves began to relax and foften, a mafter was allowed to chaftife his flave with rods and imprifonment, and, if death accidentally enfued, he was guilty of no crime : but if he ftruck him with a club or a ftone, and thereby occafioned his death ; or if in any other yet groffer manner " *immoderate fuo jure utatur, tunc reus homicidii fit.*"

B u t, to proceed. A tilt or tournament, the martial diverfion of our anceftors, was however an unlawful act ; and fo are boxing and fwordplaying, the fucceeding amufement of their pofterity : and therefore if a knight in the former cafe, or a gladiator in the latter, be killed, fuch killing is felony of manflaughter. But, if the king command or permit fuch diverfion, it is faid to be only mifadventure ; for then the act is lawful [g]. In like manner as, by the laws both of Athens and Rome, he who killed another in the *pancratium,* or public games, authorized or permitted by the ftate, was not held to be guilty of homicide [h]. Likewife to whip another's horfe, whereby he runs over a child and kills him, is held to be accidental in the rider, for he has done nothing unlawful ; but manflaughter in the perfon who whipped him, for the act was a trefpafs, and at beft a piece of idlenefs, of inevitably dangerous confequence [i]. And in general, if death enfues in confequence of any idle, dangerous, and unlawful fport, as fhooting or cafting ftones in a town, or the barbarous diverfion of cock-throwing, in thefe and fimilar cafes, the flayer is guilty of manflaughter, and not mifadventure only, for thefe are unlawful acts [k].

2. H o m i c i d e in *felf-defence,* or *fe defendendo,* upon a fudden affray, is alfo excufable rather than juftifiable, by the Englifh law. This fpecies of felf-defence muft be diftinguifhed from that juft now mentioned, as calculated to hinder the perpetra-

[f] *Cod. l.* 9. *t.* 14.
[g] 1 Hal. P. C. 473. 1 Hawk. P. C. 74.
[h] Plato *de LL. lib.* 7. *Ff.* 9. 2. 7.
[i] Hawk. P. C. 73.
[k] *Ibid.* 74. 1 Hal. P. C. 472. Foft. 261.

tion of a capital crime; which is not only a matter of excuse, but of justification. But the self-defence, which we are now speaking of, is that whereby a man may protect himself from an assault, or the like, in the course of a sudden brawl or quarrel, by killing him who assaults him. And this is what the law expresses by the word *chance-medley*, or (as some rather chuse to write it) *chaud-medley*; the former of which in it's etymology signifies a *casual* affray, the latter an affray in the *heat* of blood or passion: both of them of pretty much the same import; but the former is in common speech too often erroneously applied to any manner of homicide by misadventure; whereas it appears by the statute 24 Hen. VIII. c. 5. and our antient books[1], that it is properly applied to such killing, as happens in self-defence upon a sudden rencounter[m]. This right of natural defence does not imply a right of attacking: for, instead of attacking one another for injuries past or impending, men need only have recourse to the proper tribunals of justice. They cannot therefore legally exercise this right of preventive defence, but in sudden and violent cases; when certain and immediate suffering would be the consequence of waiting for the assistance of the law. Wherefore, to excuse homicide by the plea of self-defence, it must appear that the slayer had no other possible means of escaping from his assailant.

I n some cases this species of homicide (upon *chance-medley* in self-defence) differs but little from manslaughter, which also happens frequently upon *chance-medley* in the proper legal sense of the word[n]. But the true criterion between them seems to be this: when both parties are actually combating at the time when the mortal stroke is given, the slayer is then guilty of manslaughter; but if the slayer hath not begun to fight, or (having begun) endeavours to decline any farther struggle, and afterwards, being closely pressed by his antagonist, kills him to avoid his own destruction, this is homicide excusable by self-defence[o]. For which reason the law requires, that the person, who kills another

---

[1] Staundf. P. C. 16.
[m] 3 Inst. 55. 57. Fost. 275, 276.

[n] 3 Inst. 55.
[o] Fost. 277.

in his own defence, fhould have retreated as far as he conveniently or fafely can, to avoid the violence of the affault, before he turns upon his affailant; and that, not fictitioufly, or in order to watch his opportunity, but from a real tendernefs of fhedding his brother's blood. And though it may be cowardice, in time of war between two independent nations, to flee from an enemy; yet between two fellow fubjects the law countenances no fuch point of honour: becaufe the king and his courts are the *vindices injuriarum*, and will give to the party wronged all the fatisfaction he deferves [p]. In this the civil law alfo agrees with ours, or perhaps goes rather farther; " *qui cum aliter tueri fe non poffunt,* " *damni culpam dederint, innoxii funt* [q]. The party affaulted muft therefore flee as far as he conveniently can, either by reafon of fome wall, ditch, or other impediment; or as far as the fiercenefs of the affault will permit him [r]: for it may be fo fierce as not to allow him to yield a ftep, without manifeft danger of his life, or enormous bodily harm; and then in his defence he may kill his affailant inftantly. And this is the doctrine of univerfal juftice [s], as well as of the municipal law.

AND, as the *manner* of the defence, fo is alfo the *time* to be confidered: for if the perfon affaulted does not fall upon the aggreffor till the affray is over, or when he is running away, this is revenge and not defence. Neither, under the colour of felf defence, will the law permit a man to fcreen himfelf from the guilt of deliberate murder: for if two perfons, A and B, agree to fight a duel, and A gives the firft onfet, and B retreats as far as he fafely can, and then kills A, this is murder; becaufe of the previous malice and concerted defign [t]. But if A upon a fudden quarrel affaults B firft, and upon B's returning the affault, A really and *bona fide* flees; and, being driven to the wall, turns again upon B and kills him; this may be *fe defendendo* according to fome of our writers [u]:

[p] 1 Hal. P. C. 481. 483.   [s] Puff. b. 2. c. 5. §. 13.

[q] *Ff.* 9. 2. 45.   [t] 1 Hal. P. C. 479.

[r] 1 Hal. P. C. 483.   [u] 1 Hal. P. C. 482.

though others [w] have thought this opinion too favourable; inasmuch as the neceffity, to which he is at laft reduced, originally arofe from his own fault. Under this excufe of felf-defence, the principal civil and natural relations are comprehended; therefore mafter and fervant, parent and child, hufband and wife, killing an affailant in the neceffary defence of each other refpectively, are excufed; the act of the relation affifting being conftrued the fame as the act of the party himfelf [x].

THERE is one fpecies of homicide *fe defendendo*, where the party flain is equally innocent as he who occafions his death : and yet this homicide is alfo excufable from the great univerfal principle of felf-prefervation, which prompts every man to fave his own life preferably to that of another, where one of them muft inevitably perifh. As, among others, in that cafe mentioned by lord Bacon [y], where two perfons, being fhipwrecked, and getting on the fame plank, but finding it not able to fave them both, one of them thrufts the other from it, whereby he is drowned. He who thus preferves his own life at the expence of another man's, is excufable though unavoidable neceffity, and the principle of felf-defence; fince their both remaining on the fame weak plank is a mutual, though innocent, attempt upon, and an endangering of, each other's life.

LET us next take a view of thofe circumftances wherein thefe two fpecies of homicide, by mifadventure and felf-defence, agree; and thofe are in their blame and punifhment. For the law fets fo high a value upon the life of a man, that it always intends fome mifbehaviour in the perfon who takes it away, unlefs by the command or exprefs permiffion of the law. In the cafe of mifadventure, it prefumes negligence, or at leaft a want of fufficient caution in him who was fo unfortunate as to commit it; who therefore is not altogether faultlefs [a]. And as to the neceffity which excufes a man who kills another *fe defendendo,*

[w] 1 Hawk. P. C. 75.   [y] Elem. c. 5. See alfo 1 Hawk. P. C. 73.
[x] 1 Hal. P. C. 484.   [z] 1 Hawk. P. C. 72.

lord

lord Bacon[a] entitles it *necessitas culpabilis*, and thereby distinguishes
it from the former necessity of killing a thief or a malefactor.
For the law intends that the quarrel or assault arose from some
unknown wrong, or some provocation, either in word or deed:
and since in quarrels both parties may be, and usually are, in
some fault; and it scarce can be tried who was originally in the
wrong; the law will not hold the survivor intirely guiltless. But
it is clear, in the other case, that where I kill a thief that breaks
into my house, the original default can never be upon my side.
The law besides may have a farther view, to make the crime of
homicide more odious, and to caution men how they venture to
kill another upon their own private judgment; by ordaining,
that he who slays his neighbour, without an express warrant
from the law so to do, shall in no case be absolutely free from
guilt.

NOR is the law of England singular in this respect. Even
the slaughter of enemies required a solemn purgation among the
Jews; which implies that the death of a man, however it happens, will leave some stain behind it. And the mosaical law[b]
appointed certain cities of refuge for him " who killed his neigh-
" bour unawares; as if a man goeth into the wood with his
" neighbour to hew wood, and his hand fetcheth a stroke with
" the ax to cut down a tree, and the head slippeth from the
" helve, and lighteth upon his neighbour that he die, he shall
" flee unto one of these cities and live." But it seems he was
not held wholly blameless, any more than in the English law;
since the avenger of blood might slay him before he reached his
asylum, or if he afterwards stirred out of it till the death of the
high priest. In the imperial law likewise[c] casual homicide was
excused, by the indulgence of the emperor signed with his own
sign manual, " *adnotatione principis:*" otherwise the death of a
man, however committed, was in some degree punishable.
Among the Greeks[d] homicide by misfortune was expiated by

[a] Elem. c. 5.
[b] Numb. c. 35. and Deut. c. 19.
[c] Cod. 9. 16. 5.
[d] Plato *de Leg. lib.* 9.

voluntary

volutary banifhment for a year [e]. In Saxony a fine is paid to the kindred of the flain; which alfo, among the weftern Goths, was little inferior to that of voluntary homicide [f]: and in France [g] no perfon is ever abfolved in cafes of this nature, without a largefs to the poor, and the charge of certain maffes for the foul of the party killed.

THE penalty inflicted by our laws is faid by fir Edward Coke to have been antiently no lefs than death [h]; which however is with reafon denied by later and more accurate writers [i]. It feems rather to have confifted in a forfeiture, fome fay of all the goods and chattels, others of only part of them, by way of fine or *weregild* [k]: which was probably difpofed of, as in France, *in pios ufus*, according to the humane fuperftition of the times, for the benefit of *his* foul, who was thus fuddenly fent to his account, with all his imperfections on his head. But that reafon having long ceafed, and the penalty (efpecially if a total forfeiture) growing more fevere than was intended, in proportion as perfonal property has become more confiderable, the delinquent has now, and has had as early as our records will reach [l], a pardon and writ of reftitution of his goods as a matter of courfe and right, only paying for fuing out the fame [m]. And indeed, to prevent this expenfe, in cafes where the death has notorioufly happened by mifadventure or in felf-defence, the judges will ufually permit (if not direct) a general verdict of acquittal [n].

III. FELONIOUS homicide is an act of a very different nature from the former, being the killing of a human creature, of any

---

[e] To this expiation by banifhment the fpirit of Patroclus in Homer may be thought to allude, when he reminds Achilles, in the twenty third Iliad, that, when a child, he was obliged to flee his country for cafually killing his playfellow; " νηπιος, ἀκ ἰθελων."

[f] Stiernh. *de jure Goth. l.* 3. *c.* 4.

[g] De-Mornay on the digeft.

[h] 2 Inft. 148. 315.

[i] 1 Hal. P. C. 425. 1 Hawk. P. C. 75. Foft. 282, &c.

[k] Foft. 287.

[l] Foft. 283.

[m] 2 Hawk. P. C. 381.

[n] Foft. 288.

age or fex, without juftification or excufe. This may be done, either by killing one's felf, or another man.

SELF-MURDER, the pretended heroifm, but real cowardice, of the Stoic philofophers, who deftroyed themfelves to avoid thofe ills which they had not the fortitude to endure, though the attempting it feems to be countenanced by the civil law [o], yet was punifhed by the Athenian law with cutting off the hand, which committed the defperate deed [p]. And alfo the law of England wifely and religioufly confiders, that no man hath a power to deftroy life, but by commiffion from God, the author of it : and, as the fuicide is guilty of a double offence ; one fpiritual, in invading the prerogative of the Almighty, and rufhing into his immediate prefence uncalled for ; the other temporal, againft the king, who hath an intereft in the prefervation of all his fub-jects ; the law has therefore ranked this among the higheft crimes, making it a peculiar fpecies of felony, a felony commit-ted on onefelf. A *felo de fe* therefore is he that deliberately puts an end to his own exiftence, or commits any unlawful malicious act, the confequence of which is his own death : as if, attempt-ing to kill another, he runs upon his antagonift's fword ; or, fhooting at another, the gun burfts and kills himfelf [q]. The party muft be of years of difcretion, and in his fenfes, elfe it is no crime. But this excufe ought not to be ftrained to that length, to which our coroners' juries are apt to carry it, *viz.* that the very act of fuicide is an evidence of infanity ; as if every man who acts contrary to reafon, had no reafon at all : for the fame argument would prove every other criminal *non compos*, as well as the felf-murderer. The law very rationally judges, that every melancholy or hypochondriac fit does not deprive a man of the capacity of difcerning right from wrong ; which is neceffary, as was obferved in a former chapter [r], to form a legal excufe. And

---

[o] " *Si quis impatientia doloris, aut taedio* " *vitae, aut morbo, aut furore, aut pudore,* " *mori maluit, non animadvertatur in eum.*" *Ff.* 49. 16. 6.

[p] Pott. Antiqu. b. 1. c. 26.
[q] 1 Hawk. P. C. 68.   1 Hal. P. C. 413.
[r] See pag. 24.

there-

therefore, if a real lunatic kills himfelf in a lucid interval, he is a *felo de fe* as much as another man [a].

BUT now the queftion follows, what punifhment can human laws inflict on one who has withdrawn himfelf from their reach? They can only act upon what he has left behind him, his reputation and fortune : on the former, by an ignominious burial in the highway, with a ftake driven through his body ; on the latter, by a forfeiture of all his goods and chattels to the king : hoping that his care for either his own reputation, or the welfare of his family, would be fome motive to reftrain him from fo defperate and wicked an act. And it is obfervable, that this forfeiture has relation to the time of the act done in the felon's lifetime, which was the caufe of his death. As if hufband and wife be poffeffed jointly of a term of years in land, and the hufband drowns himfelf; the land fhall be forfeited to the king, and the wife fhall not have it by furvivorfhip. For by the act of cafting himfelf into the water he forfeits the term ; which gives a title to the king, prior to the wife's title by furvivorfhip, which could not accrue till the inftant of her hufband's death [b]. And, though it muft be owned that the letter of the law herein borders a little upon feverity, yet it is fome alleviation that the power of mitigation is left in the breaft of the fovereign, who upon this (as on all other occafions) is reminded by the oath of his office to execute judgment in mercy.

THE other fpecies of criminal homicide is that of killing another man. But in this there are alfo degrees of guilt, which divide the offence into *manflaughter*, and *murder*. The difference between which may be partly collected from what has been incidentally mentioned in the preceding articles, and principally confifts in this, that manflaughter arifes from the fudden heat of the paffions, murder from the wickednefs of the heart.

[a] 1 Hal. P. C. 412.   [b] Finch. L. 216.

1. MAN-

1. MANSLAUGHTER is therefore thus defined [u], the unlawful killing of another, without malice either exprefs or implied: which may be either voluntarily, upon a fudden heat; or involuntarily, but in the commiffion of fome unlawful act. Thefe were called in the Gothic conftitutions " *homicidia vulgaria; quae* " *aut cafu, aut etiam fponte committuntur, fed in fubitaneo quodam* " *iracundiae calore et impetu* [u]." And hence it follows, that in manflaughter there can be no acceffories before the fact; becaufe it muft be done without premeditation.

As to the firft, or *voluntary* branch: if upon a fudden quarrel two perfons fight, and one of them kills the other, this is manflaughter: and fo it is, if they upon fuch an occafion go out and fight in a field; for this is one continued act of paffion [x]: and the law pays that regard to human frailty, as not to put a hafty and a deliberate act upon the fame footing with regard to guilt. So alfo if a man be greatly provoked, as by pulling his nofe, or other great indignity, and immediately kills the aggreffor, though this is not excufable *fe defendendo*, fince there is no abfolute neceffity for doing it to preferve himfelf; yet neither is it murder, for there is no previous malice; but it is manflaughter [y]. But in this, and in every other cafe of homicide upon provocation, if there be a fufficient cooling-time for paffion to fubfide and reafon to interpofe, and the perfon fo provoked afterwards kills the other, this is deliberate revenge and not heat of blood, and accordingly amounts to murder [z]. So, if a man takes another in the act of adultery with his wife, and kills him directly upon the fpot; though this was allowed by the laws of Solon [a], as likewife by the Roman civil law, (if the adulterer was found in the hufband's own houfe [b]) and alfo among the antient Goths [c]; yet in England it is not abfolutely ranked in the clafs

[u] 1 Hal. P. C. 466.
[w] Stiernh. *de jure Goth. l.* 3. *c.* 4.
[x] 1 Hawk. P. C. 82.
[y] Kelyng. 135.

[z] Foft 296.
[a] Plutarch. *in vit. Solon.*
[b] *Ff.* 48. 5. 24.
[c] Stiernh. *de jure Goth. l.* 3. *c.* 2.

of juftifiable homicide, as in cafe of a forcible rape, but it is manflaughter [d]. It is however the loweft degree of it: and therefore in fuch a cafe the court directed the burning in the hand to be gently inflicted, becaufe there could not be a greater provocation [e]. Manflaughter therefore on a fudden provocation differs from excufable homicide *fe defendendo* in this: that in one cafe there is an apparent neceffity, for felf-prefervation, to kill the aggreffor; in the other no neceffity at all, being only a fudden act of revenge.

THE fecond branch, or *involuntary* manflaughter, differs alfo from homicide excufable by mifadventure, in this; that mif-adventure always happens in confequence of a lawful act, but this fpecies of manflaughter in confequence of an unlawful one. As if two perfons play at fword and buckler, unlefs by the king's command, and one of them kills the other: this is manflaughter, becaufe the original act was unlawful; but it is not murder, for the one had no intent to do the other any perfonal mifchief [f]. So where a perfon does an act, lawful in itfelf, but in an unlaw-ful manner, and without due caution and circumfpection: as when a workman flings down a ftone or piece of timber into the ftreet, and kills a man; this may be either mifadventure, man-flaughter, or murder, according to the circumftances under which the original act was done: if it were in a country village, where few paffengers are, and he calls out to all people to have a care, it is mifadventure only: but if it were in London, or other po-pulous town, where people are continually paffing, it is man-flaughter, though he gives loud warning [g]; and murder, if he knows of their paffing and gives no warning at all, for then it is malice againft all mankind [h]. And, in general, when an invo-luntary killing happens in confequence of an unlawful act, it will be either murder or manflaughter according to the nature of the act which occafioned it. If it be in profecution of a felonious

[d] 1 Hal. P. C. 486.
[e] Sir T. Raym. 212.
[f] 3 Inft. 56.

[g] Kel. 40.
[h] 3 Inft. 57.

intent,

intent, it will be murder; but if no more was intended than a mere trefpafs, it will only amount to manflaughter[i].

NEXT, as to the *punifhment* of this degree of homicide: the crime of manflaughter amounts to felony, but within the benefit of clergy; and the offender fhall be burnt in the hand, and forfeit all his goods and chattels.

BUT there is one fpecies of manflaughter, which is punifhed as murder, the benefit of clergy being taken away from it by ftatute; namely, the offence of mortally *ftabbing* another, though done upon fudden provocation. For by ftatute 1 Jac. I. c. 8. when one thrufts or ftabs another, not then having a weapon drawn, or who hath not then firft ftricken the party ftabbing, fo that he dies thereof within fix months after, the offender fhall not have the benefit of clergy, though he did it not of malice aforethought. This ftatute was made on account of the frequent quarrels and ftabbings with fhort daggers, between the Scotch and the Englifh, at the acceffion of James the firft[k]; and, being therefore of a temporary nature, ought to have expired with the mifchief, which it meant to remedy. For, in point of folid and fubftantial juftice, it cannot be faid that the mode of killing, whether by ftabbing, ftrangling or fhooting, can either extenuate or enhance the guilt: unlefs where, as in the cafe of poifoning, it carries with it an internal evidence of cool and deliberate malice. But the benignity of the law hath conftrued the ftatute fo favourably in behalf of the fubject, and fo ftrictly when againft him, that the offence of ftabbing ftands almoft upon the fame footing, as it did at the common law[l]. Thus, (not to repeat the cafes before-mentioned, of ftabbing an adulterefs, &c. which are barely manflaughter, as at common law) in the conftruction of this ftatute it hath been doubted, whether, if the deceafed had ftruck at all before the mortal blow given, this takes it out of the ftatute, though in the preceding quarrel the

[i] Fofter. 258.
[k] 1 Lord Raym. 140.
[l] Foft. 299, 300.

ſtabber had given the firſt blow; and it ſeems to be the better opinion, that this is not within the ſtatute[m]. Alſo it hath been reſolved, that the killing a man by throwing a hammer or other weapon is not within the ſtatute; and whether a ſhot with a piſtol be ſo or not, is doubted[n]. But if the party ſlain had a cudgel in his hand, or had thrown a pot or a bottle, or diſcharged a piſtol at the party ſtabbing, this is a ſufficient having a weapon drawn on his ſide within the words of the ſtatute[o].

2. WE are next to conſider the crime of deliberate and wilful *murder*; a crime at which human nature ſtarts, and which is I believe puniſhed almoſt univerſally throughout the world with death. The words of the moſaical law (over and above the general precept to Noah[p], that "whoſo ſheddeth man's blood, by "man ſhall his blood be ſhed") are very emphatical in prohibiting the pardon of murderers[q]. "Moreover ye ſhall take no ſa-"tisfaction for the life of a murderer, who is guilty of death, "but he ſhall ſurely be put to death; for the land cannot be "cleanſed of the blood that is ſhed therein, but by the blood "of him that ſhed it." And therefore our law has provided one courſe of proſecution, (that by appeal, of which hereafter) wherein the king himſelf is excluded the power of pardoning murder: ſo that, were the king of England ſo inclined, he could not imitate that Poliſh monarch mentioned by Puffendorf[r]; who thought proper to remit the penalties of murder to all the nobility, in an edict with this arrogant preamble, "*nos, divini* "*juris rigorem moderantes, &c.*" But let us now conſider the definition of this great offence.

THE name of *murder* was antiently applied only to the ſecret killing of another[s]; (which the word, *moërda*, ſignifies in the Teutonic language[t]) and it was defined "*homicidium quod nullo*

[m] Foſt. 301. 1 Hawk. P. C. 77.　　　[q] Numb. xxxv. 31.
[n] 1 Hal. P. C. 470.　　　[r] L. of N. b. 8. c. 3.
[o] 1 Hawk. P. C. 77.　　　[s] *Dialog. de Scacch. l.* 1. *c.* 10.
[p] Gen. ix. 6.　　　[t] Stiernh. *de jure Sueon. l.* 3. *c.* 3.

"*vidente,*

" *vidente, nullo fciente, clam perpetratur*[u]:" for which the vill
wherein it was committed, or (if that were too poor) the whole
hundred, was liable to a heavy amercement; which amercement
itfelf was alfo denominated *murdrum*[w]. This was an antient ufage
among the Goths in Sweden and Denmark; who fuppofed the
neighbourhood, unlefs they produced the murderer, to have perpetrated or at leaft connived at the murder[x]: and, according to
Bracton[y], was introduced into this kingdom by king Canute, to
prevent his countrymen the Danes from being privily murdered
by the Englifh; and was afterwards continued by William the
conqueror, for the like fecurity to his own Normans[z]. And
therefore if, upon inquifition had, it appeared that the perfon
found flain was an Englifhman, (the prefentment whereof was
denominated *englefcherie*[a]) the country feems to have been excufed from this burthen. But, this difference being totally
abolifhed by ftatute 14 Edw. III. c. 4. we muft now (as is obferved by Staundforde[b]) define murder in quite another manner,
without regarding whether the party flain was killed openly or
fecretly, or whether he was of Englifh or foreign extraction.

MURDER is therefore now thus defined, or rather defcribed,
by fir Edward Coke[c]; " when a perfon, of found memory and
" difcretion, unlawfully killeth any reafonable creature in being
" and under the king's peace, with malice aforethought, either
" exprefs or implied." The beft way of examining the nature
of this crime will be by confidering the feveral branches of this
definition.

FIRST, it muft be committed by *a perfon of found memory and
difcretion:* for a lunatic or infant, as was formerly obferved, are
incapable of committing any crime; unlefs in fuch cafes where

[u] Glanv. *l.* 14. *c.* 3.
[w] Bract. *l.* 3. *tr.* 2. *c.* 15. §. 7. Stat. Marlbr.
c. 26. Foft. 281.
[x] Stiernh. *l.* 3. *c.* 4.
[y] *l.* 3. *tr.* 2. *c.* 15.

[z] 1 Hal. P. C. 447.
[a] Bract. *ubi fupr.*
[b] P. C. *l.* 1. *c.* 10.
[c] 3 Inft. 47.

they

they ſhew a conſciouſneſs of doing wrong, and of courſe a diſcretion, or diſcernment, between good and evil.

NEXT, it happens when a perſon of ſuch ſound diſcretion
unlawfully killeth. The unlawfulneſs ariſes from the killing without warrant or excuſe : and there muſt alſo be an actual killing
to conſtitute murder; for a bare aſſault, with intent to kill, is
only a great miſdemeſnor, though formerly it was held to be
murder [d]. The killing may be by poiſoning, ſtriking, ſtarving,
drowning, and a thouſand other forms of death, by which human
nature may be overcome. Of theſe the moſt deteſtable of all is
poiſon; becauſe it can of all others be the leaſt prevented either
by manhood or forethought [e]. And therefore by the ſtatute
22 Hen.VIII. c. 9. it was made treaſon, and a more grievous and
lingering kind of death was inflicted on it than the common law
allowed; namely, boiling to death : but this act did not live
long, being repealed by 1 Edw.VI. c. 12. There was alſo, by
the antient common law, one ſpecies of killing held to be murder, which is hardly ſo at this day, nor has there been an inſtance wherein it has been held to be murder for many ages
paſt [f] : I mean by bearing falſe witneſs againſt another, with
an expreſs premeditated deſign to take away his life, ſo as the
innocent perſon be condemned and executed [g]. The Gothic
laws puniſhed in this caſe, both the judge, the witneſſes, and
the proſecutor; " *peculiari poena judicem puniunt; peculiari*
" *teſtes, quorum fides judicem ſeduxit; peculiari denique et maxima*
" *auctorem, ut homicidam* [h]." And, among the Romans, the *lex
Cornelia, de ſicariis*, puniſhed the falſe witneſs with death, as
being guilty of a ſpecies of aſſaſſination [i]. And there is no doubt

[d] 1 Hal. P. C. 425.

[e] 3 Inſt. 48.

[f] Foſt. 132. In the caſe of Macdaniel
and Berry, reported by ſir Michael Foſter,
though the attorney general declined to ar-
gue this point of law, I have grounds to believe it was not from any apprehenſion that
the point was not maintainable, but from

other prudential reaſons. Nothing therefore ſhould be concluded from the waiving
of that proſecution.

[g] Mirror. c. 1. §. 9. Britt. c.5. Bracton.
l. 3. *c.* 4.

[h] Stiernh. *de jure Goth. l.* 3. *c.* 3.

[i] *Ff.* 48. 8. 1.

but

but this is equally murder *in foro confcientiae* as killing with a
fword; though the modern law (to avoid the danger of deterring witneffes from giving evidence upon capital profecutions,
if it muft be at the peril of their own lives) has not yet punifhed it as fuch. If a man however does fuch an act, of which
the probable confequence may be, and eventually is, death;
fuch killing may be murder, although no ftroke be ftruck by
himfelf: as was the cafe of the unnatural fon, who expofed
his fick father to the air, againft his will, by reafon whereof he
died[k]; and, of the harlot, who laid her child in an orchard,
where a kite ftruck it and killed it[l]. So too, if a man hath a
beaft that is ufed to do mifchief; and he, knowing it, *fuffers* it
to go abroad, and it kills a man; even this is manflaughter in
the owner: but if he had purpofely *turned it loofe*, though
barely to frighten people and make what is called fport, it is
with us (as in the Jewifh law) as much murder, as if he had
incited a bear or a dog to worry them[m]. If a phyfician or furgeon gives his patient a potion or plaifter to cure him, which
contrary to expectation kills him, this is neither murder, nor
manflaughter, but mifadventure; and he fhall not be punifhed
criminally, however liable he might formerly have been to a
civil action for neglect or ignorance[n]: but it hath been holden,
that if it be not a *regular* phyfician or furgeon, who adminifters
the medicine or performs the operation, it is manflaughter at
the leaft[o]. Yet fir Matthew Hale very juftly queftions the law
of this determination; fince phyfic and falves were in ufe before licenfed phyficians and furgeons: wherefore he treats this
doctrine as apocryphal, and fitted only to gratify and flatter li-
centiates and doctors in phyfic; though it may be of ufe to
make people cautious and wary, how they meddle too much in
fo dangerous an employment[p]. In order alfo to make the killing murder, it is requifite that the party die within a year and
a day after the ftroke received, or caufe of death adminiftred;

---

[k] 1 Hawk. P. C. 78.
[l] 1 Hal. P. C. 432.
[m] *Ibid.* 431.

[n] Mirr. c. 4. §. 16. See Vol. III. pag. 122.
[o] Britt. c. 5. 4 Init. 251.
[p] 1 Hal. P. C. 430.

in

in the computation of which, the whole day upon which the the hurt was done fhall be reckoned the firft [q].

FARTHER; the perfon killed muft be " *a reafonable creature* " *in being, and under the king's peace,*" at the time of the killing. Therefore to kill an alien, a Jew, or an outlaw, who are all under the king's peace or protection, is as much murder as to kill the moft regular born Englifhman; except he be an alien-enemy, in time of war [r]. To kill a child in it's mother's womb, is now no murder, but a great mifprifion: but if the child be born alive, and dieth by reafon of the potion or bruifes it recei-ved in the womb, it is murder in fuch as adminiftred or gave them [s]. But, as there is one cafe where it is difficult to prove the child's being born alive, namely, in the cafe of the murder of baftard children by the unnatural mother, it is enacted by ftatute 21 Jac. I. c. 27. that if any woman be delivered of a child, which if born alive fhould by law be a baftard; and en-deavours privately to conceal it's death, by burying the child or the like; the mother fo offending fhall fuffer death as in the cafe of murder, unlefs fhe can prove by one witnefs at leaft that the child was actually born dead. This law, which favours pretty ftrongly of feverity, in making the concealment of the death almoft conclufive evidence of the child's being murdered by the mother, is neverthelefs to be alfo met with in the cri-minal codes of many other nations of Europe; as the Danes, the Swedes, and the French [t]: but I apprehend it has of late years been ufual with us in England, upon trials for this offence, to require fome fort of prefumptive evidence that the child was born alive, before the other conftrained prefumption (that the child, whofe death is concealed, was therefore killed by it's parent) is admitted to convict the prifoner.

LASTLY, the killing muft be committed *with malice afore-thought,* to make it the crime of murder. This is the grand cri-

---

[q] 1 Hawk. P. C. 79.
[r] 3 Inft. 50. 1 Hal. P. C. 433.

[s] 3 Inft. 50. 1 Hawk. P. C. 80.
[t] See Barrington on the ftatutes. 425.

terion, which now diftinguifhes murder from other killing : and this malice prepenfe, *malitia praecogitata*, is not fo properly fpite or malevolence to the deceafed in particular, as any evil defign in general ; the dictate of a wicked, depraved, and malignant heart[u]; *un difpofition a faire un male chofe*[w]. and it may be either *exprefs*, or *implied* in law. Exprefs malice is when one, with a fedate deliberate mind and formed defign, doth kill another : which formed defign is evidenced by external circumftances dif-covering that inward intention ; as lying in wait, antecedent menaces, former grudges, and concerted fchemes to do him fome bodily harm[x]. This takes in the cafe of deliberate duelling, where both parties meet avowedly with an intent to murder : thinking it their duty, as gentlemen, and claiming it as their right, to wanton with their own lives and thofe of their fellow creatures ; without any warrant or authority from any power either divine or human, but in direct contradiction to the laws both of God and man : and therefore the law has juftly fixed the crime and punifhment of murder, on them, and on their feconds alfo[y]. Yet it requires fuch a degree of paffive valour, to combat the dread of even undeferved contempt, ari-fing from the falfe notions of honour too generally received in Europe, that the ftrongeft prohibitions and penalties of the law will never be intirely effectual to eradicate this unhappy cuftom ; till a method be found out of compelling the original aggreffor to make fome other fatisfaction to the affronted party, which the world fhall efteem equally reputable, as that which is now given at the hazard of the life and fortune, as well of the perfon infulted, as of him who hath given the infult. Alfo, if even upon a fudden provocation one beats another in a cruel and un-ufual manner, fo that he dies, though he did not intend his death, yet he is guilty of murder by exprefs malice ; that is, by an exprefs evil defign, the genuine fenfe of *malitia*. As when a park-keeper tied a boy, that was ftealing wood, to a horfe's tail, and dragged him along the park ; when a mafter corrected his

[u] Fofter. 256.
[w] 2 Roll. Rep. 461.

[x] 1 Hal. P. C. 451.
[y] 1 Hawk. P. C. 82.

fervant

fervant with an iron bar, and a fchoolmafter ftamped on his
fcholar's belly; fo that each of the fufferers died; thefe were
juftly held to be murders, becaufe the correction being exceffive,
and fuch as could not proceed but from a bad heart, it was equivalent to a deliberate act of flaughter². Neither fhall he be
guilty of a lefs crime, who kills another in confequence of fuch
a wilful act, as fhews him to be an enemy to all mankind in
general; as going deliberately with a horfe ufed to ftrike, or dif-
charging a gun, among a multitude of people³. So if a man
refolves to kill the next man he meets, and does kill him, it is
murder, although he knew him not; for this is univerfal malice. And, if two or more come together to do an unlawful act
againft the king's peace, of which the probable confequence
might be bloodfhed; as to beat a man, to commit a riot, or to
rob a park; and one of them kills a man; it is murder in them
all, becaufe of the unlawful act, the *malitia praecogitata*, or evil
intended beforehand ᵇ.

ALSO in many cafes where no malice is expreffed, the law
will imply it: as, where a man wilfully poifons another, in fuch
a deliberate act the law prefumes malice, though no particular
emnity can be proved ᶜ. And if a man kills another fuddenly,
without any, or without a confiderable, provocation, the law
implies malice; for no perfon, unlefs of an abandoned heart,
would be guilty of fuch an act, upon a flight or no apparent
caufe. No affront, by words, or geftures only, is a fufficient
provocation, fo as to excufe or extenuate fuch acts of violence as
manifeftly endanger the life of another ᵈ. But if the perfon fo
provoked had unfortunately killed the other, by beating him in
fuch a manner as fhewed only an intent to chaftife and not to
kill him, the law fo far confiders the provocation of contumelious behaviour, as to adjudge it only manflaughter, and not
murder ᵉ. In like manner if one kills an officer of juftice, either

---

ᶻ 1 Hal. P. C. 454. 47 .4 .

ᵃ 1 Hawk. P. C. 74.

ᵇ *Ibid.* 84.

ᶜ 1 Hal. P. C. 455.

ᵈ 1 Hawk. P. C. 82. 1 Hal. P. C. 455, 456.

ᵉ Foft. 291.

civil

civil or criminal, in the execution of his duty, or any of his assistants endeavouring to conserve the peace, or any private person endeavouring to suppress an affray or apprehend a felon, knowing his authority or the intention with which he interposes, the law will imply malice, and the killer shall be guilty of murder[f]. And if one intends to do another felony, and undesignedly kills a man, this is also murder[g]. Thus if one shoots at A and misses *him*, but kills B, this is murder; because of the previous felonious intent, which the law transfers from one to the other. The same is the case, where one lays poison for A; and B, against whom the prisoner had no malicious intent, takes it, and it kills him; this is likewise murder[h]. It were endless to go through all the cases of homicide, which have been adjudged either expressly, or impliedly, malicious: these therefore may suffice as a specimen; and we may take it for a general rule, that all homicide is malicious, and of course amounts to murder, unless where *justified* by the command or permission of the law; *excused* on a principle of accident or self-preservation; or *alleviated* into manslaughter, by being either the involuntary consequence of some act, not strictly lawful, or (if voluntary) occasioned by some sudden and sufficiently violent provocation. And all these circumstances of justification, excuse, or alleviation, it is incumbent upon the prisoner to make out, to the satisfaction of the court and jury: the latter of whom are to decide whether the circumstances alleged be proved to have actually existed; the former, how far they extend to take away or mitigate the guilt. For all homicide is presumed to be malicious, until the contrary appeareth upon evidence[i].

THE punishment of murder, and that of manslaughter, were formerly one and the same; both having the benefit of clergy: so that none but unlearned persons, who least knew the guilt of

[f] 1 Hal. P. C. 457. Foster. 308, &c.
[g] 1 Hal. P. C. 465.
[h] 1 Hal. P. C. 466.
[i] Fost. 255.

it, were put to death for this enormous crime [k]. But now, by statute 23 Hen. VIII. c. 1. and 1 Edw. VI. c. 12. the benefit of clergy is taken away from murder though malice prepenfe. In atrocious cafes it was frequently ufual for the court to direct the murderer, after execution, to be hung upon a gibbet in chains, near the place where the fact was committed : but this was no part of the legal judgment; and the like is ftill fometimes practiced in the cafe of notorious thieves. This, being quite contrary to the exprefs command of the mofaical law [l], feems to have been borrowed from the civil law; which, befides the terror of the example, gives alfo another reafon for this practice, *viz.* that it is a comfortable fight to the relations and friends of the deceafed [m]. But now in England, it is enacted by ftatute 25 Geo. II. c. 37. that the judge, before whom a murderer is convicted, fhall in paffing fentence direct him to be executed on the next day but one, (unlefs the fame fhall be funday, and then on the monday following) and that his body be delivered to the furgeons to be diffected and anatomized [n]; and that the judge may direct his body to be afterwards hung in chains, but in no wife to be buried without diffection. And, during the fhort but awful interval between fentence and execution, the prifoner fhall be kept alone, and fuftained with only bread and water. But a power is allowed to the judge, upon good and fufficient caufe, to refpite the execution, and relax the other reftraints of this act.

By the Roman law, *parricide,* or the murder of one's parents or children, was punifhed in a much feverer manner than any other kind of homicide. After being fcourged, the delinquents were fewed up in a leathern fack, with a live dog, a cock, a vi-

---

[k] 1 Hal. P. C. 450.

[l] " The body of a malefactor fhall not " remain all night upon the tree; but thou " fhalt in any wife bury him in that day, " that the land be not defiled." Deut. xxi. 23.

[m] " Famofos latrones, in his locis, ubi graf-

" fati funt, furca figendos placuit; ut, et con-- " fpectu deterreantur alii, et folatio fit cogna- " tis interemptorum, eodem loco poena reddita, " in quo latrones homicidia feciffent." Ff. 48. 19. 28. §. 15.

[n] Foft. 107.

per, and an ape, and so cast into the sea[o]. Solon, it is true, in his laws, made none against parricide; apprehending it impossible that any one should be guilty of so unnatural a barbarity[p]. And the Persians, according to Herodotus, entertained the same notion, when they adjudged all persons who killed their reputed parents to be bastards. And, upon some such reason as this, must we account for the omission of an exemplary punishment for this crime in our English laws; which treat it no otherwise than as simple murder, unless the child was also the servant of his parent[q].

FOR, though the breach of natural relation is unobserved, yet the breach of civil or ecclesiastical connexions, when coupled with murder, denominates it a new offence; no less than a species of treason, called *parva proditio,* or *petit treason:* which however is nothing else but an aggravated degree of murder[r]; although, on account of the violation of private allegiance, it is stigmatized as an inferior species of treason[s]. And thus, in the antient Gothic constitution, we find the breach both of natural and civil relations ranked in the same class with crimes against the state and the sovereign[t].

PETIT treason, according to the statute 25 Edw. III. c. 2. may happen three ways: by a servant killing his master, a wife her husband, or an ecclesiastical person (either secular, or regular) his superior, to whom he owes faith and obedience. A servant who kills his master whom he has left, upon a grudge conceived against him during his service, is guilty of petit treason: for the traiterous intention was hatched while the relation subsisted between them; and this is only an execution of that intention[u]. So if a wife be divorced *a mensa et thoro,* still the *vinculum ma-*

[o] *Ff.* 48. 9. 9.
[p] Cic. *pro S. Roscio.* §. 25.
[q] 1 Hal. P. C. 380.
[r] Foster. 107. 324. 336.
[s] See pag. 75.
[t] " *Omnium gravissima censetur vi. facta*

" *ab incolis in patriam, subditis in regem,*
" *liberis in parentes, maritis in uxores, (et*
" *vice versa) servis in dominos, aut etiam*
" *ab homine in semet ipsum.*" Stiernh. *de jure*
Goth. *l.* 3. *c.* 3.
[u] 1 Hawk. P. C. 89. 1 Hal. P. C. 380.

　　　　　　　trimonii

trimonii fubfifts ; and if fhe kills fuch divorced hufband, fhe is a traitrefs[w]. And a clergyman is underftood to owe canonical obe-dience, to the bifhop who ordained him, to him in whofe dio-cefe he is beneficed, and alfo to the metropolitan of fuch fuffra-gan or diocefan bifhop : and therefore to kill any of thefe is petit treafon[x]. As to the reft, whatever has been faid, or re-mains to be obferved hereafter, with refpect to wilful murder, is alfo applicable to the crime of petit treafon, which is no other than murder in it's moft odious degree : except that the trial fhall be as in cafes of high treafon, before the improve-ments therein made by the ftatutes of William III[y]; and alfo except in it's punifhment.

THE punifhment of petit treafon, in a man, is to be drawn and hanged, and, in a woman, to be drawn and burned[z]: the idea of which latter punifhment feems to have been handed down to us from the laws of the antient Druids, which condemned a woman to be burned for murdering her hufband[a]; and it is now the ufual punifhment for all forts of treafons committed by thofe of the female fex[b]. Perfons guilty of petit treafon were firft debarred the benefit of clergy by ftatute 12 Hen. VII. c. 7.

[w] 1 Hal. P. C. 381.
[x] *Ibid.*
[y] Foft. 337.

[z] 1 Hal. P. C. 382. 3 Inft. 311.
[a] Caefar *de bell. Gall. l.* 6. *c.* 18.
[b] See pag. 93.

CHAPTER THE FIFTEENTH.

OF OFFENCES AGAINST THE PERSONS OF INDIVIDUALS.

HAVING in the preceding chapter confidered the principal crime, or public wrong, that can be committed againſt
a private ſubjeۥ, namely, by deſtroying his life; I proceed now
to enquire into ſuch other crimes and miſdemeſnors, as more
peculiarly affeۥ the ſecurity of his perſon, while living.

OF theſe ſome are felonious, and in their nature capital;
others are ſimple miſdemeſnors, and puniſhable with a lighter
animadverſion. Of the felonies the firſt is that of *mayhem*.

I. MAYHEM, *mahemium,* was in part confidered in the preceding volume [a], as a civil injury: but it is alſo looked upon in
a criminal light by the law; being an atrocious breach of the
king's peace, and an offence tending to deprive him of the aid
and aſſiſtance of his ſubjeۥs. For mayhem is properly defined
to be, as we may remember, the violently depriving another of
the uſe of ſuch of his members, as may render him the leſs able
in fighting, either to defend himſelf, or to annoy his adverſary [b].
And therefore the cutting off, or diſabling, or weakening a man's

---

[a] See Vol. III. pag. 121,　　　[b] Brit. *l.* 1. *c.* 25. 1 Hawk. P. C. 111.

hand or finger, or ftriking out his eye or foretooth, or depriving him of thofe parts, the lofs of which in all animals abates their courage, are held to be mayhems. But the cutting off his ear, or nofe, or the like, are not held to be mayhems at common law; becaufe they do not weaken but only disfigure him.

By the antient law of England he that maimed any man, whereby he loft any part of his body, was fentenced to lofe the like part; *membrum pro membro*[c]: which is ftill the law in Sweden[d]. But this went afterwards out of ufe: partly becaufe the law of retaliation, as was formerly fhewn[e], is at beft an inadequate rule of punifhment; and partly becaufe upon a repetition of the offence the punifhment could not be repeated. So that, by the common law, as it for a long time ftood, mayhem was only punifhable with fine and imprifonment[f]; unlefs perhaps the offence of mayhem by caftration, which all our old writers held to be felony; " *et fequitur aliquando poena capitalis,* " *aliquando perpetuum exilium, cum omnium bonorum ademptione*[g]." And this, although the mayhem was committed upon the higheft provocation[h].

But fubfequent ftatutes have put the crime and punifhment of mayhem more out of doubt. For, firft, by ftatute 5 Hen. IV. c. 5. to remedy a mifchief that then prevailed, of beating, wounding, or robbing a man, and then cutting out his *tongue* or putting out his *eyes*, to prevent him from being an evidence againft them, this offence is declared to be felony, if done of malice prepenfe; that is, as fir Edward Coke[i] explains it, voluntarily

[c] 3 Inft. 118. — *Mes, fi la pleynte foit faite de femme qu' avera tollet a home fes membres, en tiel cafe perdra la feme la une meyn par jugement, come le membre dount ele avera trefpaffe.* (Brit. c. 25.)

[d] Stiernhook *de jure Sueon. l. 3. c. 3.*

[e] See pag. 12.

[f] 1 Hawk. P. C. 112.

[g] Bract. *fol.* 144.

[h] Sir Edward Coke (3 Inft. 62.) has tranf-cribed a record of Henry the third's time, (*Clauf.* 13 *Hen. III. m.* 9.) by which a gentleman of Somerfetfhire and his wife appear to have been apprehended and committed to prifon, being indicted for dealing thus with John the monk, who was caught in adultery with the wife.

[i] 3 Inft. 62.

and

and of fet purpofe, though done upon a fudden occafion. Next, in order of time, is the ftatute 37 Hen. VIII. c. 6. which directs, that if a man fhall malicioufly and unlawfully cut off the *ear* of any of the king's fubjects, he fhall not only forfeit treble damages to the party grieved, to be recovered by action of tref-pafs at common law, as a civil fatisfaction; but alfo 10 *l.* by way of fine to the king, which was his criminal amercement. The laft ftatute, but by far the moft fevere and effectual of all, is that of 22 & 23 Car. II. c. 1. called the Coventry act; being occa-fioned by an affault on fir John Coventry in the ftreet, and flit-ting his nofe, in revenge (as was fuppofed) for fome obnoxious words uttered by him in parliament. By this ftatute it is enacted, that if any perfon fhall of malice aforethought, and by lying in wait, unlawfully cut out or difable the tongue, put out an eye, flit the nofe, cut off a nofe or lip, or cut off or difable any limb or member of any other perfon, *with intent to maim or to disfigure him;* fuch perfon, his counfellors, aiders, and abettors, fhall be guilty of felony without benefit of clergy[k].

[k] On this ftatute Mr Coke, a gentleman of Suffolk, and one Woodburn, a labourer, were indicted in 1722; Coke for hiring and abetting Woodburn, and Woodburn for the actual fact, of flitting the nofe of Mr Crifpe, Coke's brother in law. The cafe was fome-what fingular. The murder of Crifpe was intended, and he was left for dead, being terribly hacked and disfigured with a hedge bill; but he recovered. Now the bare in-tent to murder is no felony: but to disfigure, with an intent to disfigure, is made fo by this ftatute; on which they were therefore in-dicted. And Coke, who was a difgrace to the profeffion of the law, had the effron-tery to reft his defence upon this point, that the affault was not committed with an in-tent to disfigure, but with an intent to mur-der; and therefore not within the ftatute. But the court held, that if a man attacks another to murder him with fuch an inftru-ment as a hedge bill, which cannot but en-danger the disfiguring him; and in fuch at-tack happens not to kill, but only to disfigure him; he may be indicted on this ftatute: and it fhall be left to the jury whether it were not a defign to murder by disfiguring, and confequently a malicious intent to disfi-gure as well as to murder. Accordingly the jury found them guilty of fuch previous intent to disfigure, in order to effect their principal intent to murder, and they were both con-demned and executed. (State Trials. VI. 212.)

Thus

THUS much for the felony of mayhem : to which may be
added the offence of wilfully and malicioufly fhooting at any
perfon, which may endanger either killing or maiming him.
This, though no fuch evil confequence enfues, is made felony
without benefit of clergy by ftatute 9 Geo. I. c. 22. and thereupon one Arnold was convicted in 1723, for fhooting at lord
Onflow ; but, being half a madman, was never executed, but
confined in prifon, where he died about thirty years after.

II. THE fecond offence, more immediately affecting the perfonal fecurity of individuals, relates to the female part of his
majefty's fubjects ; being that of their *forcible abduction* and *mar-*
riage ; which is vulgarly called *ftealing an heirefs*. For by ftatute
3 Hen. VII. c. 2. it is enacted, that if any perfon fhall for lucre
take any woman, maid, widow, or wife, having fubftance either
in goods or lands, or being heir apparent to her anceftors, contrary to her will ; and afterwards fhe be married to fuch mif-
doer, or by his confent to others, or defiled ; fuch perfon, and
all his acceffories, fhall be deemed principal felons : and by ftatute 39 Eliz. c. 9. the benefit of clergy is taken away from all
fuch felons, except acceffories *after* the offence.

IN the conftruction of this ftatute it hath been determined,
1. That the indictment muft allege that the taking was for lucre,
for fuch are the words of the ftatute[1]. 2. In order to fhew this,
it muft appear that the woman has fubftance either real or perfonal, or is an heir apparent[m]. 3. It muft appear that fhe was
taken away againft her will. 4. It muft alfo appear, that fhe
was afterwards married, or defiled. And though poffibly the
marriage or defilement might be by her fubfequent confent, being won thereunto by flatteries after the taking, yet this is felony, if the firft taking were againft her will[n] : and fo *vice*

---

[1] 1 Hawk. P. C. 110.
[m] 1 Hal. P. C. 660. 1 Hawk. P. C. 109.
[n] 1 Hal. P. C. 660.

verfa,

verfa, if the woman be originally taken away with her own confent, yet if fhe afterwards refufe to continue with the offender, and be forced againft her will, fhe may, from that time, as properly be faid to be taken againft her will, as if fhe never had given any confent at all; for, till the force was put upon her, fhe was in her own power°.   5. It is held that a woman, thus taken away and married, may be fworn and give evidence againft the offender, though he is her hufband *de facto*; contrary to the general rule of law: becaufe he is no hufband *de jure*, in cafe the actual marriage was alfo againft her will[p].   In cafes indeed where the actual marriage is good, by the confent of the inveigled woman obtained after her forcible abduction, fir Matthew Hale feems to queftion how far her evidence fhould be allowed: but other authorities[q] feem to agree, that it fhould even then be admitted; efteeming it abfurd, that the offender fhould thus take advantage of his own wrong, and that the very act of marriage, which is a principal ingredient of his crime, fhould (by a forced conftruction of law) be made ufe of to ftop the mouth of the moft material witnefs againft him.

An inferior degree of the fame kind of offence, but not attended with force, is punifhed by the ftatute 4 & 5 Ph. & Mar. c. 8. which enacts, that if any perfon, above the age of fourteen, unlawfully fhall convey or *take away any woman child unmarried,* (which is held[r] to extend to baftards as well as to legitimate children) within the age of fixteen years, from the poffeffion and againft the will of the father, mother, guardians, or governors, he fhall be imprifoned two years, or fined at the difcretion of the juftices: and if he deflowers fuch maid or woman child, or, without the confent of parents, contracts matrimony with her, *he* fhall be imprifoned five years, or fined at the difcretion of the juftices, and *fhe* fhall forfeit all her lands to her next of kin, during the life of her faid hufband. So that

---

° 1 Hawk. P. C. 110.
p 1 Hal. P. C. 661.

q Cro. Car. 488.   3 Keb. 193.   State Trials. V. 455.
r Stra. 1162.

as thefe ftolen marriages, under the age of fixteen, were ufually upon mercenary views, this act, befides punifhing the feducer, wifely removed the temptation. But this latter part of the act is now rendered almoft ufelefs, by provifions of a very different kind, which make the marriage totally void[t], in the ftatute 26 Geo. II. c. 33.

III. A THIRD offence, againft the female part alfo of his majefty's fubjects, but attended with greater aggravations than that of forcible marriage, is the crime of *rape, raptus mulierum,* or the carnal knowlege of a woman forcibly and againft her will. This, by the Jewifh law[t], was punifhed with death, in cafe the damfel was betrothed to another man; and, in cafe fhe was not betrothed, then a heavy fine of fifty fhekels was to be paid to the damfel's father, and fhe was to be the wife of the ravifher all the days of his life; without that power of divorce, which was in general permitted by the mofaic law.

THE civil law[u] punifhes the crime of ravifhment with death and confifcation of goods: under which it includes both the offence of forcible abduction, or taking away a woman from her friends, of which we laft fpoke; and alfo the prefent offence of forcibly difhonouring them; either of which, without the other, is in that law, fufficient to conftitute a capital crime. Alfo the ftealing away a woman from her parents or guardians, and debauching her, is equally penal by the emperor's edict, whether fhe confent or is forced: " *five volentibus, five nolentibus mulie-* " *ribus, tale facinus fuerit perpetratum.*" And this, in order to take away from women every opportunity of offending in this way; whom the Roman laws fuppofe never to go aftray, without the feduction and arts of the other fex: and therefore, by reftraining and making fo highly penal the folicitations of the men, they meant to fecure effectually the honour of the women.

[t] See Vol. I. pag. 437, &c.   [u] *Cod. 9. tit.* 13.
[t] Deut. xxii. 25.

" *Si*

" *Si enim ipſi raptores metu, vel atrocitate poenae, ab hujuſmodi fa-*
" *cinore ſe temperaverint, nulli mulieri, ſive volenti, ſive nolenti,*
" *peccandi locus relinquetur ; quia hoc ipſum velle mulierum, ab in-*
" *ſidiis nequiſſimi hominis, qui meditatur rapinam, inducitur. Niſi*
" *etenim eam ſolicitaverit, niſi odioſis artibus circumvenerit, non*
" *faciet eam velle in tantum dedecus ſeſe prodere.*" But our Engliſh law does not entertain quite ſuch ſublime ideas of the honour of either ſex, as to lay the blame of a mutual fault upon
one of the tranſgreſſors only : and therefore makes it a neceſſary
ingredient in the crime of rape, that it muſt be againſt the woman's will.

RAPE was puniſhed by the Saxon laws, particularly thoſe of
king Athelſtan [w], with death : which was alſo agreeable to the
old Gothic or Scandinavian conſtitution [x]. But this was afterwards thought too hard : and in it's ſtead another ſevere, but
not capital, puniſhment was inflicted by William the conqueror ;
viz, caſtration and loſs of eyes [y]; which continued till after
Bracton wrote, in the reign of Henry the third. But in order
to prevent malicious accuſations, it was then the law, (and, it
ſeems, ſtill continues to be ſo in appeals of rape [z]) that the woman
ſhould immediately after, " *dum recens fuerit maleficium,*" go to
the next town, and there make diſcovery to ſome credible perſons
of the injury ſhe has ſuffered ; and afterwards ſhould acquaint
the high conſtable of the hundred, the coroners, and the ſheriff
with the outrage [a]. This ſeems to correſpond in ſome degree with
the laws of Scotland and Arragon [b], which require that complaint
muſt be made within twenty four hours : though afterwards by
ſtatute Weſtm. 1. c. 13. the time of limitation in England was
extended to forty days. At preſent there is no time of limitation
fixed : for, as it is uſually now puniſhed by indictment at the
ſuit of the king, the maxim of law takes place, that *nullum tem-*
pus occurrit regi : but the jury will rarely give credit to a ſtale

---

[w] Bracton. *l.* 3. *c.* 28.
[x] Stiernh. *de jure Sueon. l.* 3. *c.* 2.
[y] *LL. Guil. Conqu. c.* 19.

[z] 1 Hal. P. C. 632.
[a] Glanv. *l.* 14. *c.* 6. Bract. *l.* 3. *c.* 28.
[b] Barrington. 107.

　　　　　　　complaint.

complaint. During the former period alſo it was held for law[c], that the woman (by conſent of the judge and her parents) might redeem the offender from the execution of his ſentence, by accepting him for her huſband ; if he alſo was willing to agree to the exchange, but not otherwiſe.

In the 3 Edw. I. by the ſtatute Weſtm. 1. c. 13. the puniſhment of rape was much mitigated : the offence itſelf being reduced to a treſpaſs, if not proſecuted by the woman within forty days, and ſubjecting the offender only to two years impriſonment, and a fine at the king's will. But, this lenity being productive of the moſt terrible conſequences, it was in ten years afterwards, 13 Edw. I. found neceſſary to make the offence of rape felony, by ſtatute Weſtm. 2. c. 34. And by ſtatute 18 Eliz. c. 7. it is made felony without benefit of clergy : as is alſo the abominable wickedneſs of carnally knowing or abuſing any woman child under the age of ten years ; in which caſe the conſent or non-conſent is immaterial, as by reaſon of her tender years ſhe is incapable of judgment and diſcretion. Sir Matthew Hale is indeed of opinion, that ſuch profligate actions committed on an infant under the age of *twelve* years, the age of female diſcretion by the common law, either with or without conſent, amount to rape and felony ; as well ſince as before the ſtatute of queen Elizabeth [d] : but the law has in general been held only to extend to infants under *ten*.

A male infant, under the age of fourteen years, is preſumed by law incapable to commit a rape, and therefore it ſeems cannot be found guilty of it. For though in other felonies *malitia ſupplet aetatem*, as has in ſome caſes been ſhewn ; yet, as to this particular ſpecies of felony, the law ſuppoſes an imbecillity of body as well as mind[e].

[c] Glanv. *l.* 14. *c.* 6. Bract. *l.* 3. *c.* 28.   [e] *Ibid.*
[d] 1 Hal. P. C. 631.

THE

THE civil law feems to fuppofe a proftitute or common harlot incapable of any injuries of this kind[f]: not allowing any
punifhment for violating the chaftity of her, who hath indeed no
chaftity at all, or at leaft hath no regard to it. But the law of
England does not judge fo hardly of offenders, as to cut off all
opportunity of retreat even from common ftrumpets, and to treat
them as never capable of amendment. It therefore holds it to
be felony to force even a concubine or harlot; becaufe the woman may have forfaken that unlawful courfe of life[g]: for, as
Bracton well obferves[h], "*licet meretrix fuerit antea, certe tunc*
"*temporis non fuit, cum reclamando nequitiae ejus confentire noluit.*"

AS to the material facts requifite to be given in evidence and
proved upon an indictment of rape, they are of fuch a nature,
that though neceffary to be known and fettled, for the conviction
of the guilty and prefervation of the innocent, and therefore
are to be found in fuch criminal treatifes as difcourfe of thefe
matters in detail, yet they are highly improper to be publicly
difcuffed, except only in a court of juftice. I fhall therefore
merely add upon this head a few remarks from fir Matthew Hale,
with regard to the competency and credibility of witneffes;
which may, *falvo pudore*, be confidered.

AND, firft, the party ravifhed may give evidence upon oath,
and is in law a competent witnefs; but the credibility of her
teftimony, and how far forth fhe is to be believed, muft be left
to the jury upon the circumftances of fact that concur in that
teftimony. For inftance: if the witnefs be of good fame; if
fhe prefently difcovered the offence, and made fearch for the offender; if the party accufed fled for it; thefe and the like are
concurring circumftances, which give greater probability to her
evidence. But, on the other fide, if fhe be of evil fame, and
ftands unfupported by others; if fhe concealed the injury for any
confiderable time after fhe had opportunity to complain; if the

---

[f] *Cod.* 9. 9. 22. *Ff.* 47. 2. 39.   [h] *fol.* 147.
[g] 1 Hal. P. C. 629. 1 Hawk. P. C. 108.

place,

place, where the fact was alleged to be committed, was where it was possible she might have been heard, and she made no outcry; these and the like circumstances carry a strong, but not conclusive, presumption that her testimony is false or feigned.

MOREOVER, if the rape be charged to be committed on an infant under twelve years of age, she may still be a competent witness, if she hath sense and understanding to know the nature and obligations of an oath; and, even if she hath not, it is thought by sir Matthew Hale[i] that she ought to be heard without oath, to give the court information; though that alone will not be sufficient to convict the offender. And he is of this opinion, first, because the nature of the offence being secret, there may be no other possible proof of the actual fact; though afterwards there may be concurrent circumstances to corroborate it, proved by other witnesses: and, secondly, because the law allows what the child told her mother, or other relations, to be given in evidence, since the nature of the case admits frequently of no better proof; and there is much more reason for the court to hear the narration of the child herself, than to receive it at second hand from those who swear they heard her say so. And indeed it is now settled, that infants of any age are to be heard; and, if they have any idea of an oath, to be also sworn: it being found by experience that infants of very tender years often give the clearest and truest testimony. But in any of these cases, whether the child be sworn or not, it is to be wished, in order to render her evidence credible, that there should be some concurrent testimony, of time, place and circumstances, in order to make out the fact; and that the conviction should not be grounded singly on the unsupported accusation of an infant under years of discretion. There may be therefore, in many cases of this nature, witnesses who are competent, that is, who may be admitted to be heard; and yet, after being heard, may prove not to be credible, or such as the jury is bound to believe. For one excel-

i 1 Hal. P. C. 634.

lence of the trial by jury is, that the jury are triors of the credit of the witneſſes, as well as of the truth of the fact.

" I T is true, ſays this learned judge [k], that rape is a moſt " deteſtable crime, and therefore ought ſeverely and impartially " to be puniſhed with death ; but it muſt be remembered, that " it is an accuſation eaſy to be made, hard to be proved, but " harder to be defended by the party accuſed, though innocent." He then relates two very extraordinary caſes of malicious proſe-cutions for this crime, that had happened within his own obſer-vation ; and concludes thus : " I mention theſe inſtances, that " we may be the more cautious upon trials of offences of this " nature, wherein the court and jury may with ſo much eaſe be " impoſed upon, without great care and vigilance ; the heinouſ-" neſs of the offence many times tranſporting the judge and jury " with ſo much indignation, that they are overhaſtily carried to " the conviction of the perſon accuſed thereof, by the confident " teſtimony of ſometimes falſe and malicious witneſſes."

IV. WH A T has been here obſerved, eſpecially with regard to the manner of proof, which ought to be the more clear in proportion as the crime is the more deteſtable, may be applied to another offence, of a ſtill deeper malignity ; the infamous *crime againſt nature*, committed either with man or beaſt. A crime, which ought to be ſtrictly and impartially proved, and then as ſtrictly and impartially puniſhed. But it is an offence of ſo dark a nature, ſo eaſily charged, and the negative ſo difficult to be proved, that the accuſation ſhould be clearly made out : for, if falſe, it deſerves a puniſhment inferior only to that of the crime itſelf.

I WI L L not act ſo diſagreeable part, to my readers as well as myſelf, as to dwell any longer upon a ſubject, the very mention of which is a diſgrace to human nature. It will be more eligible to imitate in this reſpect the delicacy of our Engliſh law, which

[k] 1 Hal. P. C. 635.

treats

treats it, in it's very indictments, as a crime not fit to be named; *" peccatum illud horribile, inter christianos non nominandum."* A taciturnity obſerved likewiſe by the edict of Conſtantius and Conſtans[1]: *" ubi ſcelus eſt id, quod non proficit ſcire, jubemus inſur-* *" gere leges, armari jura gladio ultore, ut exquiſitis poenis ſubdan-* *" tur infames, qui ſunt, vel qui futuri ſunt, rei."* Which leads me to add a word concerning it's puniſhment.

THIS the voice of nature and of reaſon, and the expreſs law of God[m], determine to be capital. Of which we have a ſignal inſtance, long before the Jewiſh diſpenſation, by the deſtruction of two cities by fire from heaven: ſo that this is an univerſal, not merely a provincial, precept. And our antient law in ſome degree imitated this puniſhment, by commanding ſuch miſcreants to be burnt to death[n]; though Fleta[o] ſays they ſhould be buried alive: either of which puniſhments was indifferently uſed for this crime among the antient Goths[p]. But now the general puniſhment of all felonies is the ſame, namely, by hanging: and this offence (being in the times of popery only ſubject to eccleſiaſtical cenſures) was made ſingle felony by the ſtatute 25 Hen.VIII. c. 6. and felony without benefit of clergy by ſtatute 5 Eliz. c. 17. And the rule of law herein is, that, if both are arrived at years of diſcretion, *agentes et conſentientes pari poena plectantur*[q].

THESE are all the felonious offences, more immediately againſt the perſonal ſecurity of the ſubject. The inferior offences, or miſdemeſnors, that fall under this head, are *aſſaults, batteries, wounding, falſe impriſonment,* and *kidnapping.*

V, VI, VII. WITH regard to the nature of the three firſt of theſe offences in general, I have nothing farther to add to what has already been obſerved in the preceding book of theſe com-

---

[1] *Cod.* 9. 9. 31.
[m] Levit. xx. 13. 15.
[n] Brit. *c.* 9.

[o] *l.* 1. *c.* 37.
[p] Stiernh. *de jure Goth. l.* 3. *c.* 2.
[q] 3 Inſt. 59.

mentaries[r];

mentaries[r]; when we confidered them as private wrongs, or civil injuries, for which a fatisfaction or remedy is given to the party aggrieved. But, taken in a public light, as a breach of the king's peace, an affront to his government, and a damage done to his fubjects, they are alfo indictable and punifhable with fine and imprifonment; or with other ignominious corporal penalties, where they are committed with any very atrocious defign[s]. As in cafe of an affault with an intent to murder, or with an intent to commit either of the crimes laft fpoken of; for which intentional affaults, in the two laft cafes, indictments are much more ufual, than for the abfolute perpetration of the facts themfelves, on account of the difficulty of proof : and herein, befides heavy fine and imprifonment, it is ufual to award judgment of the pillory.

THERE is alfo one fpecies of battery, more atrocious and penal than the reft, which is the beating of a clerk in orders, or clergyman; on account of the refpect and reverence due to his facred character, as the minifter and embaffador of peace. Accordingly it is enacted by the ftatute called *articuli cleri*, 9 Edw. II. c. 3. that if any perfon lay violent hands upon a clerk, the amends for the peace broken fhall be before the king; that is by indictment in the king's courts : and the affailant may alfo be fued before the bifhop, that excommunication or bodily penance may be impofed : which if the offender will redeem by money, to be given to the bifhop, or the party grieved, it may be fued for before the bifhop; whereas otherwife to fue in any fpiritual court, for civil damages for the battery, falls within the danger of *praemunire*[t]. But fuits are, and always were, allowable in the fpiritual court, for money agreed to be given as a commutation for penance[u]. So that upon the whole it appears, that a perfon guilty of fuch brutal behaviour to a clergyman, is fubject to three kinds of profecution, all of which may be purfued for one and the fame offence : an indictment, for the breach

---

[r] See Vol. III. pag. 120.
[s] 1 Hawk. P. C. 65.

[t] 2 Inft. 492. 620.
[u] *Artic. Cler.* 9 *Edw. II.* c. 4. F. N. B. 53.

of the king's peace by such assault and battery; a civil action, for the special damage sustained by the party injured; and a suit in the ecclesiastical court, first, *pro correctione et salute animae* by *enjoining* penance, and then again for such sum of money as shall be agreed on for *taking off* the penance enjoined : it being usual in those courts to exchange their spiritual censures for a round compensation in money[v]; perhaps because poverty is generally esteemed by the moralists the best medicine *pro salute animae.*

VIII. THE two remaining crimes and offences, against the persons of his majesty's subjects, are infringements of their natural liberty : concerning the first of which, *false imprisonment,* it's nature and incidents, I must content myself with referring the student to what was observed in the preceding volume[w], when we considered it as a mere civil injury. But, besides the private satisfaction given to the individual by action, the law also demands public vengeance for the breach of the king's peace, for the loss which the state sustains by the confinement of one of it's members, and for the infringement of the good order of society. We have before seen[x], that the most atrocious degree of this offence, that of sending any subject of this realm a prisoner into parts beyond the seas, whereby he is deprived of the friendly assistance of the laws to redeem him from such his captivity, is punished with the pains of *praemunire*, and incapacity to hold any office, without any possibility of pardon[y]. Inferior degrees of the same offence of false imprisonment are also punishable by indictment (like assaults and batteries) and the delinquent may be fined and imprisoned[z]. And indeed[a] there can be no doubt, but that all kinds of crimes of a public nature, all disturbances of the peace, all oppressions, and other misdemesnors whatsoever, of a notoriously evil example, may be indicted at the suit of the king.

[v] 2 Rol. Rep. 384.
[w] See Vol. III. pag. 127.
[x] See pag. 116.

[y] Stat. 31 Car. II. c. 2.
[z] West. Symbol. part 2. pag. 92.
[a] 1 Hawk. P. C. 210.

IX. THE

IX. The other remaining offence, that of *kidnapping*, being the forcible abduction or stealing away of man, woman, or child from their own country, and selling them into another, was capital by the Jewish law. " He that stealeth a man, and selleth " him, or if he be found in his hand, he shall surely be put to " death [b]." So likewise in the civil law, the offence of spiriting away and stealing men and children, which was called *plagium*, and the offenders *plagiarii*, was punished with death [c]. This is unquestionably a very heinous crime, as it robs the king of his subjects, banishes a man from his country, and may in it's consequences be productive of the most cruel and disagreeable hardships; and therefore the common law of England has punished it with fine, imprisonment, and pillory [d]. And also the statute 11 & 12 W. III. c. 7. though principally intended against pirates, has a clause that extends to prevent the leaving of such persons abroad, as are thus kidnapped or spirited away; by enacting, that if any captain of a merchant vessel shall (during his being abroad) force any person on shore, or wilfully leave him behind, or refuse to bring home all such men as he carried out, if able and desirous to return, he shall suffer three months imprisonment. And thus much for offences that more immediately affect the *persons* of individuals.

[b] Exod. xxi. 16.
[c] *Ff.* 48. 15. 1.

[d] Raym. 474. 3 Show. 221. Skinn. 47. Comb. 10.

C H A P T E R   T H E   S I X T E E N T H.

Of OFFENCES against the HABITATIONS of INDIVIDUALS.

T HE only two offences, that more immediately affect the *habitations* of individuals or private fubjects, are thofe of *arfon* and *burglary*.

I. Arson, *ab ardendo,* is the malicious and wilful burning of the houfe or outhoufes of another man. This is an offence of very great malignity, and much more pernicious to the public than fimple theft: becaufe, firft, it is an offence againft that right, of habitation, which is acquired by the law of nature as well as by the laws of fociety; next, becaufe of the terror and confufion that neceffarily attends it; and, laftly, becaufe in fimple theft the thing ftolen only changes it's mafter, but ftill remains *in effe* for the benefit of the public, whereas by burning the very fubftance is abfolutely deftroyed. It is alfo frequently more deftructive than murder itfelf, of which too it is often the caufe: fince murder, atrocious as it is, feldom extends beyond the felonious act defigned; whereas fire too frequently involves in the common calamity perfons unknown to the incendiary, and not intended to be hurt by him, and friends as well as enemies.

For

For which reafon the civil law[a] punifhes with death fuch as malicioufly fet fire to houfes in towns, and contiguous to others; but is more merciful to fuch as only fire a cottage, or houfe, ftanding by itfelf.

Our Englifh law alfo diftinguifhes with much accuracy upon this crime. And therefore we will enquire, firft, what is fuch a houfe as may be the fubject of this offence; next, wherein the offence itfelf confifts, or what amounts to a burning of fuch houfe; and, laftly, how the offence is punifhed.

1. Not only the bare dwelling houfe, but all outhoufes that are parcel thereof, though not contiguous thereto, nor under the fame roof, as barns and ftables, may be the fubject of arfon[b]. And this by the common law : which alfo accounted it felony to burn a fingle barn in the field, if filled with hay or corn, though not parcel of the dwelling houfe[c]. The burning of a ftack of corn was antiently likewife accounted arfon[d]. And indeed all the niceties and diftinctions which we meet with in our books, concerning what fhall, or fhall not, amount to arfon, feem now to be taken away by a variety of ftatutes; which will be mentioned in the next chapter, and have made the punifhment of wilful burning equally extenfive as the mifchief. The offence of arfon (ftrictly fo called) may be committed by wilfully fetting fire to one's own houfe, provided one's neighbour's houfe is thereby alfo burnt; but if no mifchief is done but to one's own, it does not amount to felony, though the fire was kindled with intent to burn another's[e]. For by the common law no intention to commit a felony amounts to the fame crime; though it does, in fome cafes, by particular ftatutes. However fuch wilful firing one's own houfe, *in a town*, is a high mifdemefnor, and punifhable by fine, imprifonment, pillory, and perpetual fureties for the good behaviour[f]. And if a landlord or reverfioner fets fire

---

[a] *Ff.* 48. 19. 28. §. 12.
[b] 1 Hal. P. C. 567.
[c] 3 Inft. 69.

[d] 1 Hawk. P. C. 105.
[e] Cro. Car. 377.
[f] 1 Hal. P. C. 568. 1 Hawk. P. C. 106.

to his own houfe, of which another is in poffeffion under a leafe from himfelf or from thofe whofe eftate he hath, it fhall be accounted arfon; for, during the leafe, the houfe is the property of the tenant[s].

2. As to what fhall be faid a *burning*, fo as to amount to arfon : a bare intent, or attempt to do it, by actually fetting fire to an houfe, unlefs it abfolutely *burns*, does not fall within the defcription of *incendit et combuffit*; which were words neceffary, in the days of law-latin, to all indictments of this fort. But the burning and confuming of any part is fufficient; though the fire be afterwards extinguifhed[h]. Alfo it muft be a *malicious* burning; otherwife it is only a trefpafs : and therefore no negligence or mifchance amounts to it. For which reafon, though an unqualified perfon, by fhooting with a gun, happens to fet fire to the thatch of a houfe, this fir Matthew Hale determines not to be felony, contrary to the opinion of former writers[i]. But by ftatute 6 Ann. c. 31. any fervant, negligently fetting fire to a houfe or outhoufes, fhall forfeit 100 *l*, or be fent to the houfe of correction for eighteen months : in the fame manner as the Roman law directed " *eos, qui negligenter ignes apud fe* " *habuerint, fuftibus vel flagellis caedi*[k]."

3. The *punifhment* of arfon was death by our antient Saxon laws[l]. And, in the reign of Edward the firft, this fentence was executed by a kind of *lex talionis*; for the incendiaries were burnt to death[m]: as they were alfo by the Gothic conftitutions[n]. The ftatute 8 Hen.VI. c.6. made the wilful burning of houfes, under fome fpecial circumftances therein mentioned, amount to the crime of high treafon. But it was again reduced to felony by the general acts of Edward VI and queen Mary : and now the punifhment of all capital felonies is uniform, namely, by fufpenfion. The offence of arfon was denied the benefit of clergy by ftatute

---

[s] Poft. 115.
[h] 1 Hawk. P. C. 106.
[i] 1 Hal. P. C. 569.
[k] Ff. 1. 15. 4.

[l] LL. Inae. c. 7.
[m] Britt. c. 9.
[n] Stiernh. *de jure Goth. l. 3. c. 6.*

21 Hen. VIII. c. 1. but that ftatute was repealed by 1 Edw. VI. c. 12. and arfon was afterwards held to be oufted of clergy, with refpect to the principal offender, only by inference and deduction from the ftatute 4 & 5 P. & M. c. 4. which expreffly denied it to the acceffory[o]; though now it is expreffly denied to the principal alfo, by ftatute 9 Geo. I. c. 22.

II. BURGLARY, or nocturnal houfebreaking, *burgi latrocinium*, which by our antient law was called *hamefecken*, as it is in Scotland to this day, has always been looked upon as a very heinous offence : not only becaufe of the abundant terror that it naturally carries with it, but alfo as it is a forcible invafion and difturbance of that right of habitation, which every individual might acquire even in a ftate of nature; an invafion, which in fuch a ftate, would be fure to be punifhed with death, unlefs the affailant were the ftronger. But in civil fociety, the laws alfo come in to the affiftance of the weaker party : and, befides that they leave him this natural right of killing the aggreffor, if he can, (as was fhewn in a former chapter[p]) they alfo protect and avenge him, in cafe the might of the affailant is too powerful. And the law of England has fo particular and tender a regard to the immunity of a man's houfe, that it ftiles it his caftle, and will never fuffer it to be violated with impunity : agreeing herein with the fentiments of antient Rome, as expreffed in the words of Tully[q]; " *quid enim fanctius, quid omni religione muni-* " *tius, quam domus uniufcujufque civium ?*" For this reafon no doors can in general be broken open to execute any civil procefs; though, in criminal caufes, the public fafety fuperfedes the private. Hence alfo in part arifes the animadverfion of the law upon eaves-droppers, nufancers, and incendiaries : and to this principle it muft be affigned, that a man may affemble people together lawfully (at leaft if they do not exceed eleven) without danger of raifing a riot, rout, or unlawful affembly, in order to

---

[o] 11 Rep. 35. 2 Hal. P. C. 346, 347.   [p] See pag. 180.
Fofter. 336.   [q] *pro domo*, 41.

protect

protect and defend his houfe; which he is not permitted to do in any other cafe[r].

THE definition of a burglar, as given us by fir Edward Coke[s], is, " he that by night breaketh and entreth into a manfion-" houfe, with intent to commit a felony." In this definition there are four things to be confidered; the *time*, the *place*, the *manner*, and the *intent*.

1. THE *time* muft be by night, and not by day; for in the day time there is no burglary. We have feen[t], in the cafe of juftifiable homicide, how much more heinous all laws made an attack by night, rather than by day; allowing the party attacked by night to kill the affailant with impunity. As to what is reckoned night, and what day, for this purpofe: antiently the day was accounted to begin only at funrifing, and to end imme-diately upon funfet; but the better opinion feems to be, that if there be daylight or *crepufculum* enough, begun or left, to dif-cern a man's face withal, it is no burglary[u]. But this does not extend to moonlight; for then many midnight burglaries would go unpunifhed: and befides, the malignity of the offence does not fo properly arife from it's being done in the dark, as at the dead of night; when all the creation, except beafts of prey, are at reft; when fleep has difarmed the owner, and rendered his caftle defencelefs.

2. As to the *place*. It muft be, according to fir Edward Coke's definition, in a *manfion* houfe; and therefore to account for the reafon why breaking open a church is burglary, as it undoubtedly is, he quaintly obferves that it is *domus manfionalis Dei*[w]. But it does not feem abfolutely neceffary, that it fhould in all cafes be a manfion-houfe; for it may alfo be committed by breaking the

[r] 1 Hal. P. C. 547.
[s] 3 Inft. 63.
[t] See pag. 180, 181.

[u] 3 Inft. 63. 1 Hal. P. C. 550. 1 Hawk. P. C. 101.
[w] 3 Inft. 64.

gates

gates or walls of a *town* in the night[x]; though that perhaps fir Edward Coke would have called the manfion-houfe of the garrifon or corporation. Spelman defines burglary to be, " *nocturna* " *diruptio alicujus habitaculi, vel ecclefiae, etiam murorum portarumve* " *burgi, ad feloniam perpetrandam.*" And therefore we may fafely conclude, that the requifite of it's being *domus manfionalis* is only in the burglary of a private houfe; which is the moft frequent, and in which it is indifpenfably neceffary to form it's guilt, that it muft be in a manfion or dwelling houfe. For no diftant barn, warehoufe, or the like, are under the fame privileges, nor looked upon as a man's caftle of defence: nor is a breaking open of houfes wherein no man refides, and which therefore for the time being are not manfion-houfes, attended with the fame circumftances of midnight terror. A houfe however, wherein a man fometimes refides, and which the owner hath only left for a fhort feafon, *animo revertendi*, is the object of burglary; though no one be in it, at the time of the fact committed[y]. And if the barn, ftable, or warehoufe be parcel of the manfionhoufe, though not under the fame roof or contiguous, a burglary may be committed therein; for the capital houfe protects and privileges all it's branches and appurtenants, if within the curtilage or homeftall[z]. A chamber in a college or an inn of court, where each inhabitant hath a diftinct property, is, to all other purpofes as well as this, the manfion-houfe of the owner[a]. So alfo is a room or lodging, in any private houfe, the manfion for the time being of the lodger. The houfe of a corporation, inhabited in feparate apartments by the officers of the body corporate, is the manfion-houfe of the corporation. and not of the refpective officers[b]. But if I hire a fhop, parcel of another man's houfe, and work or trade in it, but never lie there; it is no dwellinghoufe, nor can burglary be committed therein: for by the leafe it is fevered from the reft of the houfe, and therefore is not the dwellinghoufe of him who occupies the other part;

[x] Spelm. *Gloff. t. Burglary.* 1 Hawk. P. C. 103.

[y] 1 Hal. P. C. 566. Foft. 77.

[z] 1 Hal. P. C. 558. 1 Hawk. P. C. 104.

[a] 1 Hal. P. C. 556.

[b] Fofter. 38, 39.

　　　　　　　　　neither

neither can I be said to dwell therein, when I neves lie there[c]. Neither can burglary be committed in a tent or booth erected in a market or fair; though the owner may lodge therein[d]: for the law regards thus highly nothing but permanent edifices; a house, or church, the wall, or gate of a town; and it is the folly of the owner to lodge in so fragile a tenement: but his lodging there no more makes it burglary to break it open, than it would be to uncover a tilted waggon in the same circumstances.

3. As to the *manner* of committing burglary: there must be both a breaking and an entry to complete it. But they need not be both done at once: for, if a hole be broken one night, and the same breakers enter the next night through the same, they are burglars[e]. There must be an actual breaking; not a mere legal *clausum fregit*, (by leaping over invisible ideal boundaries, which may constitute a civil trespass) but a substantial and forcible irruption. As at least by breaking, or taking out the glass of, or otherwise opening, a window; picking a lock, or opening it with a key; nay, by lifting up the latch of a door, or unloosing any other fastening which the owner has provided. But if a person leaves his doors or windows open, it is his own folly and negligence; and if a man enters therein, it is no burglary: yet, if he afterwards unlocks an inner or chamber door, it is so[f]. But to come down a chimney is held a burglarious entry; for that is as much closed, as the nature of things will permit[g]. So also to knock at a door, and upon opening it to rush in, with a felonious intent; or, under pretence of taking lodgings, to fall upon the landlord and rob him; or to procure a constable to gain admittance, in order to search for traitors, and then to bind the constable and rob the house; all these entries have been adjudged burglarious, though there was no actual breaking: for the law will not suffer itself to be trifled with by such evasions, especially under the cloke of legal process[h]. And so, if a servant

[c] 1 Hal. P. C. 558.
[d] 1 Hawk. P. C. 104.
[e] 1 Hal. P. C. 551.

[f] *Ibid.* 553.
[g] 1 Hawk. P. C. 102.　1 Hal. P. C. 552.
[h] Hawk. P. C. 102.

opens

opens and enters his master's chamber door with a felonious design; or if any other person lodging in the same house, or in a public inn, opens and enters another's door, with such evil intent; it is burglary. Nay, if the servant conspires with a robber, and lets him into the house by night, this is burglary in both [i]: for the servant is doing an unlawful act, and the opportunity afforded him, of doing it with greater ease, rather aggravates than extenuates the guilt. As for the entry, any the least degree of it, with any part of the body, or with an instrument held in the hand, is sufficient: as, to step over the threshold, to put a hand or a hook in at a window to draw out goods, or a pistol to demand one's money, are all of them burglarious entries [k]. The entry may be before the breaking, as well as after: for by statute 12 Ann. c. 7. if a person enters into, or is within, the dwelling house of another, without breaking in, either by day or by night, with intent to commit felony, and shall in the night break out of the same, this is declared to be burglary; there having before been different opinions concerning it: lord Bacon [l] holding the affirmative, and sir Matthew Hale [m] the negative. But it is universally agreed, that there must be both a breaking, either in fact or by implication, and also an entry, in order to complete the burglary.

4. As to the *intent*; it is clear, that such breaking and entry must be with a felonious intent, otherwise it is only a trespass. And it is the same, whether such intention be actually carried into execution, or only demonstrated by some attempt or overt act, of which the jury is to judge. And therefore such a breach and entry of a house as has been before described, by night, with intent to commit a robbery, a murder, a rape, or any other felony, is burglary; whether the thing be actually perpetrated or not. Nor does it make any difference, whether the offence were felony at common law, or only created so by statute; since

[i] 1 Hal. P. C. 553. 1 Hawk. P. C. 103.   [l] Elem 65.
[k] 1 Hal. P. C. 555. 1 Hawk. P. C. 103.   [m] 1 Hal. P. C. 554.
Foft. 108.

that

that ſtatute, which makes an offence felony, gives it incidentally all the properties of a felony at common law [n].

Thus much for the nature of burglary; which is, as has been ſaid, a felony at common law, but within the benefit of clergy. The ſtatute however of 18 Eliz. c. 7. takes away clergy from the principals, and that of 3 & 4 W. & M. c. 9. from all acceſſories before the faƈt. And, in like manner, the laws of Athens, which puniſhed no ſimple theft with death, made burglary a capital crime [o].

[n] 1 Hawk. P. C. 105.   [o] Pott. Antiq. b. 1. c. 26.

CHAPTER THE SEVENTEENTH.

OF OFFENCES AGAINST PRIVATE PROPERTY.

THE next, and laft, fpecies of offences againft private fub-jects, are fuch as more immediately affect their property. Of which there are two, which are attended with a breach of the peace; *larciny*, and *malicious mifchief*: and one, that is equally injurious to the rights of property, but attended with no act of violence; which is the crime of *forgery*. Of thefe three in their order.

I. LARCINY, or *theft*, by contraction for latrociny, *latroci-nium*, is diftinguifhed by the law into two forts; the one called *fimple* larciny, or plain theft unaccompanied with any other atro-cious circumftance; and *mixt* or *compound* larciny, which alfo includes in it the aggravation of a taking from one's houfe or perfon.

AND, firft, of *fimple* larciny: which, when it is the fteal-ing of goods above the value of twelvepence, is called *grand* larciny; when of goods to that value, or under, is *petit* larciny: offences, which are confiderably diftinguifhed in their punifh-ment, but not otherwife. I fhall therefore firft confider the nature of fimple larciny in general; and then fhall obferve the different degrees of punifhment, inflicted on it's two feveral branches.

SIMPLE

SIMPLE larciny then is " the felonious taking, and carrying
" away, of the perfonal goods of another." This offence certainly commenced then, whenever it was, that the bounds of
property, or laws of *meum* and *tuum*, were eftablifhed. How
far fuch an offence can exift in a ftate of nature, where all things
are held to be common, is a queftion that may be folved with
very little difficulty. The difturbance of any individual, in the
occupation of what he has feifed to his prefent ufe, feems to be
the only offence of this kind incident to fuch a ftate. But, unqueftionably, in focial communities, when property is eftablifhed, the neceffity whereof we have formerly feen [a], any violation
of that property is fubject to be punifhed by the laws of fociety :
though how far that punifhment fhould extend, is matter of confiderable doubt. At prefent we will examine the nature of theft,
or larciny, as laid down in the foregoing definition.

1. IT muft be a *taking*. This implies the confent of the
owner to be wanting. Therefore no delivery of the goods from
the owner to the offender, upon truft, can ground a larciny.
As if A lends B a horfe, and he rides away with him ; or, if I
fend goods by a carrier, and he carries them away ; thefe are no
larcinies [b]. But if the carrier opens a bale or pack of goods, or
pierces a veffel of wine, and takes away part thereof, or if he
carries it to the place appointed, and afterwards takes away the
whole, thefe are larcinies [c] : for here the *animus furandi* is manifeft ; fince in the firft cafe he had otherwife no inducement to
open the goods, and in the fecond the truft was determined, the
delivery having taken it's effect. But bare non-delivery fhall not
of courfe be intended to arife from a felonious defign ; fince
that may happen from a variety of other accidents. Neither by
the common law was it larciny in any fervant to run away with
the goods committed to him to keep, but only a breach of civil
truft. But by ftatute 33 Hen. VI. c. 1. the fervants of perfons

[a] See Vol. II. pag. 8, &c.　　　　　[c] 3 Inft. 107.
[b] 1 Hal. P. C. 504.

deceafed,

deceafed, accufed of embezzling their mafter's goods, may by writ out of chancery (iffued by the advice of the chief juftices and chief baron, or any two of them) and proclamation made thereupon, be fummoned to appear perfonally in the court of king's bench, to anfwer their mafter's executors in any civil fuit for fuch goods; and fhall, on default of appearance, be attainted of felony. And by ftatute 21 Hen. VIII. c. 7. if any fervant embezzles his mafter's goods to the value of forty fhillings, it is made felony; except in ap; rentices, and fervants under eighteen years old. But if he had not the poffeffion, but only the care and overfight of the goods, as the butler of plate, the fhepherd of fheep, and the like, the embezzling of them is felony at common law[d]. So if a gueft robs his inn or tavern of a piece of plate, it is larciny; for he hath not the poffeffion delivered to him, but merely the ufe[e]: and fo it is declared to be by ftatute 3 & 4 W. & M. c. 9. if a lodger runs away with the goods from his ready furnifhed lodgings. Under fome circumftances alfo a man may be guilty of felony in taking his own goods: as if he fteals them from a pawnbroker, or any one to whom he hath delivered and entrufted them, with intent to charge fuch bailee with the value; or if he robs his own meffenger on the road, with intent to charge the hundred with the lofs according to the ftatute of Winchefter[f].

2. THERE muft not only be a taking, but a *carrying away: cepit et afportavit* was the old law-latin. A bare removal from the place in which he found the goods, though the thief does not quite make off with them, is a fufficient afportation, or carrying away. As if a man be leading another's horfe out of a clofe, and be apprehended in the fact; or if a gueft, ftealing goods out of an inn, has removed them from his chamber down ftairs; thefe have been adjudged fufficient carryings away, to conftitute a larciny[g]. Or if a thief, intending to fteal plate, takes it out of a

---

[d] 1 Hal. P. C. 506.
[e] 1 Hawk. P. C. 90.

[f] Fofter. 123, 124.
[g] 3 Inft. 108, 109.

cheft

cheft in which it was, and lays it down upon the floor, but is furprized before he can make his efcape with it; this is larciny[h].

3. **T h i s** taking, and carrying away, muft alfo be *felonious*; that is, done *animo furandi*: or, as the civil law exprefles it, *lucri caufa*[i]. This requifite, befides excufing thofe who labour under incapacities of mind or will, (of whom we fpoke fufficiently at the entrance of this book[k]) indemnifies alfo mere trefpaffers, and other petty offenders. As if a fervant takes his mafter's horfe, without his knowlege, and brings him home again: if a neighbour takes another's plough, that is left in the field, and ufes it upon his own land, and then returns it: if, under colour of arrear of rent, where none is due, I diftrein another's cattel, or feife them: all thefe are mifdemefnors and trefpaffes, but no felonies[l]. The ordinary difcovery of a felonious intent is where the party doth it clandeftinely; or being charged with the fact, denies it. But this is by no means the only criterion of criminality: for in cafes that may amount to larciny the variety of circumftances is fo great, and the complications thereof fo mingled, that it is impoffible to recount all thofe, which may evidence a felonious intent, or *animum furandi*: wherefore they muft be left to the due and attentive confideration of the court and jury.

4. **T h i s** felonious taking and carrying away muft be *of the perfonal goods of another*: for if they are things *real*, or favour of the realty, larciny at the common law cannot be committed of them. Lands, tenements, and hereditaments (either corporeal or incorporeal) cannot in their nature be taken and carried away. And of things likewife that adhere to the freehold, as corn, grafs, trees, and the like, or lead upon a houfe, no larciny could be committed by the rules of the common law; but the feverance of them was, and in many things is ftill, merely a trefpafs: which depended on a fubtilty in the legal notions of

[h] 1 Hawk. P. C. 93.
[i] *Inft.* 4. 1. 1.

[k] See pag. 20.
[l] 1 Hal. P. C. 509

our

our anceftors. Thefe things were parcel of the real eftate; and therefore, while they continued fo, could not by any poffibility be the fubject of theft, being abfolutely fixed and immoveable[m]. And if they were fevered by violence, fo as to be changed into moveables; and at the fame time, by one and the fame continued act, carried off by the perfon who fevered them; they could never be faid to be taken *from* the *proprietor*, in this their newly acquired ftate of mobility (which is effential to the nature of lar-ciny) being never, as fuch, in the actual or conftructive poffeffion of any one, but of him who committed the trefpafs. He could not in ftrictnefs be faid to have taken what at that time were the perfonal goods of another, fince the very act of taking was what turned them into perfonal goods. But if the thief fevers them at *one* time, whereby the trefpafs is completed, and they are converted into perfonal chattels, in the conftructive poffeffion of him on whofe foil they are left or laid; and comes again at *an-other* time, when they are fo turned into perfonalty, and takes them away; it is larciny: and fo it is, if the owner, or any one elfe, has fevered them[n]. And now, by the ftatute 4 Geo. II. c. 32. to fteal, or fever with intent to fteal, any lead or iron fixed to a houfe, or in any court or garden thereunto belonging, is made felony, liable to tranfportation for feven years: and to fteal underwood or hedges, and the like, to rob orchards or gar-dens of fruit growing therein, to fteal or otherwife deftroy any turnips or the roots of madder when growing, are by the fta-tutes 43 Eliz. c. 7. 15 Car. II. c. 2. 23 Geo. II. c. 26. and 31 Geo. II. c. 35. punifhable criminally, by whipping, fmall fines, imprifonment, and fatisfaction to the party wronged, ac-cording to the nature of the offence. Moreover, the ftealing by night of any trees, or of any roots, fhrubs, or plants to the value of 5 s, is by ftatute 6 Geo. III. c. 36. made felony in the prin-cipals, aiders, and abettors, and in the purchafers thereof know-ing the fame to be ftolen: and by ftatute 6 Geo. III. c. 48. the ftealing of any timber trees therein fpecified[o], and of any root,

---

[m] See Vol. II. pag. 16.
[n] 3 Inft. 109. 1 Hal. P. C. 510.

[o] Oak, beech, chefnut, walnut, afh, elm, cedar, fir, afp, lime, fycamore, and birch.

ſhrub, or plant, by day or night, is liable to pecuniary penalties for the two firſt offences, and for the third is conſtituted a felony liable to tranſportation for ſeven years. Stealing ore out of mines is alſo no larciny, upon the ſame principle of adherence to the freehold; with an exception only to mines of black lead, the ſtealing of ore out of which is felony without benefit of clergy by ſtatute 25 Geo. II. c. 10. Upon nearly the ſame principle the ſtealing of writings relating to a real eſtate is no felony, but a treſpaſs [p]: becauſe they concern the land, or (according to our technical language) *ſavour* of the *realty*, and are conſidered as part of it by the law; ſo that they deſcend to the heir together with the land which they concern [q].

BONDS, bills, and notes, which concern mere *choſes in action*, were alſo at the common law held not to be ſuch goods whereof larciny might be committed; being of no intrinſic value [r], and not importing any property in the *poſſeſſion* of the perſon from whom they are taken. But by the ſtatute 2 Geo. II. c. 25. they are now put upon the ſame footing, with reſpect to larcinies, as the money they were meant to ſecure. And, by ſtatute 7 Geo. III. c. 50. if any officer or ſervant of the poſt-office ſhall ſecrete, embezzle, or deſtroy any letter or pacquet, containing any bank note or other valuable paper particularly ſpecified in the act, or ſhall ſteal the ſame out of any letter or pacquet, he ſhall be guilty of felony without benefit of clergy. Or, if he ſhall deſtroy any letter or pacquet with which he has received money for the poſtage, or ſhall advance the rate of poſtage on any letter or pacquet ſent by the poſt, and ſhall ſecrete the money received by ſuch advancement, he ſhall be guilty of ſingle felony. Larciny alſo could not at common law be committed of treaſure-trove, or wreck, till ſeiſed by the king or him who hath the franchiſe; for till ſuch ſeiſure no one hath a determinate property therein. But by ſtatute 26 Geo. II. c. 19. plundering, or ſtealing from, any ſhip in diſtreſs (whether wreck or no wreck)

[p] 1 Hal. P. C. 510. Stra. 1137.   [r] 8 Rep. 33.
[q] See Vol. II. pag. 438.

is

is felony without benefit of clergy: in like manner as, by the civil law[s], this inhumanity is also punished in the same degree as the most atrocious theft.

LARCINY also cannot be committed of such animals, in which there is no property either absolute or qualified; as of beasts that are *ferae naturae*, and unreclaimed, such as deer, hares, and conies, in a forest, chase, or warren; fish in an open river or pond; or wild fowls at their natural liberty[t]. But if they are reclaimed or confined, and may serve for food, it is otherwise, even at common law: for of deer so inclosed in a park that they may be taken at pleasure, fish in a trunk, and pheasants or partridges in a mew, larciny may be committed[u]. And now, by statute 9 Geo. I. c. 22. to kill or steal any deer in a forest, or other place, enclosed; to rob a warren; or to steal fish from a river or pond, being in this last case armed and disguised; these are felonies without benefit of clergy. And by statute 13 Car. II. c. 10. to steal deer in any forest, though uninclosed, is a forfeiture of 20 l. for the first offence, and by statute 10 Geo. II. c. 32. seven years transportation for the second offence: which punishment is also inflicted for the first offence upon such as come to hunt there armed with offensive weapons. Also by statute 5 Geo. III. c. 14. the penalty of transportation for seven years is inflicted on persons stealing or taking fish in any water within a park, paddock, orchard, or yard; and on the receivers, aiders, and abettors: and the like punishment, or whipping, fine, or imprisonment, is provided for the taking or killing of conies[w] in open warrens. And a forfeiture of five pounds to the owner of the fishery is made payable by persons taking or destroying (or *attempting* so to do) any fish in any river or other water within any inclosed ground being private property. Stealing hawks, in disobedience to the rules prescribed by the statute 37 Edw. III. c. 19. is also felony[x]. It is also said[y], that, if swans

---

[s] *Cod.* 6. 2. 18.
[t] 1 Hal. P. C. 511. Fost. 366.
[u] 1 Hawk. P. C. 94. 1 Hal. P. C. 511.

[w] See stat. 22 & 23 Car. II. c. 25.
[x] 3 Inst. 98.
[y] Dalt. Just. c. 156.

be lawfully marked, it is felony to ſteal them, though at large in a public river; and that it is likewiſe felony to ſteal them, though unmarked, if in any private river or pond : otherwiſe it is only a treſpaſs. But, of all valuable domeſtic animals, as horſes, and of all animals *domitae naturae*, which ſerve for food, as ſwine, ſheep, poultry, and the like, larciny may be committed; and alſo of the fleſh of ſuch as are *ferae naturae*, when killed[z]. As to thoſe animals, which do not ſerve for food, and which therefore the law holds to have no intrinſic value, as dogs of all ſorts, and other creatures kept for whim and pleaſure, though a man may have a baſe property therein, and maintain a civil action for the loſs of them[a], yet they are not of ſuch eſtimation, as that the crime of ſtealing them amounts to larciny[b].

NOTWITHSTANDING however that no larciny can be committed, unleſs there be ſome property in the thing taken, and an owner; yet, if the owner be unknown, provided there be a property, it is larciny to ſteal it; and an indictment will lie, for the goods of a perſon unknown[c]. In like manner as, among the Romans, the *lex Hoſtilia de furtis* provided, that a proſecution for theft might be carried on without the intervention of the owner[d]. This is the caſe of ſtealing a ſhrowd out of a grave; which is the property of thoſe, whoever they were, that buried the deceaſed : but ſtealing the corpſe itſelf, which has no owner, (though a matter of great indecency) is no felony, unleſs ſome of the gravecloths be ſtolen with it[e]. Very different from the law of the Franks, which ſeems to have reſpected both as equal offences; when it directed that a perſon, who had dug a corpſe out of the ground in order to ſtrip it, ſhould be baniſhed from ſociety, and no one ſuffered to relieve his wants, till the relations of the deceaſed conſented to his readmiſſion[f].

[z] 1 Hal. P. C. 511.
[a] See Vol. II. pag. 393.
[b] 1 Hal. P. C. 512.
[c] *Ibid.*

[d] Gravin. *l.* 3. §. 106.
[e] See Vol. II. pag. 429.
[f] Monteſq. Sp. L. b. 30. ch. 19.

HAVING

HAVING thus confidered the general nature of fimple larciny, I come next to treat of it's *punifhment*. Theft, by the
Jewifh law, was only punifhed with a pecuniary fine, and fatisfaction to the party injured [g]. And in the civil law, till fome
very late conftitutions, we never find the punifhment capital.
The laws of Draco at Athens punifhed it with death: but his
laws were faid to be written in blood; and Solon afterwards
changed the penalty to a pecuniary mulct. And fo the Attic laws
in general continued [h]; except that once, in a time of dearth,
it was made capital to break into a garden, and fteal figs: but
this law, and the informers againft the offence, grew fo odious,
that from them all malicious informers were ftiled fycophants;
a name, which we have much perverted from it's original meaning. From thefe examples, as well as the reafon of the thing,
many learned and fcrupulous men have queftioned the propriety,
if not lawfulnefs, of inflicting capital punifhment for fimple
theft [i]. And certainly the natural punifhment for injuries to
property feems to be the lofs of the offender's own property:
which ought to be univerfally the cafe, were all men's fortunes
equal. But as thofe, who have no property themfelves, are generally the moft ready to attack the property of others, it has
been found neceffary inftead of a pecuniary to fubftitute a corporal punifhment: yet how far this corporal punifhment ought
to extend, is what has occafioned the doubt. Sir Thomas More[i],
and the marquis Beccaria [k], at the diftance of more than two
centuries, have very fenfibly propofed that kind of corporal

---

[g] Exod. c. xxii.

[h] Petit. *LL. Attic. l. 7. tit. 5.*

[i] *Eft enim ad vindicanda furta nimis atrox,
nec tamen ad refraenanda fufficiens: quippe neque furtum fimplex tam ingens facinus eft, ut
capite debeat plecti; neque ulla poena eft tanta,
ut ab latrociniis cohibeat eos, qui nullam aliam
artem quaerendi victus habent.* (Mori *Utopia.
edit. Glafg.* 1750. *pag.* 21.) — *Denique, cum
lex Mofaica, quanquam inclemens et afpera, tamen pecunia furtum, haud morte, mulctavit;
ne putemus Deum, in noxia lege clementiae qua
pater imperat filiis, majorem indulfiffe nobis in-
vicem faeviendi licentiam. Haec funt cur non
licere putem: quam vero fit abfurdum, atque
etiam perniciofum reipublicae, furem atque homicidam ex aequo puniri, nemo eft (opinor) qui
nefciat.* (Ibid. 39.)

[i] *Utop. pag.* 42.

[k] ch. 22.

punifh-

punifhment, which approaches the neareft to a pecuniary fatisfaction; *viz.* a temporary imprifonment, with an obligation to
labour, firft for the party robbed, and afterwards for the public,
in works of the moft flavifh kind: in order to oblige the offender to repair, by his induftry and diligence, the depredations
he has committed upon private property and public order. But,
notwithftanding all the remonftrances of fpeculative politicians
and moralifts, the punifhment of theft ftill continues, throughout the greateft part of Europe, to be capital: and Puffendorf[l],
together with fir Matthew Hale[m], are of opinion that this muft
always be referred to the prudence of the legiflature; who are
to judge, fay they, when crimes are become fo enormous as to
require fuch fanguinary reftrictions[n]. Yet both thefe writers
agree, that fuch punifhment fhould be cautioufly inflicted, and
never without the utmoft neceffity.

OUR antient Saxon laws nominally punifhed theft with death,
if above the value of twelvepence: but the criminal was permitted to redeem his life by a pecuniary ranfom; as, among their
anceftors the Germans, by a ftated number of cattle[o]. But in
the ninth year of Henry the firft, this power of redemption was
taken away, and all perfons guilty of larciny above the value of
twelvepence were directed to be hanged; which law continues
in force to this day[p]. For though the inferior fpecies of theft,
or petit larciny, is only punifhed by whipping at common law[q],
or by ftatute 4 Geo. I. c. 11. may be extended to tranfportation
for feven years, yet the punifhment of grand larciny, or the
ftealing above the value of twelvepence, (which fum was the
ftandard in the time of king Athelftan, eight hundred years ago)
is at common law regularly death. Which, confidering the great
intermediate alteration in the price or denomination of money,
is undoubtedly a very rigorous conftitution; and made fir Henry
Spelman (above a century fince, when money was at twice it's

[l] L. of N. b. 8. c. 3.
[m] 1 Hal. P. C. 13.
[n] See pag. 9.

[o] Tac. *de mor. Germ. c.* 12.
[p] 1 Hal. P. C. 12. 3 Inft. 53.
[q] 3 Inft. 218.

present

prefent rate) complain, that while every thing elfe was rifen in
it's nominal value, and become dearer, the life of man had continually grown cheaper[r]. It is true, that the mercy of juries
will often make them ftrain a point, and bring in larciny to be
under the value of twelvepence, when it is really of much greater
value : but this is a kind of pious perjury, and does not at all excufe our common law in this refpect from the imputation of feverity, but rather ftrongly confeffes the charge. It is likewife
true, that, by the merciful extenfions of the benefit of clergy
by our modern ftatute law, a perfon who commits a fimple larciny to the value of thirteen pence or thirteen hundred pounds,
though guilty of a capital offence, fhall be excufed the pains of
death : but this is only for the firft offence. And in many cafes of
fimple larciry the benefit of clergy is taken away by ftatute : as
from horfeftealing[s]; taking woollen cloth from off the tenters[t],
or linen from the place of manufacture[v]; ftealing fheep or other
cattle fpecified in the acts[u]; thefts on navigable rivers above the
value of forty fhillings[w]; plundering veffels in diftrefs, or that
have fuffered fhipwreck[x]; ftealing letters fent by the poft[y]; and
alfo ftealing deer, hares, and conies under the peculiar circumftances mentioned in the Waltham black act[z]. Which additional
feverity is owing to the great malice and mifchief of the theft
in fome of thefe inftances ; and, in others, to the difficulties
men would otherwife lie under to preferve thofe goods, which
are fo eafily carried off. Upon which laft principle the Roman
law punifhed more feverely than other thieves the *abigei*, or
ftealers of cattle[a]; and the *balnearii*, or fuch as ftole the cloaths
of perfons who were wafhing in the public baths[b] : both which
conftitutions feem to be borrowed from the laws of Athens[c].

[r] *Gl 0ff.* 350.
[s] Stat. 1 Edw. VL c. 12. 2 & 3 Edw. VI. c. 33. 31 Eliz. c. 12.
[t] Stat. 22 Car. IL c. 5.
[v] Stat. 18 Geo. II. c. 27.
[u] Stat. 14 Geo. II. c. 6. 15 Geo. II. e. 34.
[w] Stat. 24 Geo. II. c. 45.

[x] Stat. 12 Ann. ft. 2. c. 18. 26 Geo. II. c. 19.
[y] Stat. 7 Geo. III. c. 50.
[z] Stat. 9 Geo. I. c. 22.
[a] *Ff.* 47. *t.* 14.
[b] *Ibid. t.* 17.
[c] Pott. Antiqu. b. 1. c. 26.

And

And fo too the antient Goths punifhed with unrelenting feverity thefts of cattle, or of corn that was reaped and left in the field : fuch kind of property (which no human induftry can fufficiently guard) being efteemed under the peculiar cuftody of heaven [d]. And thus much for the offence of *fimple* larciny.

Mixed, or *compound* larciny is fuch as has all the properties of the former, but is accompanied with one of, or both, the aggravations of a taking from one's *houfe* or *perfon*. Firft therefore of larciny from the *houfe*, and then of larciny from the *perfon*.

1. Larciny from the *houfe*, though it feems (from the confiderations mentioned in the preceding chapter [e]) to have a higher degree of guilt than fimple larciny, yet is not at all diftinguifhed from the other at common law [f] : unlefs where it is accompanied with the circumftance of breaking the houfe by night ; and then we have feen that it falls under another defcription, *viz.* that of burglary. But now by feveral acts of parliament (the hiftory of which is very ingenioufly deduced by a learned modern writer [g], who hath fhewn them to have gradually arifen from our improvements in trade and opulence) the benefit of clergy is taken from larcinies committed in an houfe in almoft every inftance [h]. The multiplicity of which acts are apt to create fome confufion ; but upon comparing them diligently we may collect, that the benefit of clergy is denied upon the following domeftic aggravations of larciny ; *viz.* 1. In all larcinies above the value of twelvepence, from a church, or from a dwelling-houfe, or booth, any perfon being therein. 2. In all larcinies to the value of 5 s. committed by breaking the dwelling-houfe, though no perfon be therein. 3. In all larcinies to the value of 40 s. from a dwelling-houfe, or it's outhoufes, without breaking in, and whether any perfon be

[d] Stiernh. *de jure Goth. l.* 3. *c.* 5.
[e] See pag. 223.
[f] 1 Hawk. P. C. 98.
[g] Barr. 375, *&c.*

[h] Stat. 23 Hen. VIII. c. 1. 25 Hen. VIII. c. 3. 1 Edw. VI. c. 12. 5 & 6 Edw. VI. c. 9. 39 Eliz. c. 15. 3 & 4 W. & M. c. 9. 10 & 11 W. III. c. 23. 12 Ann. c. 7.

therein

therein or no. 4. In all larcinies to the value of 5 s. from any shop, warehouse[i], coachhouse, or stable; whether the same be broken open or not, and whether any person be therein or no. In all these cases, whether happening by day or by night, the benefit of clergy is taken away from the offenders.

2. LARCINY from the *person* is either by *privately* stealing; or by open and violent assault, which is usually called *robbery*.

THE offence of *privately* stealing from a man's *person*, as by picking his pocket or the like, without his knowlege, was debarred of the benefit of clergy, so early as by the statute 8 Eliz. c. 14. But then it must be such a larciny, as stands in need of the benefit of clergy, *viz.* of above the value of twelvepence; else the offender shall not have judgment of death. For the statute creates no new offence; but only takes away the benefit of clergy, which was a matter of grace, and leaves the thief to the regular judgment of the antient law[k]. This severity (for a most severe law it certainly is) seems to be owing to the ease with which such offences are committed, and the difficulty of guarding against them : besides that this is an infringement of property, in the manual occupation or corporal possession of the owner, which was an offence even in a state of nature. And therefore the *faccularii*, or cutpurses, were more severely punished than common thieves by the Roman and Athenian laws[l].

OPEN and violent larciny from the *person*, or *robbery*, the *rapina* of the civilians, is the felonious and forcible taking, from the person of another, of goods or money to any value, by putting him in fear[m]. 1. There must be a taking, otherwise it is no robbery. A mere attempt to rob was indeed held to be felony, so late as Henry the fourth's time[n]: but afterwards it was taken to be only a misdemesnor, and punishable with fine and imprison-

---

[i] See Foster. 78, 79. Barr. 379.
[k] 1 Hawk. P. C. 98.
[l] Ff. 47. 11. 7. Pott. Antiqu. l. 1. c. 26.

[m] 1 Hawk. P. C. 95.
[n] 1 Hal. P. C. 532.

ment; till the ſtatute 7 Geo. II. c. 21. which makes it a felony tranſportable for ſeven years. If the thief, having once taken a purſe, returns it, ſtill it is a robbery: and ſo it is whether the taking be ſtrictly from the perſon of another, or in his preſence only; as where a robber by menaces and violence puts a man in fear, and drives away his ſheep or his cattle before his face[o]. 2. It is immaterial of what value the thing taken is: a penny as well as a pound, thus forcibly extorted, makes a robbery[p]. 3. Laſtly, the taking muſt be by force, or a previous putting in fear; which makes the violation of the perſon more atrocious than privately ſtealing. For, according to the maxim of the civil law[q], "*qui vi rapuit, fur improbior eſſe videtur.*" This previous putting in fear is the criterion that diſtinguiſhes robbery from other larcinies. For if one privately ſteals ſixpence from the perſon of another, and afterwards keeps it by putting him in fear, this is no robbery, for the fear is ſubſequent[r]: neither is it capital, as privately ſtealing, being under the value of twelvepence. Yet this putting in fear does not imply, that any great degree of terror or affright in the party robbed is neceſſary to conſtitute a robbery: it is ſufficient that ſo much force, or threatening by word or geſture, be uſed, as might create an apprehenſion of danger, or oblige a man to part with his property without or againſt his conſent[s]. Thus, if a man be knocked down without previous warning, and ſtripped of his property while ſenſeleſs, though ſtrictly he cannot be ſaid to be *put in fear*, yet this is undoubtedly a robbery. Or, if a perſon with a ſword drawn begs an alms, and I give it him through miſtruſt and apprehenſion of violence, this is a felonious robbery[t]. So if, under a pretence of ſale, a man forcibly extorts money from another, neither ſhall this ſubterfuge avail him. But it is doubted[u], whether the forcing a higler, or other chapman, to ſell his wares, and giving him the full value of them, amounts to ſo heinous a crime as robbery.

[o] 1 Hal. P. C. 533.
[p] 1 Hawk. P. C. 97.
[q] *Ff.* 4. 2. 14. §. 12.
[r] 1 Hal. P. C. 534.
[s] Foſt. 128.
[t] 1 Hawk. P. C. 96.
[u] *Ibid.* 97.

THIS

THIS species of larciny is debarred of the benefit of clergy by statute 23 Hen. VIII. c. 1. and other subsequent statutes; not indeed in general, but only when committed in or near the king's highway. A robbery therefore in a distant field, or footpath, was not punished with death [w]; but was open to the benefit of clergy, till the statute 3 & 4 W. & M. c. 9. which takes away clergy from robbery wheresoever committed.

II. MALICIOUS *mischief*, or damage, is the next species of injury to private property, which the law considers as a public crime. This is such as is done, not *animo furandi*, or with an intent of gaining by another's loss; which is some, though a weak, excuse: but either out of a spirit of wanton cruelty, or black and diabolical revenge. In which it bears a near relation to the crime of arson; for as that affects the habitation, so this does the other property, of individuals. And therefore any damage arising from this mischievous disposition, though only a trespass at common law, is now by a multitude of statutes made penal in the highest degree. Of these I shall extract the contents in order of time.

AND, first, by statute 22 Hen. VIII. c. 11. perversely and maliciously to cut down or destroy the powdike, in the fens of Norfolk and Ely, is felony. By statute 43 Eliz. c. 13. (for preventing rapine on the northern borders) to burn any barn or stack of corn or grain; or to prey, or make spoil, of the persons or goods of the subject upon deadly feud, in the four northern counties of Northumberland, Westmorland, Cumberland, and Durham; or to give or take any money or contribution, there called *blackmail*, to secure such goods from rapine; is felony without benefit of clergy. By statute 22 & 23 Car. II. c. 7. to burn any ricks or stacks of corn, hay, or grain, barns, houses, buildings, or kilns; or maliciously, unlawfully, and willingly to kill any horses, sheep, or other cattle, in the night time, is fe-

[w] 1 Hal. P. C. 535.

lony;

lony; but the offender may make his election to be tranſported
for ſeven years: and to maim or hurt ſuch cattle is a treſpaſs,
for which treble damages ſhall be recovered. By ſtatute 1 Ann.
ſt. 2. c. 9. captains and mariners belonging to ſhips, and deſtroying the ſame, to the prejudice of the owners, (and by 4 Geo. I.
c. 12. to the prejudice of inſurers alſo) are guilty of felony
without benefit of clergy. And by ſtatute 12 Ann. c. 18. making any hole in a ſhip in diſtreſs, or ſtealing her pumps, or
wilfully doing any thing tending to the immediate loſs of ſuch
ſhip, is felony without benefit of clergy. By ſtatute 1 Geo. I,
c. 48. maliciouſly to ſet on fire any underwood, wood, or cop-
pice, is made ſingle felony. By ſtatute 6 Geo. I. c. 23. the wilful and malicious tearing, cutting, ſpoiling, burning, or defacing
of the garments or cloaths of any perſon paſſing in the ſtreets
or highways, is felony. This was occaſioned by the inſolence
of certain weavers and others; who, upon the introduction of
ſome Indian faſhions prejudicial to their own manufactures, made
it their practice to caſt *aqua fortis* in the ſtreets upon ſuch as
wore them. By ſtatute 9 Geo. I. c. 22. commonly called the
Waltham black act, occaſioned by the devaſtations committed in
Epping foreſt, near Waltham in Eſſex, by perſons in diſguiſe or
with their faces blacked; (who ſeem to have reſembled the Ro-
berdſmen, or followers of Robert Hood, that in the reign of
Richard the firſt committed great outrages on the borders of
England and Scotland [x];) by this black act, I ſay, which has in
part been mentioned under the ſeveral heads of riots, mayhem,
and larciny, it is farther enacted, that unlawfully and maliciouſly
to ſet fire to any houſe, barn, or outhouſe, or to any hovel, cock,
mow, or ſtack of corn, ſtraw, hay, or wood; or to break down
the head of any fiſhpond, whereby the fiſh ſhall be loſt; or to
kill, maim, or wound any cattle; or to cut down, or deſtroy,
any trees planted in an avenue, or growing in a garden, orchard,
or plantation, for ornament, ſhelter, or profit; all theſe malicious acts are felonies without benefit of clergy: and the hundred ſhall be chargeable for the damages, unleſs the offender be

[x] 3 Inſt. 197.

con-

convicted. In like manner by the Roman law to cut down trees, and especially vines, was punished in the same degree as robbery [y]. By statutes 6 Geo. II. c. 37. and 10 Geo. II. c. 32. it is also made felony without the benefit of clergy, maliciously to cut down any river or sea bank, whereby lands may be over-flowed; or to cut any hop-binds growing in a plantation of hops, or wilfully and maliciously to set fire to any mine or delph of coal. By statute 28 Geo. II. c. 19. to set fire to any gofs, furze, or fern, growing in any forest or chase, is subject to a fine of five pounds. And by statute 6 Geo. III. c. 36 & 48. wilfully to spoil or destroy any timber or other trees, roots, shrubs, or plants, is for the two first offences liable to pecuniary penalties; and for the third if in the day time, and even for the first if at night, the offender shall be guilty of felony, and liable to transportation for seven years. And these are the punishments of malicious mischief.

III. FORGERY, or the *crimen falsi*, is an offence, which was punished by the civil law with deportation or banishment, and sometimes with death [z]. It may with us be defined (at common law) to be, " the fraudulent making or alteration of a wri-" ting to the prejudice of another man's right:" for which the offender may suffer fine, imprisonment, and pillory. And also by a variety of statutes, a more severe punishment is inflicted on the offender in many particular cases, which are so multiplied of late as almost to become general. I shall mention the principal instances.

BY statute 5 Eliz. c. 14. to forge or make, or knowingly to publish or give in evidence, any forged deed, court roll, or will, with intent to affect the right of real property, either freehold or copyhold, is punished by a forfeiture to the party grieved of double costs and damages; by standing in the pillory, and having both his ears cut off, and his nostrils slit, and seared; by forfeiture to the crown of the profits of his lands, and by perpetual impri-

[y] *Ff.* 47. 7. 2.　　　　　　　[z] *Inst.* 4. 18. 7.

sonment.

sonment. For any forgery relating to a term of years, or annuity, bond, obligation, acquittance, releafe, or difcharge of any debt or demand of any perfonal chattels, the fame forfeiture is given to the party grieved; and on the offender is inflicted the pillory, lofs of one of his ears, and half a year's imprifonment: the fecond offence in both cafes being felony without benefit of clergy.

Besides this general act, a multitude of others, fince the revolution, (when paper credit was firft eftablifhed) have inflicted capital punifhment on the forging or altering of bank bills or notes, or other fecurities[a]; of bills of credit iffued from the exchequer[b]; of fouth fea bonds, &c[c]; of lottery orders[d]; of army or navy debentures[e]; of Eaft India bonds[f]; of writings under feal of the London, or royal exchange, affurance[g]; of a letter of attorney or other power to receive or transfer ftock or annuities, or for the perfonating a proprietor thereof, to receive or transfer fuch annuities, ftock, or dividends[h]: to which may be added, though not ftrictly reducible to this head, the counterfeiting of mediterranean paffes, under the hands of the lords of the admiralty, to protect one from the piratical ftates of Barbary[i]; the forging or imitating any ftamps to defraud the ftamp office[k]; and the forging any marriage regifter or licence[l]: all which are by diftinct acts of parliament made felonies without benefit of clergy. And by ftatute 31 Geo. II. c. 32. forging or counterfeiting any ftamp or mark to denote the ftandard of gold and filver plate, and certain other offences of the like tendency, are made felony, but not without benefit of clergy.

[a] Stat. 7 & 8 W. III. c. 31. 8 & 9 W. III. c. 20. 11 Geo. I. c. 9. 12 Geo. I. c. 32. 15 Geo. II. c. 13.

[b] See the feveral acts for iffuing them.

[c] Stat. 9 Ann. c. 21. 6 Geo. I. c. 4. & 11. 12 Geo. I. c. 32.

[d] See the feveral acts for the lotteries.

[e] Stat. 5 Geo. I. c. 14. 9 Geo. I. c. 5.

[f] Stat. 12 Geo. I. c. 32.

[g] Stat. 6 Geo. I. c. 18.

[h] Stat. 8 Geo. I. c. 22. 9 Geo. I. c. 12.

[i] Stat. 4 Geo. II. c. 18.

[k] See the feveral ftamp acts.

[l] Stat. 26 Geo. II. c. 33.

There

THERE are also two other general laws, with regard to forgery; the one 2 Geo. II. c. 35. whereby the first offence in forging or publishing any forged deed, will, writing obligatory, bill of exchange, promissory note, indorsement or assignment thereof, or any acquittance or receipt for money or goods, with intention to defraud any person, is made felony without benefit of clergy. And by statute 7 Geo. II. c. 22. it is equally penal to forge or utter a counterfeit acceptance of a bill of exchange, or the number of any accountable receipt for any note, bill, or any other security for money; or any warrant or order for the payment of money, or delivery of goods. So that, I believe, through the number of these general and special provisions, there is now hardly a case possible to be conceived, wherein forgery, that tends to defraud, whether in the name of a real or fictitious person[m], is not made a capital crime.

THESE are the principal infringements of the rights of property; which were the last species of offences against individuals or private subjects, which the method of our distribution has led us to consider. We have before examined the nature of all offences against the public, or commonwealth; against the king or supreme magistrate, the father and protector of that community; against the universal law of all civilized nations; together with some of the more atrocious offences, of publicly pernicious consequence, against God and his holy religion. And these several heads comprehend the whole circle of crimes and misdemesnors, with the punishment annexed to each, that are cognizable by the laws of England.

[m] Fost. 116, &c.

Chapter the Eighteenth.

Of the means of PREVENTING offences.

WE are now arrived at the fifth general branch or head, under which I propofed to confider the fubject of this book of our commentaries; *viz.* the means of *preventing* the commiffion of crimes and mifdemefnors. And really it is an honour, and almoft a fingular one, to our Englifh laws, that they furnifh a title of this fort : fince *preventive* juftice is upon every principle, of reafon, of humanity, and of found policy, preferable in all refpects to *punifhing* juftice [a]; the execution of which, though neceffary, and in it's confequences a fpecies of mercy to the commonwealth, is always attended with many harfh and difagreeable circumftances.

THIS preventive juftice confifts in obliging thofe perfons, whom there is probable ground to fufpect of future mifbehaviour, to ftipulate with and to give full affurance to the public, that fuch offence as is apprehended fhall not happen; by finding pledges or fecurities for keeping the peace, or for their good behaviour. This requifition of fureties has been feveral times mentioned before, as part of the penalty inflicted upon fuch as have been guilty of certain grofs mifdemefnors : but there alfo it muft be underftood rather as a caution againft the repetition of the offence, than any immediate pain or punifhment. And

[a] Beccar. ch 41.

indeed,

indeed, if we confider all human punifhments in a large and extended view, we fhall find them all rather calculated to prevent future crimes, than to expiate the paft: fince, as was obferved in a former chapter [b], all punifhments inflicted by temporal laws may be claffed under three heads; fuch as tend to the amendment of the offender himfelf, or to deprive him of any power to do future mifchief, or to deter others by his example: all of which conduce to one and the fame end, of preventing future crimes, whether that be effected by amendment, difability, or example. But the caution, which we fpeak of at prefent, is fuch as is intended merely for prevention, without any crime actually committed by the party, but arifing only from a probable fufpicion, that fome crime is intended or likely to happen; and confequently it is not meant as any degree of punifhment, unlefs perhaps for a man's imprudence in giving juft ground of apprehenfion.

By the Saxon conftitution thefe fureties were always at hand, by means of king Alfred's wife inftitution of decennaries or frankpledges; wherein, as has more than once been obferved [c], the whole neighbourhood or tithing of freemen were mutually pledges for each others good behaviour. But, this great and general fecurity being now fallen into difufe and neglected, there hath fucceeded to it the method of making fufpected perfons find particular and fpecial fecurities for their future conduct: of which we find mention in the laws of king Edward the confeffor [d]; "*tradat fidejuffores de pace et legalitate tuenda.*" Let us therefore confider, firft, what this fecurity is; next, who may take or demand it; and, laftly, how it may be difcharged.

1. THIS fecurity confifts in being bound, with one or more fureties, in a recognizance or obligation to the king, entered on record, and taken in fome court or by fome judicial officer; whereby the parties acknowlege themfelves to be indebted to the crown in the fum required; (for inftance 100 *l*.) with condition

[b] See pag. 11.   [c] See Vol. I. pag. 113.   [d] *cap.* 18.

to be void and of none effect, if the party shall appear in court
on such a day, and in the mean time shall keep the peace : either
generally, towards the king, and all his liege people ; or particularly also, with regard to the person who craves the security.
Or, if it be for the good behaviour, then on condition that he
shall demean and behave himself well, (or be of good behaviour)
either generally or specially, for the time therein limited, as for
one or more years, or for life. This recognizance, if taken by
a justice of the peace, must be certified to the next sessions, in
pursuance of the statute 3 Hen. VII. c. 1. and if the condition of
such recognizance be broken, by any breach of the peace in the
one case, or any misbehaviour in the other, the recognizance
becomes forfeited or absolute ; and, being *estreated* or extracted
(taken out from among the other records) and sent up to the
exchequer, the party and his sureties, having now become the
king's absolute debtors, are sued for the several sums in which
they are respectively bound.

2. ANY justices of the peace, by virtue of their commission,
or those who are *ex officio* conservators of the peace, as was mentioned in a former volume[e], may demand such security according
to their own discretion : or it may be granted at the request of
any subject, upon due cause shewn, provided such demandant be
under the king's protection ; for which reason it hath been formerly doubted, whether Jews, Pagans, or persons convicted of
a *praemunire*, were intitled thereto[f]. Or, if the justice is averse
to act, it may be granted by a mandatory writ, called a *suppli-
cavit*, issuing out of the court of king's bench or chancery ;
which will compel the justice to act, as a ministerial and not as
a judicial officer : and he must make a return to such writ,
specifying his compliance, under his hand and seal[g]. But this
writ is seldom used : for, when application is made to the superior courts, they usually take the recognizances there, under the
directions of the statute 21 Jac. I. c. 8. And indeed a peer or

[e] See Vol. I. pag. 350.   [g] F. N. B. 80. 2 P. Wms. 202.
[f] 1 Hawk. P. C. 126.

peeress

peerefs cannot be bound over in any other place, than the courts of king's bench or chancery: though a juftice of the peace has a power to require fureties of any other perfon, being *compos mentis* and under the degree of nobility, whether he be a fellow juftice or other magiftrate, or whether he be merely a private man [h]. Wives may demand it againft their hufbands; or hufbands, if neceffary, againft their wives [j]. But feme-coverts, and infants under age, ought to find fecurity by their friends only, and not to be bound themfelves: for they are incapable of engaging themfelves to anfwer any debt; which, as we obferved, is the nature of thefe recognizances or acknowlegements.

3. A RECOGNIZANCE may be difcharged, either by the demife of the king, to whom the recognizance is made; or by the death of the principal party bound thereby, if not before forfeited; or by order of the court to which fuch recognizance is certified by the juftices (as the quarter feffions, affifes, or king's bench) if they fee fufficient caufe: or if he at whofe requeft it was granted, if granted upon a private account, will releafe it, or does not make his appearance to pray that it may be continued [i].

THUS far what has been faid is applicable to both fpecies of recognizances, for the *peace,* and for the *good behaviour; de pace, et legalitate, tuenda,* as expreffed in the laws of king Edward. But as thefe two fpecies of fecurities are in fome refpects different, efpecially as to the caufe of granting, or the means of forfeiting them; I fhall now confider them feparately: and firft, fhall fhew for what caufe fuch a recognizance, with fureties for the *peace,* is grantable; and then, how it may be forfeited.

1. ANY juftice of the peace may, *ex officio,* bind all thofe to keep the peace, who in his prefence make any affray; or threaten to kill or beat another; or contend together with hot

---

h 1 Hawk. P. C. 127.　　　　　i 1 Hawk. P. C. 129.
j 2 Stra. 1207.

and angry words; or go about with unufual weapons or attendance, to the terror of the people; and all fuch as he knows to
be common barretors; and fuch as are brought before him by
the conftable for a breach of the peace in his prefence; and all
fuch perfons, as, having been before bound to the peace, have
broken it and forfeited their recognizances[k]. Alfo, wherever any
private man hath juft caufe to fear, that another will burn his
houfe, or do him a corporal injury, by killing, imprifoning, or
beating him; or that he will procure others fo to do; he may
demand furety of the peace againft fuch perfon : and every juftice
of the peace is bound to grant it, if he who demands it will
make oath, that he is actually under fear of death or bodily harm;
and will fhew that he has juft caufe to be fo, by reafon of the
other's menaces, attempts, or having lain in wait for him; and
will alfo farther fwear, that he does not require fuch furety out
of malice or for mere vexation[l]. This is called *fwearing the
peace* againft another : and, if the party does not find fuch fureties, as the juftice in his difcretion fhall require, he may immediately be committed till he does[m].

2. SUCH recognizance for keeping the peace, when given,
may be forfeited by any actual violence, or even an affault, or
menace, to the perfon of him who demanded it, if it be a fpecial recognizance : or, if the recognizance be general, by any
unlawful action whatfoever, that either is or tends to a breach
of the peace; or, more particularly, by any one of the many
fpecies of offences which were mentioned as crimes againft the
public peace in the eleventh chapter of this book; or, by any
private violence committed againft any of his majefty's fubjects.
But a bare trefpafs upon the lands or goods of another, which is
a ground for a civil action, unlefs accompanied with a wilful
breach of the peace, is no forfeiture of the recognizance[n].
Neither are mere reproachful words, as calling a man knave or
liar, any breach of the peace, fo as to forfeit one's recognizance

[k] 1 Hawk. P. C. 126.
[l] *Ibid.* 127.
[m] *Ibid.* 128.
[n] *Ibid.* 131.

(being

(being looked upon to be merely the effect of heat and paffion) unlefs they amount to a challenge to fight °.

THE other fpecies of recognizance, with fureties, is for the *good abearance*, or *good behaviour*. This includes fecurity for the peace, and fomewhat more : we will therefore examine it in the fame manner as the other.

1. FIRST then, the juftices are empowered by the ftatute 34 Edw. III. c. 1. to bind over to the good behaviour towards the king and his people, all them *that be not of good fame*, wherever they be found ; to the intent that the people be not troubled nor endamaged, nor the peace diminifhed, nor merchants and others, paffing by the highways of the realm, be difturbed nor put in the peril which may happen by fuch offenders. Under the general words of this expreffion, *that be not of good fame*, it is holden that a man may be bound to his good behaviour for caufes of fcandal, *contra bonos mores*, as well as *contra pacem* ; as, for haunting bawdy houfes with women of bad fame; or for keeping fuch women in his own houfe; or for words tending to fcandalize the government, or in abufe of the officers of juftice, efpecially in the execution of their office. Thus alfo a juftice may bind over all night-walkers ; eaves-droppers ; fuch as keep fufpicious company, or are reported to be pilferers or robbers ; fuch as fleep in the day, and wake on the night ; common drunkards ; whoremafters ; the putative fathers of baftards ; cheats ; idle vagabonds ; and other perfons, whofe mifbehaviour may reafonably bring them within the general words of the ftatute, as perfons not of good fame : an expreffion, it muft be owned, of fo great a latitude, as leaves much to be determined by the difcretion of the magiftrate himfelf. But, if he commits a man for want of fureties, he muft exprefs the caufe thereof with convenient certainty ; and take care that fuch caufe be a good one P.

° 1 Hawk. P. C. 130.   P *Ibid.* 132.

2. A RECOGNIZANCE for the good behaviour may be for-feited by all the fame means, as one for the fecurity of the peace may be; and alfo by fome others. As, by going armed with unufual attendance, to the terror of the people; by fpeaking words tending to fedition; or, by committing any of thofe acts of mif-behaviour, which the recognizance was intended to prevent. But not by barely giving frefh caufe of fufpicion of that which perhaps may never actually happen [q]: for, though it is juft to compel fufpected perfons to give fecurity to the public againft mifbehaviour that is apprehended; yet it would be hard, upon fuch fufpicion, without the proof of any actual crime, to punifh them by a forfeiture of their recognizance.

[q] 1 Hawk. P. C. 133.

CHAPTER THE NINETEENTH.

Of COURTS of a CRIMINAL JURISDICTION.

THE fixth, and laft, object of our enquiries will be the method of *inflicting* thofe *punifhments*, which the law has annexed to particular offences ; and which I have conftantly fubjoined to the defcription of the crime itfelf. In the difcuffion of which I fhall purfue much the fame general method, that I followed in the preceding book, with regard to the redrefs of civil injuries : by, firft, pointing out the feveral *courts* of criminal jurifdiction, wherein offenders may be profecuted to punifhment ; and by, fecondly, deducing down in their natural order, and explaining, the feveral *proceedings* therein.

FIRST then, in reckoning up the feveral *courts* of criminal jurifdiction, I fhall, as in the former cafe, begin with an account of fuch, as are of a *public* and *general* jurifdiction throughout the whole realm ; and, afterwards, proceed to fuch, as are only of a *private* and *fpecial* jurifdiction, and confined to fome particular parts of the kingdom.

I. IN our enquiries into the criminal courts of *public* and *general* jurifdiction, I muft in one refpect purfue a different order from that in which I confidered the civil tribunals. For there, as the feveral courts had a gradual fubordination to each

other,

other, the fuperior correcting and reforming the errors of the
inferior, I thought it beft to begin with the loweft, and fo afcend gradually to the courts of appeal, or thofe of the moft extenfive powers.   But as it is contrary to the genius and fpirit of
the law of England, to fuffer any man to be tried twice for the
fame offence in a criminal way, efpecially if acquitted upon the
firft trial; therefore thefe criminal courts may be faid to be all
independent of each other: at leaft fo far, as that the fentence
of the loweft of them can never be controlled or reverfed by
the higheft jurifdiction in the kingdom, unlefs for error in matter of law, apparent upon the face of the record; though fometimes caufes may be removed from one to the other before trial.
And therefore as, in thefe courts of criminal cognizance, there
is not the fame chain and dependence as in the others, I fhall
rank them according to their dignity, and begin with the higheft
of all; *viz.*

    1. THE high court of *parliament*; which is the fupreme court
in the kingdom, not only for the making, but alfo for the execution, of laws; by the trial of great and enormous offenders,
whether lords or commoners, in the method of parliamentary
impeachment. As for acts of parliament to attaint particular
perfons of treafon or felony, or to inflict pains and penalties,
beyond or contrary to the common law, to ferve a fpecial purpofe, I fpeak not of them; being to all intents and purpofes
new laws, made *pro re nata,* and by no means an execution of
fuch as are already in being. But an impeachment before the
lords by the commons of Great Britain, in parliament, is a profecution of the already known and eftablifhed law, and has been
frequently put in practice; being a prefentment to the moft high
and fupreme court of criminal jurifdiction by the moft folemn
grand inqueft of the whole kingdom [a]. A commoner cannot
however be impeached before the lords for any capital offence,

<hr>

[a] 1 Hal. P. C. * 150.

but

but only for high mifdemefnors [b]: a peer may be impeached for any crime. And they ufually (in cafe of an impeachment of a peer for treafon) addrefs the crown to appoint a lord high fteward, for the greater dignity and regularity of their proceedings; which high fteward was formerly elected by the peers themfelves, though he was generally commiffioned by the king [c]; but it hath of late years been ftrenuoufly maintained [d], that the appointment of an high fteward in fuch cafes is not indifpenfably neceffary, but that the houfe may proceed without one. The articles of impeachment are a kind of bills of indictment, found by the houfe of commons, and afterwards tried by the lords; who are in cafes of mifdemefnors confidered not only as their own peers, but as the peers of the whole nation. This is a cuftom derived to us from the conftitution of the antient Germans; who in their great councils fometimes tried capital accufatons relating to the public: " *licet apud concilium accufare quoque, et difcrimen capitis intendere* [e]." And it has a peculiar propriety in the Englifh conftitution; which has much improved upon the antient model imported hither from the continent.

[b] When, in 4 Edw. III. the king demanded the earls, barons, and peers, to give judgment againft Simon de Bereford, who had been a notorious accomplice in the treafons of Roger earl of Mortimer, they came before the king in parliament, and faid all with one voice, that the faid Simon was not their *peer*; and therefore they were not bound to judge him as a peer of the land. And when afterwards, in the fame parliament, they were prevailed upon, in refpect of the notoriety and heinoufnefs of his crimes, to receive the charge and to give judgment againft him, the following proteft and provifo was entered on the parliamentroll. "And it is affented and accorded by "our lord the king, and all the great men, "in full parliament, that albeit the peers, "as judges of the parliament, have taken "upon them in the prefence of our lord the

"king to make and render the faid judg-"ment; yet the peers who now are, or "fhall be in time to come, be not bound or "charged to render judgment upon others "than peers; nor that the peers of the land "have power to do this, but thereof ought "ever to be difcharged and acquitted: and "that the aforefaid judgment now rendered "be not drawn to example or confequence "in time to come, whereby the faid peers "may be charged hereafter to judge others "than their peers, contrary to the laws of "the land, if the like cafe happen, which "God forbid." (*Rot. Parl.* 4 *Edw. III. n.* 2 *&* 6. 2 Brad. Hift. 190. Selden. judic. in parl. ch. 1.)

[c] 1 Hal. P. C. 350.

[d] Lords Journ. 12 May 1679. Com. Journ. 15 May 1679. Foft. 142, *&c.*

[e] Tacit. *de mor. Germ.* 12.

For, though in general the union of the legiſlative and judicial powers ought to be moſt carefully avoided[f], yet it may happen that a ſubject, intruſted with the adminiſtration of public affairs, may infringe the rights of the people, and be guilty of ſuch crimes, as the ordinary magiſtrate either dares not or cannot puniſh. Of theſe the repreſentatives of the people, or houſe of commons, cannot properly *judge*; becauſe their conſtituents are the parties injured : and can therefore only *impeach*. But before what court ſhall this impeachment be tried ? Not before the ordinary tribunals, which would naturally be ſwayed by the authority of ſo powerful an accuſer. Reaſon therefore will ſuggeſt, that this branch of the legiſlature, which repreſents the people, muſt bring it's charge before the other branch, which conſiſts of the nobility, who have neither the ſame intereſts, nor the ſame paſſions as popular aſſemblies[g]. This is a vaſt ſuperiority, which the conſtitution of this iſland enjoys, over thoſe of the Grecian or Roman republics; where the people were at the ſame time both judges and accuſers. It is proper that the nobility ſhould judge, to inſure juſtice to the accuſed; as it is proper that the people ſhould accuſe, to inſure juſtice to the commonwealth. And therefore, among other extraordinary circumſtances attending the authority of this court, there is one of a very ſingular nature, which was inſiſted on by the houſe of commons in the caſe of the earl of Danby in the reign of Charles II[h]; and is now enacted by ſtatute 12 & 13 W. III. c. 2. that no pardon under the great ſeal ſhall be pleadable to an impeachment by the commons of Great Britain in parliament[i].

2. THE court of the *lord high ſteward* of Great Britain[k] is a court inſtituted for the trial of peers, indicted for treaſon or felony, or for miſpriſion of either[l]. The office of this great magiſtrate is very antient; and was formerly hereditary, or at

f See Vol. I. pag. 269.
g Monteſq. Sp. L. xi. 6.
h Com. Journ. 5 May 1679.

i See chap. 31.
k 4 Inſt. 58. 2 Hawk. P. C. 5. 421.
l 1 Bulſtr. 198.

leaſt

leaſt held for life, or *dum bene ſe geſſerit :* but now it is uſually, and hath been for many centuries paſt [m], granted *pro hac vice* only ; and it hath been the conſtant practice (and therefore ſeems now to have become neceſſary) to grant it to a lord of parliament, elſe he is incapable to try ſuch delinquent peer [n]. When ſuch an indictment is therefore found by a grand jury of freeholders in the king's bench, or at the aſſiſes before the juſtices of *oyer* and *terminer*, it is to be removed by a writ of *certiorari* into the court of the lord high ſteward, which only has power to determine it.   A peer may plead a pardon before the court of king's bench, and the judges have power to allow it ; in order to prevent the trouble of appointing an high ſteward, merely for the purpoſe of receiving ſuch plea.   But he may not plead, in that inferior court, any other plea ; as *guilty*, or *not guilty*, of the indictment ; but only in this court : becauſe, in conſequence of ſuch plea, it is poſſible that judgment of death might be awarded againſt him.   The king therefore, in caſe a peer be indicted of treaſon, felony, or miſpriſion, creates a lord high ſteward *pro hac vice* by commiſſion under the great ſeal ; which recites the indictment ſo found, and gives his grace power to receive and try it *ſecundum legem et conſuetudinem Angliae.*   Then, when the indictment is regularly removed, by writ of *certiorari*, commanding the inferior court to certify it up to him, the lord high ſteward directs a precept to a ſerjeant at arms, to ſummon the lords to attend and try the indicted peer. This precept was formerly iſſued to ſummon only eighteen or twenty, ſelected from the body of the peers : then the number came to be indefinite ; and the cuſtom was, for the lord high ſteward to ſummon as many as he thought proper, (but of late years not leſs than twenty three [o]) and that thoſe lords only ſhould ſit upon the trial : which threw a monſtrous weight of

---

[m] Pryn. on 4 Inſt. 46.

[n] *Quand un ſeigneur de parlement ſerra arrein de treaſon ou felony, le roy par ſes lettres patents fera un grand et ſage ſeigneur d'eſtre le grand ſeneſchal d' Angleterre : qui ——*

doit faire un precept —— pur faire venir xx ſeigneurs, ou xviii, &c. (Yearb. 13 *Hen. VIII.* 11.)   See Staund   P. C. 152.   3 Inſt. 28. 4 Inſt. 59.   2 Hawk. P. C. 5.   Barr. 234.

[o] Kelynge. 56.

power

power into the hands of the crown, and this it's great officer, of selecting only such peers as the then predominant party should most approve of. And accordingly, when the earl of Clarendon fell into disgrace with Charles II, there was a design formed to prorogue the parliament, in order to try him by a select number of peers; it being doubted whether the whole house could be induced to fall in with the views of the court[p]. But now, by statute 7 W. III. c. 3. upon all trials of peers for treason or misprision, all the peers who have a right to sit and vote in parliament shall be summoned, at least twenty days before such trial, to appear and vote therein; and every lord appearing shall vote in the trial of such peer, first taking the oaths of allegiance and supremacy, and subscribing the declaration against popery.

DURING the session of parliament the trial of an indicted peer is not properly in the court of the lord high steward, but before the court last-mentioned, of our lord the *king in parliament*[q]. It is true, a lord high steward is always appointed in that case, to regulate and add weight to the proceedings; but he is rather in the nature of a speaker *pro tempore*, or chairman of the court, than the judge of it; for the collective body of the peers are therein the judges both of law and fact, and the high steward has a vote with the rest, in right of his peerage. But in the court of the lord high steward, which is held in the recess of parliament, he is the sole judge in matters of law, as the lords triors are in matters of fact; and as they may not interfere with him in regulating the proceedings of the court, so he has no right to intermix with them in giving any vote upon the trial[r]. Therefore, upon the conviction and attainder of a peer for murder in full parliament, it hath been holden by the judges[s], that in case the day appointed in the judgment for execution should lapse before execution done, a new time of execution may be appointed by either the high court of parliament, during it's

[p] Carte's life of Ormonde. Vol. 2.
[q] Fost. 141.
[r] State Trials, Vol. IV. 214. 232, 3.
[s] Fost. 139.

fitting,

fitting, though no high fteward be exifting; or, in the recefs of parliament, by the court of king's bench, the record being removed into that court.

IT has been a point of fome controverfy, whether the bifhops have now a right to fit in the court of the lord high fteward, to try indictments of treafon and mifprifion. Some incline to imagine them included under the general words of the ftatute of king William, "all peers, who have a right to fit and vote in parliament:" but the expreffion had been much clearer, if it had been, "all " lords," and not, "all peers;" for though bifhops, on account of the baronies annexed to their bifhopricks, are clearly lords of parliament, yet, their blood not being ennobled, they are not univerfally allowed to be peers with the temporal nobility: and perhaps this word might be inferted purpofely with a view to exclude them. However, there is no inftance of their fitting on trials for capital offences, even upon impeachments or indictments in full parliament, much lefs in the court we are now treating of; for indeed they ufually voluntarily withdraw, but enter a proteft declaring their right to ftay. It is certain that, in the eleventh chapter of the conftitutions of Clarendon, made in parliament 11 Hen. II. they are exprefly excluded from fitting and voting in trials of life or limb: " *epifcopi, ficut caeteri baro-* " *nes, debent intereffe judiciis cum baronibus, quoufque perveniatur* " *ad diminutionem membrorum, vel ad mortem :*" and Becket's quarrel with the king hereupon was not on account of the exception, (which was agreeable to the canon law) but of the general rule, that compelled the bifhops to attend at all. And the determination of the houfe of lords in the earl of Danby's cafe[t], which hath ever fince been adhered to, is confonant to thefe conftitutions; "that the lords fpiritual have a right to ftay and " fit in court in capital cafes, till the court proceeds to the vote " of guilty, or not guilty." It muft be noted, that this refolution extends only to trials *in full parliament :* for to the court of the lord high fteward (in which no vote can be given, but mere-

[t] Lords Journ. 15 May 1679.

ly

ly that of guilty or not guilty) no bishop, as such, ever was or could be summoned; and though the statute of king William regulates the proceedings in that court, as well as in the court of parliament, yet it never intended to new-model or alter it's constitution; and consequently does not give the lords spiritual any right in cases of blood which they had not before [u]. And what makes their exclusion more reasonable, is, that they have no right to be tried themselves in the court of the lord high steward [w], and therefore surely ought not to be judges there. For the privilege of being thus tried depends upon nobility of blood, rather than a seat in the house; as appears from the trials of popish lords, of lords under age, and (since the union) of the Scots nobility, though not in the number of the sixteen; and from the trials of females, such as the queen consort or dowager, and of all peeresses by birth; and peeresses by marriage also, unless they have, when dowagers, disparaged themselves by taking a commoner to their second husband.

3. THE court of *king's bench* [x], concerning the nature of which we partly enquired in the preceding book [y], was (we may remember) divided into a *crown* side, and a *plea* side. And on the crown side, or crown office, it takes cognizance of all criminal causes, from high treason down to the most trivial misdemesnor or breach of the peace. Into this court also indictments from all inferior courts may be removed by writ of *certiorari*, and tried either at bar, or at *nisi prius*, by a jury of the county out of which the indictment is brought. The judges of this court are the supreme coroners of the kingdom. And the court itself is the principal court of criminal jurisdiction (though the two former are of greater dignity) known to the laws of England. For which reason by the coming of the court of king's bench into any county, (as it was removed to Oxford on account of the sickness in 1665) all former commissions of *oyer* and ter-

[u] Fost. 248.
[w] Bro. *Abr. 1. Trial.* 142.

[x] 4 Inst. 70. 2 Hal. P. C. 2. 2 Hawk. P. C. 6.
[y] See Vol. III. pag. 41.

miner,

miner, and general gaol delivery, are at once abforbed and determined *ipfo facto :* in the fame manner as by the old Gothic and Saxon conftitutions, "*jure vetufto obtinuit, quieviffe omnia inferiora* "*judicia, dicente jus rege²*."

INTO this court of king's bench hath reverted all that was good and falutary of the jurifdiction of the court of *ftar-chamber, camera ftellata²:* which was a court of very antient original ᵇ, but new-modelled by ftatutes 3 Hen. VII. c. 1. and 21 Hen. VIII. c. 20. confifting of divers lords fpiritual and temporal, being privy counfellors, together with two judges of the courts of common law, without the intervention of any jury. Their jurifdiction extended legally over riots, perjury, mifbe-

---

z Stiernhook. *l.* 1. *c.* 2.

ª This is faid (Lamb. *Arch.* 154.) to have been fo called, either from the Saxon word ꞃꞇeoꞃan, to *fteer* or govern ; or from it's punifhing the *crimen ftellionatus*, or cofenage ; or becaufe the room wherein it fate, the old council chamber of the palace of Weftminfter, (Lamb. 148.) was full of windows ; or (to which fir Edward Coke, 4 Inft. 66. accedes) becaufe haply the roof thereof was at the firft garnifhed with gilded ftars. As all thefe are merely conjectures, (for no ftars are faid to have remained in the roof fo late as the reign of queen Elizabeth) I fhall venture to propofe another conjectural etymology, as plaufible perhaps as any of them. It is well known that, before the banifhment of the Jews under Edward I, their contracts and obligations were denominated in our antient records *ftarra* or *ftarrs*, from a corruption of the Hebrew word, *fhetàr*, a covenant. (Tovey's *Angl. judaic.* 32. Selden. tit. of hon. ii. 34. *Uxor Ebraic.* i. 14.) Thefe ftarrs, by an ordinance of Richard the firft, preferved by Hoveden, were commanded to be enrolled and depofited in chefts under three keys in

certain places; one, and the moft confiderable, of which was in the king's exchequer at Weftminfter : and no ftarr was allowed to be valid, unlefs it were found in fome of the faid repofitaries. (Madox hift. exch. c. vii. §. 4, 5, 6.) The room at the exchequer, where the chefts containing thefe ftarrs were kept, was probably called the *ftarr-chamber* ; and, when the Jews were expelled the kingdom, was applied to the ufe of the king's council, when fitting in their judicial capacity. To confirm this ; the firft time the ftar-chamber is mentioned in any record, (*Rot. clauf.* 41 *Edw. III. m.* 13.) it is faid to have been fituated near the receipt of the exchequer : that the king's council, his chancellor, treafurer, juftices, and other fages, were affembled *en la chaumbre des efteilles pres la refceipt al Weftminfter.* For in procefs of time, when the meaning of the Jewifh *ftarrs* was forgotten, the word *ftar-chamber* was naturally rendered in law-french, *la chaumbre des efteilles,* and in law-latin, *camera ftellata* ; which continued to be the ftile in latin till the diffolution of that court.

ᵇ Lamb. *Arch.* 156.

haviour

haviour of sheriffs, and other notorious misdemesnors, contrary to the laws of the land. Yet this was afterwards (as lord Clarendon informs us [c]) stretched " to the asserting of all procla-
" mations, and orders of state; to the vindicating of illegal
" commissions, and grants of monopolies; holding for honour-
" able that which pleased, and for just that which profited,
" and becoming both a court of law to determine civil rights,
" and a court of revenue to enrich the treasury: the council
" table by proclamations enjoining to the people that which
" was not enjoined by the laws, and prohibiting that which
" was not prohibited; and the star-chamber, which consisted
" of the same persons in different rooms, censuring the breach
" and disobedience to those proclamations by very great fines,
" imprisonments, and corporal severities: so that any disrespect
" to any acts of state, or to the persons of statesmen, was in
" no time more penal, and the foundations of right never more
" in danger to be destroyed." For which reasons, it was finally abolished by statute 16 Car. I. c. 10. to the general joy of the whole nation [d].

4. T H E court of *chivalry*[e], of which we also formerly spoke [f] as a military court, or court of honour, when held before the earl marshal only, is also a criminal court, when held before the lord high constable of England jointly with the earl marshal. And then it has jurisdiction over pleas of life and member, arising in matters of arms and deeds of war, as well out of the realm as within it. But the criminal, as well as civil

---

[c] Hist. of Reb. book 1 & 3.

[d] The just odium, into which this tribunal had fallen before it's dissolution, has been the occasion that few memorials have reached us of it's nature, jurisdiction, and practice; except such as, on account of their enormous oppression, are recorded in the histories of the times. There are however to be met with some reports of it's proceedings in manuscript; of which the author

hath one, for the first three years of king Charles: and there is in the British Museum (Harl. MSS. Vol. I. n°. 1226.) a very full, methodical, and accurate account of the constitution and course of this court, compiled by William Hudson of Gray's Inn, an eminent practitioner therein.

[e] 4 Inst. 123. 2 Hawk. P. C. 9.

[f] See Vol. III. pag. 68.

part

part of it's authority, is fallen into entire difuse : there having
been no permanent high conftable of England (but only *pro hac
vice* at coronations and the like) fince the atttainder and execution
of Stafford duke of Buckingham in the thirteenth year of Henry VIII ; the authority and charge, both in war and peace, being deemed too ample for a fubject : fo ample, that when the
chief juftice Fineux was afked by king Henry the eighth, how
far they extended, he declined anfwering; and faid, the decifion
of that queftion belonged to the law of arms, and not to the
law of England[s].

5. THE high court of *admiralty*[h], held before the lord high
admiral of England, or his deputy, ftiled the judge of the admiralty, is not only a court of civil, but alfo of criminal, jurifdiction.　This court hath cognizance of all crimes and offences
committed either upon the fea, or on the coafts, out of the body
or extent of any Englifh county ; and, by ftatute 15 Ric. II. c. 3.
of death and mayhem happening in great fhips being and hover-
ing in the main ftream of great rivers, below the bridges of the
fame rivers, which are then a fort of ports or havens; fuch as
are the ports of London and Glocefter, though they lie at a
great diftance from the fea.　But, as this court proceeded without jury, in a method much conformed to the civil law, the
exercife of a criminal jurifdictiion therein was contrary to the
genius of the law of England ; inafmuch as a man might be
there deprived of his life by the opinion of a fingle judge,
without the judgment of his peers.　And befides, as innocent
perfons might thus fall a facrifice to the caprice of a fingle man,
fo very grofs offenders might, and did frequently, efcape punifhment : for the rule of the civil law is, how reafonably I
fhall not at prefent enquire, that no judgment of death can be
given againft offenders, without proof by two witneffes, or a
confeffion of the fact by themfelves.　This was always a great
offence to the Englifh nation : and therefore in the eighth year
of Henry VI a remedy was endeavoured to be applied in parli-

---

[s] Duck *de authorit. jur. civ.*　　　　[h] 4 Inft. 134. 147.

ament; but it mifcarried for want of the royal affent. However, by the ftatute 28 Hen. VIII. c. 15. it was enacted, that thefe offences fhould be tried by commiffioners, nominated by the lord chancellor; namely, the admiral, or his deputy, and three or four more; (among whom two common law judges are conftantly appointed, who in effect try all the prifoners) the indictment being firft found by a grand jury of twelve men, and afterwards tried by another jury, as at common law: and that the courfe of proceedings fhould be according to the law of the land. This is now the only method of trying marine felonies in the court of admiralty: the judge of the admiralty ftill prefiding therein, juft as the lord mayor prefides at the feffions in London.

THESE five courts may be held in any part of the kingdom, and their jurifdiction extends over crimes that arife throughout the whole of it, from one end to the other. What follow are alfo of a general nature, and univerfally diffufed over the nation, but yet are of a local jurifdiction, and confined to particular diftricts. Of which fpecies is,

6. THE court of *oyer* and *terminer*, and general *gaol delivery*[i]: which is held before the king's commiffioners, among whom are ufually two judges of the courts at Weftminfter, twice in every year in every county of the kingdom; except the four northern ones, where it is held only once, and London and Middlefex, wherein it is held eight times. This was flightly mentioned in the preceding book[k]. We then obferved, that, at what is ufually called the affifes, the judges fit by virtue of five feveral authorities: two of which, the commiffion of *affife* and it's attendant jurifdiction of *nifi prius*, being principally of a civil nature, were then explained at large; to which I fhall only add, that thefe juftices have, by virtue of feveral ftatutes, a criminal jurifdiction alfo, in certain fpecial cafes[l]. The third,

---

[i] 4 Inft. 162. 168. 2 Hal. P. C. 22. 32.   [k] See Vol. III. pag. 58.
[2] Hawk. P. C. 14. 23.   [l] 2 Hal. P. C. 39. 2 Hawk. P. C. 28.

which

which is the commiffion of the *peace,* was alfo treated of in a
former volume [m], when we enquired into the nature and office
of a juftice of the peace.　I fhall only add, that all the juftices
of the peace of any county, wherein the affifes are held, are
bound by law to attend them, or elfe are liable to a fine; in
order to return recognizances, *&c,* and to affift the judges in
fuch matters as lie within their knowlege and jurifdiction, and
in which fome of them have probably been concerned, by way
of previous examination.　But the fourth authority is the commiffion of *oyer* and *terminer* [n], to hear and determine all treafons,
felonies, and mifdemefnors.　This is directed to the judges and
feveral others; but the judges only are of the *quorum,* fo that
the reft cannot act without them.　The words of the commiffion
are, " to enquire, hear, and determine:" fo that by virtue of
this commiffion they can only proceed upon an indictment found
at the fame affifes; for they muft firft enquire, by means of the
grand jury or inqueft, before they are empowered to hear and
determine by the help of the petit jury.　Therefore they have
befides, fifthly, a commiffion of general *gaol delivery* [o]; which
empowers them to try and deliver every prifoner, who fhall be
in the gaol when the judges arrive at the circuit town, whenever indicted, or for whatever crime committed.　It was antiently
the courfe to iffue fpecial writs of gaol delivery for each particular prifoner, which were called the writs *de bono et malo* [p]:
but, thefe being found inconvenient and oppreffive, a *general*
commiffion for all the prifoners has long been eftablifhed in their
ftead.　So that, one way or other, the gaols are cleared, and all
offenders tried, punifhed, or delivered, twice in every year:　a
conftitution of fingular ufe and excellence.　Sometimes alfo, upon
urgent occafions, the king iffues a fpecial or extraordinary commiffion of *oyer* and *terminer,* and *gaol delivery,* confined to thofe
offences which ftand in need of immediate inquiry and punifhment: upon which the courfe of proceeding is the fame, as
upon general and ordinary commiffions.　Formerly it was held,

[m] See Vol. I. pag. 351.　　　　　　　　[o] *Ibid.*
[n] See appendix, §. 1.　　　　　　　　　[p] 2 Inft. 43.

K k 2　　　　　　　　　　　　　　　in

in purfuance of the ftatutes 8 Ric. II. c. 2. and 33 Hen. VIII.
c. 4. that no judge or other lawyer could act in the commiffion
of *oyer* and *terminer*, or in that of gaol delivery, within his own
county, where he was born or inhabited; in like manner as
they are prohibited from being judges of affife and determining
civil caufes. But that local partiality, which the jealoufy of our
anceftors was careful to prevent, being judged lefs likely to ope-
rate in the trial of crimes and mifdemefnors, than in matters of
property and difputes between party and party, it was thought
proper by the ftatute 12 Geo. II. c. 27. to allow any man to be
a juftice of *oyer* and *terminer* and general gaol delivery within
any county of England.

7. **The** court of general *quarter feffions* of the peace [q] is a
court that muft be held in every county, once in every quarter
of a year; which by ftatute 2 Hen. V. c. 4. is appointed to be in
the firft week after michaelmas-day; the firft week after the
epiphany; the firft week after the clofe of eafter; and in the
week after the tranflation of faint Thomas a Becket, or the
feventh of July. It is held before two or more juftices of the
peace, one of which muft be of the *quorum*. The jurifdiction
of this court by ftatute 34 Edw. III. c. 1. extends to the trying
and determining all felonies and trefpaffes whatfoever: though
they feldom, if ever, try any greater offence than fmall felonies
within the benefit of clergy; their commiffion providing, that,
if any cafe of difficulty arifes, they fhall not proceed to judgment, but in the prefence of one of the juftices of the courts of
king's bench or common pleas, or one of the judges of affife.
And therefore murders, and other capital felonies, are ufually
remitted for a more folemn trial to the affifes. They cannot
alfo try any new-created offence, without exprefs power given
them by the ftatute which creates it [r]. But there are many offences, and particular matters, which by particular ftatutes belong
properly to this jurifdiction, and ought to be profecuted in this

---

[q] 4 Inft. 170. 2 Hal. P. C. 42. 2 Hawk.   [r] 4 Mod. 379. Salk. 406. Lord Raym.
P. C. 32.   1144.

court:

court : as, the fmaller mifdemefnors againft the public or commonwealth, not amounting to felony; and efpecially offences
relating to the game, highways, alehoufes, baftard children, the
fettlement and provifion for the poor, vagrants, fervants wages,
apprentices, and popifh recufants [f]. Some of thefe are proceeded
upon by indictment; and others in a fummary way by motion
and order thereupon : which order may for the moft part, unlefs
guarded againft by particular ftatutes, be removed into the court
of king's bench, by writ of *certiorari facias*, and be there
either quafhed or confirmed. The records or rolls of the feffions are committed to the cuftody of a fpecial officer denominated the *cuftos rotulorum*, who is always a juftice of the *quo-*
rum; and among them of the *quorum* (faith Lambard [s]) a man
for the moft part efpecially picked out, either for wifdom,
countenance, or credit. The nomination of the *cuftos rotulorum*
(who is the principal *civil* officer in the county, as the lord
lieutenant is the chief in *military* command) is by the king's
fign manual : and to him the nomination of the clerk of the
peace belongs; which office he is exprefsly forbidden to fell
for money [t].

I n moft corporation towns there are quarter feffions kept before juftices of their own, within their refpective limits : which
have exactly the fame authority as the general quarter feffions of
the county, except in a very few inftances; one of the moft
confiderable of which is the matter of appeals from orders of
removal of the poor, which, though they be from the orders of
corporation juftices, muft be to the feffions of the county, by
ftatute 8 & 9 W. III. c. 30. In both corporations and counties at large, there is fometimes kept a fpecial or petty feffion,
by a few juftices, for difpatching fmaller bufinefs in the neighbourhood between the times of the general feffions; as, for
licencing alehoufes, paffing the accounts of parifh officers, and
the like.

---

[f] See Lambard's *eirenarcha*, and Burn's
juftice.

[s] b. 4. c. 3.

[t] Stat. 37 Hen. VIII. c. 1.　1 W. & M.
ft. 1. c. 21.

8. The

8. THE *sheriff's tourn*^u, or rotation, is a court of record, held twice every year within a month after easter and michaelmas, before the sheriff, in different parts of the county; being indeed only the turn of the sheriff to keep a court-leet in each respective hundred ^w. This therefore is the great court-leet of the county, as the county court is the court-baron: for out of this, for the ease of the sheriff, was taken

9. THE *court-leet*, or *view of frankpledge*^x, which is a court of record, held once in the year and not oftener^y, within a particular hundred, lordship, or manor, before the steward of the leet; being the king's court granted by charter to the lords of those hundreds or manors. It's original intent was to view the frank pledges, that is, the freemen within the liberty; who (we may remember^z) according to the institution of the great Alfred, were all mutually pledges for the good behaviour of each other. Besides this, the preservation of the peace, and the chastisement of divers minute offences against the public good, are the objects both of the court-leet and the sheriff's tourn: which have exactly the same jurisdiction, one being only a larger species of the other; extending over more territory, but not over more causes. All freeholders within the precinct are obliged to attend them, and all persons commorant therein; which commorancy consists in usually lying there: a regulation, which owes it's original to the laws of king Canute^a. But persons under twelve and above sixty years old, peers, clergymen, women, and the king's tenants in antient demesne, are excused from attendance there: all others being bound to appear upon the jury, if required, and make their due presentments. It was also antiently the custom to summon all the king's subjects, as they respectively grew to years of discretion and strength, to come to

---

^u 4 Inst. 259. 2 Hal. P. C. 69. 2 Hawk. P. C. 55.
^w Mirr. c. 1. §. 13 & 16.
^x 4 Inst. 261. 2 Hawk. P. C. 72.

^y Mirror. c. 1. §. 10.
^z See Vol. III. pag. 113.
^a *part. 2. c. 19.*

the

the court-leet, and there take the oath of allegiance to the king.
The other general bufinefs of the leet and tourn, was to prefent
by jury all crimes whatfoever that happened within their jurifdiction; and not only to prefent, but alfo to punifh, all trivial
mifdemefnors, as all trivial debts were recoverable in the court-
baron, and county court: juftice, in thefe minuter matters of
both kinds, being brought home to the doors of every man by
our antient conftitution.   Thus in the Gothic conftitution, the
haereda, which anfwered to our court-leet, " *de omnibus quidem*
" *cognofcit, non tamen de omnibus judicat* [b]."   The objects of their
jurifdiction are therefore unavoidably very numerous : being fuch
as in fome degree, either lefs or more, affect the public weal,
or good governance of the diftrict in which they arife; from
common nufances and other material offences againft the king's
peace and public trade, down to eaves-dropping, waifs, and irregularities in public commons.   But both the tourn and the leet
have been for a long time in a declining way : a circumftance,
owing in part to the difcharge granted by the ftatute of Marl-
bridge, 52 Hen. III. c. 10. to all prelates, peers, and clergymen
from their attendance upon thefe courts; which occafioned them
to grow into difrepute.   And hence it is that their bufinefs hath
for the moft part gradually devolved upon the quarter feffions :
which it is particularly directed to do in fome cafes by ftatute
1 Edw. IV. c. 2.

10. THE court of the *coroner* [c] is alfo a court of record, to
enquire, when any one dies in prifon, or comes to a violent or
fudden death, by what manner he came to his end.   And this
he is only entitled to do *fuper vifum corporis.*   Of the coroner
and his office we treated at large in a former volume [d], among
the public officers and minifters of the kingdom; and therefore fhall not here repeat our enquiries : only mentioning his
court, by way of regularity, among the criminal courts of the
nation.

[b] Stiernh. *de jur. Goth. l.* 1. *c.* 2.   P. C. 42.
[c] 4 Inft. 271. 2 Hal. P. C. 53. 2 Hawk.   [d] See Vol. I, pag. 349.

11. THE

11. The court of the *clerk of the market*[e] is incident to every fair and market in the kingdom, to punifh mifdemefnors therein; as a court of *pie poudre* is, to determine all difputes relating to private or civil property. The object of this jurifdiction[f] is principally the cognizance of weights and meafures, to try whether they be according to the true ftandard thereof, or no: which ftandard was antiently committed to the cuftody of the bifhop, who appointed fome clerk under him to infpect the abufe of them more narrowly; and hence this officer, though now ufually a layman, is called the *clerk* of the market[g]. If they be not according to the ftandard, then, befides the punifhment of the party by fine, the weights and meafures themfelves ought to be burnt. This is the moft inferior court of criminal jurifdiction in the kingdom; though the objects of it's coercion were efteemed among the Romans of fuch importance to the public, that they were committed to the care of fome of their moft dignified magiftrates, the curule aediles.

II. There are a few other criminal courts of greater dignity than many of thefe, but of a more confined and partial jurifdiction; extending only to fome particular places, which the royal favour, confirmed by act of parliament, has diftinguifhed by the privilege of having peculiar courts of their own, for the punifhment of crimes and mifdemefnors arifing within the bounds of their cognizance. Thefe, not being univerfally difperfed, or of general ufe, as the former, but confined to one fpot, as well as to a determinate fpecies of caufes, may be denominated private or fpecial courts of criminal jurifdiction.

I speak not here of ecclefiaftical courts; which punifh fpiritual fins, rather than temporal crimes, by penance, contrition, and excommunication, *pro falute animae*: or, which is looked upon as equivalent to all the reft, by a fum of money to the of-

[e] 4 Inft 273.
[f] See ftat. 17 Car. II. c. 19. 22 Car. II.
c. 8. 23 Car. II. c. 12.
[g] Bacon of Englifh Gov. b. 1. c. 8.

ficers

ficers of the court by way of commutation of penance. Of these
we difcourfed fufficiently in the preceding book [h]. I am now
fpeaking of fuch courts as proceed according to the courfe of
the common law; which is a ftranger to fuch unaccountable
barterings of public juftice.

1. AND, firft, the court of the *lord fteward, treafurer*, or
comptroller of the king's *houfhold* [i], was inftituted by ftatute
3 Hen.VII. c. 14. to enquire of felony by any of the king's
fworn fervants, in the checque roll of the houfhold, under the
degree of a lord, in confederating, compaffing, confpiring, and
imagining the death or deftruction of the king, or any lord or
other of his majefty's privy council, or the lord fteward, treafurer, or comptroller of the king's houfe. The enquiry, and
trial thereupon, muft be by a jury according to the courfe of
the common law, confifting of twelve fad men (that is, fober
and difcreet perfons) of the king's houfhold.

2. THE court of the *lord fteward* of the king's *houfhold*, or
(in his abfence) of the treafurer, comptroller, and fteward of
the *marfhalfea* [k], was erected by ftatute 33 Hen. VIII. c. 12.
with a jurifdiction to enquire of, hear, and determine, all
treafons, mifprifions of treafon, murders, manflaughters,
bloodfhed, and other malicious ftrikings; whereby blood fhall
be fhed in any of the palaces and houfes of the king, or in
any other houfe where the royal perfon fhall abide. The proceedings are alfo by jury, both a grand and a petit one, as at
common law, taken out of the officers and fworn fervants of
the king's houfhold. The form and folemnity of the procefs,
particularly with regard to the execution of the fentence for
cutting off the hand, which is part of the punifhment for
fhedding blood in the king's court, is very minutely fet forth
in the faid ftatute 33 Hen. VIII. and the feveral offices of the
fervants of the houfhold in and about fuch execution are de-

---

[h] See Vol. III. pag. 61.
[i] 4 Inft. 132.

[k] Ibid. 2 Hal. P. C. 7.

fcribed; from the ferjeant of the wood-yard, who furnifhes the chopping-block, to the ferjeant farrier, who brings hot irons to fear the ftump.

3. As in the preceding book[1] we mentioned the courts of the two univerfities, or their chancellor's courts, for the redrefs of civil injuries; it will not be improper now to add a fhort word concerning the jurifdiction of their criminal courts, which is equally large and extenfive. The chancellor's court of Oxford (with which univerfity the author hath been chiefly converfant, though probably that of Cambridge hath alfo a fimilar jurifdiction) hath authority to determine all caufes of property, wherein a privileged perfon is one of the parties, except only caufes of freehold; and alfo all criminal offences or mifdemefnors, under the degree of treafon, felony, or mayhem. The prohibition of meddling with freehold ftill continues: but the trial of treafon, felony, and mayhem, by a particular charter is committed to the univerfity jurifdiction in another court, namely, the court of the *lord high fteward* of the *univerfity*.

FOR by the charter of 7 Jun. 2 Hen. IV. (confirmed, among the reft, by the ftatute 13 Eliz. c. 29.) cognizance is granted to the univerfity of Oxford of all indictments of treafons, infurrections, felony, and mayhem, which fhall be found in any of the king's courts againft a fcholar or privileged perfon; and they are to be tried before the high fteward of the univerfity, or his deputy, who is to be nominated by the chancellor of the univerfity for the time being. But, when his office is called forth into action, fuch high fteward muft be approved by the lord high chancellor of England; and a fpecial commiffion under the great feal is given to him, and others, to try the indictment then depending, according to the law of the land and

[1] See Vol. III. pag. 83.

the

the privileges of the said univerſity. When therefore an indictment is found at the aſſiſes, or elſewhere, againſt any ſcholar of the univerſity, or other privileged perſon, the vice-chancellor may claim the cognizance of it; and (when claimed in due time and manner) it ought to be allowed him by the judges of aſſiſe: and then it comes to be tried in the high ſteward's court. But the indictment muſt firſt be found by a grand jury, and then the cognizance claimed: for I take it that the high ſteward cannot proceed originally *ad inquirendum*; but only, after inqueſt in the common law courts, *ad audiendum et determinandum*. Much in the ſame manner, as, when a peer is to be tried in the court of the lord high ſteward of Great Britain, the indictment muſt firſt be found at the aſſiſes, or in the court of king's bench, and then (in conſequence of a writ of *certiorari*) tranſmitted to be finally heard and determined before his grace the lord high ſteward and the peers.

WHEN the cognizance is ſo allowed, if the offence be *inter minora crimina*, or a miſdemeſnor only, it is tried in the chancellor's court by the ordinary judge. But if it be for treaſon, felony, or mayhem, it is then, and then only, to be determined before the high ſteward, under the king's ſpecial commiſſion to try the ſame. The proceſs of the trial is this. The high ſteward iſſues one precept to the ſheriff of the county, who thereupon returns a panel of eighteen freeholders; and another precept to the bedells of the univerſity, who thereupon return a panel of eighteen matriculated laymen, " *laicos privilegio uni-* " *verſitatis gaudentes:*" and by a jury formed *de medietate*, half of freeholders, and half of matriculated perſons, is the indictment to be tried; and that in the guildhall of the city of Oxford. And if execution be neceſſary to be awarded, in conſequence of finding the party guilty, the ſheriff of the county muſt execute the univerſity proceſs; to which he is annually bound by an oath.

I HAVE been the more minute in defcribing thefe proceedings, as there has happily been no occafion to reduce them into practice for more than a century paft; though it is not a right that merely refts *in fcriptis* or theory, but has formerly often been carried into execution. There are many inftances, one in the reign of queen Elizabeth, two in that of James the firft, and two in that of Charles the firft, where indictments for murder have been challenged by the vice-chancellor at the affifes, and afterwards tried before the high fteward by jury. The commiffions under the great feal, the fheriff's and bedell's panels, and all the other proceedings on the trial of the feveral indictments, are ftill extant in the archives of that univerfity.

CHAPTER   THE   TWENTIETH.

OF SUMMARY CONVICTIONS.

WE are next, according to the plan I have laid down, to take into confideration the proceedings in the courts of criminal jurifdiction, in order to the punifhment of offences. Thefe are plain, eafy, and regular; the law not admitting any fictions, as in civil caufes, to take place where the life, the liberty, and the fafety of the fubject are more immediately brought into jeopardy. And thefe proceedings are divifible into two kinds; *fummary*, and *regular:* of the former of which I fhall briefly fpeak, before we enter upon the latter, which will require a more thorough and particular examination.

By a *fummary* proceeding I mean principally fuch as is directed by feveral acts of parliament (for the common law is a ftranger to it, unlefs in the cafe of contempts) for the conviction of offenders, and the inflicting of certain penalties created by thofe acts of parliament. In thefe there there is no intervention of a jury, but the party accufed is acquitted or condemned by the fuffrage of fuch perfon only, as the ftatute has appointed for his judge. An inftitution defigned profeffedly for the greater eafe of the fubject, by doing him fpeedy juftice, and by not harraffing the freeholders with frequent and troublefome attendances to try every minute offence. But it

has

has of late been fo far extended, as, if a check be not timely given, to threaten the difufe of our admirable and truly Englifh trial by jury, unlefs only in capital cafes. For,

I. Of this fummary nature are all trials of offences and frauds contrary to the laws of the *excife*, and other branches of the *revenue*: which are to be enquired into and determined by the commiffioners of the refpective departments, or by juftices of the peace in the country; officers, who are all of them appointed and removeable at the difcretion of the crown. And though fuch convictions are abfolutely neceffary for the due collection of the public money, and are a fpecies of mercy to the delinquents, who would be ruined by the expenfe and delay of frequent profecutions by indictment; and though fuch has ufually been the *conduct* of the commiffioners, as feldom (if ever) to afford juft grounds to complain of oppreffion; yet when we again [a] confider the various and almoft innumerable branches of this revenue, which may be in their turns the fubjects of fraud, or at leaft complaints of fraud, and of courfe the objects of this fummary and arbitrary jurifdiction; we fhall find that the *power* of thefe officers of the crown over the property of the people is increafed to a very formidable height.

II. Another branch of fummary proceedings is that before *juftices of the peace*, in order to inflict divers petty pecuniary mulcts, and corporal penalties, denounced by act of parliament for many diforderly offences; fuch as common fwearing, drunkennefs, vagrancy, idlenefs, and a vaft variety of others, for which I muft refer the ftudent to the juftice-books formerly cited [b], and which ufed to be formerly punifhed by the verdict of a jury in the court-leet. This change in the adminiftration of juftice hath however had fome mifchievous effects; as, 1. The almoft entire difufe and contempt of the court-leet, and fheriff's tourn, the king's antient courts of common law, formerly much rever-

---

[a] See Vol. I. pag. 318, &c.   [b] Lambard and Burn.

ed and refpected.   2. The burthenfome increafe of the bufinefs
of a juftice of the peace, which difcourages fo many gentlemen
of rank and character from acting in the commiffion; from an
apprehenfion that the duty of their office would take up too
much of that time, which they are unwilling to fpare from the
neceffary concerns of their families, the improvement of their
underftandings, and their engagements in other fervices of the
public. Though if *all* gentlemnn of fortune had it both in their
power, and inclinations, to act in this capacity, the bufinefs of
a juftice of the peace would be more divided, and fall the lefs
heavy upon individuals : which would remove what in the prefent fcarcity of magiftrates is really an objection fo formidable,
that the country is greatly obliged to any gentleman of figure,
who will undertake to perform that duty, which in confequence
of his rank in life he owes more peculiarly to his country.
However, this backwardnefs to act as magiftrates, arifing greatly
from this increafe of fummary jurifdiction, is productive of,
3. A third mifchief: which is, that this truft, when flighted
by gentlemen, falls of courfe into the hands of thofe who are
not fo; but the mere tools of office.   And then the extenfive
power of a juftice of the peace, which even in the hands of
men of honour is highly formidable, will be proftituted to mean
and fcandalous purpofes, to the low ends of felfifh ambition,
avarice, or perfonal refentment.   And from thefe ill confequences
we may collect the prudent forefight of our antient lawgivers,
who fuffered neither the property nor the punifhment of the fubject to be determined by the opinion of any one or two men;
and we may alfo obferve the neceffity of not deviating any farther from our antient conftitution, by ordaining new penalties
to be inflicted upon fummary convictions.

THE procefs of thefe fummary convictions, it muft be owned,
is extremely fpeedy. Though the courts of common law have
thrown in one check upon them, by making it neceffary to *fummon* the party accufed before he is condemned. This is now
held

held to be an indifpenfable requifite[c] : though the juftices long ftruggled the point ; forgetting that rule of natural reafon ex-preffed by Seneca,

> " *Qui ftatuit aliquid, parte inaudita altera,*
> " *Aequom licet ftatuerit, haud aequus fuit.*"

A rule, to which all municipal laws, that are founded on the principles of juftice, have ftrictly conformed : the Roman law requiring a citation at the leaft ; and our own common law never fuffering any fact (either civil or criminal) to be tried, till it has previoufly compelled an appearance by the party concerned. After this fummons, the magiftrate, in fummary proceedings, may go on to examine one or more witneffes, as the ftatute may require, upon oath ; and then make his conviction of the offender, in writing : upon which he ufually iffues his warrant, either to apprehend the offender, in cafe corporal punifhment is to be inflicted on him ; or elfe to levy the penalty incurred, by diftrefs and fale of his goods. This is, in general, the method of fummary proceedings before a juftice or juftices of the peace : but for particulars we muft have recourfe to the feveral ftatutes, which create the offence, or inflict the punifhment ; and which ufually chalk out the method by which offenders are to be convicted. Otherwife they fall of courfe under the general rule, and can only be convicted by indictment or information at the common law.

III. To this head, of fummary proceedings, may alfo be properly referred the method, immemorially ufed by the fuperior courts of juftice, of punifhing contempts by *attachment*, and the fubfequent proceedings thereon.

THE contempts, that are thus punifhed, are either *direct*, which openly infult or refift the powers of the courts, or the perfons of the judges who prefide there ; or elfe are *confequential*,

---

[c] Salk. 181. 2 Lord Raym. 1405.

which

which (without fuch grofs infolence or direct oppofition) plainly tend to create an univerfal difregard of their authority. The principal inftances, of either fort, that have been ufually [a] punifhed by attachment, are chiefly of the following kinds. 1. Thofe committed by inferior judges and magiftrates: by acting unjuftly, oppreffively, or irregularly, in adminiftring thofe portions of juftice which are intrufted to their diftribution; or by difobeying the king's writs iffuing out of the fuperior courts, by proceeding in a caufe after it is put a ftop to or removed by writ of prohibition, *certiorari*, error, *fuperfedeas*, and the like. For, as the king's fuperior courts (and efpecially the court of king's bench) have a general fuper-intendence over all inferior jurifdictions, any corrupt or iniquitous practices of fubordinate judges are contempts of that fuper-intending authority, whofe duty it is to keep them within the bounds of juftice. 2. Thofe committed by fheriffs, bailiffs, gaolers, and other officers of the court: by abufing the procefs of the law, or deceiving the parties, by any acts of oppreffion, extortion, collufive behaviour, or culpable neglect of duty. 3. Thofe committed by attorneys and folicitors, who are alfo officers of the refpective courts: by grofs inftances of fraud and corruption, injuftice to their clients, or other difhoneft practice. For the mal-practice of the officers reflects fome difhonour on their employers: and, if frequent or unpunifhed, creates among the people a difguft againft the courts themfelves. 4. Thofe committed by jurymen, in collateral matters relating to the difcharge of their office: fuch as making default, when fummoned; refufing to be fworn, or to give any verdict; eating or drinking without the leave of the court, and efpecially at the coft of either party; and other mifbehaviours or irregularities of a fimilar kind: but not in the mere exercife of their judicial capacities, as by giving a falfe or erroneous verdict. 5. Thofe committed by witneffes: by making default when fummoned, refufing to be fworn or examined, or prevaricating in their evidence when fworn. 6. Thofe committed by parties to any fuit

[a] 2 Hawk. P. C. 142, &c.

or proceeding before the court : as by difobedience to any rule or order, made in the progrefs of a caufe ; by non-payment of cofts awarded by the court upon a motion ; or by non-obfervance of awards duly made by arbitrators or umpires, after having entered into a rule for fubmitting to fuch determination[e]. 7. Thofe committed by any other perfons, under the degree of a peer : and even by peers themfelves, when enormous and accompanied with violence, fuch as forcible *refcous* and the like[f]; or when they import a difobedience to the king's great prerogative writs, of prohibition, *habeas corpus*[g], and the reft. Some of thefe contempts may arife in the face of the court ; as by rude and contumelious behaviour ; by obftinacy, perverfenefs, or prevarication ; by breach of the peace, or any wilful difturbance whatever : others in the abfence of the party ; as by difobeying or treating with difrefpect the king's writ, or the rules or procefs of the court ; by perverting fuch writ or procefs to the purpofes of private malice, extortion, or injuftice ; by fpeaking or writing contemptuoufly of the court, or judges, acting in their judicial capacity ; by printing falfe accounts (or even true ones without proper permiffion) of caufes then depending in judgment ; and by any thing in fhort that demonftrates a grofs want of that regard and refpect, which when once courts of juftice are deprived of, their authority (fo neceffary for the good order of the kingdom) is intirely loft among the people.

THE procefs of attachment, for thefe and the like contempts, muft neceffarily be as antient as the laws themfelves. For laws, without a competent authority to fecure their adminiftration from difobedience and contempt, would be vain and nugatory. A power therefore in the fupreme courts of juftice to fupprefs fuch contempts, by an immediate attachment of the offender, refults from the firft principles of judicial eftablifhments, and muft be an infeparable attendant upon every fuperior tribunal.

[e] See Vol. III. pag. 17.   [g] 4 Burr. 632. Lords Journ. 7 Febr.
[f] Styl. 277. 2 Hawk. P. C. 152.   8 Jun 1757.

Accord-

Accordingly we find it actually exercifed, as early as the annals of our law extend. And, though a very learned author [h] feems inclinable to derive this procefs from the ftatute of Weftm. 2. 13 Edw. I. c. 39. (which ordains, that in cafe the procefs of the king's courts be *refifted* by the power of any great man, the fheriff fhall chaftife the refifters by imprifonment, "*a qua non* "*deliberentur fine fpeciali praecepto domini regis :*" and if the fheriff himfelf be refifted, he fhall certify to the court the names of the principal offenders, their aiders, confenters, commanders, and favourers, and by a fpecial writ judicial they fhall be *attached* by their bodies to appear before the court, and if they be convicted thereof they fhall be punifhed at the king's pleafure, without any interfering by any other perfon whatfoever) yet he afterwards more juftly concludes, that it is a part of the *law of the land*; and, as fuch, is *confirmed* by the ftatute of *magna carta*.

IF the contempt be committed in the face of the court, the offender may be inftantly apprehended and imprifoned, at the difcretion of the judges, without any farther proof or examination. But in matters that arife at a diftance, and of which the court cannot have fo perfect a knowlege, unlefs by the confeffion of the party or the teftimony of others, if the judges upon *affidavit* fee fufficient ground to fufpect that a contempt has been committed, they either make a rule on the fufpected party to fhew caufe why an attachment fhould not iffue againft him [i]; or, in very flagrant inftances of contempt, the attachment iffues in the firft inftance [k]; as it alfo does, if no fufficient caufe be fhewn to difcharge, and thereupon the court confirms and makes abfolute, the original rule. This procefs of attachment is merely intended to bring the party into court : and, when there, he muft either ftand committed, or put in bail, in order to anfwer upon oath to fuch *interrogatories* as fhall be adminiftred to him, for the better information of the court with refpect to the cir-

[h] Gilb. Hift. C. P. ch 3.
[i] Styl. 277.
[k] Salk. 84. Stra. 185.

cumftances

cumſtances of the contempt. Theſe interrogatories are in the nature of a charge or accuſation, and muſt by the courſe of the
court be exhibited within the firſt four days[1]: and, if any of
the interrogatories is improper, the defendant may refuſe to anſwer it, and move the court to have it ſtruck out[m]. If the party
can clear himſelf upon oath, he is diſcharged; but, if perjured,
may be proſecuted for the perjury[n]. If he confeſſes the contempt,
the court will proceed to correct him by fine, or impriſonment, or both, and ſometimes by a corporal or infamous puniſhment[o]. If the contempt be of ſuch a nature, that,
when the fact is once acknowleged, the court can receive no
farther information by interrogatories than it is already poſſeſſed
of, (as in the caſe of a *reſcous*[p]) the defendant may be admitted
to make ſuch ſimple acknowlegement, and receive his judgment,
without anſwering to any interrogatories: but if he wilfully and
obſtinately refuſes to anſwer, or anſwers in an evaſive manner,
he is then clearly guilty of a high and repeated contempt, to
be puniſhed at the diſcretion of the court.

I T cannot have eſcaped the attention of the reader, that this
method, of making the defendant anſwer upon oath to a criminal charge, is not agreeable to the genius of the common
law in any other inſtance[q]; and ſeems indeed to have been
derived to the courts of king's bench and common pleas through
the medium of the courts of equity. For the whole proceſs
of the courts of equity, in the ſeveral ſtages of a cauſe, and
finally to enforce their decrees, was, till the introduction of
ſequeſtrations, in the nature of a proceſs of contempt; acting
only *in perſonam* and not *in rem*. And there, after the party
in contempt has anſwered the interrogatories, ſuch his anſwer
may be contradicted and diſproved by *affidavits* of the adverſe
party: whereas in the courts of law, the admiſſion of the party
to purge himſelf by oath is more favourable to his liberty,

[1] 6 Mod. 73.
[m] Stra. 444.
[n] 6 Mod. 73.
[o] Cro. Car. 146.
[p] The king *v.* Elkins. M. 8 Geo. III. B.R.
[q] See Vol. III. pag. 100, 101.

though

though perhaps not lefs dangerous to his confcience; for, if he clears himfelf by his anfwers, the complaint is totally difmiffed. And, with regard to this fingular mode of trial, thus admitted in this one particular inftance, I fhall only for the prefent ob-ferve; that as the procefs by attachment in general appears to be extremely antient[r], and has fince the reftoration been con-firmed by an exprefs act of parliament[s], fo the method of ex-amining the delinquent himfelf upon oath, with regard to the contempt alleged, is at leaft of as high antiquity[t], and by long and immemorial ufage is now become the law of the land.

[r] Yearb. 22 Edw. IV. 29.
[s] Stat. 13 Car. II. ft. 2. c. 2. §. 4.

[t] M. 5 Edw. IV. rot. 75. cited in Raft. Ent. 268. pl. 5.

O f   A R R E S T S.

WE are now to confider the regular and ordinary method of proceeding in the courts of criminal jurifdiction; which may be diftributed under twelve general heads, following each other in a progreffive order: *viz.* 1. Arreft; 2. Commitment, and bail; 3. Profecution; 4. Procefs; 5. Arraignment, and it's incidents; 6. Plea, and iffue; 7. Trial, and conviction; 8. Clergy; 9. Judgment, and it's confequences; 10. Reverfal of judgment; 11. Reprieve, or pardon; 12. Execution: all which will be difcuffed in the fubfequent part of this book.

FIRST then, of an *arreft*: which is the apprehending or reftraining of one's perfon, in order to be forthcoming to anfwer an alleged or fufpected crime. To this arreft all perfons whatfoever are, without diftinction, equally liable to all criminal cafes: but no man is to be arrefted, unlefs charged with fuch a crime, as will at leaft juftify holding him to bail, when taken. And, in general, an arreft may be made four ways: 1. By warrant: 2. By an officer without warrant: 3. By a private perfon alfo without warrant: 4. By an hue and cry.

1. A WARRANT may be granted in extraordinary cafes by the privy council, or fecretaries of ftate[a]; but ordinarily by juftices of the peace.   This they may do in any cafes where they have a jurifdiction over the offence; in order to compel the perfon accufed to appear before them[b]: for it would be abfurd to give them power to examine an offender, unlefs they had alfo a power to compel him to attend, and fubmit to fuch examination.   And this extends undoubtedly to all treafons, felonies, and breaches of the peace; and alfo to all fuch offences as they have power to punifh by ftatute.   Sir Edward Coke indeed[c] hath laid it down, that a juftice of the peace cannot iffue a warrant to apprehend a felon upon bare fufpicion; no, not even till an indictment be actually found: and the contrary practice is by others[d] held to be grounded rather upon connivance, than the exprefs rule of law; though now by long cuftom eftablifhed.   A doctrine, which would in moft cafes give a loofe to felons to efcape without punifhment; and therefore fir Matthew Hale hath combated it with invincible authority, and ftrength of reafon: maintaining, 1. That a juftice of peace hath power to iffue a warrant to apprehend a perfon *accufed* of of felony, though not yet *indicted*[e]; and 2. That he may alfo iffue a warrant to apprehend a perfon *fufpected* of felony, though the original fufpicion be not in himfelf, but in the party that prays his warrant; becaufe he is a competent judge of the probability offered to him of fuch fufpicion.   But in both cafes it is fitting to examine upon oath the party requiring a warrant, as well to afcertain that there *is* a felony or other crime actually committed, without which no warrant fhould be granted; as alfo to *prove* the caufe and probability of fufpecting the party, againft whom the warrant is prayed[f].   This warrant ought to be under the hand and feal of the juftice, fhould fet forth the time and place of making, and the caufe for which it is made,

[a] 1 Lord Raym. 65.
[b] 2 Hawk. P. C. 84.
[c] 4 Inft. 176.
[d] 2 Hawk. P. C. 84.
[e] 2 Hal. P. C. 108.
[f] *Ibid.* 110.

and fhould be directed to the conftable, or other peace officer, requiring him to bring the party either generally before *any* juftice of the peace for the county, or only before the juftice who granted it; the warrant in the latter cafe being called a *fpecial* warrant[g]. A *general* warrant to apprehend all perfons fufpected, without naming or particularly defcribing any perfon in fpecial, is illegal and void for it's uncertainty[h]; for it is the duty of the magiftrate, and ought not to be left to the officer, to judge of the ground of fufpicion. And a warrant to apprehend all perfons guilty of a crime therein fpecified, is no legal warrant: for the point, upon which it's authority refts, is a fact to be decided on a fubfequent trial; namely, whether the perfon apprehended thereupon be really guilty or not. It is therefore in fact no warrant at all: for it will not juftify the officer who acts under it[i]; whereas a lawful warrant will at all events indemnify the officer, who executes the fame minifterially. When a warrant is received by the officer, he is bound to execute it, fo far as the jurifdiction of the magiftrate and himfelf extends. A warrant from the chief, or other, juftice of the court of king's bench extends all over the kingdom: and is *tefte*'d, or dated, *England;* not Oxfordfhire, Berks, or other particular county. But the warrant of a juftice of the peace in one county, as Yorkfhire, muft be backed, that is, figned by a juftice of the peace in another, as Middlefex, before it can be executed there. Formerly, regularly fpeaking, there ought to have been a frefh

---

[g] 2 Hawk. P. C. 85.

[h] 1 Hal. P. C. 580. 2 Hawk. P. C. 82.

[i] A practice had obtained in the fecretaries office ever fince the reftoration, grounded on fome claufes in the acts for regulating the prefs, of iffuing *general* warrants to take up (without naming any perfon in particular) the authors, printers and publifhers of fuch obfcene or feditious libels, as were particularly fpecified in the warrant. When thofe acts expired in 1694, the fame practice was inadvertently continued, in every reign and under every adminiftration, except the four laft years of queen Anne, down to the year 1763: when fuch a warrant being iffued to apprehend the authors, printers and publifhers of a certain feditious libel, it's validity was difputed; and the warrant was adjudged by the whole court of king's bench to be void, in the cafe of Money *v.* Leach. *Trin.* 5 *Geo. III. B. R.* After which the iffuing of fuch general warrants was declared illegal by a vote of the houfe of commons. (Com. Journ. 22 Apr. 1766.)

warrant

warrant in every frefh county; but the practice of backing warrants had long prevailed without law, and was at laft authorized by ftatutes 23 Geo. II. c. 26. and 24 Geo. II. c. 55.

2. ARRESTS by *officers, without warrant,* may be executed, 1. By a juftice of the peace; who may himfelf apprehend, or caufe to be apprehended, by word only, any perfon committing a felony or breach of the peace in his prefence[k]. 2. The fheriff, and 3. The coroner, may apprehend any felon within the county without warrant. 4. The conftable, of whofe office we formerly fpoke[l], hath great original and inherent authority with regard to arrefts. He may, without warrant, arreft any one for a breach of the peace, and carry him before a juftice of the peace. And, in cafe of felony actually committed, or a dangerous wounding whereby felony is like to enfue, he may upon probable fufpicion arreft the felon; and for that purpofe is authorized (as upon a juftice's warrant) to break open doors, and even to kill the felon if he cannot otherwife be taken; and, if he or his affiftants be killed in attempting fuch arreft, it is murder in all concerned[m]. 5. Watchmen, either thofe appointed by the ftatute of Winchefter, 13 Edw. I. c. 4. to keep watch and ward in all towns from funfetting to funrifing, or fuch as are mere affiftants to the conftable, may *virtute officii* arreft all offenders, and particularly nightwalkers, and commit them to cuftody till the morning[n].

3. ANY private perfon (and *a fortiori* a peace officer) that is prefent when any felony is committed, is bound by the law to arreft the felon; on pain of fine and imprifonment, if he efcapes through the negligence of the ftanders by[o]. And they may juftify breaking open doors upon following fuch felon: and if *they kill him,* provided he cannot be otherwife taken, it is juftifiable; though if *they are killed* in endeavouring to make fuch arreft, it is

[k] 1 Hal. P. C. 86.　　　　　[n] *Ibid.* 98.
[l] See Vol. I. pag. 355.　　　[o] 2 Hawk. P. C. 74.
[m] 2 Hal. P. C. 88—90.

V o l. IV.　　　　　　　　N n　　　　　　　　murder[p].

murder[p]. Upon probable fuſpicion alſo a private perſon may arreſt
the felon, or other perſon ſo ſuſpected[q], but he cannot juſtify
breaking open doors to do it; and if either party kill the other
in the attempt, it is manſlaughter, and no more[r]. It is no more,
becauſe there is no malicious deſign to kill : but it amounts to
ſo much, becauſe it would be of moſt pernicious conſequence,
if, under pretence of ſuſpecting felony, any private perſon might
break open a houſe, or kill another; and alſo becauſe ſuch arreſt
upon ſuſpicion is barely *permitted* by the law, and not *enjoined,*
as in the caſe of thoſe who are preſent when a felony is committed.

4. THERE is yet another ſpecies of arreſt, wherein both officers and private men are concerned, and that is upon an *hue*
and *cry* raiſed upon a felony committed. An hue (from *huer,*
to ſhout) and cry, *huteſium et clamor,* is the old common law
proceſs of purſuing, with horn and with voice, all felons, and
ſuch as have dangerouſly wounded another[s]. It is alſo mentioned by ſtatute Weſtm. 1. 3 Edw. I. c. 9. and 4 Edw. I. *de
officio coronatoris.* But the principal ſtatute, relative to this
matter, is that of Wincheſter, 13 Edw. I. c. 1 & 4. which
directs, that from thenceforth every country ſhall be ſo well
kept, that, immediately upon robberies and felonies committed,
freſh ſuit ſhall be made from town to town, and from county
to county; and that hue and cry ſhall be raiſed upon the felons,
and they that keep the town ſhall follow with hue and cry,
with all the town and the towns near; and ſo hue and cry ſhall
be made from town to town, until they be taken and delivered
to the ſheriff. And, that ſuch hue and cry may more effectually be made, the hundred is bound by the ſame ſtatute, c. 3.
to anſwer for all robberies therein committed, unleſs they take
the felon; which is the foundation of an action againſt the

[p] 2 Hal. P. C. 77.
[q] Stat. 30 Geo. II. c. 24.
2 Hal. P. C. 82, 83.

[s] Bracton. *l.* 3. *tr.* 2. *c.* 1. §. 1. Mirr.
c. 2. §. 6.

hun-

hundred [t], in cafe of any lofs by robbery. By ftatute 27 Eliz. c. 13. no hue and cry is fufficient, unlefs made with both horfemen and footmen. And by ftatute 8 Geo. II. c. 16. the conftable or like officer refufing or neglecting to make hue and cry, forfeits 5 *l:* and the whole vill or diftrict is ftill in ftrict- nefs liable to be amerced, according to the law of Alfred, if any felony be committed therein and the felon efcapes. An in- ftitution, which hath long prevailed in many of the eaftern countries, and hath in part been introduced even into the Mogul empire, about the beginning of the laft century; which is faid to have effectually delivered that vaft territory from the plague of robbers, by making in fome places the villages, in others the officers of juftice, refponfible for all the robberies commit- ted within their refpective diftricts [u]. Hue and cry [w] may be raifed either by precept of a juftice of the peace, or by a peace officer, or by any private man that knows of a felony. The party raifing it muft acquaint the conftable of the vill with all the circumftances which he knows of the felony, and the per- fon of the felon; and thereupon the conftable is to fearch his own town, and raife all the neighbouring vills, and make pur- fuit with horfe and foot: and in the profecution of fuch hue and cry, the conftable and his attendants have the fame powers, protection, and indemnification, as if acting under the warrant of a juftice of the peace. But if a man wantonly or malicioufly raifes a hue and cry, without caufe, he fhall be feverely punifhed as a difturber of the public peace [x].

I N order to encourage farther the apprehending of certain felons, rewards and immunities are beftowed on fuch as bring them to juftice, by divers acts of parliament. The ftatute 4 & 5 W. & M. c. 8. enacts, that fuch as apprehend a high- wayman, and profecute him to conviction, fhall receive a re- ward of 40 *l.* from the public; to be paid to them (or, if killed

---

[t] See Vol. III. pag. 160.
[u] Mod. Un. Hift. vi. 383. vii. 156.

[w] 2 Hal. P. C. 100—104.
[x] 1 Hawk. P. C. 75.

in the endeavour to take him, their executors) by the sheriff of the county : to which the statute 8 Geo. II. c. 16. superadds 10 *l.* to be paid by the hundred indemnified by such taking. By statute 10 & 11 W. III. c. 23. any person apprehending and prosecuting to conviction a felon guilty of burglary or private larciny to the value of 5 *s.* from any shop, warehouse, coachhouse, or stable, shall be excused from all parish offices. And by statute 5 Ann. c. 31. any person so apprehending and prosecuting a burglar, or felonious housebreaker, (or, if killed in the attempt, his executors) shall be entitled to a reward of 40 *l.*

CHAPTER THE TWENTY SECOND.

OF COMMITMENT AND BAIL.

WHEN a delinquent is arrested by any of the means mentioned in the preceding chapter, he ought regularly to be carried before a justice of the peace. And how he is there to be treated, I shall next shew, under the second head, of *commitment* and *bail*.

THE justice, before whom such prisoner is brought, is bound immediately to examine the circumstances of the crime alleged: and to this end by statute 2 & 3 Ph. & M. c. 10. he is to take in writing the examination of such prisoner, and the information of those who bring him: which, Mr Lambard observes [a], was the first warrant given for the examination of a felon in the English law. For, at the common law, *nemo tenebatur prodere seipsum*; and his fault was not to be wrung out of himself, but rather to be discovered by other means, and other men. If upon this enquiry it manifestly appears, either that no such crime was committed, or that the suspicion entertained of the prisoner was wholly groundless, in such cases only it is lawful totally to discharge him. Otherwise he must either be committed to prison, or give bail; that is, put in securities for his appearance, to answer

[a] *Eirenarch.* b. 2. c. 7.

the

the charge againſt him. This commitment therefore being only
for ſafe cuſtody, wherever bail will anſwer the ſame intention,
it ought to be taken; as in moſt of the inferior crimes : but in
felonies, and other offences of a capital nature, no bail can be
a ſecurity equivalent to the actual cuſtody of the perſon.　For
what is there that a man may not be induced to forfeit, to ſave
his own life ? and what ſatisfaction or indemnity is it to the
public, to ſeize the effects of them who have bailed a murderer,
if the murderer himſelf be ſuffered to eſcape with impunity ?
Upon a principle ſimilar to which, the Athenian magiſtrates,
when they took a ſolemn oath, never to keep a citizen in bonds
that could give three ſureties of the ſame quality with himſelf,
did it with an exception to ſuch as had embezzled the public
money, or been guilty of treaſonable practiſes [b]. What the nature of bail is, hath been ſhewn in the preceding book [c]; *viz.*
a delivery, or bailment, of a perſon to his ſureties, upon their
giving (together with himſelf) ſufficient ſecurity for his appearance : he being ſuppoſed to continue in their friendly cuſtody,
inſtead of going to gaol.　In civil caſes we have ſeen that every
defendant is bailable; but in criminal matters it is otherwiſe.
Let us therefore enquire, in what caſes the party accuſed ought,
or ought not, to be admitted to bail.

A n d, firſt, to refuſe or delay to bail any perſon bailable, is
an offence againſt the liberty of the ſubject, in any magiſtrate, by
the common law [d]; as well as by the ſtatute Weſtm. 1. 3 Edw. I.
c. 15. and the *habeas corpus* act, 31 Car. II. c. 2. And leſt the
intention of the law ſhould be fruſtrated by the juſtices requiring bail to a greater amount than the nature of the caſe demands, it is expreſſly declared by ſtatute 1 W. & M. ſt. 2. c. 1.
that exceſſive bail ought not to be required : though what bail
ſhall be called exceſſive, muſt be left to the courts, on conſidering the circumſtances of the caſe, to determine.　And on the
other hand, if the magiſtrate takes inſufficient bail, he is liable

[b] Pott. Antiq. b. 1. c. 18.　　　　　　[d] 2 Hawk. P. C. 90.
[c] See Vol. III. pag. 290.

to be fined, if the criminal doth not appear[e]. Bail may be taken either in court, or in some particular cases by the sheriff, coroner, or other magistrate; but most usually by the justices of the peace. Regularly, in all offences either against the common law or act of parliament, that are below felony, the offender ought to be admitted to bail, unless it be prohibited by some special act of parliament[f]. In order therefore more precisely to ascertain what offences *are* bailable.

LET us next see, who may *not* be admitted to bail, or, what offences are *not* bailable. And here I shall not consider any one of those cases in which bail is ousted by statute, from prisoners *convicted* of particular offences; for then such imprisonment without bail is part of their sentence and punishment. But, where the imprisonment is only for safe custody *before* the conviction, and not for punishment *afterwards,* in such cases bail is ousted or taken away, wherever the offence is of a very enormous nature: for then the public is entitled to demand nothing less than the highest security that can be given; *viz.* the body of the accused, in order to ensure that justice shall be done upon him, if guilty. Such persons therefore, as the author of the mirror observes[g], have no other sureties but the four walls of the prison. By the antient common law, before[h] and since[i] the conquest, all felonies were bailable, till murder was excepted by statute: so that persons might be admitted to bail before conviction almost in every case. But the statute Westm. 1. 3 Edw. I. c. 15. takes away the power of bailing in treason, and in divers instances of felony. The statute 1 & 2 Ph. & Mar. c. 13. gives farther regulations in this matter: and upon the whole we may collect[k], that no justices of the peace can bail, 1. Upon an accusation of treason: nor, 2. Of murder: nor,

---

[e] 2 Hawk. P. C. 89.
[f] 2 Hal. P. C. 127.
[g] c. 2. §. 24.
[h] 2 Inst. 189.

[i] *In omnibus placitis de felonia solet accusatus per plegios dimitti, praeterquam in placito de homicidio, ubi ad terrorem aliter statutum est.* (Glanv. *l.* 14. *c.* 1.)
[k] 2 Inst. 186. 2 Hal. P. C. 129.

3. In

3. In cafe of manflaughter, if the prifoner be clearly the flayer, and not barely fufpected to be fo; or if any indictment be found againft him: nor, 4. Such as, being committed for felony, have broken prifon; becaufe it not only carries a prefumption of guilt, but is alfo fuperadding one felony to another: 5. Perfons outlawed: 6. Such as have abjured the realm: 7. Approvers, of whom we fhall fpeak in a fubfequent chapter, and perfons by them accufed: 8. Perfons taken with the mainour, or in the fact of felony: 9. Perfons charged with arfon: 10. Excommunicated perfons, taken by writ *de excommunicato capiendo:* all which are clearly not admiffible to bail. Others are of a dubious nature, as, 11. Thieves openly defamed and known: 12. Perfons charged with other felonies, or manifeft and enormous offences, not being of good fame: and 13. Acceffories to felony, that labour under the fame want of reputation. Thefe feem to be in the difcretion of the juftices, whether bailable or not. The laft clafs are fuch as *muft* be bailed upon offering fufficient furety; as, 14. Perfons of good fame, charged with a bare fufpicion of manflaughter, or other inferior homicide: 15. Such perfons, being charged with petit larciny or any felony, not before fpecified: or, 16. With being acceffory to any felony. Laftly, it is agreed that the court of king's bench (or any judge thereof in time of vacation) may bail for any crime whatfoever, be it treafon[1], murder, or any other offence, according to the circumftances of the cafe. And herein the wifdom of the law is very manifeft. To allow bail to be taken commonly for fuch enormous crimes, would greatly tend to elude the public juftice: and yet there are cafes, though they rarely happen, in which it would be hard and unjuft to confine a man in prifon, though accufed even of the greateft offence. The law has therefore provided one court, and only one, which has a difcretionary power of bailing in any cafe: except only, even to this high jurifdiction, and of courfe to all inferior ones, fuch perfons as

---

[1] In the reign of queen Elizabeth it was the unanimous opinion of the judges, that no court could bail upon a commitment, for a charge of high treafon, by any of the queen's privy council. (1 Anderf. 298.)

are

are committed by either houfe of parliament, fo long as the
feffion lafts; or fuch as are committed for contempts by any of
the king's fuperior courts of juftice.

UPON the whole, if the offence be not bailable, or the party
cannot find bail, he is to be committed to the county gaol by
the *mittimus* of the juftice, or warrant under his hand and feal,
containing the caufe of his commitment; there to abide till delivered by due courfe of law[m]. But this imprifonment, as has
been faid, is only for fafe cuftody, and not for punifhment:
therefore, in this dubious interval between the commitment and
trial, a prifoner ought to be ufed with the utmoft humanity;
and neither be loaded with needlefs fetters, or fubjected to other
hardfhips than fuch as are abfolutely requifite for the purpofe
of confinement only: though what are fo requifite, muft too
often be left to the difcretion of the gaolers; who are frequently
a mercilefs race of men, and, by being converfant in fcenes of
mifery, fteeled againft any tender fenfation. Yet the law will
not juftify them in fettering a prifoner, unlefs where he is un-
ruly, or has attempted an efcape[n]: this being the humane language of our antient lawgivers[o], " *cuftodes poenam fibi commiffo-*
" *rum non augeant, nec eos torqueant; fed omni faevitia remota,*
" *pietateque adhibita, judicia debite exequantur.*"

[m] 2 Hal. P. C. 122.   [o] Flet. *l.* 1. *c.* 26.
[n] 2 Inft. 381.   3 Inft. 34.

CHAPTER THE TWENTY THIRD.

OF THE SEVERAL MODES OF PROSECUTION.

THE next ſtep towards the puniſhment of offenders is their proſecution, or the manner of their formal accuſation. And this is either upon a previous finding of the fact by an inqueſt or grand jury; or without ſuch previous finding. The former way is either by *preſentment*, or *indictment*.

I. A preſentment, *generally* taken, is a very comprehenſive term; including not only preſentments properly ſo called, but alſo inquiſitions of office, and indictments by a grand jury. A preſentment, *properly* ſpeaking, is the notice taken by a grand jury of any offence from their own knowlege or obſervation [a], without any bill of indictment laid before them at the ſuit of the king. As, the preſentment of a nuſance, a libel, and the like; upon which the officer of the court muſt afterwards frame an indictment, before the party preſented as the author can be put to anſwer it. An inquiſition of office is the act of a jury, ſummoned by the proper officer to enquire of matters relating to the crown, upon evidence laid before them. Some of theſe are in themſelves convictions, and cannot afterwards be traverſed or denied; and therefore the inqueſt, or jury, ought to hear all

[a] Lamb. *Eirenarch. l.* 4 *c.* 5.

that

that can be alleged on both fides. Of this nature are all inquifitions of *felo de fe*; of flight in perfons accufed of felony; of
deodands, and the like; and prefentments of petty offences in
the fheriff's tourn or court-leet, whereupon the prefiding officer
may fet a fine. Other inquifitions may be afterwards traverfed
and examined; as particularly the coroner's inquifition of the
death of a man, when it finds any one guilty of homicide: for
in fuch cafes the offender fo prefented muft be arraigned upon
this inquifition, and may difpute the truth of it; which brings
it to a kind of indictment, the moft ufual and effectual means
of profecution, and into which we will therefore enquire a
little more minutely.

II. AN *indictment* [b] is a written accufation of one or more
perfons of a crime or mifdemefnor, preferred to, and prefented
upon oath by, a grand jury. To this end the fheriff of every
county is bound to return to every feffion of the peace, and
every commiffion of *oyer* and *terminer*, and of general gaol delivery, twenty four good and lawful men of the county, fome
out of every hundred, to enquire, prefent, do, and execute all
thofe things, which on the part of our lord the king fhall then
and there be commanded them [c]. They ought to be freeholders,
but to what amount is uncertain [d]: which feems to be *cafus
omiffus*, and as proper to be fupplied by the legiflature as the
qualifications of the petit jury; which were formerly equally
vague and uncertain, but are now fettled by feveral acts of parliament. However, they are ufually gentlemen of the beft figure in the county. As many as appear upon this panel, are
fworn upon the grand jury, to the amount of twelve at the leaft,
and not more than twenty three; that twelve may be a majority. Which number, as well as the conftitution itfelf, we find
exactly defcribed, fo early as the laws of king Ethelred [e]. "*Exeant*
"*feniores duodecim thani, et praefectus cum eis, et jurent fuper*
"*fanctuarium quod eis in manus datur, quod nolint ullum innocentem*

---

[b] See appendix. §. 1.
[c] 2 Hal. P. C. 154.

[d] Ibid. 155.
[e] Wilk. *LL. Angl. Sax* 117.

　　　　　　　　　　　　　　　　　　　　"*accufare,*

" *accusare, nec aliquem noxium celare.*" In the time of king Richard the first (according to Hoveden) the proceſs of electing the grand jury, ordained by that prince, was as follows: four knights were to be taken from the county at large, who choſe two more out of every hundred; which two aſſociated to them-ſelves ten other principal freemen, and thoſe twelve were to anſwer concerning all particulars relating to their own diſtrict. This number was probably found too large and inconvenient; but the traces of this inſtitution ſtill remain, in that ſome of the jury muſt be ſummoned out of every hundred. This grand jury are previouſly inſtructed in the articles of their enquiry, by a charge from the judge who preſides upon the bench. They then withdraw, to ſit and receive indictments, which are pre-ferred to them in the name of the king, but at the ſuit of any private proſecutor; and they are only to hear evidence on be-half of the proſecution: for the finding of an indictment is only in the nature of an enquiry or accuſation, which is after-wards to be tried and determined; and the grand jury are only to enquire upon their oaths, whether there be ſufficient cauſe to call upon the party to anſwer it. A grand jury however ought to be thoroughly perſuaded of the truth of an indictment, ſo far as their evidence goes; and not to reſt ſatisfied merely with remote probabilities: a doctrine, that might be applied to very oppreſſive purpoſes [f].

THE grand jury are ſworn to enquire, only for the body of the county, *pro corpore comitatus*; and therefore they cannot re-gularly enquire of a fact done out of that county for which they are ſworn, unleſs particularly enabled by act of parliament. And to ſo high a nicety was this matter antiently carried, that where a man was wounded in one county, and died in another, the offender was at common law indictable in neither, becauſe no complete act of felony was done in any one of them: but by ſtatute 2 & 3 Edw. VI. c. 24. he is now indictable in the county where the party died. And ſo in ſome other caſes: as particu-

[f] State Trials. IV. 183.

larly,

larly, where treaſon is committed out of the realm, it may be enquired of in any county within the realm, as the king ſhall direct, in purſuance of ſtatutes 26 Hen.VIII. c.13. 35 Hen.VIII. c. 2. and 5 & 6 Edw. VI. c. 11. But, in general, all offences muſt be enquired into as well as tried in the county where the fact is committed.

WHEN the grand jury have heard the evidence, if they think it a groundleſs accuſation, they uſed formerly to endorſe on the back of the bill, " *ignoramus;*" or, we know nothing of it; intimating, that though the facts might poſſibly be true, that truth did not appear to them: but now, they aſſert in Engliſh, more abſolutely, " not a true bill;" and then the party is diſcharged without farther anſwer. But a freſh bill may afterwards be preferred to a ſubſequent grand jury. If they are ſatisfied of the truth of the accuſation, they then endorſe upon it, " a " true bill;" antiently, " *billa vera.*" The indictment is then ſaid to be found, and the party ſtands indicted. But, to find a bill, there muſt at leaſt twelve of the jury agree: for ſo tender is the law of England of the lives of the ſubjects, that no man can be convicted at the ſuit of the king of any capital offence, unleſs by the unanimous voice of twenty four of his equals and neighbours: that is, by twelve at leaſt of the grand jury, in the firſt place, aſſenting to the accuſation; and afterwards, by the whole petit jury, of twelve more, finding him guilty upon his trial. But, if twelve of the grand jury aſſent, it is a good preſentment, though ſome of the reſt diſagree [g]. And the indictment, when ſo found, is publicly delivered into court.

INDICTMENTS muſt have a precife and ſufficient certainty. By ſtatute 1 Hen. V. c. 5. all indictments muſt ſet forth the chriſtian name, ſirname, and addition of the ſtate and degree, myſtery, town, or place, and the county of the offender: and all this to identify his *perſon*. The *time*, and *place*, are alſo to be aſcertained, by naming the day, and townſhip, in which the fact was committed: though a miſtake in theſe points is in general

[g] 2 Hal. P. C. 161.

not

not held to be material, provided the *time* be laid previous to the finding of the indictment, and the *place* to be within the jurisdiction of the court. But sometimes the *time* may be very material, where there is any limitation in point of time assigned for the prosecution of offenders; as by the statute 7 Will. III. c. 3. which enacts, that no prosecution shall be had for any of the treasons or misprisions therein mentioned (except an assassination designed or attempted on the person of the king) unless the bill of indictment be found within three years after the offence committed [h] : and, in case of murder, the time of the death must be laid within a year and a day after the mortal stroke was given. The *offence* itself must also be set forth with clearness and certainty : and in some crimes particular words of art must be used, which are so appropriated by the law to express the precise idea which it entertains of the offence, that no other words, however synonymous they may seem, are capable of doing it. Thus, in treason, the facts must be laid to be done, " treasonably, and against his allegiance;" antiently " *proditorie* " *et contra ligeantiae suae debitum :*" else the indictment is void. In indictments for murder, it is necessary to say that the party indicted " murdered," not " killed" or " slew," the other; which till the late statute was expressed in Latin by the word " *murdra-* " *vit* [i]. In all indictments for felonies, the adverb " feloniously, " *felonice*," must be used; and for burglaries also, " *burglariter*," or in English, " burglariously :" and all these to ascertain the intent. In rapes, the word " *rapuit*," or " ravished," is necessary, and must not be expressed by any periphrasis; in order to render the crime certain. So in larcinies also, the words " *felo-* " *nice cepit et asportavit*, feloniously took and carried away," are necessary to every indictment ; for these only can express the very offence. Also in indictments for murder, the length and depth of the wound should in general be expressed, in order that it may appear to the court to have been of a mortal nature : but if it goes through the body, then it's dimensions are immaterial, for that is apparently sufficient to have been the cause of

[h] Fost. 249.   [i] See Vol. III. pag. 321.

the

the death. Alfo where a limb, or the like, is abfolutely cut off, there fuch defcription is impoffible [k]. Laftly, in indictments the *value* of the thing, which is the fubject or inftrument of the offence, muft fometimes be expreffed. In indictments for larcinies this is neceffary, that it may appear whether it be grand or petit larciny; and whether entitled or not to the benefit of clergy: in homicide of all forts it is neceffary; as the weapon, with which it is committed, is forfeited to the king as a deodand.

THE remaining methods of profecution are without any previous finding by a jury, to fix the authoritative ftamp of verifimilitude upon the accufation. One of thefe, by the common law, was when a thief was taken *with the mainour*, that is, with the thing ftolen upon him, *in manu*. For he might, when fo detected *flagrante delicto*, be brought into court, arraigned, and tried, without indictment: as by the Danifh law he might be taken and hanged upon the fpot, without accufation or trial [l]. But this proceeding was taken away by feveral ftatutes in the reign of Edward the third [m]: though in Scotland a fimilar procefs remains to this day [n]. So that the only fpecies of proceeding at the fuit of the king, without a previous indictment or prefentment by a grand jury, now feems to be that of *information*.

III. INFORMATIONS are of two forts; firft, thofe which are partly at the fuit of the king, and partly at that of a fubject; and fecondly, fuch as are only in the name of the king. The former are ufually brought upon penal ftatutes, which inflict a penalty upon conviction of the offender, one part to the ufe of the king, and another to the ufe of the informer; and are a fort of *qui tam* actions, (the nature of which was explained in a former volume [o]) only carried on by a criminal inftead of a civil procefs: upon which I fhall therefore only obferve, that

[k] 5 Rep. 122.
[l] Stiernh. *de jure Sueon. i.* 3. *c.* 5.
[m] 2 Hal. P. C. 149.

[n] Lord Kayms. I. 331.
[o] See Vol. III. pag. 160.

by

by the ſtatute 31 Eliz. c. 5. no proſecution upon any penal ſtatute, the ſuit and benefit whereof are limited in part to the
king and in part to the proſecutor, can be brought by any common informer after one year is expired ſince the commiſſion of
the offence ; nor on behalf of the crown after the lapſe of two
years longer ; nor, where the forfeiture is originally given only
to the king, can ſuch proſecution be had after the expiration of
two years from the commiſſion of the offence.

THE informations, that are exhibited in the name of the
king alone, are alſo of two kinds : firſt, thoſe which are truly
and properly his own ſuits, and filed *ex officio* by his own immediate officer, the attorney general : ſecondly, thoſe in which,
though the king is the nominal proſecutor, yet it is at the relation of ſome private perſon or common informer ; and they are
filed by the king's coroner and attorney in the court of king's
bench, uſually called the maſter of the crown-office, who is
for this purpoſe the ſtanding officer of the public. The objects
of the king's own proſecutions, filed *ex officio* by his own attorney general, are properly ſuch enormous miſdemeſnors, as
peculiarly tend to diſturb or endanger his government, or to
moleſt or affront him in the regular diſcharge of his royal functions. For offences ſo high and dangerous, in the puniſhment
or prevention of which a moment's delay would be fatal, the
law has given to the crown the power of an immediate proſecution, without waiting for any previous application to any
other tribunal. A power, ſo neceſſary, not only to the eaſe
and ſafety but even to the very exiſtence of the executive magiſtrate, was originally reſerved in the great plan of the Engliſh
conſtitution, which has wiſely provided for the due preſervation
of all it's parts. The objects of the other ſpecies of informations, filed by the maſter of the crown-office upon the complaint or relation of a private ſubject, are any groſs and notorious miſdemeſnors, riots, batteries, libels, and other immoralities of an atrocious kind[p], not peculiarly tending to diſturb

[p] 2 Hawk. P. C. 260.

the

the government (for thofe are left to the care of the attorney general) but which, on account of their magnitude or pernicious example, deferve the moft public animadverfion. And when an information is filed, either thus, or by the attorney general *ex officio*, it muft be tried by a petit jury of the county where the offence arifes: after which, if the defendant be found guilty, he muft refort to the court for his punifhment.

THERE can be no doubt but that this mode of profecution, by information (or fuggeftion) filed on record by the king's attorney general, or by his coroner or mafter of the crown-office in the court of king's bench, is as antient as the common law itfelf[q]. For as the king was bound to profecute, or at leaft to lend the fanction of his name to a profecutor, whenever a grand jury informed him upon their oaths that there was a fufficient ground for inftituting a criminal fuit; fo, when thefe his immediate officers were otherwife fufficiently affured that a man had committed a grofs mifdemefnor, either perfonally againft the king or his government, or againft the public peace and good order, they were at liberty, without waiting for any farther intelligence, to convey that information to the court of king's bench by a fuggeftion on record, and to carry on the profecution in his majefty's name. But thefe informations (of every kind) are confined by the conftitutional law to mere mifdemefnors only: for, wherever any capital offence is charged, the fame law requires that the accufation be warranted by the oath of twelve men, before the party fhall be put to anfwer it. And, as to thofe offences, in which informations were allowed as well as indictments, fo long as they were confined to this high and refpectable jurifdiction, and were carried on in a legal and regular courfe in his majefty's court of king's bench, the fubject had no reafon to complain. The fame notice was given, the fame procefs was iffued, the fame pleas were allowed, the fame trial by jury was had, the fame judgment was given by the fame judges, as if the profecution had originally been by indictment. But

q 1 Show. 118.

when the ftatute 3 Hen. VII. c. 1. had extended the jurifdiction of the court of ftar-chamber, the members of which were the fole judges of the law, the fact, and the penalty; and when the ftatute 11 Hen. VII. c. 3. had permitted informations to be brought by any informer upon any penal ftatute, not extending to life or member, at the affifes or before the juftices of the peace, who were to hear and determine the fame according to their own difcretion; then it was, that the legal and orderly jurifdiction of the court of king's bench fell into difufe and ob-livion, and Empfon and Dudley (the wicked inftruments of king Henry VII) by hunting out obfolete penalties, and this tyranni-cal mode of profecution, with other oppreffive devices [r], conti-nually haraffed the fubject and fhamefully inriched the crown. The latter of thefe acts was foon indeed repealed by ftatute 1 Hen. VIII. c. 6. but the court of ftar-chamber continued in high vigour, and daily increafing it's authority, for more than a century longer; till finally abolifhed by ftatute 16 Car. I. c. 10.

UPON this diffolution the old common law [s] authority of the court of king's bench, as the *cuftos morum* of the nation, being found neceffary to refide fomewhere for the peace and good go-vernment of the kingdom, was again revived in practice [t]. And it is obfervable, that, in the fame act of parliament which abo-lifhed the court of ftar-chamber, a conviction by information is expreffly reckoned up, as one of the legal modes of conviction of fuch perfons, as fhould offend a third time againft the provifions of that ftatute [u]. It is true, fir Matthew Hale, who prefided in this court foon after the time of fuch revival, is faid [w] to have been no friend to this method of profecution: and, if fo, the reafon of fuch his diflike was probably the ill ufe, which the mafter of the crown-office then made of his authority, by per-mitting the fubject to be harraffed with vexatious informations,

[r] 1 And. 157.
[s] 5 Mod. 464.
[t] Styl. Rep. 217. 245. Styl. pract Reg.

tit. Information. pag. 187. (edit. 1657.)
2 Sid. 71. 1 Sid. 152.
[u] Stat. 16 Car. I. c. 10. §. 6.
[w] 5 Mod. 460.

when-

whenever applied to by any malicious or revengeful profecutor; rather than his doubt of their legality, or propriety upon urgent occafions[x]. For the power of filing informations, without any control, then refided in the breaft of the mafter: and, being filed in the name of the king, they fubjected the profecutor to no cofts, though on trial they proved to be groundlefs. This oppreffive ufe of them, in the times preceding the revolution, occafioned a ftruggle, foon after the acceffion of king William[y], to procure a declaration of their illegality by the judgment of the court of king's bench. But fir John Holt, who then prefided there, and all the judges, were clearly of opinion, that this proceeding was grounded on the common law, and could not be then impeached. And, in a few years afterwards, a more temperate remedy was applied in parliament, by ftatute 4 & 5 W. & M. c. 18. which enacts, that the clerk of the crown fhall not file any information without exprefs direction from the court of king's bench: and that every profecutor, permitted to promote fuch information, fhall give fecurity by a recognizance of twenty pounds (which now feems to be too fmall a fum) to profecute the fame with effect; and to pay cofts to the defendant, in cafe he be acquitted thereon, unlefs the judge, who tries the information, fhall certify there was reafonable caufe for filing it; and, at all events, to pay cofts, unlefs the information fhall be tried within a year after iffue joined. But there is a provifo in this act, that it fhall not extend to any other informations, than thofe which are exhibited by the mafter of the crown-office: and, confequently, informations at the king's own fuit, filed by his attorney general, are no way reftrained thereby.

THERE is one fpecies of informations, ftill farther regulated by ftatute 9 Ann. c. 20. viz. thofe in the nature of a writ of *quo warranto*; which was fhewn in the preceding volume[z], to be a remedy given to the crown againft fuch as had ufurped or intruded into any office or franchife. The modern information

[x] 1 Saund. 301. 1 Sid. 174.　　　Farr. 361. 1 Show. 106.
[y] M. 1 W. & M. 5 Mod. 459. Comb. 141.　[z] See Vol. III. pag. 262.

　　　　　　　　　　tends

tends to the fame purpofe as the antient writ, being generally made ufe of to try the civil rights of fuch franchifes; though it is commenced in the fame manner as other informations are, by leave of the court, or at the will of the attorney-general: being properly a criminal profecution, in order to fine the defendant for his ufurpation, as well as to ouft him from his office; yet ufually confidered at prefent as merely a civil proceeding.

THESE are all the methods of profecution at the fuit of the king. There yet remains another, which is merely at the fuit of the fubject, and is called an *appeal*.

IV. AN appeal, in the fenfe wherein it is here ufed, does not fignify any complaint to a fuperior court of an injuftice done by an inferior one, which is the general ufe of the word; but it here means an original fuit, at the time of it's firft commencement[a]. An appeal therefore, when fpoken of as a criminal profecution, denotes an accufation by a private fubject againft another, for fome heinous crime; demanding punifhment on account of the particular injury fuffered, rather than for the offence againft the public. As this method of profecution is ftill in force, I cannot omit to mention it: but, as it is very little in ufe, on account of the great nicety required in conducting it, I fhall treat of it very briefly; referring the ftudent for more particulars to other voluminous compilations[b].

THIS private procefs, for the punifhment of public crimes, had probably it's original in thofe times, when a private pecuniary fatisfaction, called a *weregild*, was conftantly paid to the party injured, or his relations, to expiate enormous offences. This was a cuftom derived to us, in common with other northern nations[c], from our anceftors, the antient Germans; among

---

[a] It is derived from the French, "*appel-*" *ler*," the verb active, which fignifies to call upon, fummon, or challenge one; and not the verb neuter, which fignifies the fame as the ordinary fenfe of "appeal" in Englifh.
[b] 2 Hawk. P. C. ch. 23.
[c] Stiernh. *de jure Sueon. l. 3. c. 4.*

whom

whom according to Tacitus[d], " *luitur homicidium certo armento-* " *rum ac pecorum numero ; recipitque fatisfaɛtionem univerfa do-* " *mus[e].*" In the fame manner by the Irifh Brehon law, in cafe of murder, the Brehon or judge was ufed to compound between the murderer, and the friends of the deceafed who profecuted him, by caufing the malefaɛtor to give unto them, or to the child or wife of him that was flain, a recompenfe which they called an *eriach*[f]. And thus we find in our Saxon laws (particularly thofe of king Athelftan[g]) the feveral weregilds for homicide eftablifhed in progreffive order, from the death of the ceorl or peafant, up to that of the king himfelf[h]. And in the laws of king Henry I[i], we have an account of what other offences were then redeemable by weregild, and what were not fo[k]. As therefore, during the continuance of this cuftom, a procefs was certainly given, for recovering the weregild by the party to whom it was due ; it feems that, when thefe offences by degrees grew no longer redeemable, the private procefs was ftill continued, in order to infure the infliɛtion of punifhment upon the offender, though the party injured was allowed no pecuniary compenfation for the offence.

But, though appeals were thus in the nature of profecutions for fome atrocious injury committed more immediately againft an individual, yet it alfo was antiently permitted, that any fub-

---

[d] *de M. G. c.* 21.

[e] And in another place, (*c.* 12.) " *De-* " *liɛtis, pro modo pœnarum, equorum pecorum-* " *que numera conviɛti mulɛtentur. Pars mulɛtae* " *regi vel civitati; pars ipfi qui vindicatur,* " *vel propinquis ejus, exfolvitur.*"

[f] Spenfer's ftate of Ireland, pag. 1513. *edit.* Hughes.

[g] *Judic. Civit. Lund.* Wilk. 71.

[h] The weregild of a ceorl was 266 thrymfas, that of the king 30000 ; each thrymfa being equal to about a fhilling of our prefent money. The weregild of a fubjeɛt was paid entirely to the relations of

the party flain : but that of the king was divided ; one half being paid to the public, the other to the royal family.

[i] c. 12.

[k] In Turkey this principle is ftill carried fo far, that even murder is never profecuted by the officers of the government, as with us. It is the bufinefs of the next relations, and them only, to revenge the flaughter of their kinfmen ; and if they rather choofe (as they generally do) to compound the matter for money, nothing more is faid about it. (Lady M. W. Montague. lett. 42.)

jeɛt

ject might appeal another subject of high-treason, either in the
courts of common law [1], or in parliament, or (for treasons committed beyond the seas) in the court of the high constable and
marshal. The cognizance of appeals in the latter still continues
in force; and so late as 1631 there was a trial by battel awarded
in the court of chivalry, on such an appeal of treason [m]: but the
first was *virtually* abolished [n] by the statutes 5 Edw. III. c. 9. and
25 Edw. III. c. 24. and the second *expressly* by statute 1 Hen. IV.
c. 14. So that the only appeals now in force, for things done
within the realm, are appeals of felony and mayhem.

A n appeal of *felony* may be brought for crimes committed
either against the parties themselves, or their relations. The
crimes against the parties themselves are *larciny, rape,* and *arson.*
And for these, as well as for *mayhem,* the persons robbed, ravished, maimed, or whose houses are burnt, may institute this private process. The only crime against one's relation, for which
an appeal can be brought, is that of *killing* him, by either murder or manslaughter. But this cannot be brought by every relation: but only by the wife for the death of her husband, or by
the heir male for the death of his ancestor; which heirship was
also confined, by an ordinance of king Henry the first, to the
four nearest degrees of blood [o]. It is given to the wife, on account of the loss of her husband: therefore, if she marries again,
before or pending her appeal, it is lost and gone; or, if she
marries after judgment, she shall not demand execution. The
heir, as was said, must also be heir male, and such a one as was
the next heir by the course of the common law, at the time of
the killing of the ancestor. But this rule has three exceptions:
1. If the person killed leaves an innocent wife, she only, and
not the heir, shall have the appeal: 2. If there be no wife, and
the heir be accused of the murder, the person, who next to him
would have been heir male, shall bring the appeal: 3. If the

---

[1] Britt. c. 22.

[m] By Donald lord Rea against David
Ramsey. (Rushw. vol. 2. part. 2. pag. 112.)

[n] 1 Hal. P. C. 349.

[o] Mirr. c. 2. §. 7.

wife kills her huſband, the heir may appeal her of the death. And, by the ſtatute of Glouceſter, 6 Edw. I. c. 9. all appeals of death muſt be ſued within a year and a day after the completion of the felony by the death of the party : which ſeems to be only declaratory of the old common law ; for in the Gothic conſtitutions we find the ſame " *praeſcriptio annalis, quae currit* " *adverſus actorem, ſi de homicida ei non conſtat intra annum a caede* " *facta, nec quenquam interea arguat et accuſet* [p]."

THESE appeals may be brought, previous to any indictment ; and, if the appellee be acquitted thereon, he cannot be afterwards indicted for the ſame offence. In like manner as by the old Gothic conſtitution, if any offender gained a verdict in his favour, when proſecuted by the party injured, he was alſo underſtood to be acquitted of any crown proſecution for the ſame offence [q] : but, on the contrary, if he made his peace with the king, ſtill he might be proſecuted at the ſuit of the party. And ſo, with us, if a man be acquitted on an indictment of murder, or found guilty, and pardoned by the king, ſtill he may, by virtue of ſtatute 3 Hen. VII. c. 1. be proſecuted by appeal for the ſame felony, not having as yet been puniſhed for it : though, if he hath been found guilty of manſlaughter on an indictment, and hath had the benefit of clergy, and ſuffered the judgment of the law, he cannot afterwards be appealed. For it is a maxim of law, that " *nemo bis punitur pro eodem delicto.*"

IF the appellee be found guilty, he ſhall ſuffer the ſame judgment, as if he had been convicted by indictment : but with this remarkable difference ; that on an indictment, which is at the ſuit of the king, the king may pardon and remit the execution ; on an appeal, which is at the ſuit of a private ſubject, to make an atonement for the private wrong, the king can no more pardon it, than he can remit the damages recovered on an action of battery [r]. In like manner as, while the weregild continued to

[p] Stiernh. *de jure Goth. l. 3. c. 4.*
[q] *Ibid. l. 1. c. 5.*

[r] 2 Hawk P. C. 392.

be

be paid as a fine for homicide, it could not be remitted by the king's authority [s]. And the antient ufage was, fo late as Henry the fourth's time, that all the relations of the flain fhould drag the appeliee to the place of execution [t]: a cuftom, founded upon that favage fpirit of family refentment, which prevailed univerfally through Europe, after the irruption of the northern nations, and is peculiarly attended to in their feveral codes of law; and which prevails even now among the wild and untutored inhabitants of America: as if the finger of nature had pointed it out to mankind, in their rude and uncultivated ftate. However, the punifhment of the offender may be remitted and difcharged by the concurrence of all parties interefted; and as the king by his pardon may fruftrate an indictment, fo the appellant by his releafe may difcharge an appeal [u]: "*nam quilibet poteft renunciare* "*juri, pro fe introducto.*"

THESE are the feveral methods of profecution inftituted by the laws of England for the punifhment of offences; of which that by indictment is the moft general. I fhall therefore confine my fubfequent obfervations principally to this method of profecution; remarking by the way the moft material variations that may arife, from the method of proceeding by either information or appeal.

[s] *LL. Edm.* §. 3.   [u] 1 Hal. P. C. 9.
[t] *M.* 11 *Hen. IV.* 12. 3 Inft. 131.

CHAPTER THE TWENTY FOURTH.

OF PROCESS UPON AN INDICTMENT.

WE are next, in the fourth place, to enquire into the manner of issuing *process*, after indictment found, to bring in the accused to answer it. We have hitherto supposed the offender to be in custody before the finding of the indictment; in which case he is immediately to be arraigned thereon. But if he hath fled, or secretes himself, in capital cases; or hath not, in smaller misdemesnors, been bound over to appear at the assises or sessions, still an indictment may be preferred against him in his absence; since, were he present, he could not be heard before the grand jury against it. And, if it be found, then process must issue to bring him into court; for the indictment cannot be tried, unless he personally appears: according to the rules of equity in all, and the express provision of statute 28 Edw. III. c. 3. in capital, cases; that no man shall be put to death, without being brought to answer by due process of law.

THE proper process on an indictment for any petty misdemesnor, or on a penal statute, is a writ of *venire facias*, which is in the nature of a summons to cause the party to appear. And if by the return to such *venire* it appears, that the party hath lands in the county whereby he may be distreined, then a *distress infinite* shall be issued from time to time till he appears.

But if the sheriff returns that he hath no lands in his bailiwick, then (upon his non-appearance) a writ of *capias* shall issue, which commands the sheriff to take his body, and have him at the next assises; and if he cannot be taken upon the first *capias*, a second, and a third shall issue, called an *alias*, and a *pluries capias*. But, on indictments for treason or felony, a *capias* is the first process: and, for treason or homicide, only one shall be allowed to issue[a], or two in the case of other felonies, by statute 25 Edw. III. c. 14. though the usage is to issue only one in any felony; the provisions of this statute being in most cases found impracticable[b]. And so, in the case of misdemesnors, it is now the usual practice for any judge of the court of king's bench, upon certificate of an indictment found, to award a writ of *capias* immediately, in order to bring in the defendant. But if he absconds, and it is thought proper to pursue him to an outlawry, then a greater exactness is necessary. For, in such case, after the several writs have issued in a regular number, according to the nature of the respective crimes, without any effect, the offender shall be put in the *exigent* in order to his outlawry: that is, he shall be exacted, proclaimed, or required to surrender, at five county courts; and if he be returned *quinto exactus*, and does not appear at the fifth exaction or requisition, then he is adjudged to be *outlawed*, or put out of the protection of the law; so that he is incapable of taking the benefit of it in any respect, either by bringing actions or otherwise.

The punishment for outlawries upon indictments for misdemesnors, is the same as for outlawries upon civil actions; (of which, and the previous process by writs of *capias, exigi facias,* and *proclamation,* we spoke in the preceding book[c]) *viz.* forfeiture of goods and chattels. But an outlawry in treason or felony amounts to a conviction and attainder of the offence charged in the indictment, as much as if he had been found guilty by his country[d]. His life is however still under the protection of

---

[a] See appendix. §. 1.
[b] 2 Hal. P. C. 195.

[c] See Vol. III. pag. 283, 4.
[d] 2 Hal. P. C. 205.

the

the law, as hath formerly been obferved [e] : and though antiently an outlawed felon was faid to have *caput lupinum*, and might be knocked on the head like a wolf, by any one that fhould meet him [f] ; becaufe, having renounced all law, he was to be dealt with as in a ftate of nature, when every one that fhould find him might flay him : yet now, to avoid fuch inhumanity, it is holden that no man is intitled to kill him wantonly or wilfully ; but in fo doing is guilty of murder [g], unlefs it happens in the endeavour to apprehend him [h]. For any perfon may arreft an outlaw on a criminal profecution, either of his own head, or by writ or warrant of *capias utlagatum*, in order to bring him to execution. But fuch outlawry may be frequently reverfed by writ of error ; the proceedings therein being (as it is fit they fhould be) exceedingly nice and circumftantial ; and, if any fingle minute point be omitted or mifconducted, the whole outlawry is illegal, and may be reverfed : upon which reverfal the party accufed is admitted to plead to, and defend himfelf againft, the indictment.

THUS much for procefs to bring in the offender after indictment found ; during which ftage of the profecution it is, that writs of *certiorari facias* are ufually had, though they may be had at any time before trial, to certify and remove the indictment, with all the proceedings thereon, from any inferior court of criminal jurifdiction into the court of king's bench ; which is the fovereign ordinary court of juftice in caufes criminal. And this is frequently done for one of thefe four purpofes ; either, 1. To confider and determine the validity of appeals or indictments and the proceedings thereon ; and to quafh or confirm them as there is caufe : or, 2. Where it is furmifed that a partial or infufficient trial will probably be had in the court below, the indictment is removed, in order to have the prifoner or defendant tried at the bar of the court of king's bench, or before the juftices of *nifi prius :* or, 3. It is fo removed, in order to plead the king's pardon there : or, 4. To iffue procefs of outlawry againſt the offender, in thoſe counties or places where the proceſs of the inferior judges will not reach him [i]. Such writ of *certiorari*, when iſſued and delivered to the inferior court for removing any record or other proceeding, as well upon indictment as otherwiſe, ſuperſedes the juriſdiction of ſuch inferior court, and makes all ſubſequent proceedings therein entirely erroneous and illegal ; unleſs the court of king's bench remands the record to the court below, to be there tried and determined. A *certiorari* may be granted at the inſtance of either the proſecutor or the defendant : the former as a matter of right, the latter as a matter of diſcretion; and therefore it is ſeldom granted to remove indictments from the juſtices of gaol delivery, or after iſſue joined or confeſſion of the fact in any of the courts below [k].

AT this ſtage of proſecution alſo it is, that indictments found by the grand jury againſt a peer muſt in conſequence of a writ of *certiorari* be certified and tranſmitted into the court of parliament, or into that of the lord high ſteward of Great Britain ; and that, in places of excluſive juriſdiction, as the two univerſities, indictments muſt be delivered (upon challenge and claim of cognizance) to the courts therein eſtabliſhed by charter, and confirmed by act of parliament, to be there reſpectively tried and determined.

[i] 2 Hal. P. C. 210.

[k] 2 Hawk. P. C. 287. 4 Burr. 749.

CHAPTER THE TWENTY FIFTH.

OF ARRAIGNMENT, AND IT'S INCIDENTS.

WHEN the offender either appears voluntarily to an indictment, or was before in cuſtody, or is brought in upon criminal proceſs to anſwer it in the proper court, he is immediately to be *arraigned* thereon; which is the fifth ſtage of criminal proſecution.

To arraign, is nothing elſe but to call the priſoner to the bar of the court, to anſwer the matter charged upon him in the indictment[a]. The priſoner is to be called to the bar by his name; and it is laid down in our antient books[b], that, though under an indictment of the higheſt nature, he muſt be brought to the bar without irons, or any manner of ſhackles or bonds; unleſs there be evident danger of an eſcape, and then he may be ſecured with irons. But yet in Layer's caſe, *A. D.* 1722. a difference was taken between the time of arraignment, and the time of trial; and accordingly the priſoner ſtood at the bar in chains during the time of his arraignment[c].

[a] 2 Hal. P. C. 216.
[b] Bract. *l.* 3. *de coron. c.* 18. §. 3. Mirr. *c.* 5. *ſect.* 1. § 54. Flet. *l.* 1. *c.* 31. §. 1.

Britt. *c.* 5. Staundf. P. C. 78. 3 Inſt 34. Kel. 10. 2Hal.P.C.219 2Hawk.P.C.308.
[c] State Trials. VI. 230.

WHEN he is brought to the bar, he is called upon by name to hold up his hand : which, though it may feem a trifling circumftance, yet is of this importance, that by the holding up of his hand *conftat de perfona*, and he owns himfelf to be of that name by which he is called[d]. However it is not an indifpenfable ceremony ; for, being calculated merely for the purpofe of identifying the perfon, any other acknowlegement will anfwer the purpofe as well : therefore, if the prifoner obftinately and contemptuoufly refufes to hold up his hand, but confeffes he is the perfon named, it is fully fufficient[e].

THEN the indictment is to be read to him diftinctly in the Englifh tongue (which was law, even while all other proceedings were in Latin) that he may fully underftand his charge. After which it is to be demanded of him, whether he be guilty of the crime, whereof he ftands indicted, or not guilty. By the old common law the acceffory could not be arraigned till the principal was attainted ; and therefore, if the principal had never been indicted at all, had ftood mute, had challenged above thirty five jurors peremptorily, had claimed the benefit of clergy, had obtained a pardon, or had died before attainder, the acceffory in any of thefe cafes could not be arraigned : for *non conflitit* whether any felony was committed or no, till the principal was attainted ; and it might fo happen that the acceffory fhould be convicted one day, and the principal acquitted the next, which would be abfurd. However, this abfurdity could only happen, where it was poffible, that a trial of the principal might be had, fubfequent to that of the acceffory : and therefore the law ftill continues, that the acceffory fhall not be tried, fo long as the principal remains liable to be tried hereafter. But by ftatute 1 Ann. c. 9. if the principal be once convicted, and before attainder, (that is, before he receives judgment of death or outlawry) he is delivered by pardon, the benefit of clergy, or otherwife ; or if the principal ftands mute, or challenges peremptorily

---

[d] 2 Hal. P. C. 219.   [e] Raym. 408.

above the legal number of jurors, fo as never to be convicted at
all ; in any of thefe cafes, in which no fubfequent trial can be
had of the principal, the acceffory may be proceeded againft, as
if the principal felon had been attainted ; for there is no danger
of future contradiction.　And upon the trial of the acceffory, as
well after as before the conviction of the principal, it feems to
be the better opinion, and founded on the true fpirit of juftice [f],
that the acceffory is at liberty (if he can) to controvert the guilt
of his fuppofed principal, and to prove him innocent of the
charge, as well in point of fact as in point of law.

W H E N a criminal is arraigned, he either *ftands mute,* or *confeffes* the fact ;　which circumftances we may call *incidents* to the
arraignment : or elfe he *pleads* to the indictment, which is to be
confidered as the next ftage of proceedings.　But, firft, let us
obferve thefe incidents to the arraignment, of ftanding mute,

I.　R E G U L A R L Y a prifoner is faid to ftand mute, when, being
arraigned for treafon or felony, he either, 1. Makes no anfwer
at all : or, 2. Anfwers foreign to the purpofe, or with fuch
matter as is not allowable ; and will not anfwer otherwife : or,
3　Upon having pleaded not guilty, refufes to put himfelf upon
the country [g].　If he fays nothing, the court ought *ex officio* to
impanel a jury, to enquire whether he ftands obftinately mute, or
whether he be dumb *ex vifitatione Dei.*　If the latter appears to
be the cafe, the judges of the court (who are to be of counfel
for the prifoner, and to fee that he hath law and juftice) fhall
proceed to the trial, and examine all points as if he had pleaded
not guilty [h].　But whether judgment of death can be given
againft fuch a prifoner, who hath never pleaded, and can fay
nothing in arreft of judgment, is a point yet undetermined [i].

[f] Fofter. 365, &c.
[g] 2 Hal. P. C. 316.

[h] 2 Hawk. P. C. 327.
[i] 2 Hal. P. C. 317.

I F

IF he be found to be obſtinately mute, (which a priſoner hath been held to be, that hath cut out his own tongue [k],) then, if it be on an indictment of high treaſon, it is clearly ſettled that ſtanding mute is equivalent to a conviction, and he ſhall receive the ſame judgment and execution [l]. And as in this the higheſt crime, ſo alſo in the loweſt ſpecies of felony, *viz.* in petit larciny, and in all miſdemeſnors, ſtanding mute is equivalent to conviction. But upon appeals or indictments for other felonies, or petit treaſon, he ſhall not be looked upon as convicted, ſo as to receive judgment for the felony; but ſhall, for his obſtinacy, receive the terrible ſentence of *penance,* or *peine forte et dure.*

BEFORE this is pronounced the priſoner ought to have not only *trina admonitio,* but alſo a convenient reſpite of a few hours, and the ſentence ſhould be diſtinctly read to him, that he may know his danger [m]: and, after all, if he continues obſtinate, and his offence is clergyable, he ſhall have the benefit of his clergy allowed him; even though he is too ſtubborn to pray it [n]. Thus tender has the modern law been of inflicting this dreadful puniſhment: but if no other means will prevail, and the priſoner (when charged with a capital felony) continues ſtubbornly mute, the judgment is then given againſt him, without any diſtinction of ſex or degree. A judgment, which the law has purpoſely ordained to be exquiſitely ſevere, that by that very means it might rarely be put in execution.

THE rack, or queſtion, to extort a confeſſion from criminals, is a practice of a different nature: *this* being only uſed to compel a man to put himſelf upon his trial; *that* being a ſpecies of trial in itſelf. And the trial by rack is utterly unknown to the law of England; though once when the dukes of Exeter and Suffolk, and other miniſters of Henry VI, had laid a deſign to introduce the civil law into this kingdom as the rule of govern-

[k] 3 Inſt. 178.
[l] 2 Hawk. P. C. 329. 2 Hal. P. C. 317.
[m] 2 Hal. P. C. 320.
[n] 2 Hal. P. C. 321. 2 Hawk. P. C. 332.

ment,

ment, for a beginning thereof they erected a rack for torture; which was called in derifion the duke of Exeter's daughter, and ftill remains in the tower of London°: where it was occafionally ufed as an engine of ftate, not of law, more than once in the reign of queen Elizabeth [p]. But when, upon the affaffination of Villiers duke of Buckingham by Felton, it was propofed in the privy council to put the affaffin to the rack, in order to difcover his accomplices; the judges, being confulted, declared unani-moufly, to their own honour and the honour of the Englifh law, that no fuch proceeding was allowable by the laws of England [q]. It feems aftonifhing that this ufage, of adminiftring the torture, fhould be faid to arife from a tendernefs to the lives of men: and yet this is the reafon given for it's introduction in the civil law, and it's fubfequent adoption by the French and other foreign nations [r]: viz. becaufe the laws cannot endure that any man fhould die upon the evidence of a falfe, or even a fingle, witnefs; and therefore contrived this method that inno-cence fhould manifeft itfelf by a ftout denial, or guilt by a plain confeffion. Thus rating a man's virtue by the hardinefs of his conftitution, and his guilt by the fenfibility of his nerves! But there needs only to ftate accurately [s], in order moft effectually to expofe, this inhuman fpecies of mercy: the uncertainty of which, as a teft and criterion of truth, was long ago very ele-gantly pointed out by Tully; though he lived in a ftate wherein it was ufual to torture flaves in order to furnifh evidence: " *ta-* " *men*, fays he, *illa tormenta gubernat dolor, moderatur natura* " *cujufque tum animi tum corporis, regit quaefitor, flectit libido,* " *corrumpit fpes, infirmat metus; ut in tot rerum anguftiis nihil* " *veritati loci relinquatur* [t]."

° 3 Inft. 35.

[p] Barr. 69. 385.

[q] Rufhw. Coll. i. 638.

[r] *Cod. l.* 9. *t.* 41. *l.* 8. & *t.* 47. *l.* 16. Fortefc. *de LL. Angl. c.* 22.

[s] The marquis Beccaria, (ch. 16.) in an exquifite piece of raillery, has propofed this problem, with a gravity and precifion that

are truly mathematical: " the force of the " mufcles and the fenfibility of the nerves " of an innocent perfon being given, it is " required to find the degree of pain, ne-" ceffary to make him confefs himfelf guilty " of a given crime."

[t] *Pro Sulla.* 28.

THE Englifh judgment of penance for ftanding mute [v] is as follows: that the prifoner fhall be remanded to the prifon from whence he came; and put into a low, dark chamber; and there be laid on his back, on the bare floor, naked, unlefs where decency forbids; that there be placed upon his body as great a weight of iron as he can bear, and more; that he fhall have no fuftenance, fave only, on the firft day, three morfels of the worft bread; and, on the fecond day, three draughts of ftanding water, that fhall be neareft to the prifon door; and in this fituation this fhall be alternately his daily diet, *till he dies,* as the judgment now runs, though formerly it was, *till he anfwered* [u].

IT hath been doubted whether this punifhment fubfifted at the common law [w], or was introduced in confequence of the ftatute Weftm. 1. 3 Edw. I. c. 12. [x] which feems to be the better opinion. For not a word of it is mentioned in Glanvil or Bracton, or in any antient author, cafe, or record, (that hath yet been produced) previous to the reign of Edward I: but there are inftances on record in the reign of Henry III [y], where perfons accufed of felony, and ftanding mute, were tried in a particular manner, by two fucceffive juries, and convicted; and it is afferted by the judges in 8 Hen. IV. that, by the common law before the ftatute, ftanding mute on an appeal amounted to a conviction of the felony [z]. This ftatute of Edward I directs fuch perfons, " as will not put themfelves upon inquefts of fe- " lonies before the judges at the fuit of the king, to be put " into hard and ftrong prifon *(foient mys en la prifone fort et dure)* " as thofe which refufe to be at the common law of the land." And, immediately after this ftatute, the form of the judgment appears in Fleta and Britton to have been only a very ftrait con-

---

[v] 2 Hal. P. C. 319. 2 Hawk. P. C. 329.
[u] Britton. c. 4. & 22. Flet. l. 1. c. 34. §. 33.
[w] 2 Inft. 179. 2 Hal. P. C. 322. 2 Hawk. P. C. 330.

[x] Staundf. P. C. 149. Barr. 65.
[y] Emlyn on 2 Hal. P. C. 322.
[z] *Al common ley, avant le ftatute de Weft.* 1. c. 12. *fi afcun uft eftre appeal, et uft eftre mute, il ferra convict de felony.* (M. 8 Hen. IV. 2.)

finement

finement in prifon, with hardly any degree of fuftenance; but no weight is directed to be laid upon the body, fo as to haften the death of the miferable fufferer : and indeed any furcharge of punifhment on perfons adjudged to penance, fo as to fhorten their lives, is reckoned by Horne in the mirror[a] as a fpecies of criminal homicide : to which we may add, that the record of 35 Edw. I. (cited by a learned author[b]) moft clearly proves, that the prifoner might then poffibly fubfift for forty days under this lingering punifhment. I fhould therefore imagine that the practice of loading him with weights, or, as it is ufually called, *preffing him to death*, was gradually introduced between the reign of Edward I and 8 Hen. IV, when it firft appears upon our books[c]; and was intended as a fpecies of mercy to the delinquent, by delivering him the fooner from his torment : and hence I prefume it alfo was, that the duration of the penance was then firft[d] altered; and inftead of continuing *till he anfwered*, it was directed to continue *till he died*, which muft very foon happen under an enormous preffure.

THE uncertainty of it's original, the doubts that may be conceived of it's legality, and the repugnance of it's theory (for it rarely is carried into practice) to the humanity of the laws of England, all feem to require a legiflative abolition of this cruel procefs, and a reftitution of the antient common law ; whereby the ftanding mute in felony, as well as in treafon and in trefpafs, amounted to a confeffion of the charge. Or, if the corruption of the blood and the confequent efcheat in felony were removed, the *peine forte et dure* might ftill remain, as a monument of the favage rapacity, with which the lordly tyrants of feodal antiquity hunted after efcheats and forfeitures ; but no man would ever be tempted to undergo fuch a horrid alternative. For the law is, that by ftanding mute, and fuffering this heavy penance, the judgment, and of courfe the corruption of the blood and efcheat of the *lands*, are faved in felony and petit treafon ;

---

[a] ch. 1. §. 9.
[b] Barr. 62.
[c] Yearb. 8 Hen. IV. 1.

[c] *Et fuit dit, que le contrarie avoit eftre fait devant ces heures. (Ibid. 2)*

though

though not the forfeiture of the *goods :* and therefore this lingering punishment was probably introduced, in order to extort a plea; without which it was held that no judgment of death could be given, and so the lord lost his escheat. But notwithstanding these terrors, some hardy delinquents, conscious of their guilt, and yet touched with a tender regard for their children, have rather chosen to submit to this painful death, than the easier judgment upon conviction, which might expose their offspring not only to present want, but to future incapacities of inheritance. But in high treason, as standing mute is equivalent to a conviction, the same judgment, the same corruption of blood, and the same forfeitures attend it, as in other cases of conviction [e]. And thus much for the demesnor of a prisoner upon his arraignment, by standing mute.

II. The other incident to arraignments, exclusive of the plea, is the prisoner's *confession* of the indictment. Upon a simple and plain confession, the court hath nothing to do but to award judgment : but it is usually very backward in receiving and recording such confession, out of tenderness to the life of the subject; and will generally advise the prisoner to retract it, and plead to the indictment [f].

But there is another species of confession, which we read much of in our antient books, of a far more complicated kind, which is called *approvement*. And that is when a person, indicted of treason or felony, and arraigned for the same, doth confess the fact before plea pleaded; and appeals or accuses others, his accomplices, of the same crime, in order to obtain his pardon. In this case he is called an *approver* or prover, *probator,* and the party appealed or accused is called the *appellee.* Such approvement can only be in capital offences; and it is, as it were, equivalent to an indictment, since the appellee is equally called upon to answer it : and if he hath no reasonable and legal exceptions to make to the person of the approver, which indeed

[e] 2 Hawk. P. C. 331.   [f] 2 Hal. P. C. 225.

are very numerous, he muſt put himſelf upon his trial, either by battel, or by the country; and, if vanquiſhed or found guilty, muſt ſuffer the judgment of the law, and the approver ſhall have his pardon, *ex debito juſtitiae*. On the other hand, if the appellee be conqueror, or acquitted by the jury, the approver ſhall receive judgment to be hangèd, upon his own confeſſion of the indictment; for the condition of his pardon has failed, *viz.* the convicting of ſome other perſon, and therefore his conviction remains abſolute.

BUT it is purely in the diſcretion of the court to permit the approver thus to appeal, or not; and, in fact, this courſe of admitting approvements hath been long diſuſed: for the truth was, as ſir Matthew Hale obſerves, that more miſchief hath a-riſen to good men by theſe kind of approvements, upon falſe and malicious accuſations of deſperate villains, than benefit to the public by the diſcovery and conviction of real offenders. And therefore, in the times when ſuch appeals were more frequently admitted, great ſtrictneſs and nicety were held therein[f]: though, ſince their diſcontinuance, the doctrine of approvements is become a matter of more curioſity than uſe. I ſhall only obſerve, that all the good, whatever it be, that can be expected from this method of approvement, is fully provided for in the caſes of robbery, burglary, houſebreaking, and larciny to the value of five ſhillings from ſhops, warehouſes, ſtables, and coachhouſes, by ſtatutes 4 & 5 W. & M. c. 8. 10 & 11 W. III. c. 23. and 5 Ann. c. 31. which enact, that, if any ſuch felon, being out of priſon, ſhall diſcover two or more perſons, who have committed the like felonies, ſo as they may be convicted thereof; he ſhall in moſt caſes receive a reward of 40*l*, and in general be entitled a pardon of all capital offences, excepting only murder and treaſon. And if any ſuch perſon, having feloniouſly ſtolen any lead, iron, or other metals, ſhall diſcover and convict two offenders of having illegally bought or received the ſame, he ſhall by virtue of ſtatute 29 Geo. II. c. 30. be pardoned for all *ſuch* felonies committed before ſuch diſcovery.

f 2 Hal. P. C. ch. 29. 2 Hawk. P. C. ch. 24.

C H A P T E R   T H E   T W E N T Y   S I X T H.

O f   P L E A,   a n d   I S S U E.

W E are now to confider the plea of the prifoner, or defenfive matter alleged by him on his arraignment, if he
does not confefs, or ftand mute. This is either, 1. A plea to
the jurifdiction; 2. A demurrer; 3. A plea in abatement;
4. A fpecial plea in bar; or, 5. The general iffue.

FƠRMERLY there was another plea, now abrogated, that of
fanctuary; which is however neceffary to be lightly touched upon,
as it may give fome light to many parts of our antient law: it
being introduced and continued during the fuperftitious venera-
tion, that was paid to confecrated ground in the times of popery.
Firft then, it is to be obferved, that if a perfon accufed of any
crime (except treafon, wherein the crown, and facrilege, wherein
the church, was too nearly concerned) had fled to any church
or church-yard, and within forty days after went in fackcloth
and confeffed himfelf guilty before the coroner, and declared all
the particular circumftances of the offence; and thereupon took
the oath in that cafe provided, *viz.* that he abjured the realm,
and would depart from thence forthwith at the port that fhould
be affigned him, and would never return without leave from the
king; he by this means faved his life, if he obferved the conditions of the oath, by going with a crofs in his hand and with
all

all convenient fpeed, to the port affigned, and embarking. For
if, during this forty days privilege of fanctuary, or in his road to
the fea fide, he was apprehended and arraigned in any court for
this felony, he might plead the privilege of fanctuary, and had
a right to be remanded, if taken out againſt his will [a]. But by
this abjuration his blood was attainted, and he forfeited all his
goods and chattels [b]. The immunity of thefe privileged places
was very much abridged by the ſtatutes 27 Hen.VIII. c. 19. and
32 Hen.VIII. c. 12. And now, by the ſtatute 21 Jac. I. c. 28.
all privilege of fanctuary, and abjuration confequent thereupon,
is utterly taken away and abolifhed.

FORMERLY alfo the benefit of clergy ufed to be pleaded
before trial or conviction, and was called a *declinatory* plea;
which was the name alfo given to that of fanctuary [c]. But, as
the prifoner upon a trial has a chance to be acquitted, and totally difcharged; and, if convicted of a clergyable felony, is
entitled equally to his clergy after as before conviction; this
courfe is extremely difadvantageous: and therefore the benefit of
clergy is now very rarely pleaded; but, if found requifite, is
prayed by the convict before judgment is paffed upon him.

I PROCEED therefore to the five fpecies of pleas, before-
mentioned.

I. A PLEA to the *jurifdiction*, is where an indictment is taken
before a court, that hath no cognizance of the offence; as if a
man be indicted for a rape at the fheriff's tourn, or for treafon at
the quarter feffions: in thefe or fimilar cafes, he may except to
the jurifdiction of the court, without anfwering at all to the
crime alleged [d].

II. A DEMURRER to the indictment. This is incident to
criminal cafes, as well as civil, when the fact as alleged is allowed

[a] Mirr. c. 1. §. 13.   2 Hawk. P. C. 335.   [c] 2 Hal. P. C. 236.
[b] 2 Hawk. P. C. 52.   [d] *Ibid.* 256.

to be true, but the prifoner joins iffue upon fome point of law in the indictment, by which he infifts that the fact, as ftated, is no felony, treafon, or whatever the crime is alleged to be. Thus, for inftance, if a man be indicted for *felonioufly* ftealing a greyhound; which is an animal in which no valuable property can be had, and therefore it is not felony, but only a civil trefpafs, to fteal it: in this cafe the party indicted may demur to the indictment; denying it to be felony, though he confeffes the act of taking it. Some have held[e], that if, on demurrer, the point of law be adjudged *againft* the prifoner, he fhall have judgment and execution, as if convicted by verdict. But this is denied by others[f], who hold, that in fuch cafe he fhall be directed and received to plead the general iffue, not guilty, after a demurrer determined againft him. Which appears the more reafonable, becaufe it is clear, that if the prifoner freely difcovers the fact in court, and refers it to the opinion of the court, whether it be felony, or no; and upon the fact thus fhewn in appears to be felony; the court will not record the confeffion, but admit him afterwards to plead not guilty[g]. And this feems to be a cafe of the fame nature, being for the moft part a miftake in point of law, and in the conduct of his pleading; and, though a man by mifpleading may in fome cafes lofe his property, yet the law will not fuffer him by fuch niceties to lofe his life. However, upon this doubt, demurrers to indictments are feldom ufed: fince the fame advantages may be taken upon a plea of not guilty; or afterwards, in arreft of judgment, when the verdict has eftablifhed the fact.

III. A plea in *abatement* is principally for a *mifnofmer*, a wrong name, or a falfe addition to the prifoner. As, if *James* Allen, *gentleman*, is indicted by the name of *John* Allen, *efquire*, he may plead that he has the name of James, and not of John; and that he is a gentleman, and not an efquire. And, if either fact is found by a jury, then the indictment fhall be abated, as

e 2 Hal P. C. 257.   g 2 Hal. P. C. 225.
f 2 Hawk P. C. 334.

writs

writs or declarations may be in civil actions ; of which we fpoke at large, in the preceding volume [h].   But, in the end, there is little advantage accruing to the prifoner by means of thefe dilatory pleas ;   becaufe if the exception be allowed, a new bill of indictment may be framed, according to what the prifoner in his plea avers to be his true name and addition.   For it is a rule, upon all pleas in abatement, that he, who takes advantage of a flaw, muft at the fame time fhew how it may be amended.   Let us therefore next confider a more fubftantial kind of plea, *viz.*

IV. SPECIAL pleas in *bar ;* which go to the merits of the indictment, and give a reafon why the prifoner ought not to anfwer it at all, nor put himfelf upon his trial for the crime alleged.   Thefe are of four kinds : a former acquittal, a former conviction, a former attainder, or a pardon.   There are many other pleas, which may be pleaded in bar of an appeal [i]: but thefe are applicable to both appeals and indictments.

1. FIRST, the plea of *auterfoits acquit,* or a former acquittal, is grounded on this univerfal maxim of the common law of England, that no man is to be brought into jeopardy of his life, more than once, for the fame offence.   And hence it is allowed as a confequence, that when a man is once fairly found not guilty upon any indictment, or other profecution, he may plead fuch acquittal in bar of any fubfequent accufation for the fame crime.   Therefore an acquittal on an appeal is a good bar to an indictment of the fame offence.   And fo alfo was an acquittal on an indictment a good bar to an appeal, by the common law [k] : and therefore, in favour of appeals, a general practice was introduced, not to try any perfon on an indictment of homicide, till after the year and day, within which appeals may be brought, were paft ; by which time it often happened that the witneffes died, or the whole was forgotten.   To remedy which inconvenience, the ftatute 3 Hen. VII. c. I. enacts,

[k] See Vol. III. pag. 302.
[i] 2 Hawk P. C. ch. 23.

[k] *Ibid.* 373.

that indictments shall be proceeded on, immediately, at the king's suit, for the death of a man, without waiting for bringing an appeal; and that the plea, of *auterfoits acquit* on an indictment, shall be no bar to the prosecuting of any appeal.

2. SECONDLY, the plea of *auterfoits convict*, or a former conviction for the same identical crime, though no judgment was ever given, or perhaps will be, (being suspended by the benefit of clergy or other causes) is a good plea in bar to an indictment. And this depends upon the same principle as the former, that no man ought to be twice brought in danger of his life for one and the same crime[1]. Hereupon it has been held, that a conviction of manslaughter, on an appeal, is a bar even in another appeal, and much more in an indictment, of murder; for the fact prosecuted is the same in both, though the offences differ in colouring and in degree. It is to be observed, that the pleas of *auterfoits acquit*, and *auterfoits convict*, or a former acquittal, and former conviction, must be upon a prosecution for the same identical act and crime. But the case is otherwise, in

3. THIRDLY, the plea of *auterfoits attaint*, or a former attainder; which is a good plea in bar, whether it be for the same or any other felony. For wherever a man is attainted of felony, by judgment of death either upon a verdict or confession, by outlawry, or heretofore by abjuration; and whether upon an appeal or an indictment; he may plead such attainder in bar to any subsequent indictment or appeal, for the same or for any other felony[m]. And this because, generally, such proceeding on a second prosecution cannot be to any purpose; for the prisoner is dead in law by the first attainder, his blood is already corrupted, and he hath forfeited all that he had: so that it is absurd and superfluous to endeavour to attaint him a second time. But to this general rule however, as to all others, there are some exceptions; wherein, *cessante ratione, cessat et ipsa lex*. As, 1. Where the former attainder is reversed for error, for then it

---

[1] 2 Hawk. P. C. 377.   [m] *Ibid.* 375.

is

is the fame as if it had never been. And the fame reafon holds, where the attainder is reverfed by parliament, or the judgment vacated by the king's pardon, with regard to felonies committed afterwards. 2. Where the attainder was upon indictment, fuch attainder is no bar to an appeal : for the prior fentence is pardonable by the king ; and if that might be pleaded in bar of the appeal, the king might in the end defeat the fuit of the fubject, by fuffering the prior fentence to ftop the profecution of a fecond, and then, when the time of appealing is elapfed, granting the delinquent a pardon. 3. An attainder in felony is no bar to an indictment of treafon : becaufe not only the judgment and manner of death are different, but the forfeiture is more extenfive, and the land goes to different perfons. 4. Where a perfon attainted of one felony, as robbery, is afterwards indicted as principal in another, as murder, to which there are alfo acceffories, profecuted at the fame time ; in this cafe it is held, that the plea of *auterfoits attaint* is no bar, but he fhall be compelled to take his trial, for the fake of public juftice : becaufe the acceffories to fuch fecond felony cannot be convicted till after the conviction of the principal. And from thefe inftances we may collect that the plea of *auterfoits attaint* is never good, but when a fecond trial would be quite fuperfluous.

4. Lastly, a *pardon* may be pleaded in bar ; as at once deftroying the end and purpofe of the indictment, by remitting that punifhment, which the profecution is calculated to inflict. There is one advantage that attends pleading a pardon in bar, or in arreft of judgment, *before* fentence is paft ; which gives it by much the preference to pleading it *after* fentence or attainder. This is, that by ftopping the judgment it ftops the attainder, and prevents the corruption of the blood : which, when once corrupted by attainder, cannot afterwards be reftored, otherwife than by act of parliament. But, as the title of pardons is applicable to other ftages of profecution ; and they have their refpective force and efficacy, as well after as before conviction, outlawry, or attainder ; I fhall therefore referve the more minute

　　　　nute

nute confideration of them, till I have gone through every other title, except only that of execution.

Before I conclude this head of fpecial pleas in bar, it will be neceffary once more to obferve; that, though in civil actions when a man has his election what plea in bar to make, he is concluded by that plea, and cannot refort to another if that be determined againft him; (as, if on an action of debt the defendant pleads a general releafe, and no fuch releafe can be proved, he cannot afterwards plead the general iffue, *nil debet*, as he might at firft: for he has made his election what plea to abide by, and it was his own folly to chufe a rotten defence) though, I fay, this ftrictnefs is obferved in civil actions, *quia intereft reipublicae ut fit finis litium:* yet in criminal profecutions, *in favorem vitae*, as well upon appeal as indictment, when a prifoner's plea in bar is found againft him upon iffue tried by a jury, or adjudged againft him in point of law by the court; ftill he fhall not be concluded or convicted thereon, but fhall have judgment of *refpondeat oufter*, and may plead over to the felony the general iffue, not guilty[a]. For the law allows many pleas by which a prifoner may efcape death; but only one plea, in confequence whereof it can be inflicted; *viz.* on the general iffue, after an impartial examination and decifion of the facts, by the unanimous verdict of a jury. It remains therefore that I confider,

V. The general iffue, or plea of *not guilty*[o], upon which plea alone the prifoner can receive his final judgment of death. In cafe of an indictment of felony or treafon, there can be no fpecial juftification put in by way of plea. As, on an indictment for murder, a man cannot *plead* that it was in his own defence againft a robber on the highway, or a burglar; but he muft plead the general iffue, not guilty, and give this fpecial matter in evidence. For (befides that thefe pleas do in effect amount to the general iffue; fince, if true, the prifoner is moft clearly not guilty) as the facts in treafon are laid to be done *pro-*

[a] 2 Hal. P. C. 239.　　　　　　[o] See appendix, §. 1.

ditorie-

ditorie et contra ligeantiae fuae debitum ; and, in felony, that the killing was done *felonice* ; thefe charges, of a traiterous or felonious intent, are the points and very *gift* of the indictment, and muft be anfwered directly, by the general negative, not guilty ; and the jury upon the evidence will take notice of any defenfive matter, and give their verdict accordingly, as effectually as if it were, or could be, fpecially pleaded. So that this is, upon all accounts, the moft advantageous plea for the prifoner[p].

WHEN the prifoner hath thus pleaded not guilty, *non culpabilis,* or *nient culpable* ; which was formerly ufed to be abbreviated upon the minutes, thus, " *non* (or *nient*) *cul.*" the clerk of the affife, or clerk of the arraigns, on behalf of the crown replies, that the prifoner is guilty, and that he is ready to prove him fo. This is done by two monofyllables in the fame fpirit of abbreviation, " *cul. prit.*" which fignifies firft that the prifoner is guilty, *(cul. culpable,* or *culpabilis)* and then that the king is ready to prove him fo ; *prit, praefto fum,* or *paratus verificare.* This is therefore a replication on behalf of the king *viva voce* at the bar ; which was formerly the courfe in all pleadings, as well in civil as in criminal caufes. And that was done in the concifeft manner : for when the pleader intended to demur, he expreffed his demurrer in a fingle word, " *judgment* ;" fignifying that he demanded judgment whether the writ, declaration, plea, *&c,* either in form or matter, were fufficiently good in law ; and if he meant to reft on the truth of the facts pleaded, he expreffed that alfo in a fingle fyllable, " *prit* ;" fignifying that he was ready to prove his affertions ; as may be obferved from the yearbooks and other antient repofitories of law[q]. By this replication the king and the prifoner are therefore at iffue : for we may remember, in our ftrictures upon pleadings in the preceding book[r], it was obferved, that when the parties come to a fact, which is affirmed on one fide and denied on the other, then they are faid to be at iffue in point of fact : which is evidently

[p] 2 Hal. P. C. 258.
[q] North's life of lord Guilford. 98.
[r] See Vol. III. pag. 312.

the

the cafe here, in the plea of *non cul.* by the prifoner ; and the replication of *cul.* by the clerk. And we may alfo remember, that the ufual conclufion of all affirmative pleadings, as this of *cul.* or *guilty* is, was by an averment in thefe words, "and this "he is *ready* to verify ; *et hoc paratus eſt verificare:*" which fame thing is here expreffed by the fingle word, "*prit.*"

How our courts came to exprefs a matter of this importance in fo odd and obfcure a manner, "*rem tantam tam negligenter,*" can hardly be pronounced with certainty. It may perhaps, however, be accounted for by fuppofing, that thefe were at firſt fhort notes, to help the memory of the clerk, and remind him what he was to reply ; or elfe it was the fhort method of taking down in court, upon the minutes, the replication and averment; "*cul.* "*prit:*" which afterwards the ignorance of fucceeding clerks adopted for the very words to be by them fpoken ˢ.

But however it may have arifen, the joining of iffue (which, though now ufually entered on the record ᵗ, is no otherwife joined ᵘ in any part of the proceedings) feems to be clearly the meaning of this obfcure expreffion ʷ; which has puzzled our moſt ingenious etymologiſts, and is commonly underſtood as if the clerk of the arraigns, immediately on plea pleaded, had fixed an opprobrious name on the prifoner, by afking him, "*culprit,* "how wilt thou be tried?" for immediately upon iffue joined it is enquired of the prifoner, by what trial he will make his innocence appear. This form has at prefent reference to appealˢ and approvements only, wherein the appellee has his choice, either to try the accufation by battel or by jury. But upon in-

---

ˢ Of this ignorance we may fee daily inſtances, in the abufe of two legal terms of antient French ; one, the prologue to all proclamations, "*oyez,* or hear ye," which is generally pronounced moſt unmeaningly "O yes:" the other, a more pardonable miſtake, *viz.* when a jury are all fworn,

the officer bids the crier number them, for which the word in law-french is, "*coun-* "*tez;*" but we now hear it pronounced in very good Englifh, "count thefe."

ᵗ See appendix, §. 1.

ᵘ 2 Hawk. P. C. 399.

ʷ 2 Hal. P. C. 258.

dictments,

dictments, since the abolition of ordeal, there can be no other trial but that by jury, *per pais*, or by the country : and therefore, if the prisoner refuses to put himself upon the inquest in the usual form, that is, to answer that he will be tried by God and the country[x], if a commoner ; and, if a peer, by God and his peers[y] ; the indictment, if in treason, is taken *pro confesso :* and the prisoner, in cases of felony, is adjudged to stand mute, and, if he perseveres in his obstinacy, shall be condemned to the *peine fort et dure.*

WHEN the prisoner has thus put himself upon his trial, the clerk answers in the humane language of the law, which always hopes that the party's innocence rather than his guilt may appear, " God send thee a good deliverance." And then they proceed, as soon as conveniently may be, to the trial ; the manner of which will be considered at large in the next chapter.

[x] A learned author, who is very seldom mistaken in his conjectures, has observed that the proper answer is " *by God* or *the country*," that is, either by *ordeal* or by *jury* ; because the question supposes an option in the prisoner. And certainly it gives some countenance to this observation, that the trial by *ordeal* used formerly to be called *judicium Dei*. But it should seem, that when the question gives the prisoner an option, his answer must be positive ; and not in the disjunctive, which returns the option back to the prosecutor.

[y] Kelynge. 57. State Trials, *passim*

CHAPTER THE TWENTY SEVENTH.

OF TRIAL, AND CONVICTION.

THE feveral methods of trial and conviction of offenders, eftablifhed by the laws of England, were formerly more numerous than at prefent, through the fuperftition of our Saxon anceftors: who, like other northern nations, were extremely addicted to divination; a character, which Tacitus obferves of the antient Germans [a]. They therefore invented a confiderable number of methods of purgation or trial, to preferve innocence from the danger of falfe witneffes, and in confequence of a notion that God would always interpofe miraculoufly, to vindicate the guiltlefs.

I. THE moft antient fpecies of trial was that by *ordeal*; which was peculiarly diftinguifhed by the appellation of *judicium Dei*; and fometimes *vulgaris purgatio*, to diftinguifh it from the canonical purgation, which was by the oath of the party. This was of two forts [b], either *fire*-ordeal, or *water*-ordeal; the former being confined to perfons of higher rank, the latter to the common people [c] Both thefe might be performed by deputy:

---

[a] *de mor. Germ.* 10.

[b] Mirr. c. 3. §. 23.

[c] *Tenetur fe purgare is qui accufatur, per Dei judicium; fcilicet, per calidum ferrum,* *vel per aquam, pro diverfitate conditionis hominum: per ferrum calidum, fi fuerit homo liber; per aquam, fi fuerit rufticus.* (Glanv. l. 14. c. 1)

but

but the principal was to anfwer for the fuccefs of the trial; the deputy only venturing fome corporal pain, for hire, or perhaps for friendfhip[d]. Fire-ordeal was performed either by taking up in the hand, unhurt, a piece of red hot iron, of one, two, or three pounds weight; or elfe by walking, barefoot, and blindfold, over nine redhot plowfhares, laid lengthwife at unequal diftances: and if the party efcaped being hurt, he was adjudged innocent; but if it happened otherwife, as without collufion it ufually did, he was then condemned as guilty. However, by this latter method queen Emma, the mother of Edward the confeffor, is mentioned to have cleared her character, when fufpected of familiarity with Alwyn bifhop of Winchefter[e].

WATER-ordeal was performed, either by plunging the bare arm up to the elbow in boiling water, and efcaping unhurt thereby: or by cafting the perfon fufpected into a river or pond of cold water: and, if he floated therein without any action of fwimming, it was deemed an evidence of his guilt; but, if he funk, he was acquitted. It is eafy to trace out the traditional relics of this water-ordeal, in the ignorant barbarity ftill practifed in many countries to difcover witches, by cafting them into a pool of water, and drowning them to prove their innocence. And in the Eaftern empire the fire-ordeal was ufed to the fame purpofe by the emperor Theodore Lafcaris; who, attributing his ficknefs to magic, caufed all thofe whom he fufpected to handle the hot iron: thus joining (as has been well remarked[f]) to the moft dubious crime in the world, the moft dubious proof of innocence.

AND indeed this purgation by ordeal feems to have been very antient, and very univerfal, in the times of fuperftitious barbarity. It was known to the antient Greeks: for in the Antigone of

[d] This is ftill exprefled in that common form of fpeech, of " going through fire and " water to ferve another."

[e] Tho. Rudborne *Hift. maj. Winton. l.* 4. *c.* 1.

[f] *Sp. L. b.* 12. *c.* 5.

Sophocles [g], a perſon, fuſpected by Creon of a miſdemeſnor, declares himſelf ready " to handle hot iron and to walk over fire,"
in order to manifeſt his innocence ; which, the ſcholiaſt tells
us, was then a very uſual purgation.   And Grotius [h] gives us
many inſtances of water-ordeal in Bithynia, Sardinia, and other
places.   There is alſo a very peculiar ſpecies of water-ordeal,
ſaid to prevail among the Indians on the coaſt of Malabar ;
where a perſon accuſed of any enormous crime is obliged to ſwim
over a large river abounding with crocodiles, and, if he eſcapes
unhurt, he is reputed innocent.   As in Siam, beſides the uſual
methods of fire and water ordeal, both parties are ſometimes
expoſed to the fury of a tiger let looſe for that purpoſe : and, if
the beaſt ſpares either, that perſon is accounted innocent ; if
neither, both are held to be guilty ; but if he ſpares both, the
trial is incomplete, and they proceed to a more certain criterion [i].

O N E cannot but be aſtoniſhed at the folly and impiety of
pronouncing a man guilty, unleſs he was cleared by a miracle ;
and of expecting that all the powers of nature ſhould be ſuſpended, by an immediate interpoſition of providence to ſave the
innocent, whenever it was preſumptuouſly required.   And yet
in England, ſo late as king John's time, we find grants to the
biſhops and clergy to uſe the *judicium ferri, aquae, et ignis* [k].
And, both in England and Sweden, the clergy preſided at this
trial, and it was only performed in the churches or in other
conſecrated ground : for which Stiernhook [l] gives the reaſon ;
" *non defuit illis operae et laboris pretium ; ſemper enim ab ejuſ-*
" *modi judicio aliquid lucri ſacerdotibus obveniebat.*"   But, to give
it it's due praiſe, we find the canon law very early declaring
againſt trial by ordeal, or *vulgaris purgatio*, as being the fabric
of the devil, " *cum ſit contra praeceptum Domini, non tentabis*
" *Dominum Deum tuum* [m]."   Upon this authority, though the

[g] v. 270.
[h] On Numb. v. 17.
[i] Mod. Univ. Hiſt. vii. 266.
[k] Spelm. *Gloſſ*. 435.

[l] *de jure Sueonum, l.* 1. *c.* 8.
[m] *Decret. part.* 2. *cauſ.* 2. *qu.* 5. *diſt.* 7.
Decretal. lib. 3. *tit.* 50. *c.* 9. *& Gloſſ. ibid.*

canons

canons themfelves were of no validity in England, it was thought proper (as had been done in Denmark above a century before[n]) to difufe and abolifh this trial entirely in our courts of juftice, by an act of parliament in 3 Hen. III. according to fir Edward Coke[o], or rather by an order of the king in council[p].

II. ANOTHER fpecies of purgation, fomewhat fimilar to the former, but probably fprung from a prefumptuous abufe of revelation in the ages of dark fuperfttion, was the *corfned*, or morfel of execration : being a piece of cheefe or bread, of about an ounce in weight, which was confecrated with a form of exorcifm; defiring of the Almighty that it might caufe convulfions and palenefs, and find no paffage, if the man was really guilty; but might turn to health and nourifhment, if he was innocent[q]: as the water of jealoufy among the Jews[r] was, by God's efpecial appointment, to caufe the belly to fwell and the thigh to rot, if the woman was guilty of adultery. This corfned was then given to the fufpected perfon; who at the fame time alfo received the holy facrament[s]: if indeed the corfned was not, as fome have fufpected, the facramental bread itfelf; till the fubfequent invention of tranfubftantiation preferved it from profane ufes with a more profound refpect than formerly. Our hiftorians affure us, that Godwyn, earl of Kent in the reign of king Edward the confeffor, abjuring the death of the king's brother, at laft appealed to his corfned, " *per buccellam deglutiendam abjuravit*[t]," which ftuck in his throat and killed him. This cuftom has been long fince gradually abolifhed, though the remembrance of it ftill fubfifts in certain phrafes of abjuration retained among the common people[u].

[n] Mod. Un. Hift. xxxii. 105.

[o] 9 Rep. 32.

[p] 1 Rym. *Foed.* 228. Spelm. *Gloff.* 326. 2 Pryn. Rec. Append. 20. Seld. *Eadm. fol.* 48.

[q] Spelm. *Gl.* 439.

[r] Numb. ch. v.

[s] *LL. Canut. c.* 6.

[t] Ingulph.

[u] As, " I will take the facrament upon " upon it; may this morfel be my laft ;" and the like.

How-

H o w e v e r we cannot but remark, that though in European countries this cuſtom moſt probably aroſe from an abuſe of revealed religion, yet credulity and ſuperſtition will, in all ages and in all climates, produce the ſame or ſimilar effects. And therefore we ſhall not be ſurprized to find, that in the kingdom of Pegu there ſtill ſubſiſts a trial by the corſned, very ſimilar to that of our anceſtors, only ſubſtituting raw rice inſtead of bread[w]. And, in the kingdom of Monomopata, they have a method of deciding lawſuits equally whimſical and uncertain. The witneſs for the plaintiff chews the bark of a tree, endued with an emetic quality, which, being ſufficiently maſticated, is then infuſed in water, which is given the defendant to drink. If his ſtomach rejects it, he is condemned: if it ſtays with him, he is abſolved, unleſs the plaintiff will drink ſome of the ſame water; and, if it ſtays with him alſo, the ſuit is left undetermined[x].

T h e s e two antiquated methods of trial were principally in uſe among our Saxon anceſtors. The next, which ſtill remains in force, though very rarely in uſe, owes it's introduction among us to the princes of the Norman line. And that is

III. T h e trial by *battel*, duel, or ſingle combat: which was another ſpecies of preſumptuous appeals to providence, under an expectation that heaven would unqueſtionably give the victory to the innocent or injured party. The nature of this trial in caſes of civil injury, upon iſſue joined in a writ of right, was fully diſcuſſed in the preceding book[y]: to which I have only to add, that the trial by battel may be demanded at the election of the appellee, in either an appeal or an approvement; and that it is carried on with equal ſolemnity as that on a writ of right: but with this difference, that there each party might hire a champion, but here they muſt fight in their proper perſons. And therefore if the appellant or approver be a woman, a prieſt, an infant, or

[w] Mod. Univ. Hiſt. vii 129.
[x] *Ibid.* xv. 464.

[y] See Vol. III. pag. 337.

of

of the age of fixty, or lame, or blind, he or fhe may counterplead and refufe the wager of battel; and compel the appellee to put himfelf upon the country. Alfo peers of the realm, bringing an appeal, fhall not be challenged to wage battel, on account of the dignity of their perfons; nor the citizens of London, by fpecial charter, becaufe fighting feems foreign to their education and employment. So likewife if the crime be notorious; as if the thief be taken with the *mainour*, or the murderer in the room with a bloody knife, the appellant may refufe the tender of battel from the appellee[z]; for it is unreafonable that an innocent man fhould ftake his life againft one who is already half-convicted.

THE form and manner of waging battel upon appeals are much the fame as upon a writ of right; only the oaths of the two combatants are vaftly more ftriking and folemn[a]. The appellee, when appealed of felony, pleads *not guilty*, and throws down his glove, and declares he will defend the fame by his body: the appellant takes up the glove, and replies that he is ready to make good the appeal, body for body. And thereupon the appellee, taking the book in his right hand, and in his left the right hand of his antagonift, fwears to this effect. " *Hoc* " *audi, homo, quem per manum teneo,*" &c: " hear this, O man " whom I hold by the hand, who calleft thyfelf John by the " name of baptifm, that I, who call myfelf Thomas by the name " of baptifm, did not felonioufly murder thy father, William " by name, nor am any way guilty of the faid felony. So help " me God, and the faints; and this I will defend againft thee " by my body, as this court fhall award." To which the appellant replies, holding the bible and his antagonift's hand in the fame manner as the other: " hear this, O man whom I hold " by the hand, who calleft thyfelf Thomas by the name of bap- " tifm, that thou art perjured; and therefore perjured, becaufe " that thou felonioufly didft murder my father, William by " name. So help me God and the faints; and this I will prove

z 2 Hawk. P. C. 427.   a Flet. *l.* 1. *c.* 34. 2 Hawk. P. C. 426.

" againft

" againſt thee by my body, as this court ſhall award [b]." The battel is then to be fought with the ſame weapons, *viz.* batons, the ſame ſolemnity, and the ſame oath againſt amulets and ſorcery, that are uſed in the civil combat: and if the appellee be ſo far vanquiſhed, that he cannot or will not fight any longer, he ſhall be adjudged to be hanged immediately; and then, as well as if he be killed in battel, providence is deemed to have determined in favour of the truth, and his blood ſhall be attainted. But if he kills the appellant, or can maintain the fight from ſunriſing till the ſtars appear in the evening, he ſhall be acquitted. So alſo if the appellant becomes recreant, and pronounces the horrible word of *craven*, he ſhall loſe his *liberam legem*, and become infamous; and the appellee ſhall recover his damages, and alſo be for ever quit, not only of the appeal, but of all indictments likewiſe for the ſame offence.

IV. THE fourth method of trial uſed in criminal caſes is that by the peers of Great Britain, in the court of parliament, or the court of the lord high ſteward, when a peer is capitally indicted. Of this enough has been ſaid in a former chapter [c]; to which I ſhall now only add, that, in the method and regulations of it's proceedings, it differs little from the trial *per patriam*, or by jury: except that the peers need not all agree in their verdict; but the greater number, conſiſting of twelve at the leaſt, will conclude, and bind the minority [d].

V. THE trial by jury, or the country, *per patriam*, is alſo that trial by the peers of every Engliſhman, which, as the grand bulwark of his liberties, is ſecured to him by the great

---

[b] There is a ſtriking reſemblance between this proceſs, and that of the court of *Areopagus* at Athens, for murder; wherein the proſecutor and priſoner were both ſworn in the moſt ſolemn manner: the proſecutor, that he was related to the deceaſed (for none but near relations were permitted to proſecute in that court) and that the priſoner was the e of his death; the priſoner, that he was innocent of the charge againſt him. (Pott. Antiqu. b. 1. c. 19.)

[c] See pag. 259.

[d] Kelynge. 56. Stat. 7W. III. c. 3. §. 11. Foſter. 247.

charter [e],

charter [e], " *nullus liber homo capiatur, vel imprifonetur, aut exulet,*
" *aut aliquo alio modo deftruatur, nifi per legale judicium parium*
" *fuorum, vel per legem terrae.*"

THE antiquity and excellence of this trial, for the fettling of
civil property, has before been explained at large [f]. And it will
hold much ftronger in criminal cafes; fince, in times of difficulty and danger, more is to be apprehended from the violence
and partiality of judges appointed by the crown, in fuits between
the king and the fubject, than in difputes between one individual
and another, to fettle the metes and boundaries of private property. Our law has therefore wifely placed this ftrong and twofold barrier, of a prefentment and a trial by jury, between
the liberties of the people, and the prerogative of the crown.
It was neceffary, for preferving the admirable ballance of our
conftitution, to veft the executive power of the laws in the
prince: and yet this power might be dangerous and deftructive
to that very conftitution, if exerted without check or control, by
juftices of *oyer* and *terminer* occafionally named by the crown;
who might then, as in France or Turkey, imprifon, difpatch,
or exile any man that was obnoxious to the government, by an
inftant declaration, that fuch is their will and pleafure. But the
founders of the Englifh laws have with excellent forecaft contrived, that no man fhould be called to anfwer to the king for
any capital crime, unlefs upon the preparatory accufation of
twelve or more of his fellow fubjects, the grand jury: and that
the truth of every accufation, whether preferred in the fhape of
indictment, information, or appeal, fhould afterwards be confirmed by the unanimous fuffrage of twelve of his equals and
neighbours, indifferently chofen, and fuperior to all fufpicion.
So that the liberties of England cannot but fubfift, fo long as this
palladium remains facred and inviolate, not only from all open
attacks, (which none will be fo hardy as to make) but alfo from
all fecret machinations, which may fap and undermine it; by
introducing new and arbitrary methods of trial, by juftices of

[e] 9 Hen III. c. 29.   [f] See Vol. III. pag. 379.

the

the peace, commiffioners of the revenue, and courts of confcience. And however *convenient* thefe may appear at firft, (as
doubtlefs all arbitrary powers, well executed, are the moft *convenient*) yet let it be again remembered, that delays, and little
inconveniences in the forms of juftice, are the price that all free
nations muft pay for their liberty in more fubftantial matters ;
that thefe inroads upon this facred bulwark of the nation are
fundamentally oppofite to the fpirit of our conftitution ; and
that, though begun in trifles, the precedent may gradually increafe and fpread, to the utter difufe of juries in queftions of the
moft momentous concern.

WH A T was faid of juries in general, and the trial thereby,
in *civil* cafes, will greatly fhorten our prefent remarks, with
regard to the trial of *criminal* fuits ; indictments, informations,
and appeals : which trial I fhall confider in the fame method
that I did the former ; by following the order and courfe of the
proceedings themfelves, as the moft clear and perfpicuous way
of treating it.

WH E N therefore a prifoner on his arraignment has pleaded
not guilty, and for his trial hath put himfelf upon the country,
which country the jury are, the fheriff of the county muft return a panel of jurors, *liberos et legales homines, de vicineto ;*
that is, freeholders, without juft exception, and of the *vifne* or
neighbourhood ; which is interpreted to be of the county where
the fact is committed [s]. If the proceedings are before the court
of king's bench, there is time allowed, between the arraignment and the trial, for a jury to be impanelled by writ of *venire
facias* to the fheriff, as in civil caufes : and the trial in cafe of a
mifdemefnor is had at *nifi prius,* unlefs it be of fuch confequence
as to merit a trial at bar ; which is always invariably had when
the prifoner is tried for any capital offence. But, before commiffioners of *oyer* and *terminer* and gaol delivery, the fheriff by
virtue of a general precept directed to him beforehand, returns

[s] 2 Hal. P. C. 264.　2 Hawk. P. C. 403.

to

to the court a panel of forty eight jurors, to try all felons that may be called upon their trial at that feffion: and therefore it is there ufual to try all felons immediately, or foon, after their arraignment. But it is not cuftomary, nor agreeable to the general courfe of proceedings, unlefs by confent of parties, to try perfons indicted of fmaller mifdemefnors at the fame court in which they have pleaded *not guilty*, or *traverfed* the indictment. But they ufually give fecurity to the court, to appear at the next affifes or feffion, and then and there to try the traverfe, giving notice to the profecutor of the fame.

I N cafes of high treafon, whereby corruption of blood may enfue, or mifprifion of fuch treafon, it is enacted by ftatute 7 W. III. c. 3. firft, that no perfon fhall be tried for any fuch treafon, except an attempt to affaffinate the king, unlefs the indictment be found within three years after the offence committed: next, that the prifoner fhall have a copy of the indictment, but not the names of the witneffes, five days at leaft before the trial; that is, upon the true conftruction of the act, before his arraignment[h]; for then is his time to take any exceptions thereto, by way of plea or demurrer: thirdly, that he fhall alfo have a copy of the panel of jurors two days before his trial: and, laftly, that he fhall have the fame compulfive procefs to bring in his witneffes *for* him, as was ufual to compel their appearance *againft* him. And, by ftatute 7 Ann. c. 21. (which did not take place till after the deceafe of the late pretender) all perfons, indicted for high treafon or mifprifion thereof, fhall have not only a copy of the indictment, but a lift of all the witneffes to be produced, and of the jurors impanelled, with their profeffions and places of abode, delivered to him ten days before the trial, and in the prefence of two witneffes; the better to prepare him to make his challenges and defence. But this laft act, fo far as it affected indictments for the inferior fpecies of high treafon, refpecting the coin and the royal feals, is repealed by the ftatute 6 Geo. III. c. 53. elfe it had been im-

[h] Foft. 230.

poſſible to have tried thoſe offences in the ſame circuit in which they are indicted : for ten clear days, between the finding and the trial of the indictment, will exceed the time uſually allotted for any ſeſſion of *oyer* and *terminer* [i]. And no perſon indicted for felony is, or (as the law ſtands) ever can be, entitled to ſuch copies, before the time of his trial [k].

WHEN the trial is called on, the jurors are to be ſworn, as they appear, to the number of twelve, unleſs they are challenged by the party.

CHALLENGES may here be made, either on the part of the king, or on that of the priſoner; and either to the whole array, or to the ſeparate polls, for the very ſame reaſons that they may be made in civil cauſes [l]. For it is here at leaſt as neceſſary, as there, that the ſheriff or returning officer be totally indifferent; that where an alien is indicted, the jury ſhould be *de medietate*, or half foreigners; (which does not indeed hold in treaſons [m], aliens being very improper judges of the breach of allegiance to the king) that on every panel there ſhould be a competent number of hundredors; and that the particular jurors ſhould be *omni exceptione majores*; not liable to objection either *propter honoris reſpectum, propter defectum, propter affectum,* or *propter delictum.*

CHALLENGES upon any of the foregoing accounts are ſtiled challenges *for cauſe;* which may be without ſtint in both criminal and civil trials. But in criminal caſes, or at leaſt in capital ones, there is, *in favorem vitae,* allowed to the priſoner an arbitrary and capricious ſpecies of challenge to a certain number of jurors, without ſhewing any cauſe at all; which is called a *peremptory* challenge: a proviſion full of that tenderneſs and humanity to priſoners, for which our Engliſh laws are juſtly famous. This is grounded on two reaſons. 1. As every one

---

i Foſt. 250.

k 2 Hawk. P. C. 410.

l See Vol. III. pag. 359.

m 2 Hawk. P. C. 420. 2 Hal. P. C. 271.

muſt

muſt be ſenſible, what ſudden impreſſions and unaccountable prejudices we are apt to conceive upon the bare looks and geſtures
of another; and how neceſſary it is, that a priſoner (when put to
defend his life) ſhould have a good opinion of his jury, the want
of which might totally diſconcert him; the law wills not that
he ſhould be tried by any one man againſt whom he has conceived a prejudice, even without being able to aſſign a reaſon for
ſuch his diſlike. 2. Becauſe, upon challenges for cauſe ſhewn,
if the reaſon aſſigned prove inſufficient to ſet aſide the juror,
perhaps the bare queſtioning his indifference may ſometimes provoke a reſentment; to prevent all ill conſequences from which,
the priſoner is ſtill at liberty, if he pleaſes, peremptorily to ſet
him aſide.

THIS privilege, of peremptory challenges, though granted
to the priſoner, is denied to the king by the ſtatute 33 Edw. I.
ſt. 4. which enacts, that the king ſhall challenge no jurors
without aſſigning a cauſe certain, to be tried and approved by
the court. However it is held, that the king need not aſſign
his cauſe of challenge, till all the panel is gone through, and
unleſs there cannot be a full jury without the perſons ſo challenged. And then, and not ſooner, the king's counſel muſt
ſhew the cauſe: otherwiſe the juror ſhall be ſworn [n].

THE peremptory challenges of the priſoner muſt however have
ſome reaſonable boundary; otherwiſe he might never be tried.
This reaſonable boundary is ſettled by the common law to be the
number of thirty five; that is, one under the number of three
full juries. For the law judges that five and thirty are fully
ſufficient to allow the moſt timorous man to challenge through
mere caprice; and that he who peremptorily challenges a greater
number, or three full juries, has no intention to be tried at all.
And therefore it dealt with one, who peremptorily challenges
above thirty five, and will not retract his challenge, as with one
who ſtands mute or refuſes his trial; by ſentencing him to the

---

[n] 2 Hawk. C. P. 413. 2 Hal. P. C. 271.

　　　　　　　　　　　　　　　peine

peine forte et dure in felony, and by attainting him in treaſon [o]. And ſo the law ſtands at this day with regard to treaſon, of any kind.

BUT by ſtatute 22 Hen. VIII. c. 14. (which, with regard to felonies, ſtands unrepealed by ſtatute 1 & 2 Ph. & Mar. c. 10.) by this ſtatute, I ſay, no perſon, arraigned for felony, can be admitted to make any more than *twenty* peremptory challenges. But how if the priſoner will peremptorily challenge twenty one? what ſhall be done? The old opinion was, that judgment of *peine forte et dure* ſhould be given, as where he challenged thirty ſix at the common law [p]: but the better opinion ſeems to be [q], that ſuch challenge ſhall only be diſregarded and overruled. Becauſe, firſt, the common law doth not inflict the judgment of penance for challenging twenty one, neither doth the ſtatute inflict it; and ſo heavy a judgment ſhall not be impoſed by implication. Secondly, the words of the ſtatute are, "that he be "not *admitted* to challenge more than twenty;" the evident conſtruction of which is, that any farther challenge ſhall be diſallowed or prevented: and therefore, being null from the beginning, and never in fact a challenge, it can ſubject the priſoner to no puniſhment; but the juror ſhall be regularly ſworn.

IF, by reaſon of challenges or the default of the jurors, a ſufficient number cannot be had of the original panel, a *tales* may be awarded as in civil cauſes [r], till the number of twelve is ſworn, "well and truly to try, and true deliverance make, be- "tween our ſovereign lord the king, and the priſoner whom "they have in charge; and a true verdict to give, according to "their evidence."

WHEN the jury is ſworn, if it be a cauſe of any conſequence, the indictment is uſually opened, and the evidence marſhalled, examined, and enforced by the counſel for the crown, or proſe-

[o] 2 Hal. P. C. 268.
[p] 2 Hawk. P. C. 414.
[q] 3 Inſt. 227. 2 Hal. P. C. 270.
[r] See Vol. III. pag. 364.

cution.

cution. But it is a fettled rule at common law, that no counfel fhall be allowed a prifoner upon his trial, upon the general iffue, in any capital crime, unlefs fome point of law fhall arife proper to be debated [s]. A rule, which (however it may be palliated under cover of that noble declaration of the law, when rightly under-ftood, that the judge fhall be counfel for the prifoner; that is, fhall fee that the proceedings againft him are legal and ftrictly regular [t]) feems to be not at all of a piece with the reft of the humane treatment of prifoners by the Englifh law. For upon what face of reafon can that affiftance be denied to fave the life of a man, which yet is allowed him in profecutions for every petty trefpafs? Nor indeed is it ftrictly fpeaking a part of our antient law: for the mirrour [u], having obferved the neceffity of counfel in civil fuits, "who know how to forward and defend "the caufe, by the rules of law and cuftoms of the realm," immediately afterwards fubjoins; "and more neceffary are they "for defence upon indictments and appeals of felony, than upon "other venial caufes [w]." And, to fay the truth, the judges themfelves are fo fenfible of this defect in our modern practice, that they feldom fcruple to allow a prifoner counfel to ftand by

[s] 2 Hawk. P. C. 400.

[t] Sir Edward Coke (3 Inft. 137.) gives another additional reafon for this refufal, "becaufe the evidence to convict a prifoner "fhould be fo manifeft, as it could not be "contradicted." It was therefore thought too dangerous an experiment, to let an advocate try, whether it could be contradicted or no.

[u] c. 3. §. 1.

[w] Father Parfons the jefuit, and after him bifhop Ellys, (of Englifh liberty. ii. 26.) have imagined, that the benefit of counfel to plead for them was firft denied to prifoners by a law of Henry I, meaning (I prefume) chapters 47 and 48 of the code which is ufually attributed to that prince. "De caufis criminalibus vel capitalibus nemo "quaerat confilium; quin implicitatus ftatim

"perneget, fine omni petitione confilii. —— In "aliis omnibus poteft et debet uti confilio." But this confilium, I conceive, fignifies only an imparlance, and the petitio confilii is craving leave to imparl; (See Vol. III. pag. 298.) which is not allowable in any criminal profecution. This will be manifeft by comparing this law with a co-temporary paffage in the grand couftumier of Normandy, (ch. 85.) which fpeaks of imparlances in perfonal actions. "Apres ce, eft tenu le "querelle a refpondre; et aura congie de foy "confeiller, s'il le demande: et, quand il fera "confeille, il peut nyer le fait dont il eft ac-"cufe." Or, as it ftands in the Latin text, (edit. 1539.) "Querelatus autem poftea tene-"tur refpondere; et habebit licentiam confu-"lendi, fi requirat: habito autem confilio, de-"bet factum negare quo accufatus eft."

him

him at the bar, and inſtruct him what queſtions to aſk, or even to aſk queſtions for him, with reſpect to matters of fact: for as to matters of law, ariſing on the trial, they are *intitled* to the aſſiſtance of counſel. But ſtill this is a matter of too much importance to be left to the good pleaſure of any judge, and is worthy the interpoſition of the legiſlature; which has ſhewn it's inclination to indulge priſoners with this reaſonable aſſiſtance, by enacting in ſtatute 7 W. III. c. 3. that perſons *indicted* for ſuch high treaſon, as works a corruption of the blood, or miſ-priſion thereof, may make their full defence by counſel, not ex-ceeding two, to be named by the priſoner and aſſigned by the court or judge: and this indulgence, by ſtatute 20 Geo. II. c. 30. is extended to parliamentary *impeachments* for high treaſon, which were excepted in the former act.

THE doctrine of evidence upon pleas of the crown is, in moſt reſpects, the ſame as that upon civil actions. There are however a few leading points, wherein, by ſeveral ſtatutes and reſolutions, a difference is made between civil and criminal evidence.

FIRST, in all caſes of high treaſon, petit treaſon, and miſ-priſion of treaſon, by ſtatutes 1 Edw. VI. c. 12. 5 & 6 Edw. VI. c. 11. and 1 & 2 Ph. & Mar. c. 10. *two* lawful witneſſes are re-quired to convict a priſoner; except in caſes of coining [x], and counterfeiting the ſeals; or unleſs the party ſhall willingly and without violence confeſs the ſame. By ſtatute 7 W. III. c. 3. in proſecutions for thoſe treaſons to which that act extends, the ſame rule is again enforced, with this addition, that the con-feſſion of the priſoner, which ſhall countervail the neceſſity of ſuch proof, muſt be in open court; and it is declared that both witneſſes muſt be to the ſame overt act of treaſon, or one to one overt act, and the other to another overt act of the ſame ſpecies of treaſon [y], and not of diſtinct heads or kinds: and no evidence ſhall be admitted to prove any overt act not expreſſly laid in the

[x] 1 Hal. P. C. 297.   [y] See St. Tr. II. 144. Foſter. 235.

indictment.   And therefore in fir John Fenwick's cafe, in king William's time, where there was but one witnefs, an act of parliament[z] was made on purpofe to attaint him of treafon, and he was executed[a].   But in almoft every other accufation one pofitive witnefs is fufficient.   Baron Montefquieu lays it down for a rule[b], that thofe laws which condemn a man to death *in any cafe* on the depofition of a fingle witnefs, are fatal to liberty : and he adds this reafon, that the witnefs who affirms, and the accufed who denies, makes an equal ballance ; there is a neceffity therefore to call in a third man to incline the fcale.   But this feems to be carrying matters too far : for there are fome crimes, in which the very privacy of their nature excludes the poffibility of having more than one witnefs : muft thefe therefore efcape unpunifhed ? Neither indeed is the bare denial of the perfon accufed equivalent to the pofitive oath of a difinterefted witnefs.   In cafes of indictments for perjury, this doctrine is better founded ; and there our law adopts it : for one witnefs is not allowed to convict a man indicted for perjury ; becaufe then there is only one oath againft another[d].   In cafes of treafon alfo there is the accufed's oath of allegiance, to counterpoife the information of a fingle witnefs ; and that may perhaps be one reafon why the law requires a double teftimony to convict him : though the principal reafon, undoubtedly, is to fecure the fubject from being facrificed to fictitious confpiracies, which have been the engines of profligate and crafty politicians in all ages.

S E C O N D L Y, though from the reverfal of colonel Sidney's attainder by act of parliament in 1689[e] it may be collected[f], that the mere fimilitude of hand-writing in two papers fhewn to a jury, without other concurrent teftimony, is no evidence that both were written by the fame perfon ; yet undoubtedly the teftimony of witneffes, well acquainted with the party's

[z] Stat. 8 W. III. c 4.
[a] St. Tr. V. 40.
[b] Sp. L. b. 12. c. 3.
[c] Beccar. c. 13.
[d] 10 Mod. 194.
[e] St. Tr. VIII. 472.
[f] 2 Hawk. P. C. 431.

hand,

hand, that they believe the paper in queſtion to have been written by him, is evidence to be left to a jury[g].

THIRDLY, by the ſtatute 21 Jac. I. c. 27. a mother of a baſtard child, concealing it's death, muſt prove by one witneſs that the child was born dead; otherwiſe ſuch concealment ſhall be evidence of her having murdered it[h].

FOURTHLY, all preſumptive evidence of felony ſhould be admitted cautiouſly : for the law holds, that it is better that ten guilty perſons eſcape, than that one innocent ſuffer. And ſir Matthew Hale in particular[j] lays down two rules, moſt prudent and neceſſary to be obſerved : 1. Never to convict a man for ſtealing the goods of a perſon unknown, merely becauſe he will give no account how he came by them, unleſs an actual felony be proved of ſuch goods : and, 2. Never to convict any perſon of murder or manſlaughter, till at leaſt the body be found dead; on account of two inſtances he mentions, where perſons were executed for the murder of others, who were then alive, but miſſing.

LASTLY, it was an antient and commonly received practice[i], (derived from the civil law, and which alſo to this day obtains in the kingdom of France[k]) that, as counſel was not allowed to any priſoner accuſed of a capital crime, ſo neither ſhould he be ſuffered to exculpate himſelf by the teſtimony of any witneſſes. And therefore it deſerves to be remembered, to the honour of Mary I, (whoſe early ſentiments, till her marriage with Philip of Spain, ſeem to have been humane and generous[l]) that when ſhe appointed ſir Richard Morgan chief juſtice of the common-pleas, ſhe injoined him, " that notwithſtanding the old error,

---

[g] Lord Preſton's caſe. *A. D.* 1690. St. Tr. IV. 453. Francia's caſe. *A. D.* 1716. St. Tr. VI. 69. Layer's caſe. *A. D.* 1722. *ibid.* 279. Henzey's caſe. *A. D.* 1758. 4 Burr. 644.

[h] See pag. 198.

[j] 2 Hal. P. C. 290.

[i] St. Tr. I. *paſſim.*

[k] Domat. publ. law. b. 3. t. 1. Monteſq. Sp. L. b. 29. c. 11.

[l] See pag. 17.

" which

"which did not admit any witnefs to fpeak, or any other matter "to be heard, in favour of the adverfary, her majefty being "party; her highnefs' pleafure was, that whatfoever could be "brought in favour of the fubject fhould be admitted to be "heard: and moreover, that the juftices fhould not perfuade "themfelves to fit in judgment otherwife for her highnefs than "for her fubject [m]. Afterwards, in one particular inftance (when embezzling the queen's military ftores was made felony by ftatute 31 Eliz. c. 4.) it was provided that any perfon, impeached for fuch felony, "fhould be received and admitted to make any "lawful proof that he could, by lawful witnefs or otherwife, "for his difcharge and defence:" and in general the courts grew fo heartily afhamed of a doctrine fo unreafonable and oppreffive, that a practice was gradually introduced of examining witneffes for the prifoner, but not upon oath [n]: the confequence of which ftill was, that the jury gave lefs credit to the prifoner's evidence, than to that produced by the crown. Sir Edward Coke [o] protefts very ftrongly againft this tyrannical practice: declaring that he never read in any act of parliament, book-cafe, or record, that in criminal cafes the party accufed fhould not have witneffes fworn for him; and therefore there was not fo much as *fcintilla juris* againft it [p]. And the houfe of commons were fo fenfible of this abfurdity, that, in the bill for abolifhing hoftilities between England and Scotland [q], when felonies committed by Englifhmen in Scotland were ordered to be tried in one of the three northern counties, they infifted on a claufe, and carried it [r] againft the efforts of both the crown and the houfe of lords, againft the practice of the courts in England, and the exprefs law of Scotland [s], "that in all fuch trials, for the better difco-"very of the truth, and the better information of the con-"fciences of the jury and juftices, there fhall be allowed to the

[m] Holingfh. 1112. St. Tr. I. 72.

[n] 2 Bulftr. 147. Cro. Car 292.

[o] 3 Inft. 79.

[p] See alfo 2 Hal. P. C. 283. and his fummary. 264.

[q] Stat. 4 Jac. I. c. 1.

[r] Com. Journ. 4, 5, 12, 13, 15, 29, 30 Jun. 1607.

[s] *Ibid.* 4 Jun. 1607.

" party arraigned the benefit of such credible witnesses, to be
" examined upon oath, as can be produced for his clearing and
" justification." At length by the statute 7 W. III. c. 3. the
same measure of justice was established throughout all the realm,
in cases of treason within the act: and it was afterwards declared by statute 1 Ann. st. 2. c. 9. that in all cases of treason and
felony, all witnesses *for* the prisoner should be examined upon
oath, in like manner as the witnesses *against* him.

WHEN the evidence on both sides is closed, the jury cannot
be discharged till they have given in their verdict; but are to
consider of it, and deliver it in, with the same forms, as upon
civil causes: only they cannot, in a criminal case, give a *privy*
verdict[t]. But an open verdict may be either general, guilty, or
not guilty; or special, setting forth all the circumstances of the
case, and praying the judgment of the court, whether, for instance, on the facts stated, it be murder, manslaughter, or no
crime at all. This is where they *doubt* the matter of law, and
therefore *chuse* to leave it to the determination of the court;
though they have an unquestionable right of determining upon
all the circumstances, and finding a general verdict, if they think
proper so to hazard a breach of their oaths: and, if their verdict
be notoriously wrong, they may be punished and the verdict set
aside by attaint at the suit of the king; but not at the suit of the
prisoner[u]. But the practice, heretofore in use, of fining, inprison-
ing, or otherwise punishing jurors, merely at the discretion of the
court, for finding their verdict contrary to the direction of the judge,
was arbitrary, unconstitutional and illegal: and is treated as such
by sir Thomas Smith, two hundred years ago; who accounted
" such doings to be very violent, tyrannical, and contrary to the
" liberty and custom of the realm of England[w]." For, as sir
Matthew Hale well observes[x], it would be a most unhappy case
for the judge himself, if the prisoner's fate depended upon his
directions: --- unhappy also for the prisoner; for, if the judge's

[t] 2 Hal. P. C. 300. 2 Hawk. P. C. 439.　　[w] Smith's commonw. l. 3. c. 1.
[u] 2 Hal. P. C. 310.　　[x] 2 Hal. P. C. 313.

opi-

opinion muſt rule the verdict, the trial by jury would be uſeleſs.
Yet in many inſtances[y], where contrary to evidence the jury have
found the priſoner guilty, their verdict hath been mercifully ſet
aſide, and a new trial granted by the court of king's bench; for
in ſuch caſe, as hath been ſaid, it cannot be ſet right by attaint.
But there hath yet been no inſtance of granting a new trial,
where the priſoner was *acquitted* upon the firſt[z].

IF the jury therefore find the priſoner not guilty, he is then
for ever quit and diſcharged of the accuſation[a]; except he be appealed of felony within the time limited by law. But if the
jury find him guilty[b], he is then ſaid to be *convicted* of the crime
whereof he ſtands indicted. Which conviction may accrue two
ways; either by his confeſſing the offence and pleading guilty;
or by his being found ſo by the verdict of his country.

WHEN the offender is thus convicted, there are two collateral circumſtances that immediately ariſe. 1. On a conviction, in general, for any felony, the reaſonable expenſes of
proſecution are by ſtatute 25 Geo. II. c. 36. to be allowed to
the proſecutor out of the county ſtock, if he petitions the judge
for that purpoſe; and by ſtatute 27 Geo. II. c. 3. poor perſons,
bound over to give evidence, are likewiſe entitled to be paid
their charges, as well without conviction as with it. 2. On
a conviction of larciny in particular, the proſecutor ſhall have
reſtitution of his goods, by virtue of the ſtatute 21 Hen. VIII.
c. 11. For by the common law there was no reſtitution of goods
upon an indictment, becauſe it is at the ſuit of the king only;
and therefore the party was enforced to bring an appeal of rob-

---

[y] 1 Lev. 9. T. Jones. 163. St. Tr. X.
416.

[z] 2 Hawk. P. C. 442.

[a] The civil law in ſuch caſe only diſ-
charges him from the ſame accuſer, but not
from the ſame accuſation. (*Ff.* 48. 2. 7.
§. 2.)

[b] In the Roman republic, when the priſoner was convicted of any capital offence
by his judges, the form of pronouncing
that conviction was ſomething peculiarly
delicate: not that he was guilty, but that
he had not been enough upon his guard;
" *parum caviſſe videtur.*" (*Feſtus.* 325.)

bery, in order to have his goods again[c]. But, it being confidered
that the party, profecuting the offender by indictment, deferves
to the full as much encouragement as he who profecutes by appeal, this ftatute was made, which enacts, that if any perfon
be convicted of larciny by the evidence of the party robbed, he
fhall have full reftitution of his money, goods, and chattels ;
or the value of them out of the offender's goods, if has any,
by a writ to be granted by the juftices. And this writ of reftitution fhall reach the goods fo ftolen, notwithftanding the property [d] of them is endeavoured to be altered by fale in market
overt[e]. And, though this may feem fomewhat hard upon the
buyer, yet the rule of law is that "*fpoliatus debet, ante omnia,*
"*reftitui ;*" efpecially when he has ufed all the diligence in his
power to convict the felon. And, fince the cafe is reduced to
this hard neceffity, that either the owner or the buyer muft fuffer ; the law prefers the right of the owner, who has done a
meritorious act by purfuing a felon to condign punifhment, to
the right of the buyer, whofe merit is only negative, that he
has been guilty of no unfair tranfaction. Or elfe, fecondly, without fuch writ of reftitution, the party may peaceably retake his
goods, wherever he happens to find them[f], unlefs a new property be fairly acquired therein. Or, laftly, if the felon be convicted and pardoned, or be allowed his clergy, the party robbed
may bring his action of trover againft him for his goods ; and
recover a fatisfaction in damages. But fuch action lies not, before profecution ; for fo felonies would be made up and healed[g]:
and alfo recaption is unlawful, if it be done with intention to
fmother or compound the larciny ; it then becoming the heinous
offence of theft-bote, as was mentioned in a former chapter[h].

It is not uncommon, when a perfon is convicted of a mifdemefnor, which principally and more immediately affects fome individual, as a battery, imprifonment, or the like, for the court

[c] 3 Inft. 242.
[d] See Vol. II. pag. 450.
[e] 1 Hal. P. C. 543.

[f] See Vol. III. pag. 4.
[g] 1 Hal. P. C. 546.
[h] See pag. 133.

to

to permit the defendant to *fpeak with the profecutor*, before any judgment is pronounced; and, if the profecutor declares himfelf fatisfied, to inflict but a trivial punifhment. This is done, to reimburfe the profecutor his expenfes, and make him fome private amends, without the trouble and circuity of a civil action. But it furely is a dangerous practice: and, though it may be intrufted to the prudence and difcretion of the judges in the fuperior courts of record, it ought never to be allowed in local or inferior jurifdictions, fuch as the quarter-feffions ; where profecutions for affaults are by this means too frequently commenced, rather for private lucre than for the great ends of public juftice. Above all, it fhould never be fuffered, where the teftimony of the profecutor himfelf is neceffary to convict the defendant : for by this means, the rules of evidence are intirely fubverted; the profecutor becomes in effect a plaintiff, and yet is fuffered to bear witnefs for himfelf. Nay even a voluntary forgivenefs, by the party injured, ought not in true policy to intercept the ftroke of juftice. " This," fays an elegant writer[i], (who pleads with equal ftrength for the *certainty* as for the *lenity* of punifhment) " may be an act of good-nature and humanity, but it is contrary " to the good of the public. For, although a private citizen " may difpenfe with fatisfaction for his private injury, he cannot " remove the neceffity of public example. The right of punifh- " ing belongs not to any one individual in particular, but to the " fociety in general, or the fovereign who reprefents that fociety: " and a man may renounce his own portion of this right, but " he cannot give up that of others."

[i] Becc. ch. 46.

CHAPTER THE TWENTY EIGHTH.

OF THE BENEFIT OF CLERGY.

AFTER trial and conviction, the judgment of the court regularly follows, unlefs fufpended or arrefted by fome intervening circumftance; of which the principal is *the benefit of clergy*: a title of no fmall curiofity as well as ufe; and concerning which I fhall therefore enquire, 1. Into it's original, and the various mutations which this privilege of clergy has fuftained. 2. To what perfons it is to be allowed at this day. 3. In what cafes. 4. The confequences of allowing it.

I. CLERGY, the *privilegium clericale*, or in common fpeech *the benefit of clergy*, had it's original from the pious regard paid by chriftian princes to the church in it's infant ftate; and the ill ufe which the popifh ecclefiaftics foon made of that pious regard. The exemptions, which they granted to the church, were principally of two kinds: 1. Exemption of *places*, confecrated to religious duties, from criminal arrefts, which was the foundation of fanctuaries: 2. Exemption of the *perfons* of clergymen from criminal procefs before the fecular judge in a few particular cafes, which was the true original and meaning of the *privilegium clericale*.

BUT

BUT the clergy, encreafing in wealth, power, honour, number, and intereft, began foon to fet up for themfelves : and that which they obtained by the favour of the civil government, they now claimed as their inherent right; and as a right of the higheft nature, indefeafible, and *jure divino*[a]. By their canons therefore and conftitutions they endeavoured at, and where they met with eafy princes obtained, a vaft extenfion of thefe exemptions : as well in regard to the crimes themfelves, of which the lift became quite univerfal[b]; as in regard to the perfons exempted, among whom were at length comprehended not only every little fubordinate officer belonging to the church or clergy, but even many that were totally laymen.

IN England however, although the ufurpations of the pope were very many and grievous, till Henry the eighth entirely exterminated his fupremacy, yet a total exemption of the clergy from fecular jurifdiction could never be thoroughly effected, though often endeavoured by the clergy[c] : and therefore, though the antient *privilegium clericale* was in *fome* capital cafes, yet it was not *univerfally*, allowed. And in thofe particular cafes, the ufe was for the bifhop or ordinary to demand his clerks to be remitted out of the king's courts, as foon as they were indicted : concerning the allowance of which demand there was for many years a great uncertainty[d] : till at length it was finally fettled in the reign of Henry the fixth, that the prifoner fhould firft be arraigned; and might either *then* claim his benefit of clergy, by way of declinatory plea; or, *after conviction*, by way of arrefting judgment. This latter way is moft ufually practiced, as it is more to the fatisfaction of the court to have the crime previoufly afcertained by confeffion or the verdict of a jury; and alfo as it is more advantageous to the prifoner himfelf, who may

[a] The principal argument, upon which they founded this exemption, was that text of fcripture; "touch not mine anointed, and "do my prophets no harm." (Keilw.181.)

[b] See Vol. III. pag. 62.
[c] Keilw. 180.
[d] 2 Hal. P. C. 377.

poſſibly be acquitted, and ſo need not the benefit of his clergy at all.

ORIGINALLY the law was held, that no man ſhould be admitted to the privilege of clergy, but ſuch as had the *habitum et tonſuram clericalem* [e]. But in proceſs of time a much wider and more comprehenſive criterion was eſtabliſhed : every one that could read (a mark of great learning in thoſe days of ignorance and her ſiſter ſuperſtition) being accounted a clerk or *clericus,* and allowed the benefit of clerkſhip, though neither initiated in holy orders, nor trimmed with the clerical tonſure. But when learning, by means of the invention of printing, and other concurrent cauſes, began to be more generally diſſeminated than formerly ; and reading was no longer a competent proof of clerkſhip, or being in holy orders ; it was found that as many laymen as divines were admitted to the *privilegium clericale :* and therefore by ſtatute 4 Hen. VII. c. 13. a diſtinction was once more drawn between mere lay ſcholars, and clerks that were really in orders. And though it was thought reaſonable ſtill to mitigate the ſeverity of the law with regard to the former, yet they were not put upon the ſame footing with actual clergy ; being ſubjected to a ſlight degree of puniſhment, and not allowed to claim the clerical privilege more than once. Accordingly the ſtatute directs, that no perſon, once admitted to the benefit of clergy, ſhall be admitted thereto a ſecond time, unleſs he produces his orders : and, in order to diſtinguiſh their perſons, all laymen who are allowed this privilege ſhall be burnt with a hot iron in the brawn of the left thumb. This diſtinction between learned laymen, and real clerks in orders, was aboliſhed for a time by the ſtatutes 28 Hen. VIII. c. 1, and 32 Hen. VIII. c. 3. but is held [f] to have been virtually reſtored by ſtatute 1 Edw. VI. c. 12. which ſtatute alſo enacts that lords of parliament, and peers of the realm, may have the benefit of their peerage, equivalent to that of clergy, for the firſt offence, (although they cannot read, and

---

[e] 2 Hal. P. C. 372. M. Paris. *A.D.* 1259.   [f] Hob. 294.
See Vol. I. pag. 24.

with-

without being burnt in the hand) for all offences then clergyable to commoners, and also for the crimes of housebreaking, high-way robbery, horse-stealing, and robbing of churches.

AFTER this burning the laity, and before it the real clergy, were discharged from the sentence of the law in the king's courts, and delivered over to the ordinary, to be dealt with according to the ecclesiastical canons. Whereupon the ordinary, not satisfied with the proofs adduced in the profane secular court, set himself formally to work to make a purgation of the offender by a new canonical trial; although he had been previously convicted by his country, or perhaps by his own confession. This trial was held before the bishop in person, or his deputy; and by a jury of twelve clerks: and there, first, the party himself was required to make oath of his own innocence; next, there was to be the oath of twelve compurgators, who swore they believed he spoke the truth; then, witnesses were to be examined upon oath, but on behalf of the prisoner only; and, lastly, the jury were to bring in their verdict upon oath, which usually acquitted the prisoner: otherwise, if a clerk, he was degraded, or put to penance[g]. A learned judge, in the beginning of the last century[h], remarks with much indignation the vast complication of perjury and subornation of perjury, in this solemn farce of a mock trial; the witnesses, the compurgators, and the jury, being all of them partakers in the guilt: the delinquent party also, though convicted before on the clearest evidence, and conscious of his own offence, yet was permitted and almost compelled to swear himself not guilty: nor was the good bishop himself, under whose countenance this scene of wickedness was daily transacted, by any means exempt from a share of it. And yet by this purgation the party was restored to his credit, his liberty, his lands, and his capacity of purchasing afresh, and was entirely made a new and an innocent man.

[g] 3 P. Wms. 447. Hob. 289.   [h] Hob. 291.

THIS scandalous proftitution of oaths, and the forms of juftice, in the almoft conftant acquittal of felonious clerks by purgation, was the occafion, that, upon very heinous and notorious circumftances of guilt, the temporal courts would not truft the ordinary with the trial of the offender, but delivered over to him the convicted clerk, *abfque purgatione facienda :* in which fituation the clerk convict could not make purgation ; but was to continue in prifon during life, and was incapable of acquiring any perfonal property, or receiving the profits of his lands, unlefs the king fhould pleafe to pardon him. Both thefe courfes were in fome degree exceptionable ; the latter being perhaps too rigid, as the former was productive of the moft abandoned perjury. As therefore thefe mock trials took their rife from factious and popifh tenets, tending to exempt one part of the nation from the general municipal law ; it became high time, when the reformation was thoroughly eftablifhed, to abolifh fo vain and impious a ceremony.

ACCORDINGLY the ftatute 18. Elix. c. 7. enacts, that, for the avoiding of fuch perjuries and abufes, after the offender has been allowed his clergy, he fhall not be delivered to the ordinary, as formerly ; but, upon fuch allowance and burning in the hand, he fhall forthwith be enlarged and delivered out of prifon ; with provifo, that the judge may, if he thinks fit, continue the offender in gaol for any time not exceeding a year. And thus the law continued, for above a century, unaltered ; except only that the ftatute 21 Jac. I. c. 6. allowed, that women convicted of fimple larcinies under the value of ten fhillings fhould, (not properly have the benefit of clergy, for they were not called upon to read ; but) be burned in the hand, and whipped, ftocked, or imprifoned for any time not exceeding a year. And a fimilar indulgence, by the ftatutes 3 & 4 W. & M. c. 9. and 4 & 5 W. & M. c. 24. was extended to women, guilty of any clergyable felony whatfoever ; who were allowed to claim the benefit of *the ftatute*, in like manner as men might claim the benefit of *clergy*,

and

and to be difcharged upon being burned in the hand, and imprifoned for any time not exceeding a year. All women, all
peers, and all commoners who could read, were therefore difcharged in fuch felonies; abfolutely, if clerks in orders; and
for the firft offence, upon burning in the hand, if lay: yet
all liable (excepting peers) if the judge faw occafion, to imprifonment not exceeding a year. And thofe men, who could not
read, if under the degree of peerage, were hanged.

AFTERWARDS indeed it was confidered, that education and
learning were no extenuations of guilt, but quite the reverfe:
and that, if the punifhment of death for fimple felony was too
fevere for thofe who had been liberally inftructed, it was, *a fortiori*, too fevere for the ignorant alfo. And thereupon by ftatute
5 Ann. c. 6. it was enacted, that the benefit of clergy fhould
be granted to all thofe who were intitled to afk it, without requiring them to read by way of conditional merit.

BUT a few years experience having fhewn, that this univerfal lenity was frequently inconvenient, and an encouragement to
commit the lower degrees of felony; and that, though capital
punifhments were too rigorous for thefe inferior offences, yet no
punifhment at all (or next to none, as branding or whipping)
was as much too gentle; it was enacted by ftatutes 4 Geo. I.
c. 11. and 6 Geo. I. c. 23. that when any perfons fhall be convicted of any larciny, either grand or petit, and fhall be entitled
to the benefit of clergy, *or*[i] liable only to the penalties of burn-

---

[i] The printed ftatute book reads *and* inftead of *or*: and, if that be the true reading, it may be doubted, and, as the confequence may in fome cafes be capital, it deferves to be explained by the legiflature,
whether *women*, and perfons convicted of
petit larciny, are ftrictly within thefe ftatutes
of George the firft; for the ftatutes, as printed, feem to extend only to fuch convicts as
are entitled to the *benefit of clergy*, which no
woman, or *petit larciner*, properly is. For,
with regard to the female fex, the ftatutes
of William and Mary (before referred to)
very anxioufly diftinguifh between the benefit of *clergy*, which extends only to *men*,
and the benefit of *the ftatute* 3 & 4W. & M.
which is allowed to be claimed by *women*:
and the ftatute of Anne (as is hereafter obferved) doth not entitle any one to the benefit of clergy but fuch as were entitled
before; as it's whole operation is merely to
difpenfe with their reading.

　　　　　　　　　　　ing

ing in the hand or whipping, the court in their diſcretion, inſtead of ſuch burning in the hand or whipping, may direct ſuch
offenders to be tranſported to America for ſeven years : and, if
they return within that time, it ſhall be felony without benefit
of clergy.

In this ſtate does the benefit of clergy at preſent ſtand ; very
conſiderably different from it's original inſtitution : the wiſdom
of the Engliſh legiſlature having, in the courſe of a long and
laborious proceſs, extracted by a noble alchemy rich medicines
out of poiſonous ingredients ; and converted, by gradual mutations, what was at firſt an unreaſonable exemption of particular
popiſh eccleſiaſtics, into a merciful mitigation of the general
law, with reſpect to capital puniſhment.

From the whole of this detail we may collect, that, however in times of ignorance and ſuperſtition that monſter in true
policy may for a while ſubſiſt, of a body of men, reſiding in the
bowels of a ſtate, and yet independent of it's laws ; yet, when
learning and rational religion have a little enlightened mens
minds, ſociety can no longer endure an abſurdity ſo groſs, as
muſt deſtroy it's very fundamentals. For, by the original contract of government, the price of protection by the united force
of individuals is that of obedience to the united will of the
community. This united will is declared in the laws of the
land : and that united force is exerted in their due, and univerſal, execution.

II. I am next to enquire, to what *perſons* the benefit of clergy
is to be allowed at this day : and this muſt be chiefly collected
from what has been obſerved in the preceding article. For, upon
the whole, we may pronounce, that all clerks in orders are, without any branding, and of courſe without any tranſportation, (for
that is only ſubſtituted in lieu of the other) to be admitted to this
privilege, and immediately diſcharged, or at moſt only confined for
one

one year: and this as often as they offend [k]. Again, all lords of parliament and peers of the realm, by the ſtatute 1 Edw. VI. c. 12. ſhall be diſcharged in all clergyable and other felonies, provided for by the act, without any burning in the hand, in the ſame manner, as real clerks convict: but this is only for the firſt offence. Laſtly, all the commons of the realm, not in orders, whether male *or female* [l], ſhall for the firſt offence be diſcharged of the puniſhment of felonies, within the benefit of clergy; upon being burnt in the hand, impriſoned for a year, or leſs; or, in caſe of larciny, being tranſported for ſeven years, if the court ſhall think proper. It hath been ſaid, that Jews, and other infidels and heretics, were not capable of the benefit of clergy, till after the ſtatute 5 Ann. c. 6. as being under a legal incapacity for orders [m]. But, with deference to ſuch reſpectable authorities, I much queſtion whether this was ever ruled for law, ſince the re-introduction of the Jews into England, in the time of Oliver Cromwell. For, if that were the caſe, the Jews are ſtill in the ſame predicament, which every day's experience will contradict: the ſtatute of queen Anne having certainly made no alteration in this reſpect; it only diſpenſing with the neceſſity of reading in thoſe perſons, who, in caſe they could read, were before the act entitled to the benefit of their clergy.

III. THE third point to be conſidered is, for what *crimes* the *privilegium clericale*, or benefit of clergy, is to be allowed. And, it is to be obſerved, that neither in high treaſon, nor in petit larciny, nor in any mere miſdemeſnors, it was indulged at the common law; and therefore we may lay it down for a rule, that it was allowable only in petit treaſon and felonies: which for the moſt part became legally intitled to this indulgence by the ſtatute *de clero*, 25 Edw. III. ſt. 3. c. 4. which provides, that clerks convict for treaſons or felonies, touching other perſons than the king himſelf or his royal majeſty, ſhall have the privilege of holy

---

[k] 2 Hal. P. C. 375.
[l] See note [l].

[m] 2 Hal. P. C. 373. 2 Hawk. P. C. 338. Foſt. 306.

church.

church. But yet it was not allowable in all felonies whatſoever: for in ſome it was denied even by the common law, viz. *inſidiatio viarum*, or lying in wait for one on the highway; *depopulatio agrorum*, or deſtroying and ravaging a country[n]; and *combuſtio domorum*, or arſon, that is, the burning of houſes[o]; all which are a kind of hoſtile acts, and in ſome degree border upon treaſon. And farther, all theſe identical crimes, together with petit treaſon, and very many other acts of felony, are ouſted of clergy by particular acts of parliament; which have in general been mentioned under the particular offences to which they belong, and therefore need not be here recapitulated. Of all which ſtatutes for excluding clergy I ſhall only obſerve, that they are nothing elſe but the reſtoring of the law to the ſame rigor of capital puniſhment in the firſt offence, that it exerted before the *privilegium clericale* was at all indulged; and which it ſtill exerts upon a ſecond offence in almoſt all kinds of felonies, unleſs committed by clerks actually in orders. We may alſo remark, that by the marine law, as declared in ſtatute 28 Hen. VIII. c. 15. the benefit of clergy is not allowed in any caſe whatſoever. And therefore when offences are committed within the admiralty-juriſdiction, which would be clergyable if committed by land, the conſtant courſe is to acquit and diſcharge the priſoner[p]. And laſtly, under this head of enquiry, we may obſerve the following rules: 1. That in all felonies, whether new created or by common law, clergy is now allowable, unleſs taken away by expreſs words of an act of parliament[q]. 2. That, where clergy is taken away from the principal, it is not of courſe taken away from the acceſſory, unleſs he be alſo particularly included in the words of the ſtatute[r]. 3. That, when the benefit of clergy is taken away from the *offence*, (as in caſe of murder, buggery, robbery, rape, and burglary) a principal in the ſecond degree, aiding and abetting the crime, is as well excluded from his clergy as he that is principal in

[n] 2 Hal. P. C. 333.   [q] 2 Hal. P. C. 330.
[o] 1 Hal. P. C. 346.   [r] 3 Hawk. P. C. 342.
[p] Moor. 756. Foſt. 288.

the

the firſt degree : but, 4. That, where it is only taken away from the *perſon committing* the offence, (as in the caſe of ſtabbing, or committing larciny in a dwelling houſe, or privately from the perſon) his aiders and abetters are not excluded ; through the tenderneſs of the law, which hath determined that ſuch ſtatutes ſhall be taken literally [s].

IV. LASTLY, we are to enquire what the conſequences are to the party, of allowing him this benefit of clergy. I ſpeak not of the branding, impriſonment, or tranſportation ; which are rather concomitant conditions, than conſequences of receiving this indulgence. The conſequences are ſuch as affect his preſent intereſt, and future credit and capacity : as having been once a felon, but now purged from that guilt by the privilege of clergy ; which operates as a kind of ſtatute pardon.

AND, we may obſerve, 1. That by his conviction he forfeits all his goods to the king; which, being once veſted in the crown, ſhall not afterwards be reſtored to the offender [t]. 2. That, after conviction, and till he receives the judgment of the law, by branding or the like, or elſe is pardoned by the king, he is to all intents and purpoſes a felon, and ſubject to all the diſabilities and other incidents of a felon [u]. 3. That, after burning or pardon, he is diſcharged for ever of that, and all other felonies before committed, within the benefit of clergy ; but not of felonies from which ſuch benefit is excluded : and this by ſtatutes 8 Eliz. c. 4. and 18 Eliz. c. 7. 4. That by the burning, or pardon of it, he is reſtored to all capacities and credits, and the poſſeſſion of his lands, as if he had never been convicted [w]. 5. That what is ſaid with regard to the advantages of commoners and laymen, ſubſequent to the burning in the hand, is equally applicable to all peers and clergymen, although never branded at all. For they have the ſame privileges, without any burning, which others are intitled to after it [x].

[s] 1 Hal. P. C. 529.　Foſter. 356.

[t] 2 Hal. P. C. 388.

[u] 3 P. Wm. 487.

[w] 2 Hal. P. C. 389. 5 Rep. 110.

[x] 2 Hal. P. C. 389, 390

Chapter the twenty ninth.

Of JUDGMENT, and it's CONSE-QUENCES.

WE are now to confider the next ftage of criminal profe-cution, after trial and conviction are paft, in fuch crimes and mifdemefnors, as are either too high or too low to be in-cluded within the benefit of clergy: which is that of *judgment.* For when, upon a capital charge, the jury have brought in their verdict, guilty, in the prefence of the prifoner; he is either im-mediately, or at a convenient time foon after, afked by the court, if he has any thing to offer why judgment fhould not be awarded againft him. And in cafe the defendant be found guilty of a mif-demefnor, (the trial of which may, and does ufually, happen in his abfence, after he has once appeared) a *capias* is awarded and iffued, to bring him in to receive his judgment; and, if he ab-fconds, he may be profecuted even to outlawry. But whenever he appears in perfon, upon either a capital or inferior conviction, he may at this period, as well as at his arraignment, offer any exceptions to the indictment, in *arreft* or ftay of judgment: as for want of fufficient certainty in fetting forth either the perfon, the time, the place, or the offence. And, if the objections be valid, the whole proceedings fhall be fet afide; but the party

may

may be indicted again [a].   And we may take notice, 1. That none of the statutes of *jeofails* [b], for amendment of errors, extend to indictments or proceedings in criminal cases; and therefore a defective indictment is not aided by a verdict, as defective pleadings in civil cases are.   2. That, in favour of life, great strictness has at all times been observed, in every point of an indictment.   Sir Matthew Hale indeed complains, " that this " strictness is grown to be a blemish and inconvenience in the " law, and the administration thereof : for that more offenders " escape by the over-easy ear given to exceptions in indictments, " than by their own innocence; and many times gross murders, " burglaries, robberies, and other heinous and crying offences, " remain unpunished by these unseemly niceties; to the reproach " of the law, to the shame of the government, to the encourage- " ment of villany, and to the dishonour of God [c]."   And yet, notwithstanding this laudable zeal, no man was more tender of life, than this truly excellent judge.

A PARDON also, as has been before said, may be pleaded in arrest of judgment : and it has the same advantage when pleaded here, as when pleaded upon arraignment; *viz.* the saving the attainder, and of course the corruption of blood : which nothing can restore but parliament, when a pardon is not pleaded till after sentence.   And certainly, upon all accounts, when a man hath obtained a pardon, he is in the right to plead it as soon as possible.

PRAYING the benefit of clergy may also be ranked among the motions in arrest of judgment; of which we spoke largely in the preceding chapter.

IF all these resources fail, the court must pronounce that judgment, which the law hath annexed to the crime, and which hath been constantly mentioned, together with the crime itself,

[a] 4 Rep. 45.
[b] See Vol. III. pag. 406.

[c] 2 Hal. P. C. 193.

in fome or other of the former chapters. Of thefe fome are capital, which extend to the life of the offender, and confift generally in being hanged by the neck till dead; though in very
atrocious crimes other circumftances of terror, pain, or difgrace
are fuperadded: as, in treafons of all kinds, being drawn or
dragged to the place of execution; in high treafon affecting the
king's perfon or government, embowelling alive, beheading, and
quartering; and in murder, a public diffection. And, in cafe
of any treafon committed by a female, the judgment is to be
burned alive. But the humanity of the Englifh nation has authorized, by a tacit confent, an almoft general mitigation of fuch
part of thefe judgments as favour of torture or cruelty: a fledge
or hurdle being ufually allowed to fuch traitors as are condemned
to be drawn; and there being very few inftances (and thofe accidental or by negligence) of any perfon's being embowelled or
burned, till previoufly deprived of fenfation by ftrangling. Some
punifhments confift in exile or banifhment, by abjuration of the
realm, or tranfportation to the American colonies: others in
lofs of liberty, by perpetual or temporary imprifonment. Some
extend to confifcation, by forfeiture of lands, or moveables, or
both, or of the profits of lands for life: others induce a difability, of holding offices or employments, being heirs, executors,
and the like. Some, though rarely, occafion a mutilation or
difmembring, by cutting off the hand or ears: others fix a
lafting ftigma on the offender, by flitting the noftrils, or branding in the hand or face. Some are merely pecuniary, by ftated
or difcretionary fines: and laftly there are others, that confift
principally in their ignominy, though moft of them are mixed
with fome degree of corporal pain; and thefe are inflicted chiefly
for crimes, which arife from indigence, or which render even
opulence difgraceful. Such as whipping, hard labour in the
houfe of correction, the pillory, the ftocks, and the ducking-
ftool.

DISGUSTING as this catalogue may feem, it will afford
pleafure to an Englifh reader, and do honour to the Englifh
law,

law, to compare it with that fhocking apparatus of death and torment, to be met with in the criminal codes of almoft every other nation in Europe. And it is moreover one of the glories of our Englifh law, that the nature, though not always the quantity or degree, of punifhment is *afcertained* for every offence ; and that it is not left in the breaft of any judge, nor even of a jury, to alter that judgment, which the law has beforehand ordained, for every fubject alike, without refpect of perfons. For, if judgments were to be the private opinions of the judge, men would then be flaves to their magiftrates; and would live in fociety, without knowing exactly the conditions and obligations which it lays them under. And befides, as this prevents oppreffion on the one hand, fo on the other it ftifles all hopes of impunity or mitigation ; with which an offender might flatter himfelf, if his punifhment depended on the humour or difcretion of the court. Whereas, where an eftablifhed penalty is annexed to crimes, the criminal may read their certain confequence in that law, which ought to be the unvaried rule, as it is the inflexible judge, of his actions.

THE difcretionary fines and difcretionary length of imprifonment, which our courts are enabled to impofe, may feem an exception to this rule. But the general nature of the punifhment, *viz.* by fine or imprifonment, is in thefe cafes fixed and determinate : though the duration and quantity of each muft frequently vary, from the aggravations or otherwife of the offence, the quality and condition of the parties, and from innumerable other circumftances. The *quantum*, in particular, of pecuniary fines neither can, nor ought to be, afcertained by any invariable law. The value of money itfelf changes from a thoufand caufes; and, at all events, what is ruin to one man's fortune, may be matter of indifference to another's. Thus the law of the twelve tables at Rome fined every perfon, that ftruck another, five and twenty *denarii* : this, in the more opulent days of the empire, grew to be a punifhment of fo little confideration, that Aulus Gellius tells a ftory of one Lucius Neratius, who made it his

Y y 2　　　　　　　diver-

diverſion to give a blow to whomever he pleaſed, and then tender them the legal forfeiture. Our ſtatute law has not therefore often aſcertained the quantity of fines, nor the common law ever; it directing ſuch an offence to be puniſhed by fine, in general, without ſpecifying the certain ſum : which is fully ſufficient, when we conſider, that however unlimited the power of the court may ſeem, it is far from being wholly arbitrary; but it's diſcretion is regulated by law. For the bill of rights [d] has particularly declared, that exceſſive fines ought not to be impoſed, nor cruel and unuſual puniſhments inflicted : (which had a retroſpect to ſome unprecedented proceedings in the court of king's bench, in the reign of king James the ſecond) and the ſame ſtatute farther declares, that all grants and promiſes of fines and forfeitures of particular perſons, before conviction, are illegal and void. Now the bill of rights was only declaratory, throughout, of the old conſtitutional law of the land : and accordingly we find it expreſſly holden, long before [e], that all ſuch previous grants are void; ſince thereby many times undue means, and more violent proſecution, would be uſed for private lucre, than the quiet and juſt proceeding of law would permit.

T H E reaſonableneſs of fines in criminal caſes has alſo been uſually regulated by the determination of *magna carta* [f], concerning amercements for miſbehaviour in matters of civil right. " *Liber homo non amercietur pro parvo delicto, niſi ſecun-* " *dum modum ipſius delicti ; et pro magno delicto, ſecundum magni-* " *tudinem delicti ; ſalvo contenemento ſuo : et mercator eodem modo,* " *ſalva mercandiſa ſua ; et villanus eodem modo amercietur, ſalvo* " *wainagio ſuo.*" A rule, that obtained even in Henry the ſecond's time [g], and means only, that no man ſhall have a larger amercement impoſed upon him, than his circumſtances or perſonal eſtate will bear : ſaving to the landholder his contenement, or land; to the trader his merchandize; and to the countryman his wainage, or team and inſtruments of huſbandry. In order

---

d Stat. 1 W. & M. ſt. 2. c. 2.   f *cap.* 14.

e 2 Inſt. 48.   g Glanv. *l.* 9 *c.* 8 & 11 .

to afcertain which, the great charter alfo directs, that the amercement, which is always inflicted in general terms ("*fit in miferi-*
"*cordia*") fhall be fet, *ponatur,* or reduced to a certainty, by the
oath of a jury. This method, of liquidating the amercement to
a precife fum, is ufually done in the court-leet and court-baron by
affeerors, or jurors fworn to *affeere,* that is, tax and moderate,
the *general* amercement according to the *particular* circumftances
of the offence and the offender. In imitation of which, in
courts fuperior to thefe, the antient practice was to enquire by a
jury, when a fine was impofed upon any man, "*quantum inde*
"*regi dare valeat per annum, falva fuftentatione fua, et uxoris,*
"*et liberorum fuorum* [h]." And, fince the difufe of fuch inqueft,
it is never ufual to affefs a larger fine than a man is able to pay,
without touching the implements of his livelyhood; but to inflict corporal punifhment, or a ftated imprifonment, which is
better than an exceffive fine, for that amounts to imprifonment
for life. And this is the reafon why fines in the king's court are
frequently denominated ranfoms, becaufe the penalty muft otherwife fall upon a man's perfon, unlefs it be redeemed or ranfomed
by a pecuniary fine [j]: according to an antient maxim, *qui non*
habet in crumena luat in corpore. Yet, where any ftatute fpeaks
both of fine and ranfom, it is holden, that the ranfom fhall be
treble to the fine at leaft [i].

WHEN fentence of death, the moft terrible and higheft judgment in the laws of England, is pronounced, the immediate infeparable confequence by the common law is *attainder.* For
when it is now clear beyond all difpute, that the criminal is no
longer fit to live upon the earth, but is to be exterminated as a
monfter and a bane to human fociety, the law fets a note of infamy upon him, puts him out of it's protection, and takes no
farther care of him than barely to fee him executed. He is
then called attaint, *attinctus,* ftained, or blackened. He is no
longer of any credit or reputation; he cannot be a witnefs in

[h] Gilb. Exch. c. 5.   [i] Dyer. 232.
[j] Mirr. c. 5. §. 3. Lamb. *Eirenarch.* 575.

any

any court; neither is he capable of performing the functions of another man : for, by an anticipation of his punishment, he is already dead in law [k]. This is after *judgment* : for there is great difference between a man *convicted*, and *attainted*; though they are frequently through inaccuracy confounded together. After conviction only, a man is liable to none of these disabilities : for there is still in contemplation of law a possibility of his innocence. Something may be offered in arrest of judgment : the indictment may be erroneous, which will render his guilt uncertain, and thereupon the present conviction may be quashed : he may obtain a pardon, or be allowed the benefit of clergy; both which suppose some latent sparks of merit, which plead in extenuation of his fault. But when judgment is once pronounced, both law and fact conspire to prove him completely guilty; and there is not the remotest possibility left of any thing to be said in his favour. Upon judgment therefore of death, and not before, the attainder of a criminal commences : or upon such circumstances as are equivalent to judgment of death; as judgment of outlawry on a capital crime, pronounced for absconding or fleeing from justice, which tacitly confesses the guilt. And therefore either upon judgment of outlawry, or of death, for treason or felony, a man shall be said to be attainted.

The consequences of attainder are forfeiture, and corruption of blood.

I. Forfeiture is twofold; of real, and personal, estates. First, as to real estates : by attainder in high treason [1] a man forfeits to the king all his lands and tenements of inheritance, whether fee-simple or fee-tail, and all his rights of entry on lands and tenements, which he held at the time of the offence committed, or at any time afterwards, to be for ever vested in the crown : and also the profits of all lands and tenements, which he had in his own right for life or years, so long as such interest

---

[k] 3 Inst. 213.   [1] Co. Litt. 392. 3 Inst. 19. 1 Hal. P. C. 240. 2 Hawk. P. C. 448.

ſhall ſubſiſt. This forfeiture relates backwards to the time of the treaſon committed; ſo as to avoid all intermediate ſales and incumbrances [m], but not thoſe before the fact: and therefore a wife's jointure is not forfeitable for the treaſon of the huſband; becauſe ſettled upon her previous to the treaſon committed. But her dower is forfeited, by the expreſs proviſion of ſtatute 5 & 6 Edw. VI. c. 11. And yet the huſband ſhall be tenant by the curteſy of the wife's lands, if the wife be attainted of treaſon [n]: for that is not prohibited by the ſtatute. But, though after attainder the forfeiture relates back to the time of the treaſon committed, yet it does not take effect unleſs an attainder be had, of which it is one of the fruits: and therefore, if a traitor dies before judgment pronounced, or is killed in open rebellion, or is hanged by martial law, it works no forfeiture of his lands; for he never was attainted of treaſon [o].

THE natural juſtice of forfeiture or confiſcation of property, for treaſon [p], is founded in this conſideration: that he who hath thus violated the fundamental principles of government, and broken his part of the original contract between king and people, hath abandoned his connexions with ſociety; and hath no longer any right to thoſe advantages, which before belonged to him purely as a member of the community: among which *ſocial* advantages the right of transferring or tranſmitting property to others is one of the chief. Such forfeitures moreover, whereby his poſterity muſt ſuffer as well as himſelf, will help to reſtrain a man, not only by the ſenſe of his duty, and dread of perſonal puniſhment, but alſo by his paſſions and natural affections; and will intereſt every dependent and relation he has, to keep him from offending: according to that beautiful ſentiment of Cicero [q], " *nec vero me fugit quam ſit acerbum, parentum ſcelera filiorum* " *poenis lui: ſed hoc praeclare legibus comparatum eſt, ut caritas* " *liberorum amiciores parentes reipublicae redderet.*" And there-

[m] 3 Inſt. 211.
[n] 1 Hal. P. C. 359.
[o] Co. Litt. 13.

[p] See Vol. I. pag. 299.
[q] *ad Brutum, ep.* 12.

fore Aulus Cafcellius, a Roman lawyer in the time of the triumvirate, ufed to boaft that he had two reafons for defpifing the power of the tyrants; his old age, and his want of children: for children are pledges to the prince of the father's obedience[r]. Yet many nations have thought, that this pofthumous punifhment favours of hardfhip to the innocent; efpecially for crimes that do not ftrike at the very root and foundation of fociety, as treafon againft the government exprefily does. And therefore, though confifcations were very frequent in the times of the earlier emperors, yet Arcadius and Honorius in every other inftance but that of treafon thought it more juft, " *ibi effe* " *poenam, ubi et noxa eft;*" and ordered that " *peccata fuos te-* " *neant auctores, nec ulterius progrediatur metus, quam reperiatur* " *delictum*[s]:" and Juftinian alfo made a law to reftrain the punifhment of relations[t]; which directs the forfeiture to go, except in the cafe of *crimen majeftatis*, to the next of kin to the delinquent. On the other hand the Macedonian laws extended even the capital punifhment of treafon, not only to the children but to all the relations of the delinquent[u]: and of courfe their eftates muft be alfo forfeited, as no man was left to inherit them. And in Germany, by the famous golden bulle[v], (copied almoft *verbatim* from Juftinian's code[w]) the lives of the fons of fuch as confpire to kill an elector are fpared, as it is exprefied, by the emperor's *particular bounty*. But they are deprived of all their effects and rights of fucceffion, and are rendered incapable of any honour ecclefiaftical or civil: " to the end that, " being always poor and neceffitous, they may for ever be accom- " panied by the infamy of their father; may languifh in conti- " nual indigence; and may find (fays this mercilefs edict) their " punifhment in living, and their relief in dying."

WITH us in England, forfeiture of lands and tenements to the crown for treafon is by no means derived from the feodal

[r] Gravin. 1. §. 68.
[s] *Cod.* 9. 47. 22.
[t] *Nov.* 134. *c.* 13.

[u] Qu. Curt. *l.* 6.
[v] *cap.* 24.
[w] *l.* 9. *t.* 8. *l.* 5.

policy,

policy, (as has been already obferved [x]) but was antecedent to the eftablifhment of that fyftem in this ifland; being tranfmitted from our Saxon anceftors [y], and forming a part of the antient Scandinavian conftitution [z]. But in fome treafons relating to the coin, (which, as we formerly obferved, feem rather a fpecies of the *crimen falfi*, than the *crimen laefae majeftatis*) it is provided by the feveral modern ftatutes which conftitute the offence, that it fhall work no forfeiture of lands. And, in order to abolifh fuch hereditary punifhment intirely, it was enacted by ftatute 7 Ann. c. 21. that, after the deceafe of the late pretender, no attainder for treafon fhould extend to the difinheriting of any heir, nor to the prejudice of any perfon, other than the traitor him-felf. By which, the law of forfeitures for high treafon would by this time have been at an end, had not a fubfequent ftatute intervened to give them a longer duration. The hiftory of this matter is fomewhat fingular and worthy obfervation. At the time of the union, the crime of treafon in Scotland was, by the Scots law, in many refpects different from that of treafon in England; and particularly in it's confequence of forfeitures of intailed eftates, which was more peculiarly Englifh: yet it feemed neceffary, that a crime fo nearly affecting government fhould, both in it's effence and confequences, be put upon the fame footing in both parts of the united kingdoms. In new-modelling thefe laws, the Scotch nation and the Englifh houfe of commons ftruggled hard, partly to maintain, and partly to acquire, a total immunity from forfeiture and corruption of blood: which the houfe of lords as firmly refifted. At length a compromife was agreed to, which is eftablifhed by this ftatute, *viz.* that the fame crimes, and no other, fhould be treafon in Scotland that are fo in England; and that the Englifh forfeitures and corrup-tion of blood, fhould take place in Scotland, till the death of the then pretender; and then ceafe throughout the whole of Great Britain [a]: the lords artfully propofing this temporary claufe, in

---

[x] See Vol. II. pag. 251.
[y] *LL. Aelfr. c.* 4. *Canut. c.* 54.

[z] Stiernh. *de jure Goth. l.*2. *c.*6. & *l.*3. *c.*3.
[a] Burnet's Hift. *A. D* 1709.

hopes (it is faid[b]) that the prudence of fucceeding parliaments would make it perpetual[c]. This has partly been done by the ftatute 17 Geo. II. c. 39. (made in the year preceding the late rebellion) the operation of thefe indemnifying claufes being thereby ftill farther fufpended, till the death of the fons of the pretender[d].

In petit treafon and felony, the offender alfo forfeits all his chattel interefts abfolutely, and the profits of all eftates of free-hold during life; and, after his death, all his lands and tene-ments in fee-fimple (but not thofe in tail) to the crown, for a very fhort period of time: for the king fhall have them for a year and a day, and may commit therein what wafte he pleafes; which is called the king's *year, day*, and *wafte*[e]. Formerly the king had only a liberty of committing wafte on the lands of felons, by pulling down their houfes, extirpating their gardens, ploughing their meadows, and cutting down their woods. And a punifhment of a fimilar fpirit appears to have obtained in the oriental countries, from the decrees of Nebuchadnezzar and Cyrus in the books of Daniel[f] and Ezra[g]; which, befides the pain of death inflicted on the delinquents there fpecified, ordain, "that their houfes "fhall be made a dunghill." But this tending greatly to the pre-judice of the public, it was agreed in the reign of Henry the firft, in this kingdom, that the king fhould have the profits of the land for one year and a day, in lieu of the deftruction he was otherwife at liberty to commit[h]: and therefore *magna carta*[i] provides, that the king fhall only hold fuch lands for a year and day, and then reftore them to the lord of the fee; without any mention made of wafte. But the ftatute 17 Edw. II. *de praero-gativa regis*, feems to fuppofe, that the king fhall have his year,

---

[b] Confid. on the law of forfeiture. 6.
[c] See Foft. 250.
[d] The juftice and expediency of this provifion were defended at the time, with much learning and ftrength of argument, in the *confiderations on the law of forfeiture*,

firft publifhed *A. D.* 1744. (See Vol. I. pag. 244)
[e] 2 Inft. 37.
[f] ch. iii. v. 29.
[g] ch. vi. v. 11.
[h] Mirr. c. 4 §. 16. Flet. *l.* 1. *c.* 28.
[i] 9 *Hen. III. c.* 22.

day,

day, *and* waste; and not the year and day *instead of* waste.
Which sir Edward Coke (and the author of the mirror, before
him) very justly look upon as an encroachment, though a very
antient one, of the royal prerogative [k]. This year, day, and
waste are now usually compounded for; but otherwise they regularly belong to the crown : and, after their expiration, the land
would naturally have descended to the heir, (as in gavelkind tenure it still does) did not it's feodal quality intercept such de-
scent, and give it by way of escheat to the lord. These forfeitures for felony do also arise only upon attainder; and therefore
a *felo de se* forfeits no lands of inheritance or freehold, for he
never is attainted as a felon [l]. They likewise relate back to the
time of the offence committed, as well as forfeitures for treason;
so as to avoid all intermediate charges and conveyances. This
may be hard upon such as have unwarily engaged with the offender : but the cruelty and reproach must lie on the part, not
of the law, but of the criminal; who has thus knowingly and
dishonestly involved others in his own calamities.

THESE are all the forfeitures of real estates, created by the
common law, as consequential upon attainders by judgment of
death or outlawry. I here omit the particular forfeitures created
by the statutes of *praemunire* and others : because I look upon
them rather as a *part* of the judgment and penalty, inflicted by
the respective statutes, than as *consequences* of such judgment;
as in treason and felony they are. But I shall just mention, under this division of real estates, the forfeiture of the profits of
lands during life : which extends to two other instances, besides
those already spoken of; misprision of treason [m], and striking in
Westminster-hall, or drawing a weapon upon a judge there,
sitting the king's courts of justice [n].

THE forfeiture of goods and chattels accrues in every one
of the higher kinds of offence : in high treason or misprision

---

[k] Mirr. c. 5. §. 2. 2 Inst 37.
[l] 3 Inst. 55.
[m] Ibid. 218.
[n] Ibid. 141.

thereof, petit treason, felonies of all sorts whether clergyable or not, self-murder or felony *de se*, petty larciny, standing mute, and the above-mentioned offence of striking in Westminster-hall. For *flight* also, on an accusation of treason, felony, or even petit larciny, whether the party be found guilty or acquitted, if the jury find the flight, the party shall forfeit his goods and chattels: for the very flight is an offence, carrying with it a strong presumption of guilt, and is at least an endeavour to elude and stifle the course of justice prescribed by the law. But the jury very seldom find the flight: forfeiture being looked upon, since the vast increase of personal property of late years, as rather too large a penalty for an offence, to which a man is prompted by the natural love of liberty.

THERE is a remarkable difference or two between the forfeiture of lands and of goods and chattels. 1. Lands are forfeited upon *attainder*, and not before: goods and chattels are forfeited by *conviction*. Because in many of the cases where goods are forfeited, there never is any attainder; which happens only where judgment of death or outlawry is given: therefore in those cases the forfeiture must be upon conviction, or not at all; and, being necessarily upon conviction in those, it is so ordered in all other cases, for the law loves uniformity. 2. In outlawries for treason or felony, lands are forfeited only by the judgment: but the goods and chattels are forfeited by a man's being first put in the *exigent*, without staying till he is *quinto exactus*, or finally outlawed; for the secreting himself so long from justice, is construed a flight in law°. 3. The forfeiture of lands has relation to the time of the fact committed, so as to avoid all subsequent sales and incumbrances: but the forfeiture of goods and chattels has no relation backwards; so that those only which a man has at the time of conviction shall be forfeited. Therefore a traitor or felon may *bona fide* sell any of his chattels, real or personal, for the sustenance of himself and family between the fact and conviction ᴾ: for personal property is of so fluctua-

° 3 Inst. 232.   ᴾ 2 Hawk. P. C. 454.

ting

ting a nature, that it paſſes through many hands in a ſhort time; and no buyer could be ſafe, if he were liable to return the goods which he had fairly bought, provided any of the prior vendors had committed a treaſon or felony. Yet if they be colluſively and not *bona fide* parted with, merely to defraud the crown, the law (and particularly the ſtatute 13 Eliz. c. 5.) will reach them; for they are all the while truly and ſubſtantially the goods of the offender: and as he, if acquitted, might recover them himſelf, as not parted with for a good conſideration; ſo, in caſe he happens to be convicted, the law will recover them for the king.

II. A N O T H E R immediate conſequence of attainder is the *corruption of blood*, both upwards and downwards; ſo that an attainted perſon can neither inherit lands or other hereditaments from his anceſtors, nor retain thoſe he is already in poſſeſſion of, nor tranſmit them by deſcent to any heir; but the ſame ſhall eſcheat to the lord of the fee, ſubject to the king's ſuperior right of forfeiture: and the perſon attainted ſhall alſo obſtruct all deſcents to his poſterity, wherever they are obliged to derive a title through him to a remoter anceſtor [q].

T H I S is one of thoſe notions which our laws have adopted from the feodal conſtitutions, at the time of the Norman conqueſt; as appears from it's being unknown in thoſe tenures which are indiſputably Saxon, or gavelkind: wherein, though by treaſon, according to the antient Saxon laws, the land is forfeited to the king, yet no corruption of blood, no impediment of deſcents, enſues; and on judgment of mere felony no eſcheat accrues to the lord. And therefore, as every other oppreſſive mark of feodal tenure is now happily worn away in theſe kingdoms, it is to be hoped, that this *corruption of blood*, with all it's connected conſequences, not only of preſent eſcheat, but of future incapacities of inheritance even to the twentieth generation, may in proceſs of time be aboliſhed by act of parliament: as it ſtands upon a very different footing from the forfeiture of lands for

[q] See Vol. II. pag. 251.

high

high treaſon, affecting the king's perſon or government. And indeed the legiſlature has, from time to time, appeared very inclinable to give way to ſo equitable a proviſion; by enacting, that, in treaſons reſpecting the papal ſupremacy[r] and counterfeiting the public coin[s], and in many of the new-made felonies, created ſince the reign of Henry the eighth by act of parliament, corruption of blood ſhall be ſaved. But as in ſome of the acts for creating felonies (and thoſe not of the moſt atrocious kind) this ſaving was neglected, or forgotten, to be made, it ſeems to be highly reaſonable and expedient to antiquate the whole of this doctrine by one undiſtinguiſhing law : eſpecially as by the afore-mentioned ſtatute of 7 Ann. c. 21. (the operation of which is poſtponed by ſtatute 17 Geo. II. c. 39.) after the death of the ſons of the late pretender, no attainder for treaſon will extend to the diſinheriting any heir, nor the prejudice of any perſon, other than the offender himſelf; which virtually aboliſhes all corruption of blood for treaſon, though (unleſs the legiſlature ſhould interpoſe) it will ſtill continue for many ſorts of felony.

[r] Stat. 5 Eliz. c. 1.

[s] Stat. 5 Eliz. c. 11. 18 Eliz. c. 1. 8 & 9 W. III. c. 26. 15 & 16 Geo. II. c. 28.

CHAPTER THE THIRTIETH.

OF REVERSAL OF JUDGMENT.

WE are next to confider how judgments, with their feveral connected confequences, of attainder, forfeiture, and
corruption of blood, may be fet afide. There are two ways of
doing this ; either by falfifying or reverfing the judgment, or
elfe by reprieve or pardon.

A JUDGMENT may be falfified, reverfed, or voided, in the
firft place, *without a writ of error*, for matters foreign to or *de-
bors* the record, that is, not apparent upon the face of it ; fo that
they cannot be affigned for error in the fuperior court, which
can only judge from what appears in the record itfelf : and
therefore, if the whole record be not certified, or not truly certified, by the inferior court ; the party injured thereby (in both
civil and criminal cafes) may allege a *diminution* of the record,
and caufe it to be rectified. Thus, if any judgment whatever
be given by perfons, who had no good commiffion to proceed
againft the perfon condemned, it is void ; and may be falfified
by fhewing the fpecial matter, without writ of error. As, where
a commiffion iffues to A and B, and twelve others, or any two
of them, of which A or B fhall be one, to take and try indictments ; and any of the other twelve proceed without the interpo-

fition or prefence of either A, or B: in this cafe all proceedings, trials, convictions, and judgments are void for want of a proper authority in the commiffioners, and may be falfified upon bare infpection without the trouble of a writ of error [a]; it being a high mifdemefnor in the judges fo proceeding, and little (if any thing) fhort of murder in them all, in cafe the perfon fo attainted be executed and fuffer death. So likewife if a man purchafes land of another; and afterwards the vendor is, either by outlawry, or his own confeffion, convicted and attainted of treafon or felony previous to the fale or alienation; whereby fuch land becomes liable to forfeiture or efcheat: now, upon any trial, the purchafor is at liberty, without bringing any writ of error, to falfify not only the time of the felony or treafon fuppofed, but the very point of the felony or treafon itfelf; and is not concluded by the confeffion or the outlawry of the vendor; though the vendor himfelf is concluded, and not fuffered now to deny the fact, which he has by confeffion or flight acknowleged. But if fuch attainder of the vendor was by verdict, on the oath of his peers, the alienee cannot be received to falfify or contradict the *fact* of the crime committed; though he is at liberty to prove a miftake in *time*, or that the offence was committed after the alienation, and not before [b].

SECONDLY, a judgment may be reverfed, *by writ of error*: which lies from all inferior criminal jurifdictions to the court of king's bench, and from the king's bench to the houfe of peers; and may be brought for notorious miftakes in the judgment or other parts of the record: as where a man is found guilty of perjury and receives the judgment of felony, or for other lefs palpable errors; fuch as any irregularity, omiffion, or want of form in the procefs of outlawry, or proclamations; the want of a proper *addition* to the defendant's name, according to the ftatute of additions; for not properly naming the fheriff or other officer of the court, or not duly defcribing where his county court was held; for laying an offence, committed in the time of

[a] 2 Hawk. P. C. 459.　　　　　　[b] 3 Inft. 231.　1 Hal. P. C. 361.

the

the late king, to be done againſt the peace of the preſent; and for many other ſimilar cauſes, which (though allowed out of tenderneſs to life and liberty) are not much to the credit or advancement of the national juſtice. Theſe writs of error, to reverſe judgments in caſe of miſdemeſnors, are not to be allowed of courſe, but on ſufficient probable cauſe ſhewn to the attorney-general; and then they are underſtood to be grantable of common right, and *ex debito juſtitiae*. But writs of error to reverſe attainders in capital caſes are only allowed *ex gratia*; and not without expreſs warrant ınder the king's ſign manual, or at leaſt by the conſent of the attorney-general[c]. Theſe therefore can rarely be brought by the party himſelf, eſpecially where he is attainted for an offence againſt the ſtate: but they may be brought by his heir, or executor, after his death, in more favourable times; which may be ſome conſolation to his family. But the eaſier, and more effectual way, is

Lastly, to reverſe the attainder by act of parliament. This may be and hath been frequently done, upon motives of compaſſion, or perhaps the zeal of the times, after a ſudden revolution in the government, without examining too cloſely into the truth or validity of the errors aſſigned. And ſometimes, though the crime be univerſally acknowleged and confeſſed, yet the merits of the criminal's family ſhall after his death obtain a reſtitution in blood, honours, and eſtate, or ſome, or one of them, by act of parliament; which (ſo far as it extends) has all the effect of reverſing the attainder, without caſting any reflections upon the juſtice of the preceding ſentence.

The effect of falſifying, or reverſing, an outlawry is that the party ſhall be in the ſame plight as if he had appeared upon the *capias*: and, if it be before plea pleaded, he ſhall be put to plead to the indictment; if after conviction, he ſhall receive the ſentence of the law: for all the other proceedings, except only the proceſs of outlawry for his non-appearance, remain good and

[c] 1 Vern. 170. 175.

effectual as before. But when judgment, pronounced upon conviction, is falsified or reversed, all former proceedings are absolutely set aside, and the party stands as if he had never been at all accused; restored in his credit, his capacity, his blood, and his estates: with regard to which last, though they be granted away by the crown, yet the owner may enter upon the grantee, with as little ceremony as he might enter upon a disseisor[d]. But he still remains liable to another prosecution for the same offence: for, the first being erroneous, he never was in jeopardy thereby.

[d] 2 Hawk. P. C. 462.

Chapter the Thirty First.

Of REPRIEVE, and PARDON.

THE only other remaining ways of avoiding the execution of the judgment are by a reprieve, or a pardon; whereof the former is temporary only, the latter permanent.

I. A REPRIEVE, from *reprendre*, to take back, is the withdrawing of a sentence for an interval of time; whereby the execution is suspended. This may be, first, *ex arbitrio judicis*; either before or after judgment: as, where the judge is not satisfied with the verdict, or the evidence is suspicious, or the indictment is insufficient, or he is doubtful whether the offence be within clergy; or sometimes if it be a small felony, or any favourable circumstances appear in the criminal's character, in order to give room to apply to the crown for either an absolute or conditional pardon. These arbitrary reprieves may be granted or taken off by the justices of gaol delivery, although their session be finished, and their commission expired: but this rather by common usage, than of strict right [a].

REPRIEVES may also be *ex necessitate legis*: as, where a woman is capitally convicted, and pleads her pregnancy; though this is no cause to stay the judgment, yet it is to respite the execution till she be delivered. This is a mercy dictated by the

[a] 2 Hal. P. C. 412.

law

law of nature, *in favorem prolis*; and therefore no part of the bloody proceedings, in the reign of queen Mary, hath been more juftly detefted than the cruelty, that was exercifed in the ifland of Guernfey, of burning a woman big with child : and, when through the violence of the flames the infant fprang forth at the ftake, and was preferved by the byftanders, after fome deliberation of the priefts who affifted at the facrifice, they caft it again into the fire as a young heretic [b]. A barbarity which they never learned from the laws of *antient* Rome; which di-rect [c], with the fame humanity as our own, " *quod praegnantis* " *mulieris damnatae poena differatur, quoad pariat* :" which doc-trine has alfo prevailed in England, as early as the firft memo-rials of our law will reach [d]. In cafe this plea be made in ftay of execution, the judge muft direct a jury of twelve matrons or difcreet women to enquire the fact : and if they bring in their verdict *quick with child* (for barely, *with child*, unlefs it be alive in the womb, is not fufficient) execution fhall be ftaid generally till the next feffion; and fo from feffion to feffion, till either fhe is delivered, or proves by the courfe of nature not to have been with child at all. But if fhe once hath had the benefit of this reprieve, and been delivered, and afterwards becomes pregnant again, fhe fhall not be intitled to the benefit of a farther refpite for that caufe [e]. For fhe may now be executed before the child is quick in the womb; and fhall not, by her own incontinence, evade the fentence of juftice.

ANOTHER caufe of regular reprieve is, if the offender become *non compos*, between the judgment and the award of execution [f]: for regularly, as was formerly [g] obferved, though a man be *com-pos* when he commits a capital crime, yet if he becomes *non compos* after, he fhall not be indicted; if after indictment, he fhall not be convicted; if after conviction, he fhall not receive judgment; if after judgment, he fhall not be ordered for exe-

---

[b] Fox, Acts and Mon.
[c] *Ff*. 48. 19. 3.
[d] Flet. *l*. 1. *c*. 38.

[e] 1 Hal. P. C. 369.
[f] *Ibid*. 370.
[g] See pag. 24.

cution :

cution : for "*furiofus folo furore punitur*," and the law knows
not but he might have offered fome reafon, if in his fenfes, to
have ftayed thefe refpective proceedings. It is therefore an invariable rule, when any time intervenes between the attainder and
the award of execution, to demand of the prifoner what he
hath to allege, why execution fhould not be awarded againft
him : and, if he appears to be infane, the judge in his difcretion may and ought to reprieve him. Or, he may *plead* in bar
of execution; which plea may be either pregnancy, the king's
pardon, an act of grace, or diverfity of perfon, *viz.* that he is not
the fame that was attainted, and the like. In this laft cafe a jury
fhall be impanelled to try this collateral iffue, namely, the iden-
tity of his perfon; and not whether guilty or innocent; for that
has been decided before. And in thefe collateral iffues the trial
fhall be *inftanter*[h], and no time allowed the prifoner to make his
defence or produce his witneffes, unlefs he will make oath that
he is not the perfon attainted[i] : neither fhall any peremptory
challenges of the jury be allowed the prifoner[k]; though formerly fuch challenges were held to be allowable, whenever a
man's life was in queftion[l].

II. If neither pregnancy, infanity, non-identity, nor other
plea will avail to avoid the judgment, and ftay the execution
confequent thereupon, the laft and fureft refort is in the king's
moft gracious *pardon*; the granting of which is the moft
amiable prerogative of the crown. Laws (fays an able writer)
cannot be framed on principles of compaffion to guilt : yet juftice, by the conftitution of England, is bound to be adminiftred
in mercy : this is promifed by the king in his coronation oath,
and it is that act of his government, which is the moft perfonal,
and moft entirely his own[m]. The king himfelf condemns no
man; that rugged tafk he leaves to his courts of juftice : the
great operation of his fceptre is mercy. His power of par-

[h] 1 Sid. 72.
[i] Foft. 42.
[k] 1 Lev. 61. Foft. 42. 46.

[l] Staundf. P. C.163. Co. Litt.157. Hal.
Sum. 259.
[m] Law of Forfcit. 99.

doning

doning was faid by our Saxon anceftors[n] to be derived *a lege fuae dignitatis:* and it is declared in parliament, by ftatute 27 Hen. VIII. c. 24. that no other perfon hath power to pardon or remit any treafon or felonies whatfoever; but that the king hath the whole and fole power thereof, united and knit to the imperial crown of this realm.

THIS is indeed one of the great advantages of monarchy in general, above any other form of government; that there is a magiftrate, who has it in his power to extend mercy, wherever he thinks it is deferved : holding a court of equity in his own breaft, to foften the rigour of the general law, in fuch criminal cafes as merit an exemption from punifhment. Pardons (according to fome theorifts[o]) fhould be excluded in a perfect legiflation, where punifhments are mild but certain : for that the clemency of the prince feems a tacit difapprobation of the laws. But the exclufion of pardons muft neceffarily introduce a very dangerous power in the judge or jury, that of conftruing the criminal law by the fpirit inftead of the letter[p]; or elfe it muft be holden, what no man will ferioufly avow, that the fituation and circumftances of the offender (though they alter not the effence of the crime) ought to make no diftinction in the punifhment. In democracies, however, this power of pardon can never fubfift; for there nothing higher is acknowleged than the magiftrate who adminifters the laws : and it would be impolitic for the power of judging and of pardoning to center in one and the fame perfon. This (as the prefident Montefquieu obferves[q]) would oblige him very often to contradict himfelf, to make and to unmake his decifions : it would tend to confound all ideas of right among the mafs of the people; as they would find it difficult to tell, whether a prifoner were difcharged by his innocence, or obtained a pardon through favour. In Holland therefore, if there be no ftadtholder, there is no power of pardoning lodged in any other member of the ftate. But in monarchies the king acts in

[n] *LL. Edw. Conf. c.* 18.　　[p] *Ibid.* ch. 4.
[o] Beccar. ch. 46.　　　　　　[q] Sp. L. b. 6. c. 5.

a fupe-

a superior sphere; and, though he regulates the whole government as the first mover, yet he does not appear in any of the disagreeable or invidious parts of it. Whenever the nation see him personally engaged, it is only in works of legislature, magnificence, or compassion. To him therefore the people look up as the fountain of nothing but bounty and grace; and these repeated acts of goodness, coming immediately from his own hand, endear the sovereign to his subjects, and contribute more than any thing to root in their hearts that filial affection, and personal loyalty, which are the sure establishment of a prince.

UNDER this head, of pardons, let us briefly consider, 1. The *object* of pardon: 2. The *manner* of pardoning: 3. The method of *allowing* a pardon: 4. The *effect* of such pardon, when allowed.

1. AND, first, the king may pardon all offences merely against the crown, or the public; excepting, 1. That, to preserve the liberty of the subject, the committing any man to prison out of the realm, is by the *habeas corpus* act, 31 Car. II. c. 2. made a *praemunire*, unpardonable even by the king. Nor, 2. Can the king pardon, where private justice is principally concerned in the prosecution of offenders: "*non potest rex gratiam facere* "*cum injuria et damno aliorum*ʳ." Therefore in appeals of all kinds (which are the suit, not of the king, but of the party injured) the prosecutor may release, but the king cannot pardonˢ. Neither can he pardon a common nusance, while it remains unredressed, or so as to prevent an abatement of it; though afterwards he may remit the fine: because, though the prosecution is vested in the king to avoid multiplicity of suits, yet (during it's continuance) this offence favours more of the nature of a *private* injury to each individual in the neighbourhood, than of a *public* wrongᵗ. Neither, lastly, can the king pardon an offence against a popular or penal statute, after information brought:

ʳ 3 Inst. 236.   ᵗ 2 Hawk. P. C. 391.
ˢ *Ibid.* 237.

for thereby the informer hath acquired a private property in his part of the penalty [u].

THERE is also a restriction of a peculiar nature, that affects the prerogative of pardoning, in case of parliamentary impeachments ; viz. that the king's pardon cannot be *pleaded* to any such impeachment, so as to impede the inquiry, and stop the prosecution of great and notorious offenders. Therefore when, in the reign of Charles the second, the earl of Danby was impeached by the house of commons of high treason and other misdemesnors, and pleaded the king's pardon in bar of the same, the commons alleged [w], " that there was no precedent, that ever any pardon " was granted to any person impeached by the commons of high " treason, or other high crimes, *depending the impeachment* ;" and therefore resolved [x], " that the pardon so pleaded was illegal and " void, and ought not to be allowed *in bar* of the impeachment " of the commons of England :" for which resolution they as- signed [y] this reason to the house of lords, " that the setting up a " pardon to be a *bar* of an impeachment defeats the whole use " and effect of impeachments : for should this point be admit- " ted, or stand doubted, it would totally discourage the exhibit- " ing any for the future ; whereby the chief institution for the " preservation of the government would be destroyed." Soon after the revolution, the commons renewed the same claim, and voted [z], " that a pardon is not *pleadable in bar* of an impeach- " ment." And, at length, it was enacted by the act of settle- ment, 12 & 13 W.III. c. 2. " that no pardon under the great seal of " England shall be *pleadable* to an impeachment by the commons " in parliament." But, after the impeachment has been solemnly heard and determined, it is not understood that the king's royal grace is farther restrained or abridged : for, after the impeach- ment and attainder of the six rebel lords in 1715, three of them

[u] 3 Inst. 238.
[w] Com. Journ. 28 Apr. 1679.
[x] *Ibid.* 5 May 1679.

[y] *Ibid.* 26 May 1679.
[z] *Ibid.* 6 Jun. 1689.

were

were from time to time reprieved by the crown, and at length received the benefit of the king's moſt gracious pardon.

2. A s to the *manner* of pardoning : it is a general rule, that, wherever it may reaſonably be preſumed the king is deceived, the pardon is void[a]. Therefore any ſuppreſſion of truth, or ſuggeſtion of falſhood, in a charter of pardon, will vitiate the whole; for the king was miſinformed[b]. General words have alſo a very imperfect effect in pardons. A pardon of all felonies will not pardon a conviction or attainder of felony; (for it is preſumed the king knew not of thoſe proceedings) but the conviction or attainder muſt be particularly mentioned[c]: and a pardon of felonies will not include piracy[d]; for that is no felony puniſhable at the common law. It is alſo enacted by ſtatute 13 Ric. II. ſt. 2. c. 1. that no pardon for treaſon, murder, or rape, ſhall be allowed, unleſs the offence be particularly ſpecified therein; and particularly in murder it ſhall be expreſſed, whether it was committed by lying in wait, aſſault, or malice prepenſe. Upon which ſir Edward Coke obſerves[e], that it was not the intention of the parliament that the king ſhould ever pardon murder under theſe aggravations; and therefore they prudently laid the pardon under theſe reſtrictions, becauſe they did not conceive it poſſible that the king would ever excuſe an offence by name, which was attended with ſuch high aggravations. And it is remarkable enough, that there is no precedent of a pardon in the regiſter for any other homicide, than that which happens *ſe defendendo* or *per infortunium:* to which two ſpecies the king's pardon was expreſſly confined by the ſtatutes 2 Edw. III. c. 2. and 14 Edw. III. c. 15. which declare that no pardon of homicide ſhall be granted, but only where the king may do it *by the oath of his crown*; that is to ſay, where a man ſlayeth another in his own defence, or by misfortune. But the ſtatute of Richard the ſecond, before-mentioned, enlarges by implication the royal power; provided the king is not deceived in the intended object

---

[a] 2 Hawk. P. C. 383.
[b] 3 Inſt. 238.
[c] 2 Hawk. P. C. 383.

[d] 1 Hawk. P. C 99.
[e] 3 Inſt. 236.

of his mercy. And therefore pardons of murder were always granted with a *non obſtante* of the ſtatute of king Richard, till the time of the revolution ; when, the doctrine of *non obſtante*'s ceaſing, it was doubted whether murder could be pardoned generally : but it was determined by the court of king's bench [f], that the king may pardon on an indictment of murder, as well as a ſubject may diſcharge an appeal. Under theſe and a few other reſtrictions, it is a general rule, that a pardon ſhall be taken moſt beneficially *for* the ſubject, and moſt ſtrongly *againſt* the king.

A PARDON may alſo be *conditional :* that is, the king may extend his mercy upon what terms he pleaſes ; and may annex to his bounty a condition either precedent or ſubſequent, on the performance whereof the validity of the pardon will depend : and this by the common law [g]. Which prerogative is daily exerted in the pardon of felons, on condition of tranſportation to ſome foreign country (uſually to ſome of his majeſty's colonies and plantations in America) for life, or for a term of years ; ſuch tranſportation or baniſhment [h] being allowable and warranted by the *habeas corpus* act, 31 Car. II. c. 2. §. 14. and rendered more eaſy and effectual by ſtatute 8 Geo. III. c. 15.

3. WITH regard to the manner of *allowing* pardons ; we may obſerve, that a pardon by act of parliament is more beneficial than by the king's charter : for a man is not bound to plead it, but the court muſt *ex officio* take notice of it [i] ; neither can he loſe the benefit of it by his own *laches* or negligence, as he may of the king's charter of pardon [k]. The king's charter of pardon muſt be ſpecially pleaded, and that at a proper time : for if a man is indicted, and has a pardon in his pocket, and afterwards puts himſelf upon his trial by pleading the general iſſue, he has waived the benefit of ſuch pardon [l]. But, if a man avails himſelf

[f] Salk. 499.

[g] 2 Hawk. P. C. 394.

[h] Tranſportation is ſaid (Barr. 352.) to have been firſt inflicted, as a puniſhment,

by ſtatute 39 Eliz. c. 4.

[i] Foſt. 43.

[k] 2 Hawk. P. C. 397.

[l] *Ibid.* 396.

thereof

thereof as foon as by courfe of law he may, a pardon may either
be pleaded upon arraignment, or in arreft of judgment, or in
the prefent ftage of proceedings, in bar of execution. Antiently,
by ftatute 10 Edw. III. c. 2. no pardon of felony could be allowed, unlefs the party found fureties for the good behaviour
before the fheriff and coroners of the county [m]. But that ftatute
is repealed by the ftatute 5 & 6 W. & M. c. 13. which, inftead
thereof, gives the judges of the court a difcretionary power to
bind the criminal, pleading fuch pardon, to his good behaviour,
with two fureties, for any term not exceeding feven years.

4. LASTLY, the *effect* of fuch pardon by the king, is to
make the offender a new man ; to acquit him of all corporal
penalties and forfeitures annexed to that offence for which he
obtains his pardon ; and not fo much to reftore his former, as
to give him a new, credit and capacity. But nothing can reftore
or purify the blood when once corrupted, if the pardon be not
allowed till after attainder, but the high and tranfcendent power
of parliament. Yet if a perfon attainted receives the king's pardon, and afterwards hath a fon, that fon may be heir to his father ; becaufe the father, being made a new man, might tranfmit new inheritable blood : though, had he been born before
the pardon, he could never have inherited at all [n].

[m] Salk. 499.   [n] See Vol. II. pag. 254.

C H A P T E R   T H E   T H I R T Y   S E C O N D.

O f   E X E C U T I O N.

THERE now remains nothing to fpeak of, but *execution*; the completion of human punifhment. And this, in all cafes, as well capital as otherwife, muft be performed by the legal officer, the fheriff or his deputy; whofe warrant for fo doing was antiently by precept under the hand and feal of the judge, as it is ftill practifed in the court of the lord high fteward, upon the execution of a peer[a]: though, in the court of the peers in parliament, it is done by writ from the king[b]. Afterwards it was eftablifhed[c], that, in cafe of life, the judge may command execution to be done without any writ. And now the ufage is, for the judge to fign the calendar, or lift of all the prifoners' names, with their feparate judgments in the margin, which is left with the fheriff. As, for a capital felony, it is written oppofite to the prifoner's name, " hanged by the " neck ;" formerly, in the days of Latin and abbreviation[d], " *fuf. per coll.*" for " *fufpendatur per collum.*" And this is the only warrant that the fheriff has, for fo material an act as taking away the life of another[e]. It may certainly afford matter of fpeculation, that in civil caufes there fhould be fuch a variety of writs of execution to recover a trifling debt, iffued in the king's

---

[a] 2 Hal. P. C. 409.
[b] See appendix. §. 5.
[c] Finch. L. 478.

[d] Staundf. P. C. 182.
[e] 5 Mod. 22.

name,

name, and under the feal of the court, without which the fheriff cannot legally ftir one ftep; and yet that the execution of a man, the moft important and terrible tafk of any, fhould depend upon a marginal note.

THE fheriff, upon receipt of his warrant, is to do execution within a convenient time; which in the country is aifo left at large. In London indeed a more folemn and becoming exactnefs is ufed, both as to the warrant of execution, and the time of executing thereof: for the recorder, after reporting to the king in perfon the cafe of the feveral prifoners, and receiving his royal pleafure, that the law muft take it's courfe, iffues his warrant to the fheriffs; directing them to do execution on the day and at the place affigned [f]. And, in the court of king's bench, if the prifoner be tried at the bar, or brought there by *habeas corpus*, a rule is made for his execution; either fpecifying the time and place [g], or leaving it to the difcretion of the fheriff [h]. And, throughout the kingdom, by ftatute 25 Geo. II. c. 37. it is enacted that, in cafe of murder, the judge fhall in his fentence direct execution to be performed on the next day but one after fentence paffed [i]. It has been well obferved [k], that it is of great importance, that the punifhment fhould follow the crime as early as poffible; that the profpect of gratification or advantage, which tempts a man to commit the crime, fhould inftantly awake the attendant idea of punifhment. Delay of execution ferves only to feparate thefe ideas; and then the execution itfelf affects the minds of the fpectators rather as a terrible fight, than as the neceffary confequence of tranfgreffion.

THE fheriff cannot alter the manner of the execution by fubftituting one death for another, without being guilty of felony himfelf, as has been formerly faid [l]. It is held alfo by fir Ed-

[f] See appendix, §. 4.
[g] St. Trials. VI. 332. Fost. 43.
[h] See appendix, §. 3.

[i] See pag. 202.
[k] Beccar. ch. 19.
[l] See pag. 179.

ward

ward Coke[m] and fir Matthew Hale[n], that even the king cannot change the punifhment of the law, by altering the hanging or burning into beheading; though, when beheading is part of the fentence, the king may remit the reft. And, notwithftanding fome examples to the contrary, fir Edward Coke ftoutly maintains, that "*judicandum eft legibus, non exemplis.*" But others have thought[o], and more juftly, that this prerogative, being founded in mercy and immemorially exercifed by the crown, is part of the common law. For hitherto, in every inftance, all thefe exchanges have been for more merciful kinds of death; and how far this may alfo fall within the king's power of granting conditional pardons, (*viz.* by remitting a fevere kind of death, on condition that the criminal fubmits to a milder) is a matter that may bear confideration. It is obfervable, that when lord Stafford was executed for the popifh plot in the reign of king Charles the fecond, the then fheriffs of London, having received the king's writ for beheading him, petitioned the houfe of lords, for a command or order from their lordfhips, how the faid judgment fhould be executed: for, he being profecuted by impeachment, they entertained a notion (which is faid to have been countenanced by lord Ruffel) that the king could not pardon any part of the fentence[p]. The lords refolved[q], that the fcruples of the fheriffs were unneceffary, and declared, that the king's writ ought to be obeyed. Difappointed of raifing a flame in that affembly, they immediately fignified[r] to the houfe of commons by one of the members, that they were not fatisfied as to the power of the faid writ. That houfe took two days to confider of it; and then[s] fullenly refolved, that the houfe was *content* that the fheriff do execute lord Stafford by fevering his head from his body. It is farther related, that when afterwards the fame lord Ruffel was condemned for high treafon upon indictment, the king, while he remitted the ignominious part of the

[m] 3 Inft. 52.
[n] 2 Hal. P. C. 412.
[o] Foft. 270.
[p] 2 Hume Hift. of G. B. 328.

[q] Lords Journ. 21 Dec. 1680.
[r] Com. Journ. 21 Dec. 1680.
[s] *Ibid.* 23 Dec. 1680.

fentence,

sentence, obferved, " that his lordfhip would now find he was
" poffeffed of that prerogative, which in the cafe of lord Staf-
" ford he had denied him ʰ." One can hardly determine (at this
diftance from thofe turbulent times) which moft to difapprove
of, the indecent and fanguinary zeal of the fubject, or the cool
and cruel farcafm of the fovereign.

To conclude : it is clear, that if, upon judgment to be hanged
by the neck till he is dead, the criminal be not thoroughly killed, but revives, the fheriff muft hang him again ᵘ. For the
former hanging was no execution of the fentence; and, if a falfe
tendernefs were to be indulged in fuch cafes, a multitude of col-
lufions might enfue. Nay, even while abjurations were in force ʷ,
fuch a criminal, fo reviving, was not allowed to take fanctuary
and abjure the realm; but his fleeing to fanctuary was held an
efcape in the officer ˣ.

AND, having thus arrived at the *laft* ftage of criminal proceedings, or execution, the end and completion of human *punifhment*, which was the fixth and laft head to be confidered under
the divifion of *public wrongs*, the fourth and laft object of the
laws of England; it may now feem high time to put a period to
thefe commentaries, which, the author is very fenfible, have already
fwelled to too great a length. But he cannot difmifs the ftudent,
for whofe ufe alone thefe rudiments were originally compiled,
without endeavouring to recal to his memory fome principal
outlines of the legal conftitution of this country; by a fhort hif-
torical review of the moft confiderable revolutions, that have
happened in the laws of England, from the earlieft to the prefent times. And this tafk he will attempt to difcharge, however
imperfectly, in the next or concluding chapter.

ᵗ 2 Hume. 360.
ᵘ 2 Hal. P. C. 412. 2 Hawk. P. C. 463.
ʷ See pag. 326.
ˣ Fitzh. *Abr. t. corone.* 335. Finch. L. 46ᵐ.

CHAPTER THE THIRTY THIRD.

OF THE RISE, PROGRESS, AND GRADUAL IMPROVEMENTS, OF THE LAWS OF ENGLAND.

BEFORE we enter on the subject of this chapter, in which I propose, by way of supplement to the whole, to attempt an historical review of the most remarkable changes and alterations, that have happened in the laws of England, I must first of all remind the student, that the rise and progress of many principal points and doctrines have been already pointed out in the course of these commentaries, under their respective divisions: these having therefore been particularly discussed already, it cannot be expected that I should re-examine them with any degree of minuteness; which would be a most tedious undertaking. What I therefore at present propose, is only to mark out some outlines of an English juridical history, by taking a chronological view of the state of our laws, and their successive mutations at different periods of time.

THE several periods, under which I shall consider the state of our legal polity, are the following six: 1. From the earliest times to the Norman conquest: 2. From the Norman conquest to the reign of king Edward the first: 3. From thence to the refor-

reformation : 4. From the reformation to the reſtoration of king
Charles the ſecond : 5. From thence to the revolution in 1688 :
6. From the revolution to the preſent time.

I. A N D, firſt, with regard to the antient Britons, the *abori-
gines* of our iſland, we have ſo little handed down to us concerning them with any tolerable certainty, that our enquiries
here muſt needs be very fruitleſs and defective. However, from
Caeſar's account of the tenets and diſcipline of the antient
Druids in Gaul, in whom centered all the learning of theſe
weſtern parts, and who were, as he tells us, ſent over to Britain,
(that is, to the iſland of Mona or Angleſey) to be inſtructed ; we
may collect a few points, which bear a great affinity and reſemblance to ſome of the modern doctrines of our Engliſh law.
Particularly, the very notion itſelf of an oral unwritten law, delivered down from age to age, by cuſtom and tradition merely,
ſeems derived from the practice of the Druids, who never committed any of their inſtructions to writing : poſſibly for want of
letters ; ſince it is remarkable that in all the antiquities, unqueſtionably Britiſh, which the induſtry of the moderns has diſcovered, there is not in any of them the leaſt trace of any character or letter to be found. The partible quality alſo of lands,
by the cuſtom of gavelkind, which ſtill obtains in many parts
of England, and did univerſally over Wales till the reign of
Henry VIII, is undoubtedly of Britiſh original. So likewiſe is
the antient diviſion of the goods of an inteſtate between his
widow and children, or next of kin ; which has ſince been revived by the ſtatute of diſtributions. And we may alſo remember an inſtance of a ſlighter nature mentioned in the preſent volume ; where the ſame cuſtom has continued from Caeſar's time
to the preſent, that of burning a woman guilty of the crime of
petit treaſon by killing her huſband.

T H E great variety of nations, that ſucceſſively broke in upon,
and deſtroyed both the Britiſh inhabitants and conſtitution, the

Romans, the Picts, and, after them, the various clans of Saxons and Danes, must necessarily have caused great confusion and uncertainty in the laws and antiquities of the kingdom; as they were very soon incorporated and blended together, and therefore, we may suppose, mutually communicated to each other their respective usages[a], in regard to the rights of property and the punishment of crimes. So that it is morally impossible to trace out, with any degree of accuracy, *when* the several mutations of the common law were made, or what was the respective original of those several customs we at present use, by any chemical resolution of them to their first and component principles. We can seldom pronounce, that *this* custom was derived from the Britons; *that* was left behind by the Romans; *this* was a necessary precaution against the Picts; *that* was introduced by the Saxons, discontinued by the Danes, but afterwards restored by the Normans.

WHEREVER this can be done, it is matter of great curiosity, and some use: but this can very rarely be the case; not only from the reason above-mentioned, but also from many others. First, from the nature of traditional laws in general; which, being accommodated to the exigences of the times, suffer by degrees insensible variations in practice[b]: so that, though upon comparison we plainly discern the alteration of the law from what it was five hundred years ago, yet it is impossible to define the precise period in which that alteration accrued, any more than we can discern the changes of the bed of a river, which varies it's shores by continual decreases and alluvions. Secondly, this becomes impracticable from the antiquity of the kingdom and it's government: which alone, though it had been disturbed by no foreign invasions, would make it an impossible thing to search out the original of it's laws; unless we had as authentic monuments thereof, as the Jews had by the hand of Moses[c].

[a] Hal. Hist. C. L. 62.   [c] Ibid. 59.
[b] Ibid. 57.

Thirdly,

Thirdly, this uncertainty of the true origin of particular cuftoms muft alfo in part have arifen from the means, whereby chriftianity was propagated among our Saxon anceftors in this ifland ; by learned foreigners brought over from Rome and other countries : who undoubtedly carried with them many of their own national cuftoms ; and probably prevailed upon the ftate to abrogate fuch ufages as were inconfiftent with our holy religion, and to introduce many others that were more conformable thereto. And this perhaps may have partly been the caufe, that we find not only fome rules of the mofaical, but alfo of the imperial and pontificial laws, blended and adopted into our own fyftem.

A FARTHER reafon may alfo be given for the great variety, and of courfe the uncertain original, of our antient eftablifhed cuftoms ; even after the Saxon government was firmly eftablifhed in this ifland : viz. the fubdivifion of the kingdom into an heptarchy, confifting of feven independent kingdoms, peopled and governed by different clans and colonies. This muft neceffarily create an infinite diverfity of laws : even though all thofe colonies, of Jutes, Angles, proper Saxons, and the like, originally fprung from the fame mother country, the great northern hive; which poured forth it's warlike progeny, and fwarmed all over Europe, in the fixth and feventh centuries. This multiplicity of laws will neceffarily be the cafe in fome degree, where any kingdom is cantoned out into provincial eftablifhments ; and not under one common difpenfation of laws, though under the fame fovereign power. Much more will it happen, where feven unconnected ftates are to form their own conftitution and fuperftructure of government, though they all begin to build upon the fame or fimilar foundations.

WHEN therefore the Weft-Saxons had fwallowed up all the reft, and king Alfred fucceeded to the monarchy of England, whereof his grandfather Egbert was the founder, his mighty genius prompted him to undertake a moft great and neceffary work, which he is faid to have executed in as mafterly a manner.

No lefs than to new-model the conftitution ; to rebuild it on a plan that fhould endure for ages ; and, out of it's old difcordant materials, which were heaped upon each other in a vaft and rude irregularity, to form one uniform and well connected whole. This he effected, by reducing the whole kingdom under one re-gular and gradual fubordination of government, wherein each man was anfwerable to his immediate fuperior for his own con-duct and that of his neareft neighbours : for to him we owe that mafterpiece of judicial polity, the fubdivifion of England into tithings, and hundreds, if not into counties ; all under the in-fluence and adminiftration of one fupreme magiftrate, the king ; in whom, as in a general refervoir, all the executive authority of the law was lodged, and from whom juftice was difperfed to every part of the nation by diftinct, yet communicating, ducts and chanels : which wife inftitution has been preferved for near a thoufand years unchanged, from Alfred's to the prefent time. He alfo, like another Theodofius, collected the various cuftoms that he found difperfed in the kingdom, and reduced and di-gefted them into one uniform fyftem or code of laws, in his bom-bec, or *liber judicialis*. This he compiled for the ufe of the court-baron, hundred, and county court, the court-leet, and fhe-riff's tourn ; tribunals, which he eftablifhed, for the trial of all caufes civil and criminal, in the very diftricts wherein the com-plaint arofe : all of them fubject however to be infpected, con-trolled, and kept within the bounds of the univerfal or common law, by the king's own courts ; which were then itinerant, be-ing kept in the king's palace, and removing with his houfhold in thofe royal progreffes, which he continually made from one end of the kingdom to the other.

T H E Danifh invafion and conqueft, which introduced new foreign cuftoms, was a fevere blow to this noble fabric : but a plan, fo excellently concerted, could never be long thrown afide. So that, upon the expulfion of thefe intruders, the Englifh re-turned to their antient law : retaining however fome few of the cuftoms of their late vifitants ; which went under the name of

Dane

Dane-Lage: as the code compiled by Alfred was called the *Weſt-Saxon-Lage*; and the local conſtitutions of the antient kingdom of Mercia, which obtained in the counties neareſt to Wales, and probably abounded with many Britiſh cuſtoms, were called the *Mercen-Lage.* And theſe three laws were, about the beginning of the eleventh century, in uſe in different counties of the realm : the provincial polity of counties, and their ſubdiviſions, having never been altered or diſcontinued through all the ſhocks and mutations of government, from the time of it's firſt inſtitution ; though the laws and cuſtoms therein uſed, have (as we ſhall ſee) often ſuffered conſiderable changes.

FOR king Edgar, (who beſides his military merit, as founder of the Engliſh navy, was alſo a moſt excellent civil governor) obſerving the ill effects of three diſtinct bodies of laws, prevailing at once in ſeparate parts of his dominions, projected and begun, what his grandſon king Edward the confeſſor afterwards completed ; *viz.* one uniform digeſt or body of laws, to be obſerved throughout the whole kingdom : being probably no more than a revival of king Alfred's code, with ſome improvements ſuggeſted by neceſſity and experience ; particularly the incorporating ſome of the Britiſh or rather Mercian cuſtoms, and alſo ſuch of the Daniſh as were reaſonable and approved, into the *Weſt-Saxon-Lage*, which was ſtill the groundwork of the whole. And this appears to me the beſt ſupported and moſt plauſible conjecture (for certainty is not to be expected) of the riſe and original of that admirable ſyſtem of maxims and unwritten cuſtoms, which is now known by the name of the *common* law, as extending it's authority univerſally over all the realm ; and which is doubtleſs of Saxon parentage.

AMONG the moſt remarkable of the Saxon laws we may reckon, 1. The conſtitution of parliaments, or rather, general aſſemblies of the principal and wiſeſt men in the nation ; the *wittena-gemote,* or *commune concilium* of the antient Germans ; which was not yet reduced to the forms and diſtinctions of our

modern

modern parliament: without whofe concurrence however, no new law could be made, or old one altered. 2. The election of their magiftrates by the people; originally even that of their kings, till dearbought experience evinced the convenience and neceffity of eftablifhing an hereditary fucceffion to the crown. But that of all fubordinate magiftrates, their military officers or heretochs, their fheriffs, their confervators of the peace, their coroners, their port-reeves, (fince changed into mayors and bailiffs) and even their tythingmen and borfholders at the leet, continued, fome till the Norman conqueft, others for two centuries after, and fome remain to this day. 3. The defcent of the crown, when once a royal family was eftablifhed, upon nearly the fame hereditary principles upon which it has ever fince continued: only that perhaps, in cafe of minority, the next of kin of full age would afcend the throne, as king, and not as protector; though, after his death, the crown immediately reverted back to the heir. 4. The great paucity of capital punifhments for the firft offence: even the moft notorious offenders being allowed to commute it for a fine or *weregild*, or, in default of payment, perpetual bondage; to which our benefit of clergy has now in fome meafure fucceeded. 5. The prevalence of certain cuftoms, as heriots and military fervices in proportion to every man's land, which much refembled the feodal conftitution; but yet were exempt from all it's rigorous hardfhips: and which may be well enough accounted for, by fuppofing them to be brought from the continent by the firft Saxon invaders, in the primitive moderation and fimplicity of the feodal law; before it got into the hands of the Norman jurifts, who extracted the moft flavifh doctrines, and oppreffive confequences, out of what was originally intended as a law of liberty. 6. That their eftates were liable to forfeiture for treafon, but that the doctrine of efcheats and corruption of blood for felony, or any other caufe, was utterly unknown amongft them. 7. The defcent of their lands was to all the males equally, without any right of primogeniture; a cuftom, which obtained among the Britons, was agreeable to the Roman law, and continued among the Saxons

till

till the Norman conqueſt : though really inconvenient, and more
eſpecially deſtructive to antient families; which are in monarchies
neceſſary to be ſupported, in order to form and keep up a nobility,
or intermediate ſtate between the prince and the common people.
8. The courts of juſtice conſiſted principally of the county
courts, and in caſes of weight or nicety the king's courts held
before himſelf in perſon, at the time of his parliaments; which
were uſually holden in different places, according as he kept the
three great feſtivals of chriſtmas, eaſter, and whitſuntide.　An
inſtitution which was adopted by king Alonſo VII of Caſtile about
a century after the conqueſt : who at the ſame three great feaſts
was wont to aſſemble his nobility and prelates in his court; who
there heard and decided all controverſies, and then, having received
his inſtructions, departed home[d].　Theſe county courts however
differed from the modern ones, in that the eccleſiaſtical and civil
juriſdiction were blended together, the biſhop and the ealdor-
man or ſheriff ſitting in the ſame county court; and alſo that
the deciſions and proceedings therein were much more ſimple
and unembarraſſed : an advantage which will always attend the
infancy of any laws, but wear off as they gradually advance to
antiquity.　9. Trials, among a people who had a very ſtrong
tincture of ſuperſtition, were permitted to be by *ordeal*, by the
corſned or morſel of execration, or by *wager of law* with compurgators, if the party choſe it; but frequently they were alſo
by *jury*: for, whether or no their juries conſiſted preciſely of
twelve men, or were bound to a ſtrict unanimity; yet the general conſtitution of this admirable criterion of truth, and moſt
important guardian both of public and private liberty, we owe
to our Saxon anceſtors.　Thus ſtood the general frame of our
polity at the time of the Norman invaſion; when the ſecond
period of our legal hiſtory commences.

II. This remarkable event wrought as great an alteration in our
laws, as it did in our antient line of kings : and, though the alteration of the former was effected rather by the conſent of the people,

[d] Mod. Un. Hiſt. xx. 114.

than

than any right of conqueft, yet that confent feems to have been partly extorted by fear, and partly given without any apprehenfion of the confequences which afterwards enfued.

1. AMONG the firft of thefe alterations we may reckon the feparation of the ecclefiaftical courts from the civil: effected in order to ingratiate the new king with the popifh clergy, who for fome time before had been endeavouring all over Europe to exempt themfelves from the fecular power; and whofe demands the conqueror, like a politic prince, thought it prudent to comply with, by reafon that their reputed fanctity had a great influence over the minds of the people; and becaufe all the little learning of the times was engroffed into their hands, which made them neceffary men, and by all means to be gained over to his interefts. And this was the more eafily effected, becaufe, the difpofal of all the epifcopal fees being then in the breaft of the king, he had taken care to fill them with Italian and Norman prelates.

2. ANOTHER violent alteration of the Englifh conftitution confifted in the depopulation of whole countries, for the purpofes of the king's royal diverfion; and fubjecting both them, and all the antient forefts of the kingdom, to the unreafonable feverities of foreft laws imported from the continent, whereby the flaughter of a beaft was made almoft as penal as the death of a man. In the Saxon times, though no man was allowed to kill or chafe the king's deer, yet he might ftart any game, purfue, and kill it, upon his own eftate. But the rigour of thefe new conftitutions vefted the fole property of all the game in England in the king alone; and no man was entitled to difturb any fowl of the air, or any beaft of the field, of fuch kinds as were fpecially referved for the royal amufement of the fovereign, without exprefs licence from the king, by a grant of a chafe or free warren: and thofe franchifes were granted as much with a view to preferve the breed of animals, as to indulge the fubject. From a fimilar principle to which, though the foreft

laws

laws are now mitigated, and by degrees grown intirely obfolete, yet from this root has fprung a baftard flip, known by the name of the game law, now arrived to and wantoning in it's higheft vigour: both founded upon the fame unreafonable notions of permanent property in wild creatures; and both productive of the fame tyranny to the commons: but with this difference; that the foreft laws eftablifhed only one mighty hunter through-out the land, the game laws have raifed a little Nimrod in every manor. And in one refpect the antient law was much lefs unreafonable than the modern: for the king's grantee of a chafe or free-warren might kill game in every part of his fran-chife; but now, though a freeholder of lefs than 100 *l.* a year is forbidden to kill a partridge upon his own eftate, yet nobody elfe (not even the lord of the manor, unlefs he hath a grant of free-warren) can do it without committing a trefpafs, and fub-jecting himfelf to an action.

3. A THIRD alteration in the Englifh laws was by narrow-ing the remedial influence of the county courts, the great feats of Saxon juftice, and extending the *original* jurifdiction of the king's jufticiars to all kinds of caufes, arifing in all parts of the kingdom. To this end the *cula regis*, with all it's multifarious authority, was erected; and a capital jufticiary appointed, with powers fo large and boundlefs, that he became at length a tyrant to the people, and formidable to the crown itfelf. The confti-tution of this court, and the judges themfelves who prefided there, were fetched from the duchy of Normandy: and the con-fequence naturally was, the ordaining that all proceedings in the king's courts fhould be carried on in the Norman, inftead of the Englifh, language. A provifion the more neceffary, becaufe none of his Norman jufticiars underftood Englifh; but as evi-dent a badge of flavery, as ever was impofed upon a conquered people. This lafted till king Edward the third obtained a double victory, over the armies of France in their own country, and their language in our courts here at home. But there was one mifchief too deeply rooted thereby, and which this caution of

king Edward came too late to eradicate. Inftead of the plain
and eafy method of determining fuits in the county courts, the
chicanes and fubtilties of Norman jurifprudence had taken poffeffion of the king's courts, to which every caufe of confequence
was drawn. Indeed that age, and thofe immediately fucceeding it,
were the aera of refinement and fubtilty. There is an active principle in the human foul, that will ever be exerting it's faculties to
the utmoft ftretch, in whatever employment, by the accidents of
time and place, the general plan of education, or the cuftoms and
manners of the age and country, it may happen to find itfelf engaged. The northern conquerors of Europe were then emerg-
ing from the groffeft ignorance in point of literature; and thofe,
who had leifure to cultivate it's progrefs, were fuch only as were
cloiftered in monafteries, the reft being all foldiers or pea-
fants. And, unfortunately, the firft rudiments of fcience which
they imbibed were thofe of Ariftotle's philofophy, conveyed
through the medium of his Arabian commentators; which were
brought from the eaft by the Saracens into Paleftine and Spain,
and tranflated into barbarous Latin. So that, though the materials
upon which they were naturally employed, in the infancy of a
rifing ftate, were thofe of the nobleft kind; the eftablifhment
of religion, and the regulations of civil polity; yet, having only
fuch tools to work with, their execution was trifling and flimfey.
Both the divinity and the law of thofe times were therefore frit-
tered into logical diftinctions, and drawn out into metaphyfical
fubtilties, with a fkill moft amazingly artificial; but which
ferves no other purpofe, than to fhew the vaft powers of the
human intellect, however vainly or prepofteroufly employed.
Hence law in particular, which (being intended for univerfal
reception) ought to be a plain rule of action, became a fcience
of the greateft intricacy; efpecially when blended with the new
refinements engrafted upon feodal property: which refinements
were from time to time gradually introduced by the Norman
practitioners, with a view to fuperfede (as they did in great meafure) the more homely, but more intelligible, maxims of diftri-
butive juftice among the Saxons. And, to fay the truth, thefe

fcholaftic

scholaftic reformers have tranfmitted their dialect and fineffes to pofterity, fo interwoven in the body of our legal polity, that they cannot now be taken out without a manifeft injury to the fub-ftance. Statute after ftatute has in later times been made, to pare off thefe troublefome excrefcences, and reftore the common law to it's priftine fimplicity and vigour; and the endeavour has greatly fucceeded : but ftill the fcars are deep and vifible ; and the liberality of our modern courts of juftice is frequently obliged to have recourfe to unaccountable fictions and circuities, in order to recover that equitable and fubftantial juftice, which for a long time was totally buried under the narrow rules and fanciful niceties of metaphyfical and Norman jurifprudence.

4. A FOURTH innovation was the introduction of the trial by combat, for the decifion of all civil and criminal queftions of fact in the laft refort. This was the immemorial practice of all the northern nations; but firft reduced to regular and ftated forms among the Burgundi, about the clofe of the fifth century : and from them it paffed to other nations, particularly the Franks and the Normans; which laft had the honour to eftablifh it here, though clearly an unchriftian, as well as moft uncertain, me-thod of trial. But it was a fufficient recommendation of it to the conqueror and his warlike countrymen, that it was the ufage of their native duchy of Normandy.

5. BUT the laft and moft important alteration, both in our civil and military polity, was the engrafting on all landed eftates, a few only excepted, the fiction of feodal tenure; which drew after it a numerous and oppreffive train of fervile fruits and ap-pendages ; aids, reliefs, primer feifins, wardfhips, marriages, efcheats, and fines for alienation ; the genuine confequences of the maxim then adopted, that all the lands in England were de-rived from, and holden, mediately or immediately, of the crown.

THE nation at this period feems to have groaned under as ab-folute a flavery, as was in the power of a warlike, an ambitious,

and

and a politic prince to create. The confciences of men were enflaved by four ecclefiaftics, devoted to a foreign power, and unconnected with the civil ftate under which they lived : who now imported from Rome for the firft time the whole *farrago* of fuperftitious novelties, which had been engendered by the blindnefs and corruption of the times, between the firft miffion of Auguftin the monk, and the Norman conqueft; fuch as tranfubftantiation, purgatory, communion in one kind, and the worfhip of faints and images; not forgetting the univerfal fupremacy and dogmatical infallibility of the holy fee. The laws too, as well as the prayers, were adminiftered in an unknown tongue. The antient trial by jury gave way to the impious decifion by battel. The foreft laws totally reftrained all rural pleafures and manly recreations. And in cities and towns the cafe was no better; all company being obliged to difperfe, and fire and candle to be extinguifhed, by eight at night, at the found of the melancholy *curfeu*. The ultimate property of all lands, and a confiderable fhare out of the prefent profits, were vefted in the king, or by him granted out to his Norman favourites; who, by a gradual progreffion of flavery, were abfolute vafals to the crown, and as abfolute tyrants to the commons. Unheard of forfeitures, talliages, aids, and fines, were arbitrarily extracted from the pillaged landholders, in purfuance of the new fyftem of tenure. And, to crown all, as a confequence of the tenure by knightfervice, the king had always ready at his command an army of fixty thoufand knights or *milites :* who were bound, upon pain of confifcating their eftates, to attend him in time of invafion, or to quell any domeftic infurrection. Trade, or foreign merchandize, fuch as it then was, was carried on by the Jews and Lombards; and the very name of an Englifh fleet, which king Edgar had rendered fo formidable, was utterly unknown to Europe : the nation confifting wholly of the clergy, who were alfo the lawyers; the barons, or great lords of the land; the knights or foldiery, who were the fubordinate landholders; and the burghers, or inferior tradefmen, who from their infignificancy happily retained, in their focage and burgage tenure, fome

points

points of their antient freedom. All the rest were villeins or bondmen.

FROM so complete and well concerted a scheme of servility, it has been the work of generations for our ancestors, to redeem themselves and their posterity into that state of liberty, which we now enjoy : and which therefore is not to be looked upon as consisting of mere incroachments on the crown, and infringements of the prerogative, as some slavish and narrow-minded writers in the last century endeavoured to maintain ; but as, in general, a gradual restoration of that antient constitution, whereof our Saxon forefathers had been unjustly deprived, partly by the policy, and partly by the force, of the Norman. How that restoration has, in a long series of years, been step by step effected, I now proceed to enquire.

WILLIAM Rufus proceeded on his father's plan, and in some points extended it ; particularly with regard to the forest laws. But his brother and successor, Henry the first, found it expedient, when first he came to the crown, to ingratiate himself with the people; by restoring (as our monkish historians tell us) the laws of king Edward the confessor. The ground whereof is this : that by charter he gave up the great grievances of marriage, ward, and relief, the beneficial pecuniary *fruits* of his feodal tenures ; but reserved the tenures themselves, for the same military purposes that his father introduced them. He also abolished the *curfeu* [e]; for, though it is mentioned in our laws a full century afterwards [f], yet it is rather spoken of as a known *time* of night (so denominated from that abrogated usage) than as a still subsisting custom. There is extant a code of laws in his name, consisting partly of those of the confessor, but with great additions and alterations of his own ; and chiefly calculated for the regulation of the county courts. It contains some directions as to crimes and their punishments, (that of theft being made capital in his reign) and a few things relating to estates, parti-

[e] Spelm. *Cod. LL. W. I.* 288. *Hen. I.* 299.　　　[f] *Stat. Civ. Lond.* 13 Edw. I.

cularly

cularly as to the defcent of lands : which being by the Saxon laws equally to all the fons, by the feodal or Norman to the eldeft only, king Henry here moderated the difference ; direct-ing the eldeft fon to have only the principal eftate, " *primum* " *patris feudum*," the reft of his eftates, if he had any others, being equally divided among them all. On the other hand, he gave up to the clergy the free election of bifhops and mitred abbots ; referving however thefe enfigns of patronage, *conge d' eflire*, cuftody of the temporalties when vacant, and homage upon their reftitution. He laftly united again for a time the ci-vil and ecclefiaftical courts, which union was foon diffolved by his Norman clergy : and, upon that final diffolution, the cog-nizance of teftamentary caufes feems to have been firft given to the ecclefiaftical court. The reft remained as in his father's time : from whence we may eafily perceive how far fhort this was of a thorough reftitution of king Edward's, or the Saxon, laws.

THE ufurper Stephen, as the manner of ufurpers is, promifed much at his acceffion, efpecially with regard to redreffing the grievances of the foreft laws, but performed no great matter either in that or in any other point. It is from his reign how-ever, that we are to date the introduction of the Roman civil and canon laws into this realm : and at the fame time was imported the doctrine of appeals to the court of Rome, as a branch of the canon law.

BY the time of king Henry the fecond, if not earlier, the charter of Henry the firft feems to have been forgotten : for we find the claim of marriage, ward, and relief, then flourifhing in full vigour. The right of primogeniture feems alfo to have ta-citly revived, being found more convenient for the public than the parcelling of eftates into a multitude of minute fubdivifions. However in this prince's reign much was done to methodize the laws, and reduce them into a regular order ; as appears from that excellent treatife of Glanvil : which, though fome of it be now antiquated and altered, yet, when compared with the code

of

of Henry the firſt, it carries a manifeſt ſuperiority [s]. Through-out his reign alſo was continued the important ſtruggle, which we have had occaſion ſo often to mention, between the laws of England and Rome; the former ſupported by the ſtrength of the temporal nobility, when endeavoured to be ſupplanted in favour of the latter by the popiſh clergy. Which diſpute was kept on foot till the reign of Edward the firſt; when the laws of England, under the new diſcipline introduced by that ſkilful commander, obtained a complete and permanent victory. In the preſent reign, of Henry the ſecond, there are four things which peculiarly me-rit the attention of a legal antiquarian : 1. The conſtitutions of the parliament at Clarendon, *A. D.* 1164. whereby the king checked the power of the pope and his clergy, and greatly nar-rowed the total exemption they claimed from the ſecular juriſ-diction : though his farther progreſs was unhappily ſtopped, by the fatal event of the diſputes between him and archbiſhop Becket. 2. The inſtitution of the office of juſtices in eyre, *in itinere*; the king having divided the kingdom into ſix circuits (a little different from the preſent) and commiſſioned theſe new created judges to adminiſter juſtice, and try writs of aſſiſe, in the ſeveral counties. Theſe remedies are ſaid to have been then firſt in-vented : before which all cauſes were uſually terminated in the county courts, according to the Saxon cuſtom; or before the king's juſticiaries in the *aula regis*, in purſuance of the Norman regulations. The latter of which tribunals, travelling about with the king's perſon, occaſioned intolerable expenſe and delay to the ſuitors; and the former, however proper for little debts and minute actions, where even injuſtice is better than procraſ-tination, were now become liable to too much ignorance of the law, and too much partiality as to facts, to determine matters of conſiderable moment. 3. The introduction and eſtabliſhment of the grand aſſiſe, or trial by a ſpecial kind of jury in a writ of right, at the option of the tenant or defendant, inſtead of the barbarous and Norman trial by battel. 4. To this time muſt alſo be referred the introduction of eſcuage, or pecuniary com-

[s] Hal. Hiſt. C. L. 138.

mutation for perfonal military fervice; which in procefs of time was the parent of the antient fubfidies granted to the crown by parliament, and the land tax of later times.

RICHARD the firft, a brave and magnanimous prince, was a fportfman as well as a foldier; and therefore inforced the foreft laws with fome rigour; which occafioned many difcontents among his people: though (according to Matthew Paris) he repealed the penalties of caftration, lofs of eyes, and cutting off the hands and feet, before inflicted on fuch as tranfgreffed in hunting; probably finding that their feverity prevented profecutions. He alfo, when abroad, compofed a body of naval laws at the ifle of Oleron; which are ftill extant, and of high authority: for in his time we began again to difcover, that (as an ifland) we were naturally a maritime power. But, with regard to civil proceedings, we find nothing very remarkable in this reign, except a few regulations regarding the jews, and the juftices in eyre: the king's thoughts being chiefly taken up by the knight errantry of a croifade againft the Saracens in the holy land.

IN king John's time, and that of his fon Henry the third, the rigours of the feodal tenures and the foreft laws were fo warmly kept up, that they occafioned many infurrections of the barons or principal feudatories: which at laft had this effect, that firft king John, and afterwards his fon, confented to the two famous charters of Englifh liberties, *magna carta*, and *carta de forefta*. Of thefe the latter was well calculated to redrefs many grievances, and encroachments of the crown, in the exertion of foreft-law: and the former confirmed many liberties of the church, and redreffed many grievances incident to feodal tenures, of no fmall moment at the time; though now, unlefs confidered attentively and with this retrofpect, they feem but of trifling concern. But, befides thefe feodal provifions, care was alfo taken therein to protect the fubject againft other oppreffions, then frequently arifing from unreafonable amercements, from illegal diftreffes or other procefs for debts or fervices due to the
crown

crown, and from the tyrannical abuſe of the prerogative of purveyance and pre-emption. It fixed the forfeiture of lands for
felony in the ſame manner as it ſtill remains ; prohibited for the
future the grants of excluſive fiſheries ; and the erection of new
bridges ſo as to oppreſs the neighbourhood. With reſpect to
private rights : it eſtabliſhed the teſtamentary power of the ſubject over part of his perſonal eſtate, the reſt being diſtributed
among his wife and children ; it laid down the law of dower,
as it hath continued ever ſince ; and prohibited the appeals of
women, unleſs for the death of their huſbands. In matters of
public police and national concern : it injoined an uniformity of
weights and meaſures ; gave new encouragements to commerce,
by the protection of merchant-ſtrangers ; and forbad the alienation of lands in mortmain. With regard to the adminiſtration
of juſtice : beſides prohibiting all denials or delays of it, it fixed
the court of commonpleas at Weſtminſter, that the ſuitors might
no longer be haraſſed with following the king's perſon in all his
progreſſes ; and at the ſame time brought the trial of iſſues home
to the very doors of the freeholders, by directing aſſiſes to be
taken in the proper counties, and eſtabliſhing annual circuits : it
alſo corrected ſome abuſes then incident to the trials by wager
of law and of battel ; directed the regular awarding of inqueſts
for life or member ; prohibited the king's inferior miniſters from
holding pleas of the crown, or trying any criminal charge,
whereby many forfeitures might otherwiſe have unjuſtly accrued
to the exchequer ; and regulated the time and place of holding
the inferior tribunals of juſtice, the county court, ſheriff's turn,
and court-leet. It confirmed and eſtabliſhed the liberties of the
city of London, and all other cities, boroughs, towns, and ports
of the kingdom. And, laſtly, (which alone would have merited
the title that it bears, of the *great* charter) it protected every
individual of the nation in the free enjoyment of his life, his
liberty, and his property, unleſs declared to be forfeited by the
judgment of his peers or the law of the land.

HOWEVER, by means of these struggles, the pope in the reign of king John gained a still greater ascendant here, than he ever before had enjoyed; which continued through the long reign of his son Henry the third: in the beginning of whose time the old Saxon trial by ordeal was also totally abolished. And we may by this time perceive, in Bracton's treatise, a still farther improvement in the method and regularity of the common law, especially in the point of pleadings [h]. Nor must it be forgotten, that the first traces which remain, of the separation of the greater barons from the less, in the constitution of parliaments, are found in the great charter of king John; though omitted in that of Henry III: and that, towards the end of the latter of these reigns, we find the first record of any writ for summoning knights, citizens, and burgesses to parliament. And here we conclude the second period of our English legal history.

III. THE third commences with the reign of Edward the first; who may justly be stiled our English Justinian. For in his time the law did receive so sudden a perfection, that sir Matthew Hale does not scruple to affirm [i], that more was done in the first thirteen years of his reign to settle and establish the distributive justice of the kingdom, than in all the ages since that time put together.

IT would be endless to enumerate all the particulars of these regulations; but the principal may be reduced under the following general heads. 1. He established, confirmed, and settled, the great charter and charter of forests. 2. He gave a mortal wound to the encroachments of the pope and his clergy, by limiting and establishing the bounds of ecclesiastical jurisdiction: and by obliging the ordinary, to whom all the goods of intestates at that time belonged, to discharge the debts of the deceased. 3. He defined the limits of the several temporal courts of the highest jurisdiction, those of the king's bench, common

[h] Hal. Hist. C. L. 156.　　　　[i] Ibid. 158.

pleas,

pleas, and exchequer; fo as they might not interfere with each
other's proper bufinefs: to do which, they muft now have recourfe to a fiction, very neceffary and beneficial in the prefent
enlarged ftate of property. 4. He fettled the boundaries of the
inferior courts in counties, hundreds, and manors: confining
them to caufes of no great amount, according to their primitive
inftitution; though of confiderably greater, than by the alteration
of the value of money they are now permitted to determine.
5. He fecured·the property of the fubject, by abolifhing all arbitrary taxes, and talliages, levied without confent of the national council. 6. He guarded the common juftice of the kingdom from abufes, by giving up the royal prerogative of fending
mandates to interfere in private caufes. 7. He fettled the form,
folemnities, and effects, of fines levied in the court of common
pleas; though the thing itfelf was of Saxon original. 8. He
firft eftablifhed a repofitory for the public records of the kingdom; few of which are antienter than the reign of his father,
and thofe were by him collected. 9. He improved upon the laws
of king Alfred, by that great and orderly method of watch and
ward, for preferving the public peace and preventing robberies,
eftablifhed by the ftatute of Winchefter. 10. He fettled and
reformed many abufes incident to tenures, and removed fome
reftraints on the alienation of landed property, by the ftatute of
quia emptores. 11. He inftituted a fpeedier way for the recovery
of debts, by granting execution not only upon goods and chattels, but alfo upon lands, by writ of *elegit*; which was of fig-
nal benefit to a trading people: and, upon the fame commercial
ideas, he alfo allowed the charging of lands in a ftatute merchant, to pay debts contracted in trade, contrary to all feodal
principles. 12. He effectually provided for the recovery of ad-
vowfons, as temporal rights; in which, before, the law was
extremely deficient. 13. He alfo effectually clofed the great
gulph, in which all the landed property of the kingdom was in
danger of being fwallowed, by his re-iterated ftatutes of mortmain; moft admirably adapted to meet the frauds that had then
been devifed, though afterwards contrived to be evaded by the

invention of uſes. 14. He eſtabliſhed a new limitation of property by the creation of eſtates tail; concerning the good policy
of which, modern times have however entertained a very different opinion. 15. He reduced all Wales to the ſubjection, not
only of the crown, but in great meaſure of the laws, of England; (which was thoroughly completed in the reign of Henry
the eighth) and ſeems to have entertained a deſign of doing the
like by Scotland, ſo as to have formed an intire and complete
union of the iſland of Great Britain.

I MIGHT continue this catalogue much farther: --- but,
upon the whole, we may obſerve, that the very ſcheme and model of the adminiſtration of common juſtice between party and
party, was entirely ſettled by this king[k]; and has continued
nearly the ſame, in all ſucceeding ages, to this day; abating
ſome few alterations, which the humour or neceſſity of ſubſequent times hath occaſioned. The forms of writs, by which
actions are commenced, were perfected in his reign, and eſtabliſhed as models for poſterity. The pleadings, conſequent upon
the writs, were then ſhort, nervous, and perſpicuous; not intricate, verboſe, and formal. The legal treatiſes, written in his
time, as Britton, Fleta, Hengham, and the reſt, are for the
moſt part, law at this day; or at leaſt *were* ſo, till the alteration
of tenures took place. And, to conclude, it is from this period,
from the exact *obſervation* of *magna carta*, rather than from it's
making or *renewal*, in the days of his grandfather and father, that
the liberty of Engliſhmen began again to rear it's head; though
the weight of the military tenures hung heavy upon it for many
ages after.

I CANNOT give a better proof of the excellence of his conſtitutions, than that from his time to that of Henry the eighth
there happened very few, and thoſe not very conſiderable, alterations in the legal *forms* of proceedings. As to matter of *ſubſtance:* the old Gothic powers of electing the principal ſubor-

[k] Hal. Hiſt. C. L. 162.

dinate magiftrates, the fheriffs, and confervators of the peace, were taken from the people in the reigns of Edward II and Edward III ; and juftices of the peace were eftablifhed inftead of the latter. In the reign alfo of Edward the third the parliament is fuppofed moft probably to have affumed it's prefent form ; by a feparation of the commons from the lords. The ftatute for defining and afcertaining treafons was one of the firft productions of this new-modelled affembly ; and the tranflation of the law proceedings from French into Latin another. Much alfo was done, under the aufpices of this magnanimous prince, for eftablifhing our domeftic manufactures; by prohibiting the exportation of Englifh wool, and the importation or wear of foreign cloth or furs; and by encouraging clothworkers from other countries to fettle here. Nor was the legiflature inattentive to many other branches of commerce, or indeed to commerce in general : for, in particular, it enlarged the credit of the merchant, by introducing the ftatute ftaple; whereby he might the more readily pledge his lands for the fecurity of his mercantile debts. And, as perfonal property now grew, by the extenfion of trade, to be much more confiderable than formerly, care was taken, in cafe of inteftacies, to appoint adminiftrators particularly nominated by the law; to diftribute that perfonal property among the creditors and kindred of the deceafed, which before had been ufually applied, by the officers of the ordinary, to ufes then denominated pious. The ftatutes alfo of *praemunire,* for effectually depreffing the civil power of the pope, were the work of this and the fubfequent reign. And the eftablifhment of a laborious parochial clergy, by the endowment of vicarages out of the overgrown poffeffions of the monafteries, added luftre to the clofe of the fourteenth century : though the feeds of the general reformation, which were thereby firft fown in the kingdom, were almoft overwhelmed by the fpirit of perfecution, introduced into the laws of the land by the influence of the regular clergy.

FROM this time to that of Henry the feventh, the civil wars and difputed titles to the crown gave no leifure for farther juri-

dical improvement : " *nam silent leges inter arma.*" --- And yet
it is to thefe very difputes that we owe the happy lofs of all the
dominions of the crown on the continent of France ; which
turned the minds of our fubfequent princes entirely to domeftic
concerns.   To thefe likewife we owe the method of barring entails by the fiction of *common recoveries;* invented originally by
the clergy, to evade the ftatutes of mortmain, but introduced
under Edward the fourth, for the purpofe of unfettering eftates,
and making them more liable to forfeiture : while, on the other
hand, the owners endeavoured to protect them by the univerfal
eftablifhment of *ufes,* another of the clerical inventions.

In the reign of king Henry the feventh, his minifters (not to
fay the king himfelf) were more induftrious in hunting out profecutions upon old and forgotten penal laws, in order to extort
money from the fubject, than in framing any new beneficial regulations.   For the diftinguifhing character of this reign was
that of amaffing treafure into the king's coffers, by every means
that could be devifed : and almoft every alteration in the laws,
however falutary or otherwife in their future confequences, had
this and this only for their great and immediate object.   To this
end the court of ftar-chamber was new-modelled, and armed
with powers, the moft dangerous and unconftitutional, over the
perfons and properties of the fubject. Informations were allowed
to be received, in lieu of indictments, at the affifes and feffions
of the peace, in order to multiply fines and pecuniary penalties.
The ftatute of fines for landed property was craftily and covertly
contrived, to facilitate the deftruction of entails, and make the
owners of real eftates more capable to forfeit as well as to aliene.
The benefit of clergy (which fo often intervened to ftop attainders and fave the inheritance) was now allowed only once to lay
offenders, who only could have inheritances to lofe.   A writ of
capias was permitted in all actions on the cafe, and the defendant
might in confequence be outlawed ; becaufe upon fuch outlawry
his goods became the property of the crown.   In fhort, there
is hardly a ftatute in this reign, introductive of a new law or
                                                              modifying

modifying the old, but what either directly or obliquely tended
to the emolument of the exchequer.

IV. This brings us to the fourth period of our legal history,
viz. the reformation of religion, under Henry the eighth, and
his children: which opens an intirely new scene in ecclesiastical
matters; the usurped power of the pope being now for ever
routed and destroyed, all his connexions with this island cut off,
the crown restored to it's supremacy over spiritual men and causes,
and the patronage of bishopricks being once more indisputably
vested in the king. And, had the spiritual courts been at this
time re-united to the civil, we should have seen the old Saxon
constitution with regard to *ecclesiastical* polity completely restored.

With regard also to our *civil* polity, the statute of wills, and
the statute of uses, (both passed in the reign of this prince) made a
great alteration as to property: the former, by allowing the *devise*
of real estates by will, which before was in general forbidden;
the latter, by endeavouring to destroy the intricate nicety of *uses*,
though the narrowness and pedantry of the courts of common
law prevented this statute from having it's full beneficial effect.
And thence the courts of equity assumed a jurisdiction, dictated
by common justice and common sense: which, however arbitrarily exercised or productive of jealousies in it's infancy, has at
length been matured into a most elegant system of rational juris-
prudence; the principles of which (notwithstanding they may differ
in forms) are now equally adopted by the courts of both law and
equity. From the statute of uses, and another statute of the
same antiquity, (which protected estates for years from being destroyed by the reversioner) a remarkable alteration took place in
the mode of conveyancing: the antient assurance by feoffment
and livery upon the land being now very seldom practiced,
since the more easy and more private invention of transferring
property, by secret conveyances to uses, and long terms of years
being now continually created in mortgages and family settle-
ments.

ments, which may be moulded to a thousand useful purposes by the ingenuity of an able artist.

THE farther attacks in this reign upon the immunity of estates-tail, which reduced them to little more than the conditional fees at the common law, before the passing of the statute *de donis*; the establishment of recognizances in the nature of a statute-staple, for facilitating the raising of money upon landed security; and the introduction of the bankrupt laws, as well for the punishment of the fraudulent, as the relief of the unfortunate, trader; all these were capital alterations of our legal polity, and highly convenient to that character, which the English began now to re-assume, of a great commercial people. The incorporation of Wales with England, and the more uniform administration of justice, by destroying some counties palatine, and abridging the unreasonable privileges of such as remained, added dignity and strength to the monarchy: and, together with the numerous improvements before observed upon, and the redress of many grievances and oppressions which had been introduced by his father, will ever make the administration of Henry VIII a very distinguished aera in the annals of juridical history.

IT must be however remarked, that (particularly in his later years) the royal prerogative was then strained to a very tyrannical and oppressive height; and, what was the worst circumstance, it's encroachments were established by law, under the sanction of those pusillanimous parliaments, one of which to it's eternal disgrace passed a statute, whereby it was enacted that the king's proclamations should have the force of acts of parliament; and others concurred in the creation of that amazing heap of wild and new-fangled treasons, which were slightly touched upon in a former chapter[e]. Happily for the nation, this arbitrary reign was succeeded by the minority of an amiable prince; during the short sunshine of which, great part of these extravagant laws were repealed. And, to do justice to the shorter reign of queen Mary,

[e] See pag. 86.

many

many falutary and popular laws, in civil matters, were made under her adminiftration; perhaps the better to reconcile the people to the bloody meafures which fhe was induced to purfue, for the re-eftablifhment of religious flavery : the well concerted fchemes for effecting which, were (through the providence of God) defeated by the feafonable acceffion of queen Elizabeth.

THE religious liberties of the nation being, by that happy event, eftablifhed (we truft) on an eternal bafis; (though obliged in their infancy to be guarded, againft papifts and other nonconformifts, by laws of too fanguinary a nature) the foreft laws having fallen into difufe; and the adminiftration of civil right in the courts of juftice being carried on in a regular courfe, according to the wife inftitutions of king Edward the firft, without any material innovations; all the principal grievances introduced by the Norman conqueft feem to have been gradually fhaken off, and our Saxon conftitution reftored, with confiderable improvements : except only in the continuation of the military tenures, and a few other points, which ftill armed the crown with a very oppreffive and dangerous prerogative. It is alfo to be remarked, that the fpirit of inriching the clergy and endowing religious houfes had (through the former abufe of it) gone over to fuch a contrary extreme, and the princes of the houfe of Tudor and their favourites had fallen with fuch avidity upon the fpoils of the church, that a decent and honourable maintenance was wanting to many of the bifhops and clergy. This produced the *reftraining* ftatutes, to prevent the alienations of lands and tithes belonging to the church and univerfities. The number of indigent perfons being alfo greatly increafed, by withdrawing the alms of the monafteries, a plan was formed in the reign of queen Elizabeth, more humane and beneficial than even feeding and cloathing of millions; by affording them the means (with proper induftry) to feed and to cloath themfelves. And, the farther any fubfequent plans for maintaining the poor have departed from this inftitution, the more impracticable and even pernicious their vifionary attempts have proved.

H o w e v e r, confidering the reign of queen Elizabeth in a great and political view, we have no reafon to regret many fubfequent alterations in the Englifh conftitution. For, though in general fhe was a wife and excellent princefs, and loved her people ; though in her time trade flourifhed, riches increafed, the laws were duly adminiftred, the nation was refpected abroad, and the people happy at home ; yet, the encreafe of the power of the ftar-chamber, and the erection of the high commiffion court in matters ecclefiaftical, were the work of her reign. She alfo kept her parliaments at a very awful diftance : and in many particulars fhe, at times, would carry the prerogative as high as her moft arbitrary predeceffors. It is true, fhe very feldom exerted this prerogative, fo as to opprefs individuals ; but ftill fhe had it to exert : and therefore the felicity of her reign depended more on her want of opportunity and inclination, than want of power, to play the tyrant. This is a high encomium on her merit ; but at the fame time it is fufficient to fhew, that thefe were not thofe golden days of genuine liberty, that we formerly were taught to believe : for, furely, the true liberty of the fubject confifts not fo much in the gracious behaviour, as in the limited power, of the fovereign.

T h e great revolutions that had happened, in manners and in property, had paved the way, by imperceptible yet fure degrees, for as great a revolution in government : yet, while that revolution was effecting, the crown became more arbitrary than ever, by the progrefs of thofe very means which afterwards reduced it's power. It is obvious to every obferver, that, till the clofe of the Lancaftrian civil wars, the property and the power of the nation were chiefly divided between the king, the nobility, and the clergy. The commons were generally in a ftate of great ignorance ; their perfonal wealth, before the extenfion of trade, was comparatively fmall ; and the nature of their landed property was fuch, as kept them in continual dependence upon their feodal lord, being ufually fome powerful baron, fome opulent abbey,

or

or fometimes the king himfelf. Though a notion of general liberty had ftrongly pervaded and animated the whole conftitution, yet the particular liberty, the natural equality, and perfonal independence of individuals, were little regarded or thought of; nay even to affert them was treated as the height of fedition and rebellion. Our anceftors heard, with deteftation and horror, thofe fentiments rudely delivered, and pufhed to moft abfurd extremes, by the violence of a Cade and a Tyler; which have fince been applauded, with a zeal almoft rifing to idolatry, when foftened and recommended by the eloquence, the moderation, and the arguments of a Sidney, a Locke, and a Milton.

BUT when learning, by the invention of printing and the progrefs of religious reformation, began to be univerfally diffeminated; when trade and navigation were fuddenly carried to an amazing extent, by the ufe of the compafs and the confequent difcovery of the Indies; the minds of men, thus enlightened by fcience and enlarged by obfervation and travel, began to entertain a more juft opinion of the dignity and rights of mankind. An inundation of wealth flowed in upon the merchants, and middling rank; while the two great eftates of the kingdom, which formerly had ballanced the prerogative, the nobility and clergy, were greatly impoverifhed and weakened. The popifh clergy, detected in their frauds and abufes, expofed to the refentment of the populace, and ftripped of their lands and revenues, ftood trembling for their very exiftence. The nobles, enervated by the refinements of luxury, (which knowlege, foreign travel, and the progrefs of the politer arts, are too apt to introduce with themfelves) and fired with difdain at being rivalled in magnificence by the opulent citizens, fell into enormous expenfes: to gratify which they were permitted, by the policy of the times, to diffipate their overgrown eftates, and alienate their antient patrimonies. This gradually reduced their power and their influence within a very moderate bound: while the king, by the fpoil of the monafteries and the great increafe of the cuftoms, grew rich, independent, and haughty: and the commons

were

were not yet fenfible of the ftrength they had acquired, nor urged to examine it's extent by new burthens or oppreffive taxations, during the fudden opulence of the exchequer. Intent upon acquiring new riches, and happy in being freed from the infolence and tyranny of the orders more immediately above them, they never dreamt of oppofing the prerogative, to which they had been fo little accuftomed; much lefs of taking the lead in oppofition, to which by their weight and their property they were now entitled. The latter years of Henry the eighth were therefore the times of the greateft defpotifm, that have been known in this ifland fince the death of William the Norman : the prerogative, as it then ftood by common law, (and much more when extended by act of parliament) being too large to be endured in a land of liberty.

Queen Elizabeth, and the intermediate princes of the Tudor line, had almoft the fame legal powers, and fometimes exerted them as roughly, as their father king Henry the eighth. But the critical fituation of that princefs with regard to her legitimacy, her religion, her enmity with Spain, and her jealoufy of the queen of Scots, occafioned greater caution in her conduct. She probably, or her able advifers, had penetration enough to difcern how the power of the kingdom had gradually fhifted it's chanel, and wifdom enough not to provoke the commons to difcover and feel their ftrength. She therefore drew a veil over the odious part of prerogative ; which was never wantonly thrown afide, but only to anfwer fome important purpofe : and, though the royal treafury no longer overflowed with the wealth of the clergy, which had been all granted out, and had contributed to enrich the people, fhe afked for fupplies with fuch moderation, and managed them with fo much oeconomy, that the commons were happy in obliging her. Such, in fhort, were her circumftances, her neceffities, her wifdom, and her good difpofition, that never did a prince fo long and fo intirely, for the fpace of half a century together, reign in the affections of the people.

On

On the acceffion of king James I, no new degree of royal power was added to, or exercifed by, him; but fuch a fceptre was too weighty to be wielded by fuch a hand. The unreafonable and imprudent exertion of what was then deemed to be prerogative, upon trivial and unworthy occafions, and the claim of a more abfolute power inherent in the kingly office than had ever been carried into practice, foon awakened the fleeping lion. The people heard with aftonifhment doctrines preached from the throne and the pulpit, fubverfive of liberty and property, and all the natural rights of humanity. They examined into the divinity of this claim, and found it weakly and fallacioufly fupported: and common reafon affured them, that, if it were of human origin, no conftitution could eftablifh it without power of revocation, no precedent could fanctify, no length of time could confirm it. The leaders felt the pulfe of the nation, and found they had ability as well as inclination to refift it : and accordingly refifted and oppofed it, whenever the pufillanimous temper of the reigning monarch had courage to put it to the trial ; and they gained fome little victories in the cafes of concealments, monopolies, and the difpenfing power. In the mean time very little was done for the improvement of private juftice, except the abolition of fanctuaries, and the extenfion of the bankrupt laws, the limitation of fuits and actions, and the regulating of informations upon penal ftatutes. For I cannot clafs the laws againft witchcraft and conjuration under the head of improvements; nor did the difpute between lord Ellefmere and fir Edward Coke, concerning the powers of the court of chancery, tend much to the advancement of juftice.

Indeed when Charles the firft fucceeded to the crown of his father, and attempted to revive fome enormities, which had been dormant in the reign of king James, the loans and benevolences extorted from the fubject, the arbitrary imprifonments for refufal, the exertion of martial law in time of peace, and other domeftic grievances, clouded the morning of that mif-

guided

guided prince's reign; which, though the noon of it began a
little to brighten, at laſt went down in blood, and left the whole
kingdom in darkneſs. It muſt be acknowleged that, by the petition of right, enacted to aboliſh theſe encroachments, the
Engliſh conſtitution received great alteration and improvement.
But there ſtill remained the latent power of the foreſt laws,
which the crown moſt unſeaſonably revived. The legal juriſdiction of the ſtar-chamber and high commiſſion courts was alſo
extremely great; though their uſurped authority was ſtill greater.
And, if we add to theſe the diſuſe of parliaments, the ill-timed
zeal and deſpotic proceedings of the eccleſiaſtical governors in
matters of mere indifference, together with the arbitrary levies
of tonnage and poundage, ſhip money, and other projects, we
may ſee grounds moſt amply ſufficient for ſeeking redreſs in a
legal conſtitutional way. This redreſs, when ſought, was alſo
conſtitutionally given: for all theſe oppreſſions were actually
aboliſhed by the king in parliament, before the rebellion broke
out, by the ſeveral ſtatutes for triennial parliaments, for aboliſh-
ing the ſtar-chamber and high commiſſion courts, for aſcertaining the extent of foreſts and foreſt-laws, for renouncing ſhip-
money and other exactions, and for giving up the prerogative of
knighting the king's tenants *in capite* in conſequence of their
feodal tenures: though it muſt be acknowleged that theſe con-
ceſſions were not made with ſo good a grace, as to conciliate the
confidence of the people. Unfortunately, either by his own miſ-
management, or by the arts of his enemies, the king had loſt the
reputation of ſincerity; which is the greateſt unhappineſs that can
befal a prince. Though he formerly had ſtrained his prerogative,
not only beyond what the genius of the preſent times would
bear, but alſo beyond the example of former ages, he had now
conſented to reduce it to a lower ebb than was conſiſtent with
monarchical government. A conduct ſo oppoſite to his temper
and principles, joined with ſome raſh actions and unguarded ex-
preſſions, made the people ſuſpect that this condeſcenſion was
merely temporary. Fluſhed therefore with the ſucceſs they had
gained, fired with reſentment for paſt oppreſſions, and dreading
the

the confequences if the king fhould regain his power, the popular leaders (who in all ages have called themfelves *the people*)
began to grow infolent and ungovernable: their infolence foon
rendered them defperate: and, joining with a fet of military
hypocrites and enthufiafts, they overturned the church and monarchy, and proceeded with deliberate folemnity to the trial and
murder of their fovereign.

I P A S S by the crude and abortive fchemes for amending the
laws in the times of confufion which followed; the moft pro-
mifing and fenfible whereof (fuch as the eftablifhment of new
trials, the abolition of feodal tenures, the act of navigation, and
fome others) were adopted in the

V. F I F T H period, which I am next to mention, *viz.* after
the reftoration of king Charles II. Immediately upon which,
the principal remaining grievance, the doctrine and confequences
of military tenures, were taken away and abolifhed, except in
the inftance of corruption of inheritable blood, upon attainder
of treafon and felony. And though the monarch, in whofe perfon the royal government was reftored, and with it our antient
conftitution, deferves no commendation from pofterity, yet in
his reign, (wicked, fanguinary, and turbulent as it was) the concurrence of happy circumftances was fuch, that from thence we
may date not only the re-eftablifhment of our church and monarchy, but alfo the complete reftitution of Englifh liberty, for
the firft time, fince it's total abolition at the conqueft. For
therein not only thefe flavifh tenures, the badge of foreign dominion, with all their oppreffive appendages, were removed from
incumbering the eftates of the fubject; but alfo an additional
fecurity of his perfon from imprifonment was obtained, by that
great bulwark of our conftitution, the *habeas corpus* act. Thefe
two ftatutes, with regard to our property and perfons, form a
fecond *magna carta*, as beneficial and effectual as that of Runing-
Mead. That only pruned the luxuriances of the feodal fyftem;
but the ftatute of Charles the fecond extirpated all it's flaveries:

except

except perhaps in copyhold tenure; and there alfo they are now in great meafure enervated by gradual cuftom, and the interpofition of our courts of juftice. *Magna carta* only, in general terms, declared, that no man fhall be imprifoned contrary to law: the *habeas corpus* act points him out effectual means, as well to releafe himfelf, though committed even by the king in council, as to punifh all thofe who fhall thus unconftitutionally mifufe him.

T o thefe I may add the abolition of the prerogatives of purveyance and pre-emption; the ftatute for holding triennial parliaments; the teft and corporation acts, which fecure both our civil and religious liberties; the abolition of the writ *de haeretico comburendo*; the ftatute of frauds and perjuries, a great and neceffary fecurity to private property; the ftatute for diftribution of inteftates' eftates; and that of amendments and *jeofails*, which cut off thofe fuperfluous niceties which fo long had difgraced our courts; together with many other wholfome acts, that were paffed in this reign, for the benefit of navigation and the improvement of foreign commerce: and the whole, when we likewife confider the freedom from taxes and armies which the fubject then enjoyed, will be fufficient to demonftrate this truth, " that the " conftitution of England had arrived to it's full vigour, and " the true balance between liberty and prerogative was happily " eftablifhed by *law*, in the reign of king Charles the fecond."

I t is far from my intention to palliate or defend many very iniquitous proceedings, *contrary to all law*, in that reign, through the artifice of wicked politicians, both in and out of employment. What feems inconteftable is this; that *by the law*[m], as it then ftood, (notwithftanding fome invidious, nay dangerous, branches of the prerogative have fince been lopped off, and the

[m] The point of time, at which I would chufe to fix this *theoretical* perfection of our public law, is the year 1679; after the *habeas corpus* act was paffed, and that for licenfing the prefs had expired: though the years which immediately followed it were times of great *practical* oppreffion.

reft

reft more clearly defined) the people had as large a portion of real liberty, as is confiftent with a ftate of fociety; and fufficient power, refiding in their own hands, to affert and preferve that liberty, if invaded by the royal prerogative. For which I need but appeal to the memorable cataftrophe of the next reign. For when king Charles's deluded brother attempted to enflave the nation, he found it was beyond his power: the people both could, and did, refift him; and, in confequence of fuch refiftance, obliged him to quit his enterprize and his throne together. Which introduces us to the laft period of our legal hiftory; *viz.*

VI. FROM the revolution in 1688 to the prefent time. In this period many laws have paffed; as the bill of rights, the toleration--act, the act of fettlement with it's conditions, the act for uniting England with Scotland, and fome others: which have afferted our liberties in more clear and emphatical terms; have regulated the fucceffion of the crown by parliament, as the exigences of religious and civil freedom required; have confirmed, and exemplified, the doctrine of refiftance, when the executive magiftrate endeavours to fubvert the conftitution; have maintained the fuperiority of the laws above the king, by pronouncing his difpenfing power to be illegal; have indulged tender confciences with every religious liberty, confiftent with the fafety of the ftate; have eftablifhed triennial, fince turned into feptennial, elections of members to ferve in parliament; have excluded certain officers from the houfe of commons; have reftrained the king's pardon from obftructing parliamentary impeachments; have imparted to all the lords an equal right of trying their fellow peers; have regulated trials for high treafon; have afforded our pofterity a hope that corruption of blood may one day be abolifhed and forgotten; have (by the defire of his prefent majefty) fet bounds to the civil lift, and placed the adminiftration of that revenue in hands that are accountable to parliament; and have (by the like defire) made the judges completely independent of the king, his minifters, and his fucceffors. Yet, though thefe provifions have, in appearance and nomi-

nally, reduced the ftrength of the executive power to a much
lower ebb than in the preceding period ; if on the other hand
we throw into the oppofite fcale (what perhaps the immoderate
reduction of the antient prerogative may have rendered in fome
degree neceffary) the vaft acquifition of force, arifing from the
riot-act, and the annual expedience of a ftanding army ; and the
vaft acquifition of perfonal attachment, arifing from the magnitude of the national debt, and the manner of levying thofe yearly
millions that are appropriated to pay the intereft ; we fhall find
that the crown has, gradually and imperceptibly, gained almoft
as much in influence, as it has apparently loft in prerogative.

THE chief alterations of moment, (for the time would fail
me to defcend to *minutiae*) in the adminiftration of private juftice
during this period, are the folemn recognition of the law of nations with refpect to the rights of embaffadors : the cutting off,
by the ftatute for the amendment of the law, a vaft number of
excrefcences, that in procefs of time had fprung out of the practical part of it : the protection of corporate rights by the improvements in writs of *mandamus*, and informations in nature of
quo warranto : the regulations of trials by jury, and the admitting
witneffes for prifoners upon oath : the farther reftraints upon
alienation of lands in mortmain : the extenfion of the benefit of
clergy, by abolifhing the pedantic criterion of reading : the
counterballance to this mercy, by the vaft encreafe of capital
punifhment : the new and effectual methods for the fpeedy recovery of rents : the improvements which have been made in eject-
ments for the trying of titles : the introduction and eftablifhment
of paper credit, by indorfments upon bills and notes, which have
fhewn the poffibility (fo long doubted) of affigning a *chofe in action :*
the tranflation of all legal proceedings into the Englifh language :
the erection of courts of confcience for recovering fmall debts,
and (which is much the better plan) the reformation of county
courts : the great fyftem of marine jurifprudence, of which the
foundations have been laid, by clearly developing the principles
on which policies of infurance are founded, and by happily applying

plying thofe principles to particular cafes : and, laftly, the liberality of fentiment, which (though late) has now taken poffeffion of our courts of common law, and induced them to adopt (where facts can be clearly afcertained) the fame principles of redrefs as have prevailed in our courts of equity, from the time that lord Nottingham prefided there ; and this, not only where fpecially impowered by particular ftatutes, (as in the cafe of bonds, mortgages, and fet-offs) but by extending the remedial influence of the equitable writ of trefpafs on the cafe, according to it's primitive inftitution by king Edward the firft, to almoft every inftance of injuftice not remedied by any other procefs. And thefe, I think, are all the material alterations, that have happened with refpect to private juftice, in the courfe of the prefent century.

THUS therefore, for the amufement and inftruction of the ftudent, I have endeavoured to delineate fome rude outlines of a plan for the hiftory of our laws and liberties; from their firft rife, and gradual progrefs, among our Britifh and Saxon anceftors, till their total eclipfe at the Norman conqueft; from which they have gradually emerged, and rifen to the perfection they now enjoy, at different periods of time. We have feen, in the courfe of our enquiries, in this and the former volumes, that the fundamental maxims and rules of the law, which regard the rights of perfons, and the rights of things, the private injuries that may be offered to both, and the crimes which affect the public, have been and are every day improving, and are now fraught with the accumulated wifdom of ages : that the forms of adminiftring juftice came to perfection under Edward the firft ; and have not been much varied, nor always for the better, fince : that our religious liberties were fully eftablifhed at the reformation : but that the recovery of our civil and political liberties was a work of longer time ; they not being throughly and completely regained, till after the reftoration of king Charles, nor fully and explicitly acknowleged and defined, till the aera of the happy revolution. Of a conftitution, fo wifely contrived, fo

ftrongly

ſtrongly raiſed, and ſo highly finiſhed, it is hard to ſpeak with that praiſe, which is juſtly and ſeverely it's due : --- the thorough and attentive contemplation of it will furniſh it's beſt panegyric. It hath been the endeavour of theſe commentaries, however the execution may have ſucceeded, to examine it's ſolid foundations, to mark out it's extenſive plan, to explain the uſe and diſtribution of it's parts, and from the harmonious concurrence of thoſe ſeveral parts to demonſtrate the elegant proportion of the whole. We have taken occaſion to admire at every turn the noble monuments of antient ſimplicity, and the more curious refinements of modern art. Nor have it's faults been concealed from view; for faults it has, left we ſhould be tempted to think it of more than human ſtructure : defects, chiefly ariſing from the decays of time, or the rage of unſkilful improvements in later ages. To ſuſtain, to repair, to beautify this noble pile, is a charge intruſted principally to the nobility, and ſuch gentlemen of the kingdom, as are delegated by their country to parliament. The protection of T H E L I B E R T Y   O F   B R I T A I N is a duty which they owe to themſelves, who enjoy it; to their anceſtors, who tranſmitted it down; and to their poſterity, who will claim at their hands this, the beſt birthright, and nobleſt inheritance of mankind.

T H E   E N D.

APPENDIX.

§. 1. RECORD *of an Indictment and Conviction of* MURDER, *at the Assises.*

Warwickshire, ⎱ 𝕭𝕰 **it remembered**, that at the general session of the
   to wit. ⎰   lord the king of *oyer* and *terminer* holden at Warwick, in and for the said county of Warwick, on Friday the twelfth
day of March in the second year of the reign of the lord George the
third, now king of Great Britain, before sir Michael Foster, knight,
one of the justices of the said lord the king assigned to hold pleas before the king himself, sir Edward Clive, knight, one of the justices
of the said lord the king of his court of common bench, and others
their fellows, justices of the said lord the king, assigned by letters patent of the said lord the king, under his great seal of Great Britain,
made to them the aforesaid justices and others, and any two or more
of them, whereof one of them the said sir Michael Foster and sir Edward Clive, the said lord the king would have to be one, to enquire
(by the oath of good and lawful men of the county aforesaid, by whom
the truth of the matter might be the better known, and by other ways,
methods, and means, whereby they could or might the better know,
as well within liberties as without) more fully the truth of all treasons,
misprisions of treasons, insurrections, rebellions, counterfeitings, clippings, washings, false coinings, and other falsities of the monies of
Great Britain, and of other kingdoms or dominions whatsoever; and
of all murders, felonies, manslaughters, killings, burglaries, rapes of
women, unlawful meetings and conventicles, unlawful uttering of
words, unlawful assemblies, misprisions, confederacies, false allegations, trespasses, riots, routs, retentions, escapes, contempts, falsities,
negligences, concealments, maintenances, oppressions, champarties,
deceits,

Session of *oyer* and *terminer*.

Commission of

deceits, and all other misdeeds, offences, and injuries whatsoever, and also the accessories of the same, within the county aforesaid, as well within liberties as without, by whomsoever and howsoever done, had, perpetrated, and committed, and by whom, to whom, when, how, and in what manner; and of all other articles and circumstances in the said letters patent of the said lord the king specified, the premises and *oyer and terminer,* every or any of them howsoever concerning; and for this time to hear and determine the said treasons and other the premises, according to *and of the peace.* the law and custom of the realm of England; and also keepers of the peace, and justices of the said lord the king, assigned to hear and determine divers felonies, trespasses, and other misdemesnors committed *Grand jury.* within the county aforesaid: by the oath of sir James Thompson, baronet, Charles Roper, Henry Dawes, Peter Wilson, Samuel Rogers, John Dawson, James Philips, John Mayo, Richard Savage, William Bell, James Morris, Laurence Hall, and Charles Carter, esquires, good and lawful men of the county aforesaid, then and there impanelled, sworn, and charged to enquire for the said lord the king and for the *Indictment.* body of the said county, it is presented, that Peter Hunt, late of the parish of Lighthorne in the said county, gentleman, not having the fear of God before his eyes, but being moved and seduced by the instigation of the devil, on the fifth day of March in the said second year of the reign of the said lord the king, at the parish of Lighthorne aforesaid, with force and arms, in and upon one Samuel Collins, in the peace of God and of the said lord the king then and there being, feloniously, wilfully, and of his malice aforethought, did make an assault; and that the said Peter Hunt with a certain drawn sword, made of iron and steel, of the value of five shillings, which he the said Peter Hunt in his right hand then and there had and held, him the said Samuel Collins in and upon the left side of the belly of him the said Samuel Collins then and there feloniously, wilfully, and of his malice aforethought, did strike, thrust, stab, and penetrate; giving unto the said Samuel Collins, then and there, with the sword drawn as aforesaid, in and upon the left side of the belly of him the said Samuel Collins, one mortal wound of the breadth of one inch, and the depth of nine inches; of which said mortal wound he the said Samuel Collins, at the parish of Lighthorne aforesaid in the said county of Warwick, from the said fifth day of March in the year aforesaid until the seventh day of the same month in the same year, did languish, and languishing did live; on which said seventh day of March, in the year aforesaid, the said Samuel Collins, at the parish of Lighthorne aforesaid in the county aforesaid, of the said mortal wound did die: and so the jurors aforesaid, upon their oath aforesaid, do say, that the said Peter Hunt him the said Samuel Collins, in manner and form aforesaid, feloniously, wilfully, and of his malice aforethought, did kill and murder, against the peace of the said

lord

lord the now king, his crown, and dignity. **Whereupon** the sheriff of *Capias.*
the county aforesaid is commanded, that he omit not for any liberty in
his bailiwick, but that he take the said Peter Hunt, if he may be found
in his bailiwick, and him safely keep, to answer to the felony and mur-
der whereof he stands indicted. **Which** said indictment the said justi- *Session of gaol-*
ces of the lord the king abovenamed, afterwards, to wit, at the deli- *delivery.*
very of the gaol of the said lord the king, holden at Warwick in and
for the county aforesaid, on Friday the sixth day of August, in the said
second year of the reign of the said lord the king, before the right honourable William lord Mansfield, chief justice of the said lord the king
assigned to hold pleas before the king himself, sir Sidney Stafford Smythe,
knight, one of the barons of the said lord the king, and others their
fellows, justices of the said lord the king, assigned to deliver his said
gaol of the county aforesaid of the prisoners therein being, by their
proper hands do deliver here in court of record in form of law to be
determined. **And afterwards**, to wit, at the same delivery of the gaol *Arraignment.*
of the said lord the king of his county aforesaid, on the said Friday the
sixth day of August, in the said second year of the reign of the said
lord the king, before the said justices of the lord the king last abovenamed and others their fellows aforesaid, here cometh the said Peter
Hunt, under the custody of William Browne, esquire, sheriff of the
county aforesaid, (in whose custody in the gaol of the county aforesaid,
for the cause aforesaid, he had been before committed) being brought
to the bar here in his proper person by the said sheriff, to whom he is
here also committed : **And** forthwith being demanded concerning the
premises in the said indictment above specified and charged upon him,
how he will acquit himself thereof, he saith, that he is not guilty there- *Plea; not guilty.*
of ; and thereof for good and evil he puts himself upon the country : *Issue.*
And John Blencowe, esquire, clerk of the assises for the county aforesaid, who prosecutes for the said lord the king in this behalf, doth the
like : **Therefore** let a jury thereupon here immediately come before *Venire.*
the said justices of the lord the king last abovementioned, and others
their fellows aforesaid, of free and lawful men of the neighbourhood of
the said parish of Lighthorne in the county of Warwick aforesaid, by
whom the truth of the matter may be the better known, and who are not
of kin to the said Peter Hunt, to recognize upon their oath, whether
the said Peter Hunt be guilty of the felony and murder in the indictment aforesaid above specified, or not guilty : because as well the said
John Blencowe, who prosecutes for the said lord the king in this behalf, as the said Peter Hunt, have put themselves upon the said jury.
And the jurors of the said jury by the said sheriff for this purpose impanelled and returned, to wit, David Williams, John Smith, Thomas
Horne, Charles Nokes, Richard May, Walter Duke, Matthew Lyon,
James White, William Bates, Oliver Green, Bartholomew Nash, and
Henry

Henry Long, being called, come; who being elected, tried, and sworn, to speak the truth of and concerning the premises, upon their oath say, **that** the said Peter Hunt is guilty of the felony and murder aforesaid, on him above charged in the form aforesaid, as by the indictment aforesaid is above supposed against him; and that the said Peter Hunt at the time of committing the said felony and murder, or at any time since to this time, had not nor hath any goods or chattels, lands or tenements, in the said county of Warwick, or elsewhere, to the knowlege of the said jurors. And upon this it is forthwith demanded of the said Peter Hunt, if he hath or knoweth any thing to say, wherefore the said justices here ought not upon the premises and verdict aforesaid to proceed to judgment and execution against him: who nothing farther saith, unless as he before had said. **Whereupon**, all and singular the premises being seen, and by the said justices here fully understood, **it is considered** by the court here, that the said Peter Hunt be taken to the gaol of the said lord the king of the said county of Warwick from whence he came, and from thence to the place of execution on Monday now next ensuing, being the ninth day of this instant August, and there be hanged by the neck until he be dead; and that afterwards his body be dissected and anatomized.

Verdict; guilty of murder.

Judgment of death,

and dissection.

§. 2. *Conviction of* Manslaughter.

Verdict; — not guilty of murder; guilty of manslaughter.

———— upon their oath say, **that** the said Peter Hunt is not guilty of the murder aforesaid, above charged upon him; but that the said Peter Hunt is guilty of the felonious slaying of the aforesaid Samuel Collins; and that he had not nor hath any goods or chattels, lands or tenements, at the time of the felony and manslaughter aforesaid, or ever afterwards to this time, to the knowlege of the said jurors. And immediately it is demanded of the said Peter Hunt, if he hath or knoweth any thing to say, wherefore the said justices here ought not upon the premises and verdict aforesaid to proceed to judgment and execution against him: **who saith** that he is a clerk, and prayeth the benefit of clergy to be allowed him in this behalf. **Whereupon**, all and singular the premises being seen, and by the said justices here fully understood, **it is considered** by the court here, that the said Peter Hunt be burned in his left hand, and delivered. And immediately he is burned in his left hand, and is delivered, according to the form of the statute.

Clergy prayed.

Judgment to be burned in the hand, and delivered.

§. 3. *Entry*

§. 3. *Entry of a Trial* inſtanter *in the Court of King's Bench, upon a col-*
lateral Iſſue ; and Rule of Court for Execution thereon.

Michaelmas term, in the ſixth year of the reign of king George
the third.

Kent: The King
againſt
Thomas Rogers.

The priſoner at the bar being brought into
this court in cuſtody of the ſheriff of the county
of Suſſex, by virtue of his majeſty's writ of *Habeas corpus.*
habeas corpus, **it is ordered** that the ſaid writ and the return thereto be filed.
And it appearing by a certain record of attainder, which hath been re- Record of attain-
moved into this court by his majeſty's writ of *certiorari,* that the pri- der read ;
ſoner at the bar ſtands attainted, by the name of Thomas Rogers, of fe- for felony and
lony for a robbery on the highway, and the ſaid priſoner at the bar robbery.
having heard the record of the ſaid attainder now read to him, is now Priſoner aſked
aſked by the court here, what he hath to ſay for himſelf, why the what he can ſay
in bar of execu-
court here ſhould not proceed to award execution againſt him upon the tion:
ſaid attainder. **He** for plea ſaith, that he is not the ſame Thomas Rogers Plea; not the
in the ſaid record of attainder named, and againſt whom judgment was ſame perſon.
pronounced : and this he is ready to verify and prove, *&c.* **To** which Replication.
ſaid plea the honourable Charles Yorke, eſquire, attorney general of our
preſent ſovereign lord the king, who for our ſaid lord the king in this
behalf proſecuteth, being now preſent here in court, and having heard
what the ſaid priſoner at the bar hath now alleged, for our ſaid lord the
king by way of reply ſaith, that the ſaid priſoner now here at the bar is averring that he
the ſame Thomas Rogers in the ſaid record of attainder named, and is.
againſt whom judgment was pronounced as aforeſaid : and this he Iſſue joined.
prayeth may be enquired into by the country ; and the ſaid priſoner at
the bar doth the like : **Therefore** let a jury in this behalf immediately *Venire* awarded
come here into court, by whom the truth of the matter will be the bet- *inſtanter.*
ter known, and who have no affinity to the ſaid priſoner, to try upon
their oath, whether the ſaid priſoner at the bar be the ſame Thomas
Rogers in the ſaid record of attainder named, and againſt whom judgment was ſo pronounced as aforeſaid, or not : becauſe as well the ſaid
Charles Yorke, eſquire, attorney general of our ſaid lord the king, who
for our ſaid lord the king in this behalf proſecutes, as the ſaid priſoner
at the bar, have put themſelves in this behalf upon the ſaid jury. **And** Jury ſworn.
immediately thereupon the ſaid jury come here into court; and being
elected, tried, and ſworn to ſpeak the truth touching and concerning
the premiſes aforeſaid, and having heard the ſaid record read to them,
do ſay upon their oath, that the ſaid priſoner at the bar is the ſame Tho- Verdict; that he
mas Rogers in the ſaid record of attainder named, and againſt whom is the ſame.

H h h judgment

judgment was fo pronounced as aforefaid, in manner and form as the
faid attorney general hath by his faid replication to the faid plea of the
faid prifoner now here at the bar alleged. And hereupon the faid attorney general on behalf of our faid lord the king now prayeth, that the
court here would proceed to award execution againft him the faid Thomas Rogers upon the faid attainder. Whereupon, all and fingular the
premifes being now feen and fully underftood by the court here, it is
ordered by the court here, that execution be done upon the faid prifoner at the bar for the faid felony in purfuance of the faid judgment,
according to due form of law: And it is laftly ordered, that he the faid
Thomas Rogers, the prifoner at the bar, be now committed to the cuftody of the fheriff of the county of Kent (now alfo prefent here in
court) for the purpofe aforefaid; and that the faid fheriff of Kent do
execution upon the faid defendant the prifoner at the bar for the faid
felony, in purfuance of the faid judgment, according to due form of
law.

*Award of execu-
tion.*

On the motion of Mr. Attorney General.

By the Court.

§. 4. *Warrant of Execution on Judgment of Death, at the general Gaol-
delivery in* London *and* Middlefex.

London
and
Middlefex.
} To the fheriffs of the city of London; and to the fheriff
of the county of Middlefex: and to the keeper of his
majefty's gaol of Newgate.

Whereas at the feffion of gaol delivery of Newgate, for the city of
London and county of Middlefex, holden at Juftice Hall in the Old
Bailey, on the nineteenth day of October laft, Patrick Mahony, Roger
Jones, Charles King, and Mary Smith, received fentence of death for
the refpective offences in their feveral indictments mentioned; Now it
is hereby ordered, that execution of the faid fentence be made and done
upon them the faid Patrick Mahony and Roger Jones, on Wednefday
the ninth day of this inftant month of November at the ufual place of
execution. And it is his majefty's command, that execution of the faid
fentence upon them the faid Charles King and Mary Smith be refpited,
until his majefty's pleafure touching them be farther known.

Given under my hand and feal this fourth day of
November, one thoufand feven hundred and fixty
eight.

James Eyre, Recorder. L. S.

§. 5. *Writ*

§. 5. *Writ of Execution upon a judgment of* Murder, *before the* King *in* Parliament.

𝕲𝕰𝕺𝕽𝕲𝕰 the second by the grace of God of Great Britain, France, and Ireland, king, defender of the faith, and so forth ; to the sheriffs of London and sheriff of Middlesex, greeting. 𝕎𝔥𝔢𝔯𝔢𝔞𝔰 Lawrence earl Ferrers, viscount Tamworth, hath been indicted of felony and murder by him done and committed, which said indictment hath been certified before us in our present parliament ; and the said Lawrence earl Ferrers, viscount Tamworth, hath been thereupon arraigned, and upon such arraignment hath pleaded not guilty ; and the said Lawrence earl Ferrers, viscount Tamworth, hath before us in our said parliament been tried, and in due form of law convicted thereof ; and whereas judgment hath been given in our said parliament, that the said Lawrence earl Ferrers, viscount Tamworth, shall be hanged by the neck till he is dead, and that his body be dissected and anatomized, the execution of which judgment yet remaineth to be done : 𝕎𝔢 require, and by these presents strictly command you, that upon Monday the fifth day of May instant, between the hours of nine in the morning and one in the afternoon of the same day, him the said Lawrence earl Ferrers, viscount Tamworth, without the gate of our tower of London (to you then and there to be delivered, as by another writ to the lieutenant of our tower of London or to his deputy directed, we have commanded) into your custody you then and there receive : and him in your custody so being, you forthwith convey to the accustomed place of execution at Tyburn : and that you do cause execution to be done upon the said Lawrence earl Ferrers, viscount Tamworth, in your custody so being, in all things according to the said judgment. And this you are by no means to omit, at your peril. 𝕎𝔦𝔱𝔫𝔢𝔰𝔰 ourself at Westminster the second day of May, in the thirty third year of our reign.

Yorke and Yorke.

T H E   E N D.

I N D E X.

☞ *The large numerals denote the volumes; the ciphers the pages of the commentaries; and the small numerals the pages of the appendix.*

INDEX.

Appen-

INDEX.

INDEX.

INDEX.

Conti-

INDEX.

Dehors,

I N D E X.

INDEX.

Embaſſadors,

INDEX.

I N D E X.

Fine

I N D E X.

Health.

INDEX.

I N D E X.

Interdictum.

I N D E X.

INDEX.

I N D E X.

INDEX.

I N D E X.

INDEX.

Office

INDEX.

I N D E X.

I N D E X.

I N D E X.

INDEX.

I N D E X.

Threats

I N D E X.

Ubiquity

I N D E X.

Wales,

INDEX.

THE END.

SUPPLEMENT

TO THE

FIRST EDITION;

CONTAINING

The moſt material CORRECTIONS and ADDITIONS in the
SECOND.

Page 46. lin. 10.

*A*FTER action *inſert*; (indifferent in
itſelf)

Page 83. lin. 2.
For Adrian *read* Clement

Page 97. lin. 29.
After union *inſert this note.*

It may juſtly be doubted, whether even ſuch
an infringement (though a manifeſt breach
of good faith, unleſs done upon the moſt preſ-
ſing neceſſity) would conſequentially diſſolve
the union : for the bare idea of a ſtate, without a power ſomewhere veſted to alter every
part of it's laws, is the height of political
abſurdity. The truth ſeems to be, that in
ſuch an *incorporate union* (which is well diſ-
tinguiſhed by a very learned prelate from a
foederate alliance, where ſuch an infringement would certainly reſcind the compact)
the two contracting ſtates are totally anni-
hilated, without any power of revival ; and
a third ariſes from their conjunction, in
which all the rights of ſovereignty, and
particularly that of legiſlation, muſt of neceſſity reſide. (See Warburton's alliance. 195.)
But the imprudent exertion of this right
would probably raiſe a very alarming fer-
ment in the minds of individuals; and therefore it is hinted above that ſuch an attempt
might *endanger* (though not certainly *deſtroy*)
the union.

Page 98. lin. 16.
Inſtead of this Paragraph, inſert the following.
The town of Berwick upon Tweed was
originally part of the kingdom of Scotland ;
VOL. I.

and, as ſuch, was for a time reduced by
king Edward I into the poſſeſſion of the
crown of England : and, during ſuch it's
ſubjection, it received from that prince a
charter, which (after it's ſubſequent ceſſion
by Edward Balliol, to be for ever united to
the crown and realm of England) was confirmed by king Edward III, with ſome additions ; particularly that it ſhould be governed by the laws and uſages which it enjoyed during the time of king Alexander,
that is, before it's reduction by Edward I.
It's conſtitution was new-modelled, and put
upon an Engliſh footing by a charter of
king James I : and all it's liberties, fran-
chiſes, and cuſtoms, were confirmed in parliament by the ſtatutes 22 Edw. IV. c. 8.
and 2 Jac. I. c. 28. Though therefore it
hath ſome local peculiarities, derived from
the antient laws of Scotland, [Hale Hiſt.
C. L. 183. 1 Sid. 382. 462. 2 Show. 365.]
yet it is clearly part of the realm of England, being repreſented by burgeſſes in the
houſe of commons, and bound by all acts
of the Britiſh parliament, whether ſpecially
named or otherwiſe. And therefore it was
(perhaps ſuperfluouſly) declared by ſtatute
20 Geo. II. c. 42. that, where England only
is mentioned in any act of parliament, the
ſame notwithſtanding hath and ſhall be
deemed to comprehend the dominion of
Wales and town of Berwick upon Tweed.
And, though certain of the king's writs or
proceſſes of the courts of Weſtminſter do
not uſually run into Berwick, any more
than the principality of Wales, yet it hath
been

been folemnly adjudged, [Cro. Jac. 543. 2 Roll. Abr. 292. Stat. 11 Geo. I. c. 4. 4 Burr. 834.] that all prerogative writs (as thofe of *mandamus*, prohibition, *habeas corpus*, *certiorari*, &c.) may iffue to Berwick as well as to every other of the dominions of the crown of England; and that indictments and other local matters arifing in the town of Berwick may be tried by a jury of the county of Northumberland.

Page 100. lin. 11.

Leave out from yearbook *to the end of the paragraph : and infert* ; " a tax " granted by the parliament of England " fhall not bind thofe of Ireland, becaufe " they are not fummoned to our parlia- " ment:" and again, " Ireland hath a par- " liament of it's own, and maketh and al- " tereth laws ; and our ftatutes do not bind " them becaufe they do not fend knights to " our parliament: but their perfons are the " king's fubjects, like as the inhabitants of " Calais, Gafcoigny, and Guienne, while " they continued under the king's fubjec- " tion." The general run of laws, enacted by the fuperior ftate, are fuppofed to be calculated for it's own internal government, and do not extend to it's diftant dependent countries ; which, bearing no part in the legiflature, are not therefore in it's ordinary and daily contemplation. But, when the fovereign legiflative power fees it neceffary to extend it's care to any of it's fubordinate dominions, and mentions them exprefsly by name or includes them under general words, there can be no doubt but then they are bound by it's laws [Yearbook 1 Hen. VII. 3. 7 Rep. 22. Calvin's cafe.]

The original method of paffing ftatutes in Ireland was nearly the fame as in England, the chief governor holding parliaments at his pleafure, which enacted fuch laws as they thought proper. [Irifh Stat. 11 Eliz. ft. 3. c. 8.] But an ill ufe being made of this liberty, particularly by lord Gormanftown, deputy-lieutenant in the reign of Edward IV, [*Ibid.* 10 Hen. VII. c. 23.] a fet of ftatutes were there enacted in the 10 Hen. VII. (fir Edward Poynings being then lord deputy, whence they are called Poynings' laws) one of which, [cap. 4. expounded by 3 & 4 Ph. & M. c 4.] in order to reftrain the power as well of the deputy as the Irifh parliament, provides, 1. That, before any parliament be fummoned or holden, the chief governor and council of

Ireland fhall certify to the king under the great feal of Ireland the confiderations and caufes thereof, and the articles of the acts propofed to be paffed therein. 2. That after the king, in his council of England, fhall have confidered, approved, or altered the faid acts or any of them, and certified them back under the great feal of England, and fhall have given licence to fummon and hold a parliament, then the fame fhall be fummoned and held ; and therein the faid acts fo certified, and no other, fhall be propofed, received, or rejected. [4 Inft. 353.] But as this precluded any law from being propofed, but fuch as were preconceived before the parliament was in being, which occafioned many inconveniences and made frequent diffolutions neceffary, it was provided by the ftatute of Philip and Mary before-cited, that any new propofitions might be certified to England in the ufual forms, even after the fummons and during the feffion of parliament. By this means however there was nothing left to the parliament in Ireland, but a bare negative or power of rejecting, not of propofing or altering, any law. But the ufage now is, that bills are often framed in either houfe, under the denomination of "heads for a " bill or bills;" and in that fhape they are offered to the confideration of the lord lieutenant and privy council : who, upon fuch parliamentary intimation, or otherwife upon the application of private perfons, receive and tranfmit fuch heads, or reject them without any tranfmiffion to England. And, with regard to Poynings' law in particular, it cannot be repealed or fufpended, unlefs the bill for that purpofe, before it be certified to England, be approved by both the houfes. [Irifh Stat. 11 Eliz. ft. 3. c. 38.]

Page 102. lin. 6, 7.
For all other courts *read* the chancery

Page 105. lin. 1.

Leave out from are *to* them *in line* 3, *and infert* ; then in being, which are the birthright of every fubject, [2 P. W^{ms}. 75.] are immediately there in force. But this muft be underftood with very many and very great reftrictions. Such colonifts carry with them only fo much of the Englifh law, as is applicable to their own fituation and the condition of an infant colony ; fuch, for inftance, as the general rules of inheritance, and of protection from perfonal injuries. The artificial refinements and diftinctions incident

SUPPLEMENT.

incident to the property of a great and commercial people, the laws of police and revenue, (such especially as are inforced by penalties) the mode of maintenance for the established clergy, the jurisdiction of spiritual courts, and a multitude of other provisions, are neither necessary nor convenient for them, and therefore are not in force. What shall be admitted and what rejected, at what times, and under what restrictions, must, in case of dispute, be decided in the first instance by their own provincial judicature, subject to the revision and controll of the king in council; the whole of their constitution being also liable to be new-modelled and reformed, by the general super-intending power of the legislature in the mother country.

Ibid. lin.16.

After particularly named *insert*;

With respect to their interior polity, our colonies are properly of three sorts. 1. Provincial establishments, the constitutions of which depend on the respective commissions issued by the crown to the governors, and the instructions which usually accompany those commissions; under the authority of which, provincial assemblies are constituted, with the power of making local ordinances, not repugnant to the laws of England. 2. Proprietary governments, granted out by the crown to individuals, in the nature of feudatory principalities, with all the inferior regalities, and subordinate powers of legislation, which formerly belonged to the owners of counties palatine: yet still with these express conditions, that the ends for which the grant was made be substantially pursued, and that nothing be attempted which may derogate from the sovereignty of the mother country. 3. Charter governments, in the nature of civil corporations, with the power of making by-laws for their own interior regulation, not contrary to the laws of England; and with such rights and authorities as are specially given them in their several charters of incorporation.

Ibid. lin. 30.

After effect *insert*; and, because several of the colonies had claimed the sole and exclusive right of imposing taxes upon themselves, the statute 6Geo.III. c.12. expressly declares, that all his majesty's colonies and plantations in America have been, are, and of right ought to be, subordinate to and dependent upon the imperial crown and

parliament of Great Britain; who have full power and authority to make laws and statutes of sufficient validity to bind the colonies and people of America, subjects of the crown of Great Britain, in all cases whatsoever.

Page 107. lin. 4.
After Wales *insert*; and Berwick,

Page 110. lin. 5.
After Church. *insert*; Yet extraparochial wastes and marsh lands, when improved and drained, are by the statute 17Geo.II. c.37. to be assessed to all parochial rates in the parish next adjoining.

Page 126. lin. 25, 26.
For are totally void in law *read* may be afterwards avoided,

Page 129. lin. 2.
After Life. *insert*; But, even in the times of popery, the law of England took no cognizance of *profession* in any foreign country, because the fact could not be tried in our courts; [Co. Litt.132.] and therefore, since the reformation, the disability is held to be abolished. [Salk. 162.]

Page 134. lin. 9.
After service: *insert*; excepting sailors and soldiers, the nature of whose employment necessarily implies an exception:

Page 143.
After 307. *(in note *) insert*; The first mention of it in our statute law is in the preamble to the statute of Westm. 1. 3 Edw. I. A. D. 1272.

Page 143. lin. 24.
After France *insert this note.* These were assembled for the last time, A. D. 1561. See Whitelocke of Parl. c. 72.

Page 147. lin. 28.
After scruple. *insert*; And yet, out of abundant caution, it was thought necessary to confirm it's acts in the next parliament, by stat. 13 Car. II. c.7. & c. 14.

Page 152. lin. 7.
After estates *insert*; And, from this want of a separate assembly and separate negative of the prelates, some writers have argued [Whitelocke on Parl. c.72. Warburt. alliance. b. 2. c.3.] very cogently, that the lords spiritual and temporal are now in reality only one estate: [Dyer. 60] which is unquestionably true in every effectual sense, though the antient distinction between them still nominally continues.

Page

§   Page 152.

After c. 6. *(in note* u*) insert*; The act of uniformity, 1 Eliz. c.2. was passed with the diffent of all the bishops; (Gibf. cod.268.) and therefore the ftile of *lords spiritual* is omitted throughout the whole.

§ *After* 6, 7. *(in note* w*) insert*; See Keilw. 184; where it is holden by the judges, 7 Hen. VIII. that the king may hold a parliament without any spiritual lords. This was alfo exemplified in fact in the two firft parliaments of Charles II; wherein no bishops were summoned, till after the repeal of the ftat. 16 Car. I. c.27. by ftat. 13 Car. II. ft. 1. c. 2.

Page 160. lin. 34.

Leave out from But *to* required *in pag.* 161. lin. 3.   Page 161. lin. 22.

⁁   *After* any other *insert*;

The only way by which courts of juftice could antiently take cognizance of privilege of parliament was by writ of privilege, in the nature of a *superfedeas*, to deliver the party out of cuftody when arrefted in a civil fuit. [Dyer. 59. 4 Pryn. Brev. Parl. 757.] For when a letter was written by the fpeaker to the judges, to ftay proceedings againft a privileged perfon, they rejected it as contrary to their oath of office. [Latch. 48. Noy. 83.] But fince the ftatute 12 W. III. c. 3. which enacts, that no privileged perfon fhall be fubject to arreft or imprifonment, it hath been held that fuch arreft is irregular *ab initio*, and that the party may be difcharged upon motion. [Stra. 989.] It is to be obferved, that there is no precedent of any fuch writ of privilege, but only in civil fuits; and that the ftatute of 1 Jac. I. c. 13. and that of king William (which remedy fome inconveniences arifing from privilege of parliament) fpeak only of civil actions. And therefore the claim of privilege hath been ufually guarded with an exception as to the cafe of indictable crimes; [Com. Journ. 17 Aug. 1641.] or, as it hath been frequently expreffed, of treafon, felony, and breach (or furety) of the peace. [4 Inft. 25. Com. Journ. 20 May. 1675.] Whereby it feems to have been underftood that no privilege was allowable to the members, their families, or fervants in any crime whatfoever; for all crimes are treated by the law as being *contra pacem domini regis*. And inftances have not been wanting, wherein privileged perfons have been convicted of mifdemefnors, and committed, or profecuted to outlawry, even in the middle of a

feffion; [*Mich.* 16 *Edw.* IV. in Scacch.—— Lord Raym. 1461.] which proceeding has afterwards received the fanction and approbation of parliament. [Com. Journ. 16 May. 1726.] To which may be added, that, a few years ago, the cafe of writing and publifhing feditious libels was refolved by both houfes [Com. Journ. 24 Nov. Lord's Journ. 29 Nov. 1763.] not to be intitled to privilege, and that the reafons, upon which that cafe proceeded, [Lords Proteft. *ibid.*] extended equally to every indictable offence. So that the chief, if not the only, privilege of parliament, in fuch cafes, feems to be the right of receiving immediate information of the imprifonment or detention of any member, with the reafon for which he is detained: a practice that is daily ufed upon the flighteft military accufations, preparatory to a trial by a court martial; [Com. Journ. 20 Apr. 1762.] and which is recognized by the feveral temporary ftatutes for fufpending the *habeas corpus* act, [particularly 17 Geo. II. c.6.] whereby it is provided, that no member of either houfe fhall be detained, till the matter of which he ftands fufpected, be firft communicated to the houfe of which he is a member, and the confent of the faid houfe obtained for his commitment or detaining. But yet the ufage has uniformly been, ever fince the revolution, that the communication has been fubfequent to the arreft.

⁁   Page 164.

After 17. *(in note* w*) insert*; See the anfwer to this cafe by fir Heneage Finch, Com. Journ. 22 Apr. 1671.

⁁   Page 174. lin. 27.

After feal, *insert*; or any other appointed by the king's commiffion: and, if none be fo appointed, the houfe of lords (it is faid) may elect.

⁁   Page 176. lin. 32.

After to, *insert*; the title to it is then fettled; which ufed to be a general one for all the acts paffed in the feffion, till in the fifth year of Henry VIII diftinct titles were introduced for each chapter. [Lord Bacon on ufes. 8°. 326.] After this,

⁁   Page 177. lin. 18.

After lords *insert*; But, when an act of grace or pardon is paffed, it is firft figned by his majefty, and then read once only in each of the houfes, without any new engroffing or amendment. [D'ewes journ. 20. 73. Com. journ. 17 June. 1747.]

Page

Page 177. lin. 20.

After assent; *insert*; except in the case of a money bill, which after receiving the concurrence of the lords is sent back to the house of commons? [Com. journ. 24 Jul. 1660.]

Page 177. lin. 34.

After upon it." *insert*; When a money bill is passed, it is carried up and presented to the king by the speaker of the house of commons; [*Rot. Parl.* 9 *Hen. IV.* in Pryn. 4 Inst. 30, 31.] and the royal assent is thus expressed, "*le roy remercie ses loyal subjects,* "*accepte lour benevolence, et aussi le veut,* the "king thanks his loyal subjects, accepts "their benevolence, and wills it so to be." In case of an act of grace, which originally proceeds from the crown and has the royal assent in the first stage of it, the clerk of the parliament thus pronounces the gratitude of the subject; "*les prelats, seigneurs, et com-* "*mons, en ce present parliament assemblees, au* "*nom de touts vous autres subjects, remercient* "*tres humblement votre majeste, et prient a* "*Dieu vous donner en sante bone vie et longue;* "the prelates, lords, and commons, in this "present parliament assembled, in the name "of all your other subjects, most humbly "thank your majesty, and pray to God to "grant you in health and wealth long to "live." [D'ewes journ. 35.]

Page 193. lin. 23.

After royal, *insert*; excepting his elder broth r Theobald, who (as earl of Blois) was already provided for.

Page 193. lin. 27.

After usurper; *insert*; and therefore he rather chose to rely on a title by election, ["*Ego Stephanus Dei gratia assensu cleri et* "*populi in regem Anglorum electus, &c.*" (*Cart. A.D.* 1136. Ric. de Haguftald 314. Hearne *ad Guil. Neubr.* 711.)]

Page 196. lin. 20.
For right *read* law

Page 208. lin. 6.
For only *read* eldest

Page 217. lin. 20.
For IV *read* VI.

Page 218. lin. 30.

After son. *insert*; But under the description of the king's *children* his *grandsons* are held to be included, without having recourse to sir Edward Coke's interpretation of *nephew*: and therefore when his late majesty created his grandson, the second son of Frederick prince of Wales deceased,

duke of York, and referred it to the house of lords to settle his place and precedence, they certified [Lords journ. 24 Apr. 1760] that he ought to have place next to the duke of Cumberland, the king's youngest son; and that he might have a seat on the left hand of the cloth of estate. But when, on the accession of his present majesty, those royal personages ceased to take place as the *children,* and ranked only as the *brother* and *uncle,* of the king, they also left their seats on the side of the cloth of estate: so that when the duke of Glocester, his majesty's second brother, took his seat in the house of peers, [*ibid.* 10 Jan. 1765.] he was placed on the upper end of the earl's bench (on which the dukes usually sit) next to his royal highness the duke of York

Page 224. lin. 13.

After council. *insert*; Whenever also a question arises between two provinces in America or elsewhere, as concerning the extent of their charters and the like, the king in his council exercises *original* jurisdiction therein, upon the principles of feodal sovereignty. And so likewise when any person claims an island or a province, in the nature of a feodal principality, by grant from the king or his ancestors, the determination of that right belongs to his majesty in council: as was the case of the earl of Derby with regard to the isle of Man in the reign of queen Elizabeth, and of the earl of Cardigan and others, as representatives of the duke of Montague, with relation to the island of St. Vincent in 1764. But from all the dominions of the crown, excepting Great Britain and Ireland, an *appellate* jurisdiction (in the last resort) is vested in the same tribunal; which usually exercises it's judicial authority in a committee of the whole privy council, who hear the allegations and proofs, and make their rep rt to his majesty in council, by whom the judgment is finally given.

Page 229. lin. 14.

After religion. *insert*; And, with respect to the latter of these three branches, we may farther remark, that by the act of union, 5 Ann. c 8. two preceding statutes are recited and confirmed; the one of the parliament of Scotland, the other of the parliament of England: which e act; the former, that every king at his accession shall take and subscribe an oath, to preserve the protestant religion and presbyterian church government in Scotland; the

latter

latter, that at his coronation he shall take and subscribe a similar oath, to preserve the settlement of the church of England within England, Ireland, Wales, and Berwick, and the territories thereunto belonging.

Page 235. lin. 18.

ſ *After* empire ; *add this note. Rex allegavit, quod ipſe omnes libertates haberet in regno ſuo, quas imperator vindicabat in imperio.* (M. Paris, *A. D.* 1095.)

Page 240. lin. 19.

ſ *After* Great Britain, *inſert*; and that the "king was a ſtranger to our language and "conſtitution."

Page 247. lin. 10.

ſ *After* of *inſert*; this country, as well as of the reſt of

Page 247. lin. 21.

ſ *Leave out from* And the truth *to* reciting *in page* 248. *lin.* 5. *and inſert*; But the truth is, ſo few caſes (if any) had ariſen, wherein the privilege was either claimed or diſputed, even with regard to civil ſuits, that our law books are ſilent upon it, previous to the reign of queen Anne; when an embaſſador from Peter the great, czar of Muſcovy, was actually arreſted, and taken out of his coach in London, [21 July. 1708. Boyer's annals of queen Anne.] for a debt of 50 *l.* which he had there contracted. Inſtead of applying to be diſcharged upon his privilege, he gave bail to the action, and the next day complained to the queen. The perſons who were concerned in the arreſt were examined before the privy council (of which the lord chief juſtice Holt was at the ſame time ſworn a member) [25 July. 1708. *ibid.*] and ſeventeen were committed to priſon : [25, 29 Jul. 1708. *ibid.*] moſt of whom were proſecuted by information in the court of queen's bench, at the ſuit of the attorney general, [23 Oct. 1708. *ibid.*] and at their trial before the lord chief juſtice were convicted of the facts by the jury; [14 Feb. 1708. *ibid*] reſerving the queſtion of law, how far thoſe facts were criminal, to be afterwards argued before the judges; which queſtion was never determined. In the mean time the czar reſented this affront very highly, and demanded that the ſheriff of Middleſex and all others concerned in the arreſt ſhould be puniſhed with inſtant death. [17 Sept. 1708. *ibid*] But the queen (to the amazement of that deſpotic court directed her ſecretary to inform him, "that "ſhe could inflict no puniſhment upon any, "the meaneſt, of her ſubjects unleſs war-

"ranted by the law of the land, and there-"fore was perſuaded that he would not in-"ſiſt upon impoſſibilities." [11 Jan. 1708. *ibid.* Mod. Un. Hiſt. xxxv.454] To ſatisfy however the clamours of the foreign miniſters, (who made it a common cauſe) as well as to appeaſe the wrath of Peter, a bill was brought into parliament, [Com. journ. 1708.] and afterwards paſſed into a law, [21 Apr. 1709. Boyer, *ibid.*] to prevent and to puniſh ſuch outrageous inſolence for the future. And with a copy of this act, elegantly engroſſed and illuminated, accompanied by a letter from the queen, an embaſſador extraordinary [Mr Whitworth.] was commiſſioned to appear at Moſcow, [8 Jan. 1709. Boyer, *ibid.*] who declared "that though her majeſty could not inflict "ſuch a puniſhment as was required, be-"cauſe of the defect in that particular of "the former eſtabliſhed conſtitutions of her "kingdom, yet, with the unanimous con-"ſent of the parliament, ſhe had cauſed a "new act to be paſſed, to ſerve as a law "for the future." This humiliating ſtep was accepted as a full ſatisfaction by the czar; and the offenders, at his requeſt, were diſcharged from all farther proſecution. This ſtatute [7 Ann. c. 12.} recites

Page 248. lin. 27.

ſ *After* now *inſert*; held to be part of the law of the land, and are

Page 252. lin. 11.

ſ *After* arms. *inſert*; But paſſports under the king's ſign manual, or licences from his embaſſadors abroad, are now more uſually obtained, and are allowed to be of equal validity.

Page 255. lin. 26.
After do it. *inſert*;

ſ It is partly upon the ſame, and partly upon a fiſcal foundation, to ſecure his marine revenue, that the king has the prerogative of appointing *ports* and *havens*, or ſuch places only, for perſons and merchandize to paſs into and out of the realm, as he in his wiſdom ſees proper. By the feodal law all navigable rivers and havens were computed among the *regalia*, [2 Feud. *t.*56. Crag. 1. 15. 15.] and were ſubject to the ſovereign of the ſtate. And in England it hath always been held, that the king is lord of the whole ſhore, [F. N. B. 113.] and particularly is the guardian of the ports and havens, which are the inlets and gates of the realm : [Dav. 9. 56.] and therefore, ſo

early

early as the reign of king John, we find ships seized by the king's officers for putting in at a place that was not a legal port. [Madox hist. exch. 530.] These legal ports were undoubtedly at first assigned by the crown; since to each of them a court of portmote is incident, [4 Inst. 148.] the jurisdiction of which must flow from the royal authority: the *great ports* of the sea are also referred to, as well known and established, by statute 4 Hen. IV. c. 20. which prohibits the landing elsewhere under pain of confiscation: and the statute 1 Eliz. c. 11. recites that the franchise of lading and discharging had been frequently granted by the crown.

But though the king had a power of granting the franchise of havens and ports, yet he had not the power of resumption, or of narrowing and confining their limits when once established; but any person had a right to load or discharge his merchandize in any part of the haven: whereby the revenue of the customs was much impaired and diminished, by fraudulent landings in obscure and private corners. This occasioned the statutes of 1 Eliz. c. 11. and 13 & 14 Car. II. c. 11. §. 14. which enable the crown by commission to ascertain the limits of all ports, and to assign proper wharfs and quays in each port, for the exclusive landing and loading of merchandize.

The erection of beacons, light-houses, and sea-marks, is also a branch of the royal prerogative: whereof the first were antiently used in order to alarm the country, in case of the approach of an enemy; and all of them are signally useful in guiding and preserving vessels at sea by night as well as by day. For this purpose the king hath the exclusive power, by commission under his great seal, [3 Inst. 204. 4 Inst. 148.] to cause them to be erected in fit and convenient places, [*Rot. Clauf.* 1 Ric. II. m. 42. Pryn. on 4 Inst. 136.] as well upon the lands of the subject as upon the demesnes of the crown: which power is usually vested by letters patent in the office of lord high admiral. [1 Sid. 158. 4 Inst. 149.] And by statute 8 Eliz. c. 13. the corporation of the trinity-house are impowered to set up any beacons or sea-marks wherever they shall think them necessary; and if the owner of the land or any other person shall destroy them, or shall take down any steeple, tree, or other known sea-mark, he shall forfeit 100 *l.* or, in case of inability to pay it, shall be *ipso facto* outlawed.

Page 259. lin. 14.
Leave out from And, *to* public *in line* 18.

Page 279. lin. 13.
After amercements *add this note.* Roger North, in his life of lord keeper North, (43, 44) mentions an eyre, or *iter*, to have been held south of Trent soon after the restoration: but I have met with no report of it's proceedings.

Page 292. lin. 2.
After deodand. *insert*; But juries have of late very frequently taken upon themselves to mitigate these forfeitures, by finding only some trifling thing, or part of an intire thing, to have been the occasion of the death. And in such cases, although the finding of the jury be hardly warrantable by law, the court of king's bench hath generally refused to interfere on behalf of the lord of the franchise, to assist so odious a claim. [Foster of homicide. 266.

Page 304. lin. 19.
After wines. *insert*; which is considerably older than the customs, being taken notice of in the great roll of the exchequer, 8 Ric. I. still extant. [Madox hist. exch. 526, 532.]

Page 321. lin. 18.
For it never in fact amounted to quite so much *read* complaints were made (in the first years at least) that it did not amount to so much

Page 323. lin. 18.
For operating on *read* being pleaded to

Page 329. lin. 22.
Leave out But *and insert*; and the king's letters patent, appointing the new sheriffs, used commonly to bear date the sixth day of November. [Stat. 12 Edw. IV. c. 1.] The statute of Cambridge, 12 Ric. II. c. 2. ordains, that the chancellor, treasurer, keeper of the privy seal, steward of the king's house, the king's chamberlain, clerk of the rolls, the justices of the one bench and the other, barons of the exchequer, and all other that shall be called to ordain, name, or make justices of the peace, *sheriffs*, and other officers of the king, shall be sworn to act indifferently, and to name no man that sueth to be put in office, but such only as they shall judge to be the best and most sufficient. And

Page 330. lin. 25.
After book, *insert*; and the statute 34 & 35 Hen. VIII. c. 26. §. 61. which expresly recognizes this to be the law of the land,

Page 331. lin. 10
After law *insert*; However, it must be

acknow-

acknowleged, that the practice of occasionally naming what are called pocket sheriffs, by the sole authority of the crown, hath been continually uniformly continued to this day.

Page 337. lin. 5.
After suddenly *infert*; or in prison,

Page 339. lin. 2.
After peace, *infert*; either claim that power by prescription; [Lamb. 15.] or were bound to exercise it by the tenure of their lands; [*ibid.* 17.] or, lastly,

Page 348. lin. 28.
After after, *infert*; (though a subsequent nomination will be valid) [Stra. 1123.]

Page 351. lin. 19.
After he *infert*; remains in England, and
Ibid. lin. 20.
Before after *infert*; in his absence, or during (perhaps) his inability, or

Page 352. lin. 13.
After unmarried, *infert*; and childless,

Page 389. lin. 1.
After lords: *infert*; and some are of opinion that there must be at least two writs of summons, and a sitting in two distinct parliaments, to evidence an hereditary barony: [Whitelocke of parl. c. 114.]

Page 400. lin. 22.
For Edmond earl of Kent being taken *read* Thomas earl of Lancaster being condemned

Page 404. lin. 27.
For their *read* nuncupative

Page 409. lin. 6.
For informal *read* nuncupative

Page 426. lin. 29.
Leave out from Idiots *to* it *in page* 427. *lin.* 2. *and infert*; It was formerly adjudged, that the issue of an idiot was legitimate, and consequently that his marriage was valid. A strange determination! since consent is absolutely requisite to matrimony, and neither idiots nor lunatics are capable of consenting to any thing. And therefore the civil law judged much more sensibly, when it made such deprivations of reason a previous impediment, though not a cause of divorce, if they happened after marriage. [*Ff* 23. *tit.* 1 *l* 8. *&* *tit.* 2. *l.* 16.] And modern resolutions have adhered to the reason of the civil law, by determining [Morrison's case, *coram Delegat.*] that the marriage of a lunatic, not being in a lucid interval, was absolutely void. But as it might be difficult to prove the exact state of the party's mind at the actual celebration of the nuptials, upon this account (concurring with some private family [See private acts 23 Geo. II. c. 6.] reasons) the stat. 15 Geo. II. c. 30. has provided, that the marriage of lunatics and persons under phrenzies (if found lunatics under a commission, or committed to the care of trustees by any act of parliament) before they are declared of sound mind by the lord chancellor or the majority of such trustees, shall be totally void.

Page 444. lin. 24.
Leave out from any *to* bastard *in line* 25. *and infert*; the presumptive heir shall be admitted to the inheritance; though liable to lose it again, on the birth of a child within forty weeks from the death of the husband. [Britton. c. 66. page 166.]

Page 453. lin. 7.
After aetatem. *infert*; So also, in much more modern times, a boy of ten years old, who was guilty of a heinous murder, was held a proper subject for capital punishment, by the opinion of all the judges. [Foster. 72.]

Page 464. lin. 7.
After circuits. *infert*; And, even though they be so approved, still if contrary to law they are void.

Ibid. lin. 28.
For It cannot be a trustee; *read* It cannot be seized of lands to the use of another; [Bro. *Abr.* tit. *Feoffm. al uses.* 40. Bacon of uses. 347.]

Page 469. lin. 15.
After authority. *add this note.* This notion is perhaps too refined. The court of king's bench, from it's general superintendent authority where other jurisdictions are deficient, has power to regulate all corporations where no special visitor is appointed. But, as it's judgments are liable to be reversed by writs of error, it wants one of the essential marks of visitatorial power.

Page 473. lin. 9.
Before a writ *infert*; an information in nature of
Ibid. lin. 16.
Leave out from sufficiently *to* charter *and infert*; in most of them were sufficiently regular: but the judgment against that of London was reversed by act of parliament [Stat 2 W. & M. c. 8.] after the revolution; and, by the same statute, it is enacted that the franchises

T H E   E N D